AF070254

The Tawny One

The Tawny One

Soma, Haoma and Ayahuasca

Matthew Clark

AEON

First published in 2017 by Muswell Hill Press. This new edition published in 2020
by Aeon Books Ltd
12 New College Parade Finchley Road
London NW3 5EP

Copyright © 2020 Matthew Clark

The right of Matthew Clark to be identified as the authors of this work has been asserted in accordance with §§ 77 and 78 of the Copyright Design and Patents Act 1988. All rights reserved. No part of this publication may be reproduced, stored in a retrieval system, or transmitted, in any form or by any means, electronic, mechanical, photocopying, recording, or otherwise, without the prior written permission of the publisher.

British Library Cataloguing in Publication Data
A C.I.P. for this book is available from the British Library ISBN-13: 978-1-91327-439-9
Printed in Great Britain

Also by Matthew Clark:

The Daśanāmī-Saṃnyāsīs: The Integration of Ascetic Orders into a Lineage. Leiden/Boston: E. J. Brill (2006)

The Origins and Practices of Yoga: A Weeny Introduction. Lulu.com (2010)

Matthew Clark (Mahabongo) is also a musician, singer and song-writer:

Swish It's Everywhere (2008): www.mahabongo.com
Minus Ridiculous (2012): http://www.cdbaby.com/cd/mahabongo2
Murmuration (2015): https://mahabongo.bandcamp.com/releases
The Banyan Tree (2016): https://mahabongo.bandcamp.com/album/the-banyan-tree

Disclaimer and warning:

This book is only for educational purposes. The author does not endorse or recommend the consumption of any plant or substance mentioned in this publication that is illegal in the jurisdiction of the consumer. Nor should any substance or plant be consumed, even if it is legal to do so, without sufficient guidance and specific instruction by an expert in its effects, possible counter-indications, and administration.

Preface

The somewhat speculative thesis presented in this book is that the Asian ritual drink known as *soma/haoma*, which can be traced to the late Bronze Age (*c.* 1600 BCE) or earlier, was most probably a concoction of plants that could induce an entheogenic/psychedelic experience; and that this concoction was most probably primarily based on an ayahuasca-like analogue. To this proposition is appended another suggestion: that the culture and knowledge of such concoctions may possibly have been more widespread in the Mediterranean region and the Middle-East than in the more apparent instantiation in the cults of the Iranian *Avesta* and the South Asian *Veda.* Should the thesis proposed—that *soma/haoma* was probably an analogue of ayahuasca—prove to be wrong or unfounded, it is nevertheless hoped that this publication will be a useful, updated summary of most of the previous research that has been undertaken into the topic of *soma/haoma.*

During the course of my research into *soma/haoma* it was a slight surprise to find out just how many people, from lay inquirers to professional academics, have engaged in this topic over the last two centuries: people are curious about a nectar of immortality. The churning of the ocean of ideas on *soma/haoma* has engendered many extraordinary notions, some worthy of serious consideration, some as unfeasible as wish-fulfilling cows. In this book independent research and quite a number of marginal opinions and eccentric suggestions have been included alongside the views and research of well-established academics and professional scientists. Also included are extensive footnotes on aspects of mythology and ritual and on some psychoactive plants and substances that are not central to the main thesis of this investigation. All of this hopefully provides both a more comprehensive picture of this multifaceted topic and a more complete cultural history of research into *soma/haoma*, its suggested identifications, and sufficient information adequately to eliminate some of the more improbable candidates for *soma/haoma.* Overall, this study is aimed not only at academics but also at readers who are not fully apprised of all the relevant background, previous arguments and suggestions concerning *soma/haoma.*

Many thanks to Simon BRODBECK, Dean BRODRICK, Yamuna GIRI and Alan PIPER for information, comments on previous drafts and corrections; to Janette BUSHELL and Desh RAJ for providing photographs of plants; to Kate ARMSTRONG, Chris BENNETT, Peter CONNOLLY, Gilad HAROUVI, Almut HINZE, Mehrbod KHANIZADEH, Suzanne NEWCOMBE, James MALLINSON, Alex MCKAY, Dennis MCKENNA and Nick PORUCZNIK for providing publications or suggestions for further reading; and to Carroll DUNHAM and Marco LEONTI for facilitating connections to other researchers; none of whom is, of course, in any way responsible for any of the errors or ideas in this book. Ralph METZNER generously allowed me to use a diagram (Appendix 5) from one of his books. Melanie-Jayne HOWES (at the Royal Botanical Gardens at Kew, London) and Simon GIBBONS (at the School of Pharmacy, University College London) very kindly conducted tests on plants for me. Great thanks are due also to the staff at the British Library, the Wellcome Institute library, Senate House library, and at the library of the School of Oriental and African Studies, who have been unfailingly helpful in retrieving publications for me. Particular thanks go to Yelena SHLYUGER in the inter-library loans section of the SOAS library for satisfying my numerous requests for publications. I am also grateful to Dave KING: in a conversation with him one evening in London a few years ago he encouraged me to write about this topic; I began keeping notes on *soma* in 2002 but it was only that evening that I decided to start writing.

Matthew Clark, Hove, UK, January 2017.

Contents

1. Introduction 1

2. *Soma* in the *Veda*s and yoga texts 7

3. *Haoma* in the *Avesta*.. 25

4. 'Substitutes' for *soma* in South Asia 37

5. What are the effects of *soma/haoma*? 49

6. The botanical identification of *soma/haoma*: an overview....... 61

7. Cannabis/hemp 65

8. Altered states of consciousness and demarcation criteria........ 77

9. Diverse theories about *soma/haoma*.. 103

10. Ephedra 113

11. Fly-agaric mushrooms (*Amanita muscaria*) 119

12. Syrian rue (*Peganum harmala*) 129

13. Many plants are *soma/haoma*.. 135

14. A renewed case for a psychedelic: ayahuasca 147

15. Vedic and ayahuasca rituals 165

16. Greek mystery rites 171

17. *Kykeōn* and the ergot hypothesis.. 181

18. Bronze Age origins of entheogenic cults 197

19. Rejoinders to the ayahuasca thesis 205

20. Concluding remarks..211

References 215

List of abbreviations... 249

Appendix 1: The Vedic sacrificial arena for *agniṣṭoma* rites 251

Appendix 2: *Arundo donax* (giant reed) 253

Appendix 3: *Darbha/Kuśa* grass.. 255

Appendix 4: Brief outline of the three largest Brazilian ayahuasca churches... 257

Appendix 5: States of consciousness (diagram from Metzner 2009:64) 259

Appendix 6: Pre-Columbian trans-Pacific contact?...................... 261

Index 265

CHAPTER 1

Introduction[1]

"The unknown herbs, which I am trying to know, I am learning to understand their inner powers" (*Atharva Veda* 8.7.18, trans. KASHYAP)

The identity of the plant known as *soma* in ancient India, and as *haoma* in the Zoroastrian tradition, has for around 250 years exercised the wits and imagination of scores of scholars. This plant is praised in the highest terms—as a kind of deity—in both Zoroastrian and Vedic texts that date from around 1700–1500 BCE; it is said to provide health, power, wisdom and even immortality. It has been variously identified by researchers as a non-psychoactive plant, as a medicine, as water, as merely a concept, as alcoholic, as a 'narcotic', as a stimulant, and as a psychedelic.[2]

Most of what is presented in the earlier part of this book is well known to any student of ancient Indian or Iranian religion; many of the references provided here have been previously iterated by former researchers; and the discussion that follows on the botanical

1. This book has undergone several revisions after receiving helpful comments on earlier drafts. The thesis is also published as a short article in KING *et al.* (2015:149–160).
2. This author is aware of the discussion concerning the appropriateness (or otherwise) of the use of the terms 'psychedelic' (famously coined in 1957 by Dr. Humphry OSMOND), 'hallucinogen' (from the Latin *alucinari*: wander in mind/ramble), and 'entheogen' ('engendering god within', coined by Carl RUCK and Jonathan OTT). Some scholars prefer 'entheogen': 'hallucinogen' and 'psychedelic' are not suitable for some classes of psychoactive drugs (see OTT 1996a:15ff.; BEYER 2010:244). In this book the terms 'entheogen' and 'psychedelic' are used interchangeably to mean both 'god-inducing' and/or 'visionary'.

identification of *soma* will also be familiar to scholars in this field. However, previous research has been summarized below in order to provide an introduction for non-specialists, and a novel suggestion is proposed for the identity of *soma/haoma*: as possibly an analogue of *ayahuasca*,[3] a preparation of psychoactive plants that is well known both to natives and anthropologists of South America and, increasingly during the last four decades or so, to the wider world.[4] Most of this latter part of the discussion may be well known to those interested in entheogens. So, apologies in advance go to those readers who find much in this publication that is already well known, and which may be redundant to scholars in the relevant fields.

In South America ayahuasca[5] is usually prepared from a mixture of two plants: the *Banisteriopsis caapi* vine and the leaves of the plant *Psychotria viridis*, though other additives are also used. The *Banisteriopsis caapi* vine contains monoamine-oxidase (MAO) inhibitors and *Psychotria viridis* contains *N-N* dimethyl-tryptamine (DMT). DMT consumed orally is inactive unless combined with an MAO inhibitor. If the two chemicals are consumed in appropriate dosages at the same time, the result is usually a powerful psychedelic trip. In the last few decades numerous plants have been discovered that contain either an MAO inhibitor or DMT, which means that a form or analogue of ayahuasca (or 'anahuasca') can be made from dozens of different plants, all combinations providing an almost identical effect. As part of the argument in this book, more attention has been paid to the effects of the plants proposed for *soma/haoma* than has sometimes hitherto been the case amongst researchers. A feature of this approach is that numerous anecdotal reports of

---

3. JAY (1999:172–173) also suggests that the number of candidates for *soma/haoma* can be, rather tentatively, extended if the idea of *ayahuasca*-like plant combinations is considered.
4. For the history of its discovery by Europeans, see OTT (1996a:206–209), MCKENNA (1999); see also LUNA (2011) for some personal reflections.
5. Throughout this book the term 'ayahuasca' is used rather loosely to refer not only to the combination of the two plants traditionally used in South America but also to other plant combinations having similar chemistry. Some commentators like to distinguish *hoasca* (the vine), *ayahuasca* (the combination), pharmahuasca (pure, combined ingredients), and anahuasca (analogues of *ayahuasca*). For a discussion of this point, see SHULGIN and SHULGIN (1997:285ff.).

experiences of various kinds of drugs, plants and compounds have been included. Generally in academic studies anecdotal evidence, without objective verification, carries little weight; but in an attempt to understand the effects of various kinds of substances, anecdotal reports are in many instances all we have to go on.

The thesis presented in this book is that *soma/haoma* was in all probability not a single plant but a combination of psychoactive plants,[6] and that in ancient Asia in the late Bronze Age (*c.* 1600 BCE) there was sufficient botanical knowledge to produce a psychedelic concoction from a variety of plants. Further, it seems probable that concoctions not only differed over time and between regions in Asia—depending on which plants were available—but, as in the living cultures of the Amazon region, other psychoactive plants may have been added to a 'basic' concoction, as boosters, enhancers or moderators.

Although definitive proof of which plants were used has not been established, and although there are several possible objections to the thesis being proposed (which are summarized towards the end of this book in the chapter on 'Rejoinders to the ayahuasca thesis'), there are, nevertheless, several important clues in the texts consulted which indicate possible, future lines of inquiry for chemical analysis of potentially psychoactive properties of particular plants. Quite a few of the plants referred to in this book, even though they may have a long history of medical applications, have never been properly analysed for psychoactive properties; and I invite interested readers to research their properties. There may be interesting discoveries to be made particularly in the effects of combinations of plants.

During the course of research for this book, tests on plants were very kindly conducted by Melanie-Jayne HOWES at the Royal Botanical Gardens at Kew and by Simon GIBBONS at the School of Pharmacy, University College London. At Kew, samples of both a banyan tree (*Ficus bengalenis/benghalensis*) and a peepal tree (*Ficus*

---

6. The idea of *soma* being many plants, from which juice could be extracted, is suggested by MUKHOPADHYAY (1978), but without elaboration or detail. This notion is also endorsed by LEONTI and CASU (2014) in an important article that provides evidence of plants used in South Asia in the 6th century CE in preparations that would be effective as ayahuasca analogues; see Chapter 13.

religiosa) were tested for harmine and harmaline, which are monoamine-oxidase inhibitors. The tests proved negative. However, it remains possible that there are other alkaloids in these plants that could work as MAOIs. Sufficient tests have not so far been conducted to determine whether or not this is the case. At the London School of Pharmacy a small sample of *kuśa* grass was tested for DMT. This test also proved negative. This could mean that *kuśa* grass contains no DMT, or merely that this sample contained no DMT. It will be further elaborated in Chapter 14 that samples of *Phalaris* grass, which is a relative of *kuśa* grass, vary widely in their alkaloid content. Some samples that have been tested contained DMT, while others contained none. Geographical location, soil constituents, the time of day and the season all influence the alkaloid content of plants. Or, it could be that *kuśa* grass growing in South Asia contains no DMT at all. This will need further tests to determine.

So, overall, perhaps this investigation is best considered as a proposition that needs further research, rather than as a definitive solution to the question of the specific botanical identities of *soma/haoma*; or it may be considered as a presentation of a balance of probabilities, given the paucity of available, historical evidence. However, if indeed it was the case that in the ancient world there was the necessary botanical knowledge to manufacture a form of ayahuasca, then a new perspective on Vedic and Zoroastrian rituals might plausibly be considered.

The argument presented in this investigation is really an attempt at answering, firstly, basic questions: if *soma/haoma* was a drug (which is now almost universally accepted by commentators), what kind would fit consumption during the duration of a (sometimes lengthy) Vedic ritual; that could be drunk every few hours without impeding the ability of highly intoxicated ritualists to recite *mantra*s precisely; that would keep participants awake; that produces no side-effects or hang-over (participants feel 'reborn' after a ritual and do not seem to be 'recovering' from a drug experience); and that could be consumed regularly throughout a consumer's life, and for many generations of participating ritualists, without any deleterious effects? These requirements seem to me incontrovertible concerning any candidate for *soma/haoma.* Secondly, if, as is argued in this book, *soma/haoma* was indeed visionary, then we need to find a psychedelic drug that fits these primary criteria. These considerations are what initially led me to the ayahuasca analogue hypothesis, as ayahuasca fulfills all of the criteria mentioned above; and further, the structure and performance of the ritual during which ayahuasca is drunk by members of one the churches that use it as a sacrament, namely the church of Santo Daime, exhibit remarkable similarities with the ritual structure of the longer, periodic Vedic rites, during which *soma* is consumed (although for many centuries prepared in substitute form). This illustrates the possibility that an ayahuasca analogue could have been consumed in Vedic or Zoroastrian ritual over many years without deleterious effects or impeding the performance of a ritual.

The ayahuasca/anahusaca hypothesis that is presented in this book is not without aspects that are either unclear or unresolved, particularly concerning the exact botanical identity of all the plants that may have been used, whether or not any kind of vine was ever used, and the exact manner of the preparation of *soma/haoma*. My interpretation of particular religious texts may also be subject to criticism; and there may well be factual errors in some of the information presented, as I lack expertise in several of the disciplines that are explored. However, even though, as already mentioned, the thesis remains unproven in several regards, having looked at the issue of *soma/haoma* in the light of current knowledge of psychedelics, the history of research into the topic, and the relevant religious and ritual texts, I cannot see any more plausible solution to its botanical identity. A commonplace in the philosophy of science is that a theory is never refuted by objections alone but only by a better, alternative theory, which more adequately explains available evidence; it is hoped that this is what is presented in this book.

The available evidence on this topic has drawn my research towards the ayahuasca analogue conjecture. However, in what aspires to be the true spirit of scientific inquiry, compelling new evidence on the historical use of another plant, or a discovery of new information on the use of any one of the alternative candidates for *soma/haoma* that has been rejected in this survey (such as hallucinogenic mushrooms, for example) could possibly necessitate a revision of the hypothesis presented.

In this book, firstly references to and descriptions of *soma/haoma* in the *Vedas*, yoga texts and the *Avesta* are briefly summarized in Chapters 2 and 3. In Chapter 3 the possible origins of the *soma/*

haoma cult in Central Asia are also explored. This is followed, in Chapter 4, by a survey of plants mentioned primarily in the *Brāhmaṇa*s as being either *soma* or as substitutes for *soma*. From references in various texts, what appear to be the effects of *soma/haoma* are explored in Chapter 5. In Chapters 6 to 12 the numerous candidates for *soma/haoma* that have been proposed are presented and discussed. In Chapter 8 an attempt is made to go some way towards achieving a distinction between properly entheogenic plants and other drugs that have different or less potent effects. The proposition that *soma/haoma* always referred to many kinds of plants is explored in Chapter 13. In Chapter 14, South American use of ayahuasca is surveyed, with particular attention paid to the ritual structure of the Santo Daime church. Comparisons between South American and Vedic rituals are tentatively explored in Chapter 15. In Chapter 16 there is a brief overview of Greek mystery rites, followed, in Chapter 17, by a consideration of the hypothesis that an ergot fungus was the basis of the ancient ritual potion known as *kykeōn*, which was used in the ancient rites that were performed at the temple of Eleusis, near Athens. In Chapter 18, the possible use of entheogenic concoctions in wider Asia in the late Bronze Age is considered. Finally, in Chapter 19, several of the possible objections to the thesis of this book are detailed.

CHAPTER 2

Soma in the *Veda*s and yoga texts

The four *Veda*s[7] are a corpus of primarily oral,[8] religious texts composed between about 1700 and 800 BCE, containing mantras and hymns that are still ritually recited (those from the *Sāmaveda* are chanted) in many brahman families both domestically and occasionally in public rituals in India[9] and Nepal. Although mantras from the *saṃhitā* portions of the *Veda*s are used in many religious and socio-religious Hindu contexts in South Asia, the original function of the mantras, which are said to have been 'received' or 'seen' by

---

7. From the Sanskrit root √*vid* (know/see/understand). The four *Veda*s, used at rituals are: *Ṛgveda* (for recitation), *Sāmaveda* (for chanting), *Yajurveda* (for performance), *Atharvaveda* (for officiating). Each *Veda* has several ancillary texts, including *Upaniṣad*s, *Āraṇyaka*s, *Brāhmaṇa*s, *Śrautasūtra*s and other texts. The *Ṛgveda*, the earliest of the four *Veda*s, was mostly composed in the Panjab region, in three layers of composition, dating between *c.* 1700 and 1200 BCE (WITZEL 1999:8) or perhaps slightly later (*c.* 1300–1000 BCE: PARPOLA 2015:15). Many of the mantras of the *Ṛgveda* appear in the other *Veda*s. The portions of the *Veda*s containing the mantras/hymns that are recited at rituals are referred to as the *saṃhitā*s. For the historical layering, ordering and geographical composition of the *Veda*s, see WITZEL (1997). The priests assigned to each of the *Veda*s are: *hotar* (*Ṛgveda*), *adhvaryu* (*Yajurveda*), *udgātar* (*Sāmaveda*), brahman (*Atharvaveda*). The brahman's original function in Vedic ritual was most probably as a poet (BRERETON 2004), but his role evolved: to oversee the recitations of the other three kinds of priest.
8. The earliest evidence of the *Veda*s being written down is in texts from Kashmir dating to *c.* 1000 CE.
9. See KNIPE (2015) for a vivid, comprehensive and detailed account of a living Vedic ritual tradition in coastal Andhra Pradesh.

ancient *ṛṣis* (seers),[10] was and remains an essential feature of the performance of Vedic ritual, known as *yajña/yāga*[11] (praise/worship/sacrifice).[12]

Many deities of various kinds and attributes people the *Vedas*, the foremost—in terms of the number of times that they are mentioned or invoked—being Indra (king of the gods), Agni (the god of fire), and Soma who is the third-most mentioned deity,[13] who is invoked many scores of times in the *Ṛgveda*,[14] and who also extensively pervades the other *Vedas*. Besides being a deity, *soma* has two other aspects: it is a plant and is the juice of a plant.[15]

---

10. The 'standard' list is of seven *ṛṣis*: see MITCHENER (1982) for further details.
11. In the brahmanical practice of Vedic ritualists in coastal Andhra Pradesh the use of this term is more restricted, referring to the first *soma* ritual (the *agniṣṭoma*, 'praise of Agni'), which is conducted outdoors, performed by an orthodox brahman, his wife and a team of Vedic ritualists (KNIPE 2015:45).
12. People calling themselves 'Ārya' (noble) migrated in successive waves from Central Asia, arriving first about 1700–1500 BCE in South Asia, bringing with them the ancestor of the Sanskrit language and the cults of *soma* and the god Indra. For the original homeland of PIE (Proto-Indo-European) speakers, see WITZEL (2000); for a discussion of alternative theories, see MALLORY (1998). Currently the majority scholarly consensus is that the PIE homeland was in Central Asia; however, RENFREW, in many publications (including 1998), favours Anatolia.
13. However, although Soma is an important god, he is somewhat dissimilar to other Vedic deities: only once is he (as 'King Soma') offered a sacrificed offering (*ṚV* 1.91.4); unlike other gods, he is not invited to the sacrifice; priests offer to other gods, but not to Soma (PATIL 1960). Nevertheless, in some rites, such as the *agnicāyana* (see below), Soma is addressed similarly to other Vedic deities (Indra, Agni, Mitra, Varuṇa, Bṛhaspati, Aditi) (see DUMONT 1961:650, 3.11.5).
14. For a concise summary of the references to, and the mythology of, *soma* in the *Vedas*, see MACDONELL (1995:104–115); see also KEITH (1925:166–172).
15. *Soma* is the object of all 114 hymns—attributed to sixty or more poets—of the 9th *maṇḍala* (circle/book) of the *Ṛgveda* and is also celebrated in four or five other hymns as a dual deity, paired with Indra, Agni, Pūṣan or Rudra. *Soma* is homologized with gods, people, animals and natural elements; and has dozens of epithets (see OBERLIES 1999:56ff., 81ff.). The 9th *maṇḍala* of the *Ṛgveda*, in which the deity Soma is almost universally identified with the *soma* plant, is primarily concerned with the ritual preparation (clarification) of *soma* (see GONDA 1975:89), which is an essential ritual activity. GONDA

Well known to any student of the *Vedas*, it is the mighty god Indra who is particularly associated with the drinking of *soma*: "As soon as he was born the young bull [Indra] liked the offering of the pressed *soma* juice".[16] Indra, born transversely and fully grown through the side of his mother, was born to drink *soma*.[17] A hero, he is always youthful; he, intoxicated after drinking thirty ponds full of *soma*, is the slayer of the three-headed snake/demon/dragon Vṛtra (*vṛtrahan*, 'slayer of resistance'),[18] with whom *soma* is occasionally identified (but only in the later *Vedas* and the *Brāhmaṇas*);[19] he is the enemy and conqueror of the people called Dāsas (or Dasyus);[20] he of

---

(1994) also notices that in sixteen *sūktas* of *ṚV* 9, Soma/*soma* is addressed but unnamed. The hymns collected in *ṚV* 9 appear to have been collected together from the other 'family books' (2–7) of the *ṚV* into one group, as a recitation to accompany the ritual pressing and 'clarification' of *soma* (KAPADIA 1959:1; RENOU 1961:1). These hymns allude to and allegorically describe the several processes in the preparation of *soma*.

16. *ṚV* 3.48.1 (trans. GONDA 1989:18). For the character of Indra in the *Ṛgveda* and his association with *soma*, see GONDA (1989).
17. *ṚV* 1.5.6.
18. *Vṛtra* also has (probably ancient) associations with a boar (DAS 2001:27–28n.39), as has the spirit/deity (*yazata*) Vĕrĕthragna (who smites destruction/evil) in ancient Iran and Armenia (RUSSELL 1987:189). In the *Avesta*, the god of victory, Vərəθrayner, in the form of a wild boar, runs before the *vazra*-(weapon-) wielding warrior god Mithra, whose counterpart in the *Vedas* is Indra (PARPOLA 2015:114). WITZEL (2012:64) includes the 'mytheme' of the killing of a dragon (who, in most instances, in various ways, releases waters/blood and fertilizes the earth) as one of the provisional fifteen core mythemes that constitute the original corpus of mythology of, roughly, the northern hemisphere, which WITZEL terms Laurasian mythology. See FONTENROSE (1959) for a comprehensive treatment of this global myth/theme of slaying the dragon/enemy; and for the slaying of Vṛtra (pp.194–205).
19. See KUIPER (1969:281); LAHIRI (1984:172ff.). '*Vṛra*' derives from the Indo-European root **u̯er*, which means primarily to cover, close or obstruct (LAHIRI pp.26–72); or 'resistance' (WITZEL 2012:150). LAHIRI (pp.182–186) speculatively suggests that the identification of *soma* and *vṛtra* ensued from the idea that *soma* contained also forces of negativity (*vṛtra*), which needed to be eliminated through the 'purification' of *soma*. *Vṛtra* is 'killed'—though this is not complete extinction—in the pressing and purification of *soma*.
20. PARPOLA (1997b; 2015:103–105) believes these people (whose name possibly derives from *daha* = 'man') are the wild, nomadic Scythians/Sakās, whose main homeland was in regions around the Black Sea. They migrated in

overwhelming power is frequently invited to be present at the *soma* rituals.[21]

According to the *Vedas*, *Brāhmaṇas*, *Śrautasūtras* and other commentarial texts, the *soma*, in the form of bundles of stalks[22] of a plant with shoots but no leaves, is usually purchased from a *śūdra* (= low-class),[23] in exchange for a preferably tawny-coloured cow and sometimes other goods in the form of gold or a goat; the deal is haggled.[24] The bundles of *soma* are examined and extraneous plants are weeded out. The seller, who brings the *soma* on a wheeled cart (or on his head),[25] is asked if the *soma* comes from Mount Mūjavat,

---

the 1st millennium BCE as far as Xinjiang province in China (for more on the Scythians, see below). Battles referred to in the *Vedas* between Indra and the Dāsas may record historical encounters between Indo-Āryans and Scythians in Central Asia (to the east of their original homeland), perhaps around 2000 BCE, when Indo-Āryans first occupied this region. Global cooling may have caused migrations of people seeking better food supplies around 2000 BCE, which is one of the four periods of global cooling in the last 4,000 years (HSÜ 1998). PARPOLA (2002:233ff.) speculates that the Dāsas may have been the elite of the Bactria Margiana Archaeological Complex (BMAC: see below) in Turkmenistan, whose triple-ringed forts were attacked (the memory of which is alluded to in the *Vedas*) by people who would subsequently migrate to South Asia, taking there the cult of *soma*. The Kāfirs of northern Pakistan may be their descendants. In the *Ṛgveda* the Dasyu people are referred to as 'riteless', indifferent to the gods, reviling the gods, not-sacrificing, and lawless: see (BHATTACHARYA 2007:67) for references.

21. In contemporary Hindu (in distinction from Vedic) understanding, Indra is now considered as a god of rain: see, for example, TIGUNĀIT (2012:117).
22. These seem to have sections with nodes or joints (*parvan*) (HILLEBRANDT 1980, Vol. 1:137–138; BHAWE 1957, Part 1:71–72; KAPADIA 1959:5).
23. Who may be beaten in the transaction, as there is an allusion to the idea that trade in *soma* might be illegal (RENOU 2004:146); or from a brahman from the Kutsa *gotra* (or from any brahman). The *Aitareya Brāhmaṇa* (1.3.1) describes the *soma* seller as 'evil'. Expiation rites are performed if any mishap befalls the purchased *soma* stalks; see GONDA (1982:11) on this point; for all Vedic expiation rites, see DANDEKAR (1958:436ff.).
24. The purchase is dealt with primarily in the *Brāhmaṇas*. It is partly mythological, as the purchase of *soma* is the purchase of a god, who then travels to the ritual enclosure as a divine king. See MALAMOUD (1991a) for the mythology of the purchase of *soma*.
25. For the details of the purchase and drinking of *soma*, see the White (*Śukla*) *Yajurveda* (books 1–9) and its appendix, the *Śatapatha Brāhmaṇa*. For

where the best quality comes from.[26] After the purchase of the *soma* by the *adhvaryu* priest, the *yajamāna*—who pays for the ritual (see below)—mutters the first part of a mantra[27] when the *adhvaryu* approaches him with the *soma* bundle. He then uncovers his right thigh, places the bundle on it, and recites the remainder of the mantra. The *soma* bundle is then tied with a cloth, covered with a turban and deposited on a black antelope skin. With the recitation of mantras, the stalks are then sprinkled with warm water to make them swell (*āpyāyana*), after which they are placed on a preferably reddish bull's hide and handfuls of stalks are pounded with stones (*adri* or *grāvan*)[28] on two planks of wood to extract the juice,[29] a process undertaken inside the Vedic ritual arena in the *havirdhāna* (see

---

references collated from these and other relevant texts, see CALAND and HENRY (1906:35–49); HILLEBRANDT (1980, Vol. 1:159–167); KANE (1997, Vol. 2, part 2:1141–1147). For details of the drinking of *soma* by priests in the *agniṣṭoma* ritual, see KANE (1997:1175–1181).

26. See STAAL (2001a:769–771), FALK (2002/3:145), WITZEL (2004:594) and STUHRMAN (2006:41n.100) on where this mountain might be: possibly, among other suggestions, (1) Muz Tagh Ata (meaning 'ice mountain father') in Kirghiz/Kyrgyz, height, 24,767 feet, which is close to the sources of the Oxus and Yarkand-Tarim rivers in the Pamir range. Muz Tagh Ata is also close to the Muzh Kol river, which runs just east of the border of Tajikistan, in the Kirghiz and Sariqoli (Sakā) lands of westernmost China; (2) Muzh Tagh in Kashmir, north-east of Skardu; (3) Girimuñja/Muñjavat, one of the holiest sites in Gandhāra (in the Swat and Kabul river valleys in northern Pakistan); this mountain, or range, is also similarly referred to (as *Muža*) in the *Avesta* (see below).
27. This mantra is a *yajus* (from the *Yajurveda*): *mitro na ehi sumitradhā / indrasyorum ā viśa dakṣiṇam / uśann uśantaṃ śyonaḥ śyonam* / (*TS* 1.2.7.1f). "Come to us as a friend, making good friends. Enter the right thigh of Indra; you willing, it willing, you gracious, it gracious": trans. STAAL (2002:49).
28. Sometimes also pressed with mortar and pestle (*ṚV* 1.28.1–4); which also have poetically sexual allusions: see SCHMIDT (2009) for comment on this point. See also, for example, *Bṛhadāraṇyaka Upaniṣad* (6.4.3), where the altar, the sacrificial grass, the *soma* press, and the ritual fire are described, metaphorically sexualized, as a woman.
29. Juice from imperfectly pressed stalks is pressed out by the presser's fingers (BHAWE 1957, Part 1:7). See BHAWE (1962, Part 3:140) for details of the pressing.

Appendix 1).[30] Pressings of *soma*[31]—which are sometimes compared with the milking of a cow—are performed three times a day, in the morning, noon and evening. The ritual pressing of *soma* was a highly esteemed activity; pressers, it seems, were considered as a select sub-caste of Vedic society (WHITAKER 2007).

The expressed juice, which is said to make a lot of noise, like a bellowing bull when it is being pressed out,[32] is passed through a sheep-wool filter, from which it issues flowing clearly/purified (*pavamāna*); *soma pavamāna* is a prevalent image in the *soma* hymns. It is then mixed[33] in a trough known as *ādhavanīya* with specially drawn water[34] and poured into wooden casks.[35] Milk and usually also curd and barley are then added to the water and the extracted *soma* juice.[36] The mixture is offered to the gods on a litter of grass that has been carried on the *soma* cart (*āsandī*, throne) to the ritual enclosure[37] and is then drunk from bowls/cups (*camasa*) by

---

30. The most important ritual events prior to the offering (to the fire) and drinking of *soma* are: 1. the purchase of *soma*; 2. the bringing of 'him' in a cart to the sacrificial shed (*havirdhāna*); 3. the reception of *soma* as a special guest; 4. the fetching of the special waters (*vasatīvarī* and *ekadhāna*: see below) to mix with *soma* juice; 5. the pressing and offering of *soma* (DANGE 2000:129).
31. Meaning 'press out', from the Sanskrit root √*su*; or (probably earlier) from the Proto-Indo-European root **sau* (PARPOLA 2015:107).
32. This is somewhat curious. The *Yajurveda* (5.22) has mantras for the preparation of four, deep, arm-length 'sound holes' (*uparavas*) beneath the wooden pressing-boards, made to increase the noise of the pounding of *soma*. It seems that the *soma* stalks made a sound when struck (BHAWE 1957, Part 1:9).
33. Unmixed *soma* is offered almost exclusively to Vāyu (the wind-god) and Indra.
34. There are two kinds of ritual-waters: *vasatīvarī* (the kind mostly referred to) which is drawn from flowing, rippling streams prior to sunset and left standing overnight; and *ekadhanā*, which is drawn the next day prior to sunrise. See DANGE (1988/9) for further details.
35. *Kalaśa*, smaller vessels; *droṇa*, larger vessels; often referred to as one compound.
36. These are the usual three additives (*tryāśiraḥ*). Other additives, for specific occasions or pressings, include butter, honey and gold (see HILLEBRANDT 1980, Vol. 1:292ff.).
37. The *soma* carts are kept in a temporary hut, the *havirdhāna*, where the *soma* is prepared.

the priests (the first to drink being the *hotar* priest) who officiate at the ritual, before which (usually) a male goat (or goats)[38] is/are sacrificed by asphyxiation[39] at the sacrificial post (*yūpa*).[40] Also prepared and offered to the gods in the ritual by standing priests are 'cakes' (*puroḍāśa*) cooked, by either frying, boiling or baking, from rice or sometimes barley, which are similar to either a small loaf or a pancake.

There are many kinds of Vedic ritual, comprising both domestic (*gṛhya*) rites,[41] which require the ritual establishment of the domestic

---

38. As many as thirty-two goats are sacrificed for the *vājapeya* (drink of strength/contest) rite, which is one of the seven *soma* rites (KNIPE 2015:215).
39. The sacrificed animals are cut open, the fat and the guts are removed, and eleven parts of the animal are roasted and apportioned to the ritual participants. In former times the animals were decapitated (KNIPE 2015:291n.38). In Kerala and Nepal, in *soma* rites vegetable offerings of rice flour in banana leaves are used instead, which provoked amusement in a brahman interviewed by KNIPE (p.215): "How can there be a sacrifice if no one dies?"
40. See KANE (1997, Vol. 2, part 2:1174) for further details. The sacrifice of goats to a deity may even pre-date Vedic ritual and have been practised previously in the Indus valley civilization. Animal sacrifice outside *soma* rites is recommended by Āpastamba (*Āpastambaśrautasūtra* 7.28.6) to be done every year for a brahman who performs *agnihotra*, though this is not current practice (KNIPE 2015:215). The *yūpa* symbolizes a cosmic tree growing from the navel of the earth, upholding the sky and leading to heaven.
41. The domestic rites require that a brahman householder, after marriage, makes morning and evening oblations (*sandhyāvandanam*) at sunrise (while standing) and sunset (while seated)—and for some rites at noon also—into the domestic fire (or three fires) (*agnihotra*), accompanied by Vedic mantras. However, owing to the expense of cow-dung cakes and firewood, many poor brahmans commonly (and historically) only set up the domestic fire (or fires) in later life (HARSHANANDA 2001:6). The domestic *śrauta* ritual complex is initially established with five hearths, which is subsequently reduced to three at the close of the setting of the fires (KNIPE 2015:195). KNIPE (2015:190) comments that only a fraction of the certified Vedic pandits and their wives in the village of Konasima in Andhra Pradesh, which he studied for thirty-five years, establish three fires, perform *agnighotra* twice daily, and move on to their first *soma* sacrifice, the *agniṣṭoma.*

fireplaces,[42] and more elaborate *śrauta* rites,[43] all of which embody the combination and amalgamation of various types of rituals and minor rites. What has been called the 'divine triumvirate' of deities associated with *śrauta* rites are Indra, Agni and Soma (LUBIN 2016:149). The *Yajurveda* is the *Veda* most closely associated with Vedic *śrauta* ritual. A review of its contents illustrates its prime concerns: the setting up the ritual arena[44] (see Appendix 1), and the purchase, preparation and drinking of *soma.* The *soma* sacrifices are the most elaborate and important rites in Yajurvedic texts, described in great detail in the *Brāhmaṇa*s and *Śrautasūtra*s. They are the most important of the *śrauta* sacrifices in Vedic ritual and have been so since the time of the *Ṛgveda,* [45] the core of which is primarily a liturgical collection of hymns for *soma* rites.[46] The fundamental and typical Vedic sacrifices are the *soma* rituals (RENOU 2004:158), which are regarded by all authorities as a distinct class of sacrifice and as

---

42. A feature of the establishment of these fires is the use of twigs of five kinds of tree: *aśvattha* (*Ficus religiosa*, peepal), *udumbara* (*Ficus glomerata/ racemosa*, cluster fig), *parṇa* (*Butea frondosa*, flame of the forest), *śamī* (*Mimosa suma* = *Acacia Polyacantha* Willd.), and from any tree burned by lightning (KNIPE 2015:193). The possible significance of the use of these trees is explored in later sections of this book.
43. From √*śru* (hear). 160 varieties of *śrauta* rites are detailed by DANDEKAR (1958). There are three main categories of ritual: obligatory (*nitya*), incidental (*naimittika*) and optional (*kāmya*), *kāmya* rites being performed for the fulfillment of specific desires. The *Gopatha Brāhmaṇa* (2012:28) classifies three kinds of ceremonies (each of which has seven varieties): *pākayajña,* in which the cooking of rice or another grain is the most important; *haviryajña,* in which the offering of ghee is most important; *somayajña,* in which the *soma* drink is most important; some participants at these rituals drink *soma* and some do not (*Gopatha Brāhmaṇa* 2.1.6). The *soma* sacrifices require a total of seventeen officiants, including the four main priests (*hotar, adhvaryu, udgātar* and brahman), each of whom has three assistants, and the *yajamāna.*
44. The outdoor ritual arena is temporary: it is set up for a ritual and then dismantled after its completion. The offerings to the fire and the *soma* sacrifices stand at the centre of the rite; the preliminary and concluding procedures are bilaterally symmetrical (STAAL *et al.* 2001b:128).
45. See DANDEKAR (1958:21); BROUGH (1971:331); HOUBEN (1991:16); BRERETON (2005:8521).
46. The bulk (originally the whole: RENOU 2004:38) of the *Aitareya Brāhmaṇa* (which pertains to the *Ṛgveda*) deals with the *soma* sacrifices.

the most important and the superior of the three basic kinds of Vedic ritual, the other two kinds being the *iṣṭi* and *paśubandha*.[47] PARPOLA (2015:130) comments that the hymn collections of the *Ṛgveda, Sāmaveda* and *Yajurveda* mainly relate to the *soma* sacrifice or other *śrauta* rituals.

Accompanied by mantras from the *Vedas*, *śrauta* rites require oblations from a wooden ladle into the (usually) three fires[48] established for the rites, of substances including ghee (which is the most important offering), rice, barley, and depending on the rite, *soma* and the fat and the omentum (*vapā*)[49] from sacrificed animals.[50] The omentum is the first offering to the deities. These rites require teams of brahmans who at an appropriate astronomical time set up

---

47. *Iṣṭi* requires vegetable oblations of rice, barley, cakes etc.; *paśubandha* requires animal sacrifice. All three kinds of ritual have many similarities. For further details of these rites, see GONDA (1982:7ff.).
48. These are the *gārhapatya, āhavanīya* and *dakṣiṇāgni* fires (see Appendix 1) in, respectively, the west, east and south of the sacrificial/offering arena. Occasionally, five fires are required. According to the White *Yajurveda* (*Kātyāyana Śrautasūtra*) these are the *sabhya* and *āvasthya* fires (WITZEL 2016:377).
49. The membrane that connects the stomach with other abdominal organs.
50. For a summarized account of a contemporary *soma* ritual (performed in Trichur, Kerala in 2003), see MAHADEVAN and STAAL (2003). This *somayāgam* contains twelve *soma* sequences, which comprise chants from the *Sāmaveda*, extensive recitations from the *Ṛgveda*, *soma* offerings to the deities, and *soma* drinking by the *yajamāna* and the priests. Traditionally, the entire ritual and all recitations are oral in character, though in contemporary rituals hand gestures are used on occasion by priests as *aides memoires.* Commentarial literature describes the seven forms of *soma* sacrifice: *agniṣṭoma, atyagniṣṭoma, ukthya, ṣodaśin, vājapeya, atirāta* and *aptoryāma* (see KANE 1997, Vol. 2, part 2:1204ff. for further details). The *agniṣṭoma* (= *jyotiṣṣtoma*, 'praise of light'), which requires twelve 'rounds' of recitation—and includes twelve *stotras* (musical performances) and twelve *śāstras* (solemn recitations)—is the basic and simplest form of the *soma* sacrifice; it lasts for one day. The other *soma* rites mentioned require elaborations (i.e. extensions) of the recitations and rites performed for the *agniṣṭoma*, and also the sacrifice of more animals; the sacrifice of animals is an important feature of *soma* rites. The name *agniṣṭoma* derives from the last chant of the twelve 'rounds', which constitute the *agniṣṭoma sāman*, which is the singing of *ṚV* 6.48. See STAAL (2008:242–245) for a concise overview of what he calls the '*soma* sequences' of the larger *soma* rituals.

the ritual arena (see Appendix 1), including the sacrificial fires that are moved in pots from the brahman's house to the outdoor arena, and the 'altar' (*vedi*), which is an hour-glass-shaped pit that is dug out two or three inches deep between the fires,[51] and covered with straw, which takes a couple of days. *Soma* sacrifices should be performed on the highest ground in the locality, as these rituals are regarded as preeminently suitable for ascending to the sphere of the gods (GONDA 1982:11). Rituals may continue for one day[52] or several days;[53] a *sattra* is a *soma* sacrifice that lasts twelve days or longer.[54] Of particular importance are the sacrifices that take place regularly on the new and full moon. RENOU (2004:154) describes Vedic sacrifice as a kind of drama, with its actors, its dialogue, its portions set to music,[55] and its interludes and climaxes.

---

51. One of the most important and elaborate Vedic rituals is the *agnicāyana* (of which there are five kinds, including less elaborate forms and forms with different configurations of the altar and the number of bricks used; see DUMONT 1951; KNIPE 2015:222ff.), which is performed together with a *soma* sacrifice, and which, in its main form, involves the construction of a raised altar comprising 10,800 bricks in the form of a large bird (*śyena*, falcon), and the performance of the twenty-nine '*soma* sequences' (see STAAL 2001b). The number 10,800 derives from a division of the year into 360 days, each day having thirty divisions (*muhūrtas*) of forty-eight minutes.
52. The two most important one-day *soma* rituals are the *vājapeya*, originally performed maybe only by warriors and kings, which used to involve a chariot race, the symbolic ascent of the sacrificer and his wife on a ladder to heaven (*svarga*), and the drinking of both *soma* and alcohol (*surā*), the latter being usually forbidden. In coastal Andhra Pradesh *surā* is brewed from rice, barley and millet, and left to ferment in milk for three days (KNIPE 2015:228, 239). The other important one-day ritual is the *rājasūya* (king's coronation), which involved a symbolic battle march and games of dice (WINTERNITZ 1981:160).
53. *Soma yāgas* are sometimes divided into three classes: one day rites (*ekāha*); rites lasting from two to twelve days (*ahīna*); rites of twelve of more days (*sattra*) (BHATTACHARYA 2007:223).
54. These days goats are sacrificed instead of, in former times, bulls, calves, cows and ewes, which are specified in the *sūtras* (KNIPE 2015:238).
55. During *soma* sacrifices, chants (*sāmans*) from the *Sāmaveda* are sung by a trio of priests: the *prastotar* (pre-lauder), who sings the first portion; the *pratihartar* (the receiver), who sings the second portion; and the *udgātar* (high chanter), who sings the most important portion, the *udgītha* ('high chant') (PARPOLA 2015:128).

The sacrificer (*yajamāna*), the patron who pays for the ritual and has to be wealthy,[56] needs first to undergo initiation, *dīkṣā* (intention to adore), consecration for the rites. This is preferably performed on the new moon, or on another suitable day (GONDA 1982:13), and may last one day, or three or four days, or even a year. He must fast (or restrict his diet or abstain from meat), observe temporary celibacy, bathe, and be shaven before a *soma* ritual, and must be accompanied by his wife. Having also undergone similar preparations, she is girdled with a rope of *darbha* grass and remains in a temporary hut in the ritual enclosure during the performance of the rites. The initiation of the sacrificer and his wife (the co-sacrificer) results in their symbolic death and rebirth; the sacrificer becomes an embryo, closing his fists like a foetus in the womb, which is represented by the temporary hut prepared for the initiate. He receives a piece of cloth representing the placenta and mimics stammering (SEN 1978:11; KNIPE 2015:45). In the first section of the *Aitareya Brāhmaṇa* (1.3), a text from *c.* 500 BCE, the symbolic rebirth of the consecrated initiate at the beginning of the *soma* rite is described. At the conclusion of the ceremony the sacrificer and his wife take a ritual bath (*avabhṛtha*). With the assistance of 'King *soma*' the sacrifice eradicates any sin or fault (*enas*) he has committed against the gods.

There is a clear distinction in the literature between those who have drunk *soma* (which requires an invitation) and those who have not, the latter sometimes compared to *śūdra*s (HILLEBRANDT 1981, Vol. 1:175). It seems that while priests may drink *soma* regularly at *soma* rituals, the *yajamāna* might drink only once or infrequently.[57] The purpose of the performance of Vedic rites is primarily that they should be performed, regardless of circumstances, for 'cosmic

56. *Manusmṛti* (XI.7–8) states: "A man who has sufficient resources to maintain his dependents for three years, or someone who has more than that, is entitled to drink Soma. If a twice-born man who possesses fewer resources than that drinks Soma, he will not reap its reward, even though he may never have drunk Soma before" (trans. OLIVELLE).

57. *Viṣṇusmṛti* (59.8–9) says that someone with a sufficient supply of food should perform the *soma* sacrifice once a year, in spring. Similarly, In Iran, in the cult of Mithra in the early centuries BCE (see below), the majority of participants participated in *haoma* only once but some participated in the *haoma* ceremony several times (BOWMAN 1970:35).

order'; but also, for the *yajamāna*, to obtain a 'better life', with good health, sons and cows. However, *soma* sacrifices are also performed for sorcery. The earliest Vedic texts that feature *soma* rites for sorcery belong to the *Sāmaveda* branch of the *Veda*s.[58]

Soma is several times said to grow on mountains (or in heaven),[59] from where it was brought by a falcon (*śyena*);[60] it is both terrestrial and celestial.[61] Adjectives used for its colour, which are not always

58. The *Ṣaḍviṃśa Brāhmaṇa* contains sorcery rites called *śyena* (falcon), *iṣu* (arrow), *saṃdaṃśa* (tongs), and *vajra* (mace/thunderbolt): see PARPLOLA (2015:134ff.) for further details.
59. *ṚV* 1.93.6; 3.48.2; 5.36.2; 5.43.4; 5.85.2; 9.18.1; 9.46.1; 9.71.4; 9.82.3; *AV* 3.21.10; or on Mount Mūjavat (*ṚV* 10.34.1); or in the Ārjīkīya country; or by the Suṣomā river; or in a valley or lake called Śaryaṇāvān (*ṚV* 8.53.11) (see HILLEBRANDT 1980, Vol. 1:175–183). PARPOLA (2015:93) tentatively identifies Suṣomā with the Sohan river, on the plains of north-west India.
60. *ṚV* 1.93.6; 4.18.13; 4.26.6–7; 4.27.3; 9.68.6; 9.77.2; 9.87.6; a bird occasionally identified as an eagle (*suparṇa*, fine-winged: 8.100.8; 10.144.4). On *śyena/suparṇa* identifications, see KNIPE (1967:331n.22). The popular myth of the falcon/eagle and *soma/haoma*, which appears in its earliest literary version in *ṚV* 4.26–27 (KNIPE 1967:328), has parallel traces in the *Avesta* and later Iranian texts. In this version of the myth (*ṚV* 4.26–27), a falcon bears Indra to heaven to fetch the coveted *soma*, to obtain which Indra had to break out of heaven's hundred 'iron forts'. Another version of the myth occurs in the *Rāmāyaṇa* (6.50), when the eagle Garuḍa flies up to heaven to obtain *amṛta*, breaking 'nets of iron' in order to steal it. The story of Garuḍa carrying off the elixir does not appear before the composition of the *Mahābhārata* (*c.* 200 BCE–200 CE) (GONDA 1997:59). The motif of an eagle who steals the nectar of immortality also occurs in the mythologies of the ancient Mediterranean and Scandinavia (see KNIPE 1967:338ff.; GONDA 1997:61ff.). In the classical Greek tradition, an eagle steals the ambrosia (which in this case is fermented mead) from a mountain. Similarly to the Indian notion of *amṛta*, *ambrosia* means 'immortal' (*am-brotos*), while 'nectar' derives from **nek* **ter*, which means 'the means to overcome death'.
61. Although in later Vedic literature *soma* is associated with the moon (see, for example, *Chāndogya Upaniṣad* 5.10; *Bṛhadāraṇyaka Upaniṣad* 6.2.16; *Śatapatha Brāhmaṇa* 2.4.2.7; *Atharvaveda* 9.6.7), in the *Ṛgveda soma* is also associated with the sun; *soma* is the bridegroom of the sun (*ṚV* 10.85.9). Some commentators maintain that early Vedic lunar associations are tenuous (MACDONELL 1995:112). See HOPKINS (1929) for a summary of the lunar associations, which HILLEBRANDT (1980, Vol. 1:200ff.) maintains obtain in the *ṚV*; but others do not agree with HILLEBRANDT on this point: see BHAWE (1957, Part 1:45), LAHIRI (1984:225–228) and GONDA (1997:38ff.). GONDA provides the most comprehensive analysis, and speculates (p.48) that the

easy to determine, include: *hari*, which may be translated as 'green', 'yellow' or 'golden'; *babhru* (brown/tawny); and *aruṇa* (red/brown/ tawny).[62] It is occasionally called 'sweet' (*madhu*, which also means both 'honey' and '[alcoholic] mead'),[63] but that seems to be only after the addition of milk, which makes it milder (ELIZARENKOVA 1996:17); otherwise it seems to be 'sharp' (*tīvra*) or bitter/piquant/ astringent (HILLEBRANDT 1980, Vol. 1:314), and in the *Veda*s[64] and *Brāhmaṇa*s—which may possibly be referring to another concoction, and not the plant itself—as foul smelling.[65]

---

life-giving functions of *soma* and the fertilizing power of the moon may have led to their eventual identification; also, like *soma*, the moon swells and is golden. The lunar aspect of *soma*, which is also a name of the moon, has further associations with an ancient binary classification, particularly in Ayurvedic medicine, of heating and cooling (such as for 'hot' and 'cold' foods), as *āgneya* (*agni*) and *saumya* (*soma*). See WUJASTYK (2004) for further details.

62. See HILLEBRANDT (1980, Vol. 1:131–135, 299) on the various colour references for *soma* in the *Veda*s and *Brāhmaṇa*s. On the tricky question of colour, see also STAAL (2001:762): besides issues of translation, it is sometimes uncertain whether colour references in the texts are to the extracted juice or to the plant itself.
63. *Madhu* is said in the *ṚV* to have intoxicating qualities and to be of eight kinds (MW:779). MAYOR (1995:40) and OTT (1998a) propose that honey used in some ancient religious rites may have had entheogenic (and not alcoholic) properties. See MAYOR (1995); RÄTSCH (2005:751–754); DEMIR AKCA and KAHVECI (2012) on intoxicating honey that can engender hallucinations, topor, 'madness' and even death. The most famous historical occurrences of honey intoxication are from the Black Sea region, when several times armies have succumbed to the effects. In 401 BCE, thousands of Greek soldiers under the general XENOPHON (430–355 BCE), who were returning from war with Persia, became like intoxicated madmen and then collapsed after eating honey from around the Black Sea (see XENOPHON in SCHLEIFFER 1979:89–90). Cases of honey intoxication have been reported from Turkey, Japan, Nepal, Brazil, North America, southern Russia and various parts of Europe. The main reagent in intoxicating honey is acetylandromedol (a grayanotoxin), which is found in two kinds of rhododendron (*R. luteum* and *R. ponticum*), and also in some varieties of Mediterranean azalea and oleander. PLINY was the first correctly to identify honey from these plants as toxic, and warned of honey from the Black Sea region (MAYOR 1995:33–35); however, it is also used as a medicine in that region for gastric pain, bowel disorders, hypertension and as an aphrodisiac.
64. LAHIRI (1984:173–174) observes that *soma* had a putrid smell.
65. See *Śatapatha Brāhmaṇa* 4.1.3.8.

Although the mythology and use of *soma* permeate the *Vedas*, it is of course difficult to determine reliable botanical evidence from religious texts. Another particular problem inherent in the interpretation of Vedic passages, which is well known to analysts, is the poetic, allusive, multivalent and polysemantic use of terms, which are open to a variety of interpretations. Some aspects of *soma* are, however, evident. One of the most common epithets for *soma*—often referred to as 'King Soma'[66]—in the *Vedas* and *Brāhmaṇas* is *aṃśu*, which may be translated as 'stem' or 'stalk'[67] (or 'section of a stalk').[68] The term *amśu* (Avestan *ąsu*) is the original name of the *soma* plant (THOMPSON 2007:67), from which juice is pressed. Other of the many epithets and attributes of *soma* in the *Vedas* include 'Lord of vision' (*dhī*), *indu* (the bright drop),[69] *andhas* (which refers to the plant and to *soma* juice),[70] *drapsa* (drop), and *pitu* (juice/drink/food). *Soma* is 'lord of the mind'.[71] *Soma* is also the 'king' of plants; its effects are compared to the strength of a bull; it is swift like a steed, brilliant like the sun, conferring immortality on gods and men; it has medicinal power and confers long life; it destroys falsehood and promotes truth; it stimulates the voice and inspires poets and the composing of hymns (*soma* is also identified as the 'divine poet'); *soma* is all knowing; (he) sees everything with a thousand eyes and kills demons and the wicked;[72] pressing *soma* engenders *ānanda* (bliss/happiness);[73] *soma* is also referred to as *amṛta* (non-death/immortal).

---

66. In one story, King Soma had thirty-three wives, the daughters of Prajāpati. For a summary of this myth, see ZYSK (1985:15). Thirty-three deities, plus Prajāpati, are the thirty-four deities of the formulae of the oblations performed at a *soma* sacrifice (see GONDA 1982:3).
67. *Tige*: RENOU (1961:17, v.4 & ff.).
68. Most probably also fibrous: see BROUGH (1971:338); GERSHEVITCH 1974:74). *Soma* stalks are without leaves or flowers (STAAL 2008:98).
69. Which refers to the moon in later literature (see below).
70. See HILLEBRANDT (1980, Vol. 1: 145–147). GONDA (1982:8) comments that *andhas* is the preferred term for the plant when those concerned are looking for it.
71. *ṚV* 9.11.8.4: *manasaspatiḥ*. This is an epithet that is unique amongst Vedic deities (DANGE 2000:138).
72. GONDA (1975:356–357) remarks that the *soma* hymns emphasize the brightness, brilliance, strength, roaring sound, and swift and restless motion of the beverage.
73. The term *ānanda* is only used in the *Ṛgveda* in connection with the pressing of *soma* (DANGE 2000:141).

ELIZARENKOVA (1996:28) observes that, strictly speaking, '*soma*' in the *Veda*s is not a proper name but is a ritual designation for a substance out of which *soma* was pressed. Similarly, MALANDRA (1983:150) remarks that in the ancient Iranian context *haoma* means simply 'the thing which has been pressed' or 'juice': "It is important to realize that this specialized word originally meant 'juice': it was not the name of a plant".[74] In a Chapter 13 the idea will be mooted that perhaps *'soma'*, also in the Vedic context, may have referred not necessarily only to a specific plant but to an effective preparation of plants.

It was observed above that one of the epithets used for *soma* in the *Veda*s is *amṛta* (immortality). Although this trope, amongst many others, of *soma* as *amṛta* appears occasionally in the *Veda*s,[75] the well-known myth of the 'churning of the ocean of milk' (*kṣīrābhdimathana*)—from which the *rasāmṛta*, the precious juice/nectar of immortality,[76] emerges—appears only later, unexpectedly and in highly developed form (LONG 1976:177) in the *Rāmāyaṇa* (*c.* 200 BCE–200 CE), *Mahābhārata* (*c.* 200 BCE–200 CE)[77] and *Purāṇa*s (*c.* 300–1200 CE).[78] This extended notion of *amṛta*, as the nectar of immortality, which appeared long after the composition of the *Veda*s,[79] has perhaps to some extent influenced discussion,

74. See also, similarly, THOMPSON (2007:67).
75. *ṚV* 6.44.16; 6.44.23; 8.48.3; 9.91.2; 9.110.4. The sacrificer becomes immortal by drinking *soma* (*ŚB* 3.3.3.10).
76. LONG (1976:18n.22) notes that in Hindu mythology *amṛta* does not always mean 'eternal life', as in the concept in the Judeo-Christian tradition, but rather a long life filled with prosperity, health, progeny and well-being.
77. However, BHATTACHARYA (1984:76ff.) illustrates how many of the specific motifs in the 'churning of the ocean' myth, as it appears in the *Mahābhārata*, have parallels, antecedents and traces in the *Veda*s (for example, the 'pressing out' of *soma*, celebrated in *ṚV* 7, having a parallel in the 'churning' of the ocean); though some the proposed correspondences seem somewhat dubious.
78. See, for example, *Bhāgavata Purāṇa*, 8.6.33–8.7.
79. This myth was yet further elaborated, probably in the early 20th century, and appended to the *Skanda Purāṇa* (CLARK 2006:287–299), to account for the current sites of the largest festival on earth, the (usually) triennial *Kumbh Melā*. This elaboration—of which there are variants—of the earlier myth describes how drops of *amṛta* fell from a pot (*kumbha*) carried by the bird Garuḍa onto the four current sites of the festival, at Haridvār, Prayāg (Allahabad), Ujjain and Tryambakeśvar (Nāsik), an account that may be found in many popular Hindi religious booklets and pamphlets (for

analysis and the identification of *soma*, some commentators (see Chapter 13) identifying *soma* simply as *amṛta*, with the general function of providing either immortality or the key to higher wisdom or consciousness. It will be suggested that this notion is in essence probably correct, though this identification may have detracted from an analysis of what exactly, in the botanical domain, *soma* may have referred to in the Vedic context.

Even though around two millennia ago in South Asia the notion of a divine, immaterial, 'non-plant' *soma* is apparent, nevertheless it is also evident that there was also a general but probably restricted awareness in medical and yogic milieux of *soma* as a drug. In the *Yogasūtra* of PATAÑJALI (4.1), which dates to the late 4th or 5th century CE, supernatural powers (*siddhi*s) are said to be obtained through birth, herbs/drugs[80] (*oṣadhi*),[81] *mantra*s, *tapas* (austerities) or *samādhi* (yogic trance).[82] In his commentary on this verse, ŚAṄKARĀCARYA states[83] that *siddhi* can be attained through taking drugs such as *soma* or the *āmalaka* plant.[84]

---

example, UPĀDHYĀY n.d.:9ff.; *Kumbh* 2001:10ff.). In *Kumbh* (p.14) the *amṛta* notion is further extended, the attainment of which becoming the aim/purpose (*lakṣya*) of those participating in the festival. Similarly, in a Norse myth, Odin stole the 'mead of inspiration' and escaped to Asgard as an eagle; *en route* some of the mead dropped to earth and thus became available for mortals (ELLIS DAVIDSON 1973:40–41).

80. Commenting on this verse, ĀRAṆYA (1985:347) notes that witches can acquire similar power by rubbing hemlock on their body; and that, "it is certain that supernormal powers on a small scale can be acquired by the application of drugs".

81. According to CARAKA (*Sūtrasthāna* 1, SHARMA and DASH 1983:50), there are four kinds of drugs of vegetable origin: *vanaspati* (having fruits only, and no flowers), *virudh* (which spread, with branches), *vānaspatya* (having flowers and fruits), and *oṣadhi* (which die out when their fruits mature).

82. *Janmauṣadhimantratapaḥsamādhijāḥ siddhayaḥ*.

83. Translation of this commentary by LEGGETT (1990). Some scholars accept this commentary as a genuine work of ŚAṄKARA (*c.* 700 CE); however, RUKMANI (1998) cogently argues that this is not one of ŚAṄKARA's genuine works.

84. The plant being referred to here is *Phyllanthus emblica* (emblic myrobalan), also known as *āmlā/āṃvlā* (Hindi) and *āmalakī* (Sanskrit). Particularly the fruits of this tree have many uses in Āyurveda. Its synonyms in Indian *material medica* include *dhatrīphala, amṛtaphala, śrīphala* and *śiva* (DASH

Interestingly, the notion of *soma* being identified as *amṛta* is reversed in some later Tantric and yoga texts, wherein the ecstasy-producing *amṛta*, which is believed to be stored (or activated or accessed) in the cranial vault, becomes identified as *soma*: *amṛta* becomes *soma*. See, for example, the *c.* 15th-century *Haṭhapradīpikā* (3.44–46): describing the *khecarī mudrā* (a yogic practice of placing the curled-back, extended tongue over the top of the palate), it is stated that:

> The knower of yoga—tongue above, steady, drinking soma—undoubtedly conquers death in half a month. Poison does not spread in the yogi whose body is filled every day with drops of soma—even when bitten by the Takshaka serpent. As the fire, the fuel, and the flame, the oily wick, so the soul does not abandon a body filled with drops of soma (trans. AKERS).

Here, what is being referred to is clearly an allegorical 'soma', rather than extracted vegetable juice. Similarly, in the *c.* 14th-century *Khecarīvidyā* of Ādinātha (2.16–26), *soma* is identified as an internal nectar (*amṛta*)—stored in eight places (*kalā*), or as eight streams/oceans—in one's head, 'drinking' which, through *khecarī mudrā*, the yogi conquers disease and acquires a diamond body (MALLINSON 2007:124). Also, in the Tamil *siddha* tradition it is believed that there is an endogenous *soma* (correlative with exogenous *soma*), which is a fluid known as *civampu* (the flowering of *civam*) that is secreted by the midbrain, and which can be activated by yoga exercises (ZVELEBIL 1996:92).85 In some Tibetan Buddhist transgressive rites (such as, for example, in the *c.* 8th-century *Cakrasamvara Tantra*), combined male and female

---

and KASHYAP 1980:451). *Āmlā* is not usually considered to be psychoactive on its own but, interestingly, it appears as one of the most important plants in over a dozen Ayurvedic formulas in the *Caraka saṃhitā* for rejuvenation (*rasāyana*) (VALIATHAN 2003:236–241); it is also one of many plants used in the preparation of *amṛta* formulas that appear in the 6th-century Bower Manuscript, a medical text discussed in Chapter 13.

85. I have come across the anecdotal notion in yoga circles that the nectar released by performing *khecarī mudrā* might be endogenous DMT, though I have not yet come across any scientific or corroborative evidence of this supposition.

sexual emissions, which are consumed, are also sometimes referred to as *soma* (GRAY 2007:151).

From the evidence presented it is apparent that *soma* was, on the one hand, used in Vedic rites in the form of the expressed juice of a plant (or plants), but that, on the other hand, *soma* became identified in later yogic and Tantric circles with a kind of internal 'nectar of immortality' providing the same or similar kinds of the *siddhi*s and bliss engendered by the drinking of real juice.

Finally, it is important to note that historically the *soma* cult related to the performance of Vedic recitation was only ever practised by a relatively very small number of people. In South Asia, it was primarily the brahman community who engaged in these rites, a community that has been estimated to comprise—both now and historically—approximately only four or five percent of the South Asian population. Around 1500–1000 BCE in South Asia, this community, who would have known the *Veda*s and of *soma*, might have numbered about 1,000.[86] It was not the case that *soma* rites were practised by the general population of South Asia. Similar observations probably hold true for early Zoroastrian *haoma* rites.[87]

---

86. The estimate for the brahman population of South Asia, which is very rough, was arrived at after examining numerous census reports in the course of previous research (it may need revising). The figure of 1,000 ancient brahman ritualists is similarly approximate, based on the best estimates of several senior Indologists.
87. SHERRATT (1995:15) remarks that the use of psychoactive substances is often culturally restricted to a fraction of the society, whether this fraction is defined by gender, status or wealth, or a combination of all three: "One reason for this is the powerful potential of such substances to accrue symbolic meanings, and to provide focal experiences in the formation of dissident communities". Interestingly, the wide-ranging studies by SIEGAL (2005) on the effects of various kinds of drugs on animals demonstrate how creatures (for example, mice) who become habituated to drug use form their own, separate sub-groups within the community.

CHAPTER 3

Haoma in the *Avesta*

Along with several other scholars, MACDONELL (1995:113–114)[88] more than a century ago[89] noted the striking similarities in depiction and mythology between *soma* in Vedic texts and *haoma* (*hōm*)[90] in the *Avesta*,[91] the corpus of texts sacred to Zoroastrians.[92] In the *Avesta*: *haoma* is placed on a mountain in Haraiti[93] by a skillful god;

88. See also EGGELING (1885:xi–xxxii [*Śatapatha Brāhmaṇa* Vol. 2 = *S.B.E.* Vol. 26]); MODI (1922: 299–300).
89. Specific comparisons between Zoroastrian and Vedic material began in the mid-19th century: see HOUBEN (2003:2.1).
90. Pahlavi (middle-Persian). The Sanskrit root √*su* = Avestan √*hu*.
91. On the ancient, common cultural ancestry of Vedic and Zoroastrian religions, see PARPOLA (1997a).
92. The teachings of Zarathustra are contained in the *Avesta* (which comprises seventy-two chapters/sections, and which is entirely mantric/mānthric in form). The earlier portion of the *Avesta* comprises seventeen *gāthā*s, believed to have been composed by the prophet himself—though the whole *Avesta* is attributed to him—and which is in a language known as Gathic Avestan. This language is similar to the Sanskrit of the *Ṛgveda* and similarly ancient, the *gāthā*s dating from perhaps around 1200–1000 BCE. The *gāthā*s comprising the seven bundles/chapters of the *Yasna Haptaŋhāiti*, which are central to the structure of the *yasna* (HINZE 2004), may possibly predate Zarathustra. *Mānthra*s recited in Gathic Avestan are believed to be more powerful. Later portions of the *Avesta* are in a language known as Younger Avestan. The oral corpus was first committed to writing in the 5th century CE. *Gāthā*s are recited in daily Zoroastrian worship, known as *yasna*. Some of the *yasna* comprises *yasht*s, which are hymns to semi-divine beings, including Hōm (i.e. *haoma*). For further details, see BOYCE (1990); KOTWAL and BOYD (1991).
93. This 'cosmic' mountain, partly mythological and partly homologized with real mountains, is an axis of transcendence; it is equivalent to Mount Meru in

it is distributed from the mountain[94] by auspicious birds; it is the mighty king of plants and a god; it comes to earth from heaven; it is both celestial and terrestrial; it is a medicine, giving health, long life and removing death and the intrigues of the wicked; it gives victory over enemies; it is light-winning and wise; it grants steeds and excellent children; its stalks (*ąsu*) are pressed (twice, according to the *Avesta*) to produce a juice that is mixed with water and milk.[95] The names of the ancient, mythological preparers of the beverage are very similar in both the Avestan and Vedic traditions.[96] The slaying of the 'cosmic' snake (*vṛtrahan*)—which is Indra's most acclaimed feat in the mythology of the *Vedas*—has a close homonym in Avestan, as *verethrajan*.[97]

---

the Indian tradition (MALANDRA 1983:11). In Iran it is identified with Mount Alburz (Av. Harā Bərəzaitī [*bərəzaitī* = lofty]), which MODI (1922:303) notes is not only a peak in the Caucasus range, but also refers to the entire range as far as the Hindu Kush. GHOSAL (1980/81:53) refers to this mountain as Haraburja, from which *soma* spreads to the whole range of the Pārsika (i.e. Persian) mountains. Elburz/Elborz/Alburz currently designates a range of mountains in northern Iran that stretches from the border of Azerbaijan along the western and entire southern coast of the Caspian Sea.

94. Also in river valleys (*Y* 10.17). References with '*Y*' refer to *yasnas* in the *Hōm Yasht* (see below). All references and translation from the *Hōm Yasht* are from JOSEPHSON (1997).
95. *Y* 10.13.
96. See MACDONELL (1995:114): Vivasat (Vivasvant) = Vivaṅhvant (Vīuuaŋᵥhaṇt); Trita Āptya = Thrita. In the *Avesta* (*Y* 9.4) Vīuuaŋᵥhaṇt was the first mortal to press *haoma*, resulting in the birth of Yima (in the *Vedas* Vivasvant is the father of Yama (the god of death): *ṚV* 10.14.1); Āthwya (the 'third' Āptya) is the second to do so, resulting in the birth of Thraētaona (see below) (in the *Vedas* his cognate, Traitana, occurs only once, at *ṚV* 1.85, as a Dāsa, a demonic creature). Thrita is the third mortal to press *haoma*, resulting in the birth of Kərəsāspa (see below) (KHANIZADEH 2016:4).
97. The ancient epithet *verethrajan* (obstruction-smashing = Vedic *vṛtrahan*), which occurs at *Y* 44.16 (its only occurrence in Old Avestan), refers to the actions of the divine being/spirit Sraoša, who protects the world of Ahura Mazda from darkness, and who, in this passage, smashes Wrath. In the *Avesta*, there is not a 'Vṛtra' that is a snake/demon/dragon, as in the *Vedas*. In ancient Zoroastrian Armenia and Iran the deity/divine being (*yazata*) Vĕrĕthraghna/Verethrajan/Vahagn smites evil, slays a dragon (similarly to Indra, who slays Vṛtra), is the personification of victory, and is a weather god who thunders above the clouds. He protects the sick and travellers and is

In the *Avesta*, chapters/sections 9–11 comprise the *Hōm Yasht* [*Yašt*], which is around 1,700 words long and contains what appear to be very ancient elements (Boyce 2012). It has litanies to *haoma* (*hōm*), which, as in the *Veda*s, is both a plant and its juice, and a form of deity/spirit being (*yazad*) who is also the 'son' of Ahura Mazda (*Y* 11.4).[98] It is collected by women,[99] and when properly prepared and praised, *haoma* bestows six gifts: bliss, health, long life, power to prevent evil, victory against enemies, and fore-warnings against thieves and "wolves" (*Y* 9.19–21). It helps barren women desiring children and gives spiritual power to students of the *Avesta*; it helps warriors going into battle (*Y* 9.22) and maidens to find husbands (*Y* 9.23).[100] *Haoma* is described as being yellow or golden-coloured (*zairi*) (*Y* 9.11), with pliant shoots (*Y* 9.16),[101] giving strength, health (*Y* 9.17, 19) and bliss.[102] It is sweet-scented (*Y* 10.4) and has branches

---

associated with righteousness and with Mithra. He is sometimes represented with fiery, golden hair, with a lion skin over his shoulder, resting on a club. In the *Avesta* the three-headed, three-mouthed, six-eyed monster/dragon, the demon *par excellence* called Aži (serpent) Dahāka, made by Angra Mainyu for the destruction of the material world, is slain by Thraētaona (*Y* 9.8) or Kərəsāspa (Russell 1987:42, 189, 198; Skærvø 2004:276–277; 2011:15), though in Pahlavi literature (unlike in the *Avesta*) Kərəsāspa does not slay the dragon but fetters him lest evil creatures emerge from his body. However, the myths of both Thraētaona and Kərəsāspa seem to originate from a single dragon-slaying story, as they share similar features (Khanizadeh 2016:4).

98. In distinction from Vedic tradition, in Zoroastrian religion there is also a white, spiritual form of *hōm*, called *gōkarn* (Av. *gaokərəna*), which produces immortals at the time of the renovation of the world. It is a mythological tree that confers immortality on the resurrected bodies of the dead at the 'end-time'.

99. "...bound in bundles by the women" (*Y* 10.17, trans. Josephson).

100. Russell (1987:439) notes the practice by Persians in the Parthian period (247–224 CE), reported by Plutarch (*De Iside* 45–47), of what seems to have been an inversion of the *haoma*-pounding ceremony: for rites to Angra Mainyu, Hadēs and darkness are invoked and a herb called *omoni* is pounded and mixed with the blood of a slaughtered wolf and thrown into a sunless place.

101. See also Modi (1922:304n.67); Gershevitch (1974:59).

102. "The first boon I ask of you, O death-destroying Haoma, the best existence of the righteous, light, with all bliss" (*Y* 9.19); "May your brilliant intoxicant [drops] come forth! Your intoxication moves lightly" (*Y* 10.19) (trans. Josephson).

and sprigs[103] (MODI 1922:304). Although *haoma* is mentioned frequently in the *Avesta* in connection with the worship of ancient Iranian deities, the *Hōm Yasht* is the only part of the *Avesta* in which *haoma* is referred to as a plant (FLATTERY and SCHWARZ 1989:54).[104] *Y* 9–11 accompanies the first ritual drinking of *haoma.*[105] This section (*Y* 9–11) of the *Avesta* and the *haoma* ceremony for which it is the liturgy probably predate the prophet Zarathustra,[106] who is believed to have lived around 1700–1500 BCE[107] (BOYCE 2001:125,18).[108] Zarathustra's miraculous birth is associated with the *haoma* plant because prior to his birth his guardian spirit (*fravaši*),[109] brought to the material world by Vohuman and Ašavahišt, is believed to have been within its stalk (DUCHESNE-GUILLEMIN 1962:339); KOTWAL and BOYD 1991:98n.94).[110]

The evidence indicates that the cult of *soma/haoma* has a common origin in the geographical region of Turkmenistan, Iran and

---

103. "You are truly the source of truth! Increase through my prayer! In every stem, in every shoot, in every branch" (*Y* 10.5) (trans. JOSEPHSON).
104. However, in the 9th century *Dēnkard* (7.2.22–23), a collection of Zoroastrian wisdom, there are references to a stem of Hōm the size of a man; to sap constantly oozing from the Hōm when it is moist; and to Hōm being connected to a tree, where it grew constantly fresh and golden-coloured (or verdant) at the summit, where there was a nest of birds (9.2.28) (WEST 2010:23–25).
105. *Y* 27 accompanies the pressing and offering of the plant(s).
106. The *Hōm Yasht* originated as the liturgy of a separate and independent *haoma* ceremony (FLATTERY and SCHWARZ 1989:88), which at some time was incorporated into the ritual of the *yasna* (JOSEPHSON 1997:23).
107. Not all scholars agree on this early date; some argue for a much more recent date in the 6th–8th centuries BCE. PARPOLA (2002:247), for example, proposes *c.* 800 BCE. For a useful, brief summary of some of the problems and contradictions concerning Zarathustra's date, see STAUSBERG 2004:4n.11).
108. According to tradition, Zarathustra had his first vision aged thirty, when, emerging 'pure' from a river, he saw a shining being, Vohuh Manah (good purpose); this led Zarathustra into the presence of Ahura Mazda—the god of light from whom Zarathustra's revelation primarily derives—and five other radiant figures, whose light obscured his own shadow (BOYCE 2001:19).
109. This is a kind of 'over-soul', related to a counterpart, earthly personality.
110. There is also a legend in the *Dēnkard* (7.2.14) that Ahura Mazda, through Hōm, transmitted the guardian spirit to Zarathustra through his parents (WEST 2010:21). Zarathustra's birth is described (*Y* 9.13) as the reward his father Pourushapa received for pressing *haoma.*

Afghanistan, even though there are several significant differences in the cultures of ancient (Zoroastrian) Iran and (Vedic) India; and there is no mention in the *Avesta* that the Vedic and Iranian people shared a common past (FALK 2002/3:141–143). THOMPSON (2007:67) maintains that the Indo-Iranians did not inherit their **sauma*[111] cult from their Indo-European linguistic ancestors, and assuming that they did not invent the cult themselves, they most probably acquired it in Central Asia.[112] In this regard he observes that the original name for **sauma* was *aṃśu/ąsu*, which appears to be a loan word from a Central Asian substrate language. On the basis of linguistic and archeological evidence, PARPOLA (1997a:370) maintains that the cult of drinking *haoma* was evidently adopted by Zoroastrianism[113] from the earlier Bronze Age religion of Central Asia and eastern Iran,[114] and suggests (2002:245) that the cults of Indra and **sauma* were adopted by what he describes as the third wave of proto-Indo-Āryan

---

111. Authors generally use the 'reconstructed' (from proto Indo-Iranian) term **sauma* when discussing *haoma* in its ancient context.
112. WITZEL (2004:595) also maintains that the name **sauma* further supports the 'foreign' origin of *soma/haoma.*
113. There is disagreement among scholars whether or not Zarathustra condemned drinking *haoma* in his reformation of Iranian religion. NYBERG (1938:189–191) maintains that Zarathustra condemned it; but see DUCHESNE-GUILLEMAN (1988) for three arguments against NYBERG's view. BOYCE (1975:216–217) is of the opinion that he did not condemn it. MALANDRA (1983:21–22) remarks that although some commentators argue for the idea that Zarathustra condemned *haoma*, "Against it is the entire history of Zoroastrianism, in which the central ritual, the yasna, is essentially a haoma sacrifice. How could it be possible for followers of Zarathusthra's teachings unashamedly to espouse a practice that their prophet so roundly condemned?" Also, for example, in the 9th century *Zādsparam* (a Pahlavi hagiography of Zarathustra by the theologian Zādsparam), Zarathustra himself presses *hōm* (20.16; 21.5) (WEST 2010:154–155).
114. See also FLATTERY and SCHWARZ (1989:52). KUIPER (1969:279) comments that, "it is not impossible that the use and worship of the *Sauma* was borrowed by the Proto-Indo-Iranian speaking people from some foreign culture at a time when they had already split off as a separate community from the other groups which spoke Indo-European languages".

speakers, who occupied BMAC[115] from *c.*1750–1500 BCE.[116] BOYCE (1982:146) also believes that it is very likely that the pressing of *haoma* goes back to pre-Zoroastrian times. HUTTER (1996:196ff.) discusses the textual evidence in the Zoroastrian tradition of a *haoma* cult prior to Zarathustra,[117] particularly amongst some Central Asian *haomavarga* (*haoma*-swilling) Scythians.[118] WITZEL (2004:594–597) similarly maintains that the cults of Indra and *haoma/soma* were probably acquired as components of Ṛgvedic religion around 2000 BCE in the southern part of Western Central Asia, close to the mountain Muzh Tagh Ata.

---

115. This is the Bactria Margiana Achaeological Complex in Turkmenistan. See Chapter 10 for further details.

116. PARPOLA (1998:126) also speculates that the cult of **sauma* may have been acquired from the Afanas'evo culture, which spread from southern Siberia to western Mongolia from *c.*3000–2000 BCE.

117. HUTTER (1996:198ff.) cites passages from the *Avesta* (*Y* 29.1; *Y* 32.12–14; *Y* 48.10), which, he maintains, indicate a former, non-Zoroastrian, intoxicating *haoma* cult—which also possibly involved blood-sacrifice and perhaps sexual rites—which was condemned by Zarathustra, who reformed and 'spiritualized' the cult. BOWMAN (1970:9–10) is of the opinion that Zarathustra merely condemned the excessive drinking of *haoma.*

118. GERSHEVITCH (1974:54–55) discusses a tribe of Sakā (i.e. Scythian) nomads occupying the Tashkent region since the 7th century BCE, referred to by DARIUS and XERXES as *haumawarga* (*hauma*-pressers/twisters), who he identifies as probably the Tūra tribe. BARTHOLOMAE (1904:1735) refers to the *haomavarka* as a branch of the Scythians; ABAEV (1975:2) refers to inscriptions in Old Persian of a Scythian tribe denominated as "*sakā hauma-varga*". For the various possible derivations of the term **varg-* that have been proposed by linguists, see SCHMITT (2015), who maintains that these *haumavargā*s were one of three groups of Sakā tribes, neighbours of 'pointed-hat' Scythians, who lived somewhere beyond the Oxus/Āmu Daryā river, in the neighbourhood of the Bactrians and Sogdians. PARPOLA (2015:102) also refers to the royal inscriptions of DARIUS and XERXES. In a list of peoples, of which there are five versions, in one short version (in an inscription of DARIUS) two kinds of Sakā are mentioned: *haumavargā* and *tigrazandā* (pointed hat). KORYAKOVA and EPIMACHOV (2014:225) comment that the Greeks knew little about these eastern nomads, whom they called Asiatic or Eastern Scythians, names which seem to have been synonymous with 'nomads'; they comprised numerous separate groups, including Sakā-Haomavarga, Sakā-Paradarayia and Sakā-Tigrakhuada.

The cult of *haoma* drinking was also central to the cult of Mithra in the latter half of the 1st millennium BCE in Central Asia, a cult that was particularly popular with soldiers and the military.[119] *Haoma* was drunk at Mithraic festivals and was used in Persepolis in Iran in the Achaemenid period at least from the time of XERXES (BOWMAN (1970:8ff.).[120] However, by the time that the Sasanian clergy translated the *Avesta* into Pahlavi, around 350 CE, the meaning of the *haoma* texts seems to have become a matter of speculation for Zoroastrians; and they seem to have been unaware that *haoma* was an intoxicating drug, inducing *madha/mada* (intoxication).[121] By the

119. BOWMAN (1970) examines a body of Aramaic inscriptions on mortars and pestles (mostly made of green chert) for pressing *haoma*, and plates found in Persepolis, dated to the 5th century BCE, many inscribed during the reign of ARTAXERXES I. For critical comment on some of BOWMAN's decipherment see HINZ (1975).

120. BEDROSIAN (2000:5,16n.40) also provides evidence that *haoma* drinking may have been undertaken annually at a festival of Mithra by Persian kings in the Achaemenid period (550–330 BCE).

121. The term 'intoxication' is problematic in relation to the effects of drugs, plants and foods in general. Anything consumed can be toxic (i.e. poisonous) if incorrectly or excessively consumed. Drinking too much water can kill someone within forty-eight hours; similarly, eating too many carrots can cause death. Terminology related to 'getting high' or experiencing other dimensions of consciousness is particularly limited in the English language, so 'intoxication' is used throughout this book for the effects of a drug (also a problematic term, probably deriving from Dutch, around 1400 CE, meaning 'dried goods': JAY 2010:54); though the author is aware of the inappropriateness of the term, particularly in relation to the use of entheogens. Reservations concerning terminology apt for the effect of *soma* pertain similarly to terms with 'negative' connotations (as of drunkenness) used by commentators in other languages, such as *Rausch* (German), *breuvage-enivrant* (French: e.g. RENOU 1961:17, v.3), or *naśā* (Hindi). For useful discussions of the unhelpfully vague demarcation between plants, drugs, foods and medicine, particularly concerning consumption by animals, see SAMORINI (2002:1–17); and also VAYNE (2006:22–27), who comments (p.24): "If we assume... that the mind is a system based on a chemical network (the brain and the body) then anything that we come into contact with might be thought of as a drug". For a scheme classifying various kinds of 'intoxication', see Appendix 5. Nearly two thousand years ago CARAKA (*Sūtrasthāna* 36.12) remarked that, "there is nothing in the world which does not have therapeutic utility in appropriate conditions and situations" (trans. SHARMA and DASH 1983:453).

9th century, the term *hōm/haoma* simply designated a non-intoxicating plant consumed in daily *yasna* rites (FLATTERY and SCHWARZ 1989:13–14).[122]

In contemporary practice of the *haoma* ritual,[123] which follows ancient performance, prayers from particular chapters of the *Avesta* are recited to the golden *haoma* plant, who is 'the sage' and the guardian spirit of Zarathustra. The *haoma* ritual, includes both the preparation and the drinking of *haoma*. It is a part of a longer two-and-a-half-hour, daily ritual performed by two priests (*zōts/zaotars*)[124] and culminates with the priests drinking the filtered[125]

The central issues of drugs and intoxication are generally confused in contemporary discussion, because while it is generally acceptable to use plants or drugs to alleviate minor or major deficiencies or illness in other bodily organs, the notion that psychedelic agents, if used scientifically and appropriately, may, through 'mystical experience' (however that is conceived of; see below) improve the health and functioning of the brain, and hence the individual in society, is generally unacceptable to many physicians and scientists, which seems to be an irrational prejudice. SIEGAL (2005) suggests that, besides sex, shelter and sustenance, intoxication is the fourth drive in humans. WEIL (1975) similarly endorses the notion of alteration of consciousness as natural behaviour. In a cross-cultural survey of 488 societies of the world, across six international zones, BOURGUIGNON (1973:11) found that an average of ninety percent of them had institutional means to alter consciousness.

122. MALANDRA (1983:150) remarks that, "in the history of Vedic and Zoroastrian rituals, a parallel process of symbolic valorization occurred whereby the symbolism of the ritual took precedence over the actual properties of the juice".

123. The current *yasna* has two preparations of *haoma*, which differ only slightly in their rituals (BOYCE 2001:125; 2012).

124. Originally eight priests were required. In some manuscripts of the *Vendidād* a diagram is given showing their placement in the ceremonial arena, in the cardinal directions. The use of two priests dates only from the 9th century CE (BOWMAN 1970:11). The title of the chief Iranian officiant, *zaotar*, is similar to the Vedic equivalent: *hotar*. Also of interest is that one of the eight priests was the *haoma* mixer (*rāeθwiškara*), which role is, it is suggested, more significant than merely someone who mixed water with milk, pomegranate and other substances. It is suggested later in this book that the accurate mixing of psychoactive plants was crucial for the safety and efficacy of the *haoma*.

125. Through a sieve made of bull's hair in former times. A lock of three, five, or

parahaoma (*parahōm*),[126] which is a mixture of consecrated water and the juice (or essence) of both the *haoma* plant and pomegranate[127] (*urwarām*) twigs.[128] This 'essence' (or juice) is extracted from three twigs of *hōm* and pomegranate twigs using the traditional method of pounding[129] with mortar and pestle.[130] The requisite items for the performance of the *yasna* of the *haoma* ritual are:[131] *haoma*, sacred bread (*drōn*), consecrated water, pure water,[132] fresh milk, a pomegranate twig, mortar and pestle, fragrant wood,[133] frankincense, a fire, and a bundle of metal wires,[134] known as *barsom*[135] (which

seven hairs from the tail of a white bull—which is tied to a metal thumb-ring that is placed into a strainer when the juice is about to be poured—appears to have replaced the bull's hair sieve (WEST 2010:71n.2).

126. For accounts of the part of the ritual of the *yasna* dedicated to *haoma* (*Y* 9–11), see DROWER (1956:208ff.); KOTWAL and BOYD (1991:97–100); MODI (1913:506–510); MODI (1922:306ff.).
127. This is one of the substitutes for *haoma*, probably on account of the visual resemblance of its seed pods to those of rue (see FLATTERY and SCHWARZ 1989:76ff., 132).
128. Goat's milk is also added to some preparations of *hōm*, but not for the *parahōm*. BOYCE (2012) comments that the addition of milk, which in later texts is said to be important, may perhaps be a later modification of the ritual. She believes that, "The doctrinal significance of the milk is plainly that the animal creation is thus represented". Whether or not milk is a later addition to the ritual, the fat of milk or milk products aid the absorption of psychoactive compounds into the bloodstream. I would suggest that this is the reason for the use of milk products with *soma* and with the Greek *kykeōn* (see Chapter 17).
129. The pounding of *haoma* is accompanied by recitation of *Y* 22–27.11 and subsequently other *yasnas* (32–33).
130. The mortar and pestle are symbolized as the 'sky of stone' in the seven-fold scheme of creation in Zoroastrianism (see BOYCE 1990:13).
131. A recitation of a list of these items is uttered by a priest and comprises the 24th chapter of the *yasna* (see MODI 1922:308).
132. As in Vedic rites, water (known as *zaothra*) from a running source is used (DROWER 1956:80).
133. Sandalwood is currently used.
134. In the *yasna* twenty-three are used; in the *visperad* thirty-five; in the *bāj* of *panj tāī* five (DROWER 1956:80).
135. The Avestan term *baresman* is probably etymologically related to *barhiṣ*, the grass used in Vedic ritual (GONDA 1985:148n.53), which is discussed below. The post-fix *men* often denotes numinal power.

was a bundle of twigs from a tree in former times),[136] whose ceremony is particularly important in the tradition. The ritual needs to be performed continuously until the time of the 'last judgment', when evil will be defeated.[137] SKJÆRVØ (2011:34) characterizes the *yasna* as the ritual re-creation of the world.

In Zoroastrian practice, for many centuries in both India and Iran, it is the ephedra plant—which is discussed in greater detail later in this book—which can be used as a mild stimulant, that has been used as *haoma* (DUCHESNE-GUILLEMIN 1962:72; BOYCE 1975:157; GNOLI 2005:3775). Although there are alternative theories to that of ephedra (see below), most scholars of Zoroastrianism are of the opinion that ephedra was the 'original' *haoma*.[138] Parsis in Mumbai used to import ephedra from Iran, but now have no supplies. About a century ago ephedra was still being imported into Mumbai, where it was ritually washed and purified and stored for up to thirteen months prior to ceremonial use, so that impurities accumulated on its journey from Persia could dissipate (MODI 1922:305). Substitutes are now being used but it is unclear what these are (BOYCE 1979:173). It has been suggested (FLATTERY and SCHWARZ 1989:45) that what is referred to generally as *haoma* is now a substitute for what may have been used in ancient Iran. However, STAAL (2008:29) believes that substitutes have always been used in Iran.

In September 2014 I had the good fortune to meet an Iranian scholar who had recently participated in a ritual in Iran with a sect of

---

136. Modern Parsis are uncertain which plant or shrub the wire twigs represent; DROWER (1956:80n.1) suggests, possibly, balsamodendron (= *Commiphora myrrha*). A fragrant gum (myrrh) exudes from the bark of this shrub, which is in the *Amyridaceae* family. Myrrh is mildly psychoactive and may, in combination with other plants, possibly have been used for intoxication in early Christian times (NEMU 2016:14).

137. A few drops of *hōm* used to be given to new-born babies but substitutes made of molasses or sugar were already usual a century ago (MODI 1922:1). BOWMAN (1970:7) notes that *haoma* was the first liquid to pass the lips of new-born babies and the last draught given to a dying person.

138. MODI (1922:303n.65) supports the view that *haoma* is ephedra: it fits descriptions in the *Avesta* and grows commonly in Afghanistan and neighbouring regions; (DROWER 1956:81) follows MODI on this point. KOTWAL and BOYD (1991:16) also—following BOYCE (1975:157)—maintain that *haoma* is a species of ephedra.

Sūfī Qalandars, who are a radical antinomian sect, who generally live *be-shār* (outside the law) and usually consume *bhāṃg* (cannabis) excessively. They first noticeably emerged in the Muslim world, principally in Syria, Iraq and Iran, in the 11th century,[139] becoming more organized in sects in the 12th and 13th centuries.[140] One of the conditions imposed upon my informant by the Qalandars for participating in a *haoma* ritual was that he ask no questions. With the Sūfīs he drank a powerful entheogenic concoction, which they call *hōm*, that had the same effect as ayahuasca (see below), with which he is very familiar. This demonstrates a living entheogenic culture in a region where people are believed to have consumed *haoma* 3,500 years ago. One of the ingredients was Syrian rue, but he was unable to determine the other ingredients. However, a report in the *Entheogen Review* (Winter 1992, DEKORNE *et al.* 2002:126), entitled 'Sufi Ayahuasca…The Soma of the Aryans?' possibly provides further information on this concoction:[141] the other plant mixed with Syrian rue appears to have been the giant reed *Arundo donax*, which is also widely distributed in India and

---

139. This is the 'standard' view; however, TORTEL (2009) proposes, perhaps somewhat speculatively, that the *qalandar*, as a social type, has much earlier roots and instantiation in Indian asceticism; though whether such parallel developments in different cultures can be conflated seems questionable.

140. For historical accounts of this sect, see DIGBY (1984); KARAMUSTAFA (2006); TORTEL (2009). For a brief, contemporary ethnography of a woman Qalandar (called Bava Sahib), living in Lahore, see EWING (1997:201–229). This account highlights the radical social dichotomy (and 'otherness' from an anthropological perspective) between Qalandars (also known as *malangs*) and orthodox Muslims.

141. "According to an acquaintance who was sworn to secrecy by a Sufi musician, *Peganum harmala* [Syrian rue] root and the roots of *Arundo donax* were and are the source of a secret entheogen long used in particular musical orders since before Islam influenced the Sufis. *A. donax* (giant reed or cane) is used in Persia for making the 'Nay', an end-blown flute, or reed pipe. The same plant is the source for reeds for clarinet, sax, oboe, bassoon, bagpipes and so on. My informant would not give me particulars of how the "mystical potion" was made…Much Sufi literature, mostly untranslated, makes many oblique references to the reed pipe and *P. harmala*". The Persian term *nāy*, for 'flute', is related to several other words meaning 'reed' (WITZEL 1999:20).

contains DMT[142] (in some varieties).[143] The mixture of this reed with Syrian rue can produce a powerful entheogen, in the form of an ayahuasca analogue. The topic of this chemical formulation is further explored in Chapter 15. In this inquiry it will be suggested that the notion of 'substitutes' for *soma/haoma* could be misleading: if a combination of plants can produce (and did produce, when used in the past) entheogenic experiences, then that is why those plants were called *soma*. Even though some of the plants that will be discussed are not entheogenic (and some only mildly psychoactive) on their own, they can be used as potentiators, as additives to an entheogenic concoction; and ephedra, long used in Zoroastrian rites, seems almost certain to have been an additive plant in some instances.

---

142. Tryptamines, including DMT, bufotenin and traces of 5-MeO-DMT, have been found in samples of *Arundo donax* (Trout 2002:27; Al-Snafi 2015:35).

143. The results of bioassays of a variety of specimens from the USA were mixed (DeKorne *et al.* 2002:126–131); some samples were found to contain no DMT; others had alkaloids that caused nausea; others tested positive for DMT. Native samples tested in India have the highest DMT content that has been found (Trout 2004c).

CHAPTER 4

'Substitutes' for *soma* in South Asia

As mentioned previously, by the end of the 19th century a general scholarly consensus had formed that *soma* and *haoma* were originally the same plant. It is also generally acknowledged that certainly in the Indian (in distinction from the Iranian) tradition, substitutes for *soma* may have been used for perhaps more that 2,800 years.

In South Asia, by the time of the early *Brāhmaṇa*s (from *c.*800 BCE) the 'original' *soma* appears to have become rare, if not unavailable; though this is not certain.[144] The *Śatapatha Brāhmaṇa* (4.5.10.2–6) mentions several substitute plants—should *soma* be taken away or stolen (*yadi somamapahareyuḥ*)—that may be pressed for *soma*, namely: one of the two kinds of *phālguna*[145] plant (having brown flowers), *śyenahṛta*,[146] *ādāra* plants,[147] brown *dūrvā* (= *dūb*)

---

144. There is a possible interpretation of *ṚV* 10.89.5 and 10.85.3 that 'substitutes' or alternatives were already being used as early as the composition of the *Ṛgveda*. HILLEBRANDT (1980, Vol. 1:159) remarks that several statements in the *ṚV* do not agree with each other, and give the impression that different plants were already being used at that time.
145. It is unclear exactly what plant this is; another reddish (*lohita*) kind of this plant is also mentioned, but it seems to be a kind of grass.
146. 'Carried away by a falcon': this plant is also obscure, though this is one the descriptions of the 'original' *soma* (e.g. *ṚV* 1.80.2; 9.87.6).
147. *Ādāra* is identified as *pūtīka* (*ŚB* 4.5.10.4; 14.1.2.12), which EGGELING (n.2) identifies as the *rohiṣa* plant (?*Guilandina bonduc* = *Caesalpinia bonduc*), a *soma* substitute. *Caesalpinia bonduc* is a pan-tropical, vine-like, prickly, flowering shrub (gray nicker). A Chinese species, *Caesalpinia sepiaria* (= *Yun-shih*) is reportedly hallucinogenic (SCHULTES and HOFMANN 1980:335). Both *Caesalpinia pulcherrima* and *C. gilliesii* have tested positive (but not always) for DMT and 5-MeO-DMT (TROUT 2002:31, 121). *Rohiṣa* is

grass[148] (which are said to be akin to *soma* plants) and yellow (or greenish) *kuśa* grass.[149] Other substitutes for *soma* mentioned in the

---

considered to be a sacred plant (PANDEY 1989:7). It is referred to (MW:890) by SUŚRUTA as a fragrant grass. ȚODARĀNANDA provides eleven synonyms for *rohiṣa tṛṇa* (grass), including *tṛṇa* and *śyāmāka* (millet) (DASH and KASHYAP 1980:471). Commenting on *TB* 1.4.7.5 and EGGELING's translation of the passage in the *ŚB* (14.1.2.12) referring to *ādāra* as *pūtīka*, KUIPER (1984:220) opines that both *ādāra* and *pūtīka* are creepers with a milky sap. So, *ādāra* might be gray nicker or a kind of grass.

148. *Dūrvā* (also known in Āyurveda as *sādvala*) is identified by GONDA (1985:108) and PANDEY (1989:14) as *Cynodon dactylon* (= *Panicum dactylon* = *Agrostis linearis*), which is known, amongst other names, as couch grass or Bermuda grass.

149. The name *kuśa* does not appear in the *saṃhitās*; *kuśa* is usually but not always identified by both ancient and modern authors as the same grass as *darbha* (GONDA 1985:97ff.), and also usually as the common grass *Desmostachya bipinnata* Stapf. (= *Eragrostis cynosuroides* = *Poa cynosuroides* Retz.) (PANDEY 1989:17; IPNI 2005), known as big cordgrass or salt reed-grass in the USA, and as halfa grass in Australia. This is the most common modern botanical identification. However, some commentators who do distinguish these grasses describe *kuśa* as short and soft with sharp, needle-like leaves, while *darbha* has broad, long, rough leaves (GONDA 1985:29). *Kuś* grass, which is identified as *darbh* grass in Hindi (MCGREGOR 1995:482) and generally by Hindi speakers (this author's inquiries), grows ubiquitously in both north and south India. I collected some growing wild in a park in Delhi and on a beach in south Goa.

It is virtually impossible to determine whether or not references in Vedic texts to *kuśa* and *darbha* refer to the same or different species of grass (GONDA 1985:107). The specific botanical identifications of the various kinds of grass that have been mentioned in this footnote are problematic, with alternative taxonomic identifications both in the Sanskrit terms and modern botanical classifications. MADHIHASSAN (1987b), for example, maintains (though with inadequate support) that *kuśa* is *Desmostachya bipinnata*, *darbha* is *Imperata cylindrica*, and *dūrvā* is *Panicum dactylon*. SHAH *et al.* (2012), however, assume that *kuśa* is *Imperata cylindrica* and that *darbha* is *Desmostachya bipinnata*. THAKUR and KUMAR (n.d.) provide what they maintain are other synonyms for *kuśa*, besides *Eragrostis cynosuroides* (Retz.) P. Beauv, *Desmostachya bipinnata* (Linn.) Stapf., and *Poa cynosuroides* (Retz.): namely the somewhat uncertain identifications with **[1]** Briza bipinnata Linn., **[2]** *Coelachyrum longiglume* (Napper), **[3]** *Cynosurus durus* (Forssk.), **[4]** *Eragrostis bipinnata* (Linn.) Schum., **[5]** *Leptochoa bipinnata* (Linn.) Hochst., **[6]** *Pogonarthria bipinnata* (Linn.) Chiov., **[7]** *Stapfiola bipinnata* (Linn.) Kuntze, and **[8]** *Uniola bipinnata*

*Brāhmaṇa*s include cultivated millet (*śyāmāka*),[150] *kattṛṇa*,[151] *parṇa* (a sacred tree),[152] and *muñja* grass (O'FLAHERTY 1968:97). *Muñja* is a grass[153] that pervades Vedic ritual. In a slightly obscure passage in the *Ṛgveda* (1.161.8), it is recommended to drink the rinsing of the *muñja* grass, which GONDA (1985:130) interprets as referring to an inferior substitute for *soma*.[154] *Somapattra*, another plant referred to, is identified by MONIER-WILLIAMS as *Saccharum cylindricum*, a species of reed-like grass. *Manusmṛti* (XI.149) states that if someone touches, gives or receives an intoxicant, or drinks water left over by a *śūdra*, he should drink water boiled with *kuśa* grass for three days.

KANE (1997, Vol. 2, part 2:1203) also details substitutes mentioned in other *Brāhmaṇa*s, including the juice of *pūtīka*s.[155]

(Linn.). PANDEY *et al.* (2013:67) identify *Desmostachya bipinnata* with **[1]**, **[2]**, **[4]**, **[5]** and **[7]**. The seed company B & T World Seeds, based in Aigues-Vives, France, classify three synonyms for *Desmostachya bipinnata* (ref. no. 515812): *Eragrostis cynosuroides*, *Poa cynosuroides* and *Uniola bipinnata* (http://b-and-t-world-seeds.com / accessed 8/3/2016). In sum, both *kuśa* and *darbha* (see n.156 below) are most commonly identified as *Desmostachya bipinnata*.

150. = *Panicum frumentaceum*.

151. MONIER-WILLIAMS identifies this plant as a fragrant grass and also as *Pistia stratiotes*; but this latter plant is usually known as water cabbage.

152. *Butea frondosa/monosperma*, the large-leafed *palāśa* (= *parṇa*) tree (flame of the forest/parrot tree) with orange flowers, whose wood is used for sacred objects. This tree is mentioned as a substitute for *soma* in *Kauśītaki Brāhmaṇa* (2.2) (SWAMY 1976:18). In the *Ṛgveda* and *Brāhamaṇa*s the eagle (*suparṇa* = beautiful feathered) fetched *soma* from heaven. The eagle was shot by Kṛśānu (the footless archer) and a feather (*parṇa*) fell to earth, becoming a blade/feather of *soma* and the essence of the *parṇa* tree, which is imbued with *soma* (BLATTER and MILLARD 1954:16; PANDEY 1989:6; PARPOLA 2002:306).

153. GONDA (1985:122) identifies this as *Saccharum arundinaceum* (= *Saccharum ciliare*).

154. GONDA is unsure what exactly the compound *muñjanejanam* refers to in this passage.

155. *Taṇḍya Brāhmaṇa* (10.3.3); *Jaiminīya Brāhmaṇa* (3.6.40; 4.3.13–17; 4.3.31); *Mimāṃsasūtra* (6.3.31ff.) and ŚABARA's *Bhāṣya* also identify *pūtīka* as a substitute. See also GONDA (1982:10) for further references to *pūtīka* plants, which may be used as substitutes if the *soma* is taken away after purchase. MODI (1922:315) cites Martin HAUG, who claims that brahmans use the stalks of *pūtīka* as a substitute for *soma*.

The commentary on *Āśvalāyana Śrautaśūtra* (6.8.5–6) states that *durva* (= *darbha*)[156] and *kuśa* [grass][157] may be mixed with *pūtīka* stalks. The identity of *pūtīka* is not certain, but HOUBEN (1991:110n.25) notes references to *pūtīka* as "dark *durva* grass" and as "the well-known kind of grass or herb". SĀYAṆA, commenting on the suitability of *pūtīka* as a substitute mentioned in the *Tāṇḍya Brāhmaṇa* (9.5.1), identifies *pūtīka* as a creeper (*latā*), and adds that a dark grass known as *arjunāni*[158] may be used (KANE 1997, Vol. 2, part 2:1203). So, several references seem to indicate a possibility that *pūtīka* refers to a kind of grass, rather than a creeper.[159] However, SHARMA and

---

156. *Darbha* may also refer to a bunch or tuft of *kuśa* grass (MONIER-WILLIAMS, p.470). As with *kuśa* grass (see above) *darbha* has been interpreted by various commentators to refer to common grasses of several kinds, including *Desmostachya bipinnata, Cynodon dactylon, Imperata arundinacea* (= *Imperata cylindrica* = *Saccharum cylindricum* [blady grass] = *Poa cynosuroides*), and *Saccharum spontaneum*. These varieties have around a dozen different botanical identifications (MEULENBELD 1974:561–562). *Darbha* is taken by GONDA (1985:52) to refer to *Imperata arundinacea*; while MADHIHASSAN (1987b) suggests *Desmostachya bipinnata. Dūrvā* is sometimes distinguished by commentators from *darbha*, though both are identified in Hindi and Sanskrit dictionaries as 'panic' or 'bent' grass. *Darbha* is also often referred to as *barhiṣ* (sacrificial grass) and as *oṣadhi* (herb) in some texts (GONDA 1985:41). *Tṛṇa* is the general term (in Sanskrit) for grasses of all kinds.

157. As mentioned above, *darbha* and *kuśa* are generally understood by most commentators to refer to the same kind of grass.

158. Identified by MONIER-WILLIAMS merely as a particular grass mentioned in the *Brāhmaṇa*s as a substitute. GONDA (1985:134) also identifies *arjuna* as a kind of grass. *Arjun*, however, also refers (in Hindi) to the tree *Terminalia arjuna* BRAHMAVARCAS (2000:84–89; 2001:1–2).

159. KRAMRISCH (1975:230ff.) identifies *pūtika* [*pūtīka*] as 'mushroom', from an erroneous derivation from the Santal word *putka*, meaning 'mushroom'. This identification is discussed in detail by KUIPER (1984), who provides the following observations: the spelling of the term in early sources is *pūtīka*, while the form *pūtika* occurs only in later texts; several sources, including *Kāṭhaka Saṃhitā* 34.3 (37,14) and *Pañcaviṃśa Brāhmaṇa* 9.5.3, prescribe, as substitutes for *soma*, *pūtīka*s, described as "a kind of creeper" (*latā*). However, DĀRILA (in his commentary on *Kauśikasūtra* 22.15) refers to *pūtikāḥ* as "well-known grasses" (*tṛṇāni prasiddhani*). MONIER-WILLIAMS (p.470) also notes *pūtīka* as referring to a bunch of *darbha* grass. *Pūtīka* is used in the making of clay pots for the *pravargya* rite, which may precede

DASH (Vol. 1 1983:58), translators of CARAKA (*Sūtrasthāna* 113), identify *pūtīka* as *Caesalpinia crista* Linn., the bark of which is said to be useful in medicine.[160]

SWAMY (1976:16–18) provides a useful table of substitutes[161] mentioned in the *Brāhmaṇa*s and *Śrautasūtra*s,[162] the relative preference for each one in the texts, and identifications (some tentative) for the following ten plants: *pūtīka, arjuna, prapōta* [sic], *phālguna, ādāra, śyenahṛta, aruṇadūrvā, kuśa, śyāmāka, parṇa.* SWAMY identifies as kinds of grass: *arjuna, phālguna* (following ROTH 1881:690),[163] *aruṇadūrvā*[164] and *kuśa. Prapōta*[165] and

the *agniṣṭoma* (HOUBEN 1991; 2003:3.1). Commenting on the *Taittirirīya Āraṇyaka* (4.2.4(13)), HOUBEN 1991:110n.25) comments that, "the Pūtīka plants appear to be grass or herbs that grow in clumps or tussocks that have some firmness". He adds that they are different from those plants referred to by the same name in later Sanskrit, when they are a kind of *oṣadhi* (a herb or a herb-like plant). ROTH (1881:689) remarks that *pūtīka* seems like an adjective or a synonym for *ādāra* (see below), and also says that there are other modern, folk identifications: the Bengali vegetable *pūī śāk* (*Basella cordifolia*), and *pūtikarañja/pūtiparṇa/pūtikarṇaka* (*Pongamia glabra*). ZYSK (1985:260) identifies *pūtīka* as *karañja*, which he identifies as *Pongamia pinnata/glabra* (Indian beech). However, MEULENBELD (1974:537) lists more than a dozen different plants that could be identified as *karañja.*

160. This is a woody shrub, a prickly vine, identified by SURYAWANSHI and PATEL (2011) as Teri pods or Fever nut. However, in some sources *Caesalpinia crista* is identified as gray nicker (= usually, *Caesalpinia bonduc*). *Caesalpinia crista* has numerous, traditional medicinal uses: including against fever, malaria and abdominal pain, and as an anthelmintic and as a tonic.

161. See also KUIPER (1984:219–220).

162. *Pañcaviṃśa, Taittirīya, Śatapatha, Tāṇḍya (Śabara Bhāṣya) Brāhmaṇa*s; *Āśvalāyana, Kātyāyana, Āpastamba, Baudhāyana, Sāñkhyāyana Śrautasūtra*s; *Taittirīya Saṃhitā.*

163. SWAMY (1976:18) also notes that CARAKA refers to *phalgu* as a fig (*Ficus carica*).

164. ROTH (1881:690) identifies *aruṇadūrvā* as the grass *Cynodon (Panicum) dactylon*, and notes the observation (of NARAHARI Paṇḍita, 17th century) in his medical treatise *Rājanighaṇṭu* (8.108ff.), that this plant is of four kinds: *nīla* [blue], *śveta* [white], *vallī* [creeper] and *gaṇḍadūrvā* [knotted together].

165. I have been unable to identify this plant in any source.

śyenahṛta[166] are not identified.[167] *Pūtīka* is identified as *Basella alba* (vine spinach or Malabar spinach), though, as discussed above, it seems also possible that *pūtīka* is either a kind of grass or gray nicker (*Caesalpinia bonduc*). Also as noted above, *ādāra* is said to be possibly a synonym for *pūtīka*, though this is uncertain. Apart from *pūtīka, śyāmāka* (cultivated millet) and *parṇa*[168] (*Butea frondosa/ monosperma*), all the other identifiable plants used as *soma* substitutes appear to be kinds of grass. This is an important point that we return to in Chapter 14, when considering the chemical and potentially psychoactive properties of several kinds of grass.

The inclusion of *śyāmāka*[169] is curious. NADKARNI (1954:477) lists one of its names in Sanskrit as *soma*, illustrating its continuing identification with *soma*. In Chapter 9 a theory by GREENE (1992) will be considered that proposes a manner whereby millet could be *soma*; but the method of preparation he proposes seems improbable. To date, I have found no plausible explanation of why millet should be considered to be *soma*, except (as a remote possibility) that it was used because it is a potential host for ergot fungus, which can be strongly psychoactive. This notion is also further explored in Chapter 17 of this book.

Intended for use by non-brahmans, other substitutes are also mentioned in the *Brāhmaṇas*. The *Aitareya Brāhmaṇa* (5.7.28–32) recommends for *kṣatriyas* the pressed tendrils of the *nyagrodha* (banyan)[170] tree and the fruits of the *udumbara* (Indian or cluster

---

166. 'Snatched by a falcon': ROTH (1881:690) identifies this plant as *khadira* (*Mimosa catechu/Acacia catechu*).

167. Another substitute mentioned (KUIPER 1984:220) in the *Jaiminīya Brāhmaṇa* (1.354–355) is *ūtika*. MONIER-WILLIAMS:221 merely mentions this plant as a *soma* substitute, and refers to *pūtīka*.

168. Also known as *kiṃśuka* (Sanskrit); *ḍhāk* (Hindi).

169. = *rāgī* in Kannaḍa and sometimes also in north India.

170. *Nyagrodha* (downwards grower) = *Ficus bengalensis/benghalensis* = *bargad/ vaṭ* (Hindi) = (also) *vaṭa* (Sanskrit). The term *vaṭa*, however, first appears in the epics (PARPOLA 2004:489). Veneration of this tree with hanging shoots is ancient. It appears on numerous artefacts from the Indus valley civilization (*c*. 2500–1500 BCE). It features frequently in the *Vedas* as a 'heavenly' tree with several mythological associations, and also in the Buddhist Jātaka tales, often as a 'child-granting' tree. In South Asia it has associations with both fertility and kingship and is the abode of tree-spirits (*yakṣas* and *yakṣiṇīs*)

fig),[171] *aśvattha* (peepal),[172] and *plakṣa* (wavy-leaf/white fig)[173] trees. The *Chāndogya Upaniṣad* (8.5.3) refers to an *aśvattha* tree[174] (in the world of *brahman*) as "*somasavana*" (*soma*-pressing), while in the *Atharvaveda* (8.7.20), *aśvattha, darbha* and *soma* are all identified with the immortal sacrifice. In the Hindu tradition there are five sacred trees: peepal, banyan, *gūlar* (*udumbara*), *pākaṛ* (*plakṣa*) and mango, the most 'holy' being the peepal (PANDEY 1989:22).[175] None of these plants is currently known to have any strongly psychoactive properties, though they all have medicinal uses.[176] Significantly, the four *Ficus* species referred to above

(PARPOLA 2004:483–494; 2015:201–204). In folk Hinduism the banyan is associated with Śiva (as Vaṭapatreśvar) and Kālī (as Vaṭapatreśvarī) (GUPTA 2010:117). In domestic Tantric rites leaves of banyan are to be used for enjoyment/gratification; peepal for obtaining a son; flame of the forest for sovereignty (SARASVATI n.d.:10).

171. *Ficus glomerata/racemosa* = *gūlar* (Hindi).

172. *Ficus religiosa* = bodhi = peepal (*pīpal*, Hindi) = *vṛkṣādana* = *mahādruma* (Sanskrit). The *Atharvaveda* (19.39.5–6, 8) connects *soma* with the *aśvattha* tree and also the *kuṣṭha* plant (usually interpreted as *Costus speciosus* = wild ginger: but see below); but by HOERNLE (2011:83) and FRAWLEY (2013:330–331) as one or another of the species of *Saussurea*, particularly *Saussurea lappa* (= costus root), or *Saussurea involucrata* (= snow lotus), which has medicinal properties. '*Kuṣṭha*' (in Sanskrit) also means 'leprosy' and 'skin disease'. Snow lotus is also identified as *Saussurea laniceps* Hand.-Mazz. and *Saussurea medusa* Maxim. in Tibetan medicine, in which it is used for pain and inflammatory conditions (YI 2010).

173. *Ficus infectoria* = *pākaṛ/plakṣ* (Hindi).

174. In translations of this passage, OLIVELLE (*Upaniṣads* 1996:170) refers to this tree as a banyan, while HUME (*Upaniṣads* 1998:267) and ROEBUCK (*Upaniṣads* 2003:197) refer to it as a fig tree. However, the Sanskrit text (LIMAYE and VADEKAR 1958:165) states that it is an *aśvattha* (peepal), which is one of the many species of *Ficus*.

175. For a summary of rights performed to (and with) this tree and for its religious associations, see MAJUPURIA (1978:71–79). The *Padma Purāṇa* (1992, part X:3431–3439) devotes a whole chapter (VII.12) to the greatness of the *aśvattha*. Either a banyan or a peepal tree typically function, particularly in the absence of a built temple, as a shrine in Indian villages, with a stone or a *liṅga* at the base of the tree. Vedic texts refer to both *aśvattha* and *nyagrodha* as the abode of the mischievous *gandharva* and *apsarasa* entities (PARPOLA 2004:486).

176. Of the four *Ficus* species referred to—out of seventy-eight species of *Ficus*

(*nyagrodha, udumbara, aśvattha* and *plakṣa*)[177] all feature as ingredients of a 6th-century recipe for *amṛta*, which we return to in Chapter 13.

In the *Śatapatha Brāhmanā* there are two references (3.4.3.13; 4.2.5.15) to a plant called *uśānā*. It is said to grow on mountains and is pressed to become *soma.*[178] This plant does not seem to be presented as a substitute for *soma* but as *soma* itself. It is not identified in either Sanskrit or Hindi dictionaries.[179] Whatever the plant was, it appears that this is an example of one of several plants that may be used to make *soma.*

DAS (2001) discusses a reference in the *Atharvaveda* (2.27) to Indra's eating the *pāṭā* plant and becoming victorious. It is synonymous with *soma* but its identity is obscure. MALANDRA (1979) maintains that in this verse *soma* is in the form of an amulet used 'magically' for victory in legalistic contexts,[180] and states

---

that are native to South Asia (BRANDIS 1907:598–610)—only *Ficus infectoria* is not reported as having aphrodisiac properties (SOOD *et al.* 2005), which is a possible but weak indication of MAOI (see below). Interestingly, two South American *Ficus* species (*Ficus insipida, Ficus ruiziana*) have been reported as admixtures to ayahuasca (see below) (OTT 1996:271, 273).

177. These four *Ficus* species and also either *parīśa* (*Thespesia populnea*), *sirīśa* (*Albizia lebbeck*), or *vetasa* (*Calamus rotang*) are known in Āyurveda as the five trees with milky sap; their bark is known as *pañcavalkala* (HOERNLE 2011:20n.64).

178. *etaddīkṣopsadbhistānūnaptrairāpyāynena somaṃ karoti* (3.4.3.13).

179. MONIER-WILLIAMS merely states that it is the name of a plant and provides a reference to *ŚB* 3.4, while APTE states that it is the plant from which *soma* juice is pressed. The root is √*vaś* (wish/desire), which affords little help. BENNETT (2010:320–321) maintains that *uśānā* is cannabis; but this is based on an improbable derivation of *uśānā* from *san*, which is one of the Hindi terms for cannabis.

180. GONDA (1980:10) notes the use of *soma* stalks as an amulet used in a battle rite to render a *kṣatriya* (soldier) and his army victorious. WHITAKER (2004) surveys the use of amulets as sources of power and prestige, observing that the use of amulets is a feature of sections of the *Atharvaveda.* Amongst substances used for amulets was *darbha* grass. Amulets were bound or fastened to the body and were made of (or contained) either gold, copper, iron, ivory, pearl, or various plants, including barley, *parṇa* (*Butea frondosa*, flame of the forest) and *udumbara* (cluster fig): see WHITAKER (2004:567) for textual references. *Parṇa, udumbara* and *darbha* are all also identified as *soma*: see below. Alongside medicinal plants, 'magical' techniques

(p.222) that the "safest interpretation" of this passage is that the amulet was made from a root or tuber.[181] DAS (2001:33n.67) also refers to the *Śāntikalpa* of the *Atharvaveda* (19.6) in which the name *pāṭā* occurs, as an amulet made from the root of the *pāṭā* plant, which is bound on. If the plant is a kind of grass,[182] then the roots or stems could be twisted and used as an amulet in the form of a wristband, which is still a common way of wearing a 'magical' amulet in South Asia. Alternatively, KAMAL (1988:22) identifies *pāṭā* as the perennial creeper *Clypea hernandifolia* (= *Stephania hernandifolia* Willd. = *Stephania japonica discolor*),[183] though the usual spelling of this plant in Sanskrit is *pāṭhā*. This plant contains around twenty recently-identified alkaloids (some of which are toxic) and is used in both Chinese medicine and Āyurveda. It appears in several medicinal formulas in the Bower Manuscript (see below). If *pāṭā* (as *soma*) in the *Atharvaveda* is taken as *pāṭhā* (a creeper), then it could also be twisted into an amulet; and I would suggest that this plant also was possibly a psychoactive ingredient of a *soma* concoction.

Discussing medically restorative treatments (*rasāyana*), for the prevention of death and decay, SUŚRUTA[184] (1963:530–538 [Vol. 2,

employing mantras, sanctified water, the smoke from burnt, fragrant plants and amulets were also used in the early Vedic world by medicine-men (*bhiṣaj*) to ward off attacks by disease-causing demons (ZYSK 2002:114).

181. However, MALANDRA also suggests that the plant appears to be a truffle or a mushroom, as it is dug up by a boar (and boars like truffles), even though he is (paradoxically) sceptical of WASSON's mushroom thesis (see below). DAS (2001:23–24) points out that there is no mention anywhere, historically, in any South Asian text of boars retrieving mushrooms or truffles; and it is unclear how a mushroom or a truffle could possibly be worn as an amulet, as they quickly decompose.

182. The Kashmiri recension of the *AV* refers to *pāṭā* as, "one which stands/rules alone" and as, "sole queen" (trans. DAS). DAS (2001:31n.52) comments that this probably means that no other plant grows in its vicinity, which would fit with patches of wild grass. Further, the Kashmiri *AV* (7.12.6) states that the plant is, "as a swimmer on/in the wind", which could fit with long grasses swaying in the wind.

183. This identification is also made by an anonymous contributor to this website (Atharva-Veda Samhita.djvu238): https://en.wikisource.org/wiki/Page:Atharva-Veda_samhita.djvu/238 (accessed 13/03/2017).

184. SUŚRUTA, together with VĀGHBAṬA and CARAKA, is one of the foundational authorities of Ayurvedic medical treatments. SUŚRUTA's compendium was

ch. XXIX]), in an oft-cited Ayurvedic passage, equates *soma* with *amṛta* (immortality) and states that there are twenty-four species of the *soma* plant,[185] which have various epithets, habitats and potencies. What is recommended is that *soma* be used in a treatment that lasts about four months for a patient[186] requiring rejuvenation, who has first undergone ritual and dietary purification (including the use of emetics). SUŚRUTA says that the bulb of the *soma* plant should be pricked to extrude a milky juice, which is to be consumed without being tasted.[187]

Some of the names for *soma* that SUŚRUTA provides are mentioned in the *Veda*s; and it is apparent that several of them (such as *agniṣṭoma* and *candramāḥ*) are Vedic epithets for *soma.* Interestingly, SUŚRUTA states (p.531) that the virtues and methods of using them are identical; that, essentially, the effects are the same. However, it is apparent that different kinds of *soma* plants are referred to. SUŚRUTA mentions that those which trail upon the ground or grow as small shrubs or in bushes should be consumed as they

---

probably compiled between the early centuries BCE and 500 CE (WUJASTYK 1998:105).

185. These names are: *aṃśumān, muñjavān, candramāḥ, rājaprabha, dūrvā soma, kanīyān, śvetākṣa, kanaka prabha, pratānavān, ṭāla vṛnta, karavira, amśavān, svayaṃprabha, mahāsoma, garuḍāhṛta, gāyatrya, traiṣṭubha, pāṃkta, jāgata, śāṃkara, agniṣṭoma, raivata, yathokta* and *udupati.* All varieties are said to have fifteen leaves, which sprout at the rate of one per day during the waxing moon of the 'bright' half of the lunar month); and which fall off over the next fifteen 'dark' days of the lunar month.

186. *Śūdra*s are not permitted to drink it.

187. After drinking *soma* the patient should not be allowed to sleep and should pass the first nights supervised by friends in a secluded room. The patient will vomit after drinking *soma,* which will purge him of worms and other obnoxious matter accumulated in the body as a result of wrong diet or conduct. For the next seven days the patient should only drink milk; he will become very thin but the vital spark of life will be maintained by *soma.* Various ointments should be applied to the body throughout the treatment. After twenty-four days the patient may start eating gruel, by now endowed with a renewed body (including a beautiful face and body and revitalized hair, skin and teeth). After a month, for the next ten days, the patient gradually spends more and more time outside the treatment chamber, eventually resuming normal life, fully endowed with great power and beauty.

are:[188] juice is not extracted from these kinds; but juice is extracted from the kinds called *aṃśumān* and *candramāḥ*, the latter being said to be the best kind of *soma*.[189] Several kinds of habitats are mentioned, most of which are mountain ranges;[190] a few are aquatic.[191]

What is one to make of SUŚRUTA's account? Is it merely fantastically imaginary? Of course, the claims by SUŚRUTA that teeth will regrow or that one can live for 10,000 years after a 'treatment' are unbelievable. However, similar claims in some yoga texts, although fantastry, often have an element of truth: in improving health, stamina, insight and awareness, even though to nothing like the degree claimed in the texts. Could the *soma* treatment indeed provide some form of rejuvenation? As a speculation, is it perhaps an ayahuasca-like treatment, or maybe just the partial or incomplete memory of such a treatment, which uses a variety of plants to produce a kind of psychedelic, near-death experience and rejuvenation in a patient, a process that is well-known amongst those who drink ayahuasca (which is further explored in Chapter 14)? If *soma* had become rare or unobtainable by the time of the *Brāhmaṇa*s, then why does SUŚRUTA mention so many plants called *soma*? Is it perhaps the case that *soma*, like ayahuasca, can be made from many species of plant, if the preparer has sufficient botanical knowledge? We return to this possibility in Chapter 13 of this book.

188. The dose is said to be four *muśti*s (= 32 *tolā*s = *c.* 350 gms).

189. Several varieties of *soma* are partially described: *aṃśumān* smells like ghee and has a bulb; *muñjavān* has leaves like those of the garlic plant; *candramāḥ* is golden-coloured and is aquatic; *garuḍāhṛta* and *śvetākṣa* are yellowish, look like the cast-off skin of a snake, and hang from the boughs of trees. All other kinds are said (p.537) to be marked with circular, motley-coloured rings, to have fifteen leaves (which grow and drop off with the waxing and waning of the moon) and a creeper-like appearance, and to secrete a milky juice.

190. Himālaya, Arvuda, Sahya, Mahendra, Malaya, Śri Parvata, Devagiri, Devasaha, Pāripātra, Vindhya.

191. In Lake Devasunda; floating on the Indus river (*candramāḥ*); in 'little' Manasa lake in Kashmir (*gāyatrī, traiṣṭubha, pāṃkta, jāgata, śāṃkara*).

CHAPTER 5

What are the effects of *soma/haoma*?

In ancient Iranian and Indian religion it is quite apparent that *soma/haoma* was central to religious practices. BOYCE (1975:156) comments that, "What distinguishes the *yajña/yasna* from other acts of worship is that it centers on the preparation and offering of *soma/haoma.* This offering has been termed the focal point of Vedic religion, and it was evidently of great importance also in pagan Iran".[192] Similarly, MALANDRA (1983:150) remarks that, "Two elements stand at the very center of Indo-Iranian ritual. They are *haoma/soma* and fire.[193] From the times of the *Avesta* and the *Veda*s down to the present day, the major Zoroastrian and Vedic rituals have been inseparable from these elements". WATKINS (1978:13) describes the *soma* ritual as, "the central cultic act of Vedic liturgy, and beyond that of Common Indo-Iranian religion". Similarly, BROCKINGTON (1996:16) remarks that, "the extraction and drinking of [the juice of soma] formed the centre of Vedic ritual". BOWMAN (1970:7) comments that, "The use of an intoxicating drink, which is called *soma* by the people of India and *haoma* by the Iranians, is one of the earliest and most persistent elements in the religion of the Indo-Iranian peoples". I would suggest that these remarks can only

---

192. BOYCE (1975:157) adds that it seems probable that although the cult of *soma/ haoma* was given enhanced significance by the Indians, it was circumscribed and subordinated in ethical Zoroastrianism, though elements of its old power survive strongly even in the reformed faith.
193. The householder brahman, when performing his twice-daily *agnihotra*, of all deities, first offers oblations to Fire, then to Soma, then to both of them together (*Manusmṛti* 3.85; trans. OLIVELLE).

be properly understood in the light of the effects of the plant (or plants) that were being used.

The effects of *soma* are frequently mentioned in the *Veda*s and also in the *Avesta* (as *haoma/hōm*), as not only exhilarating but as intoxicating (*mada/madha[maδa]*).[194] This term may be used for someone under the influence of alcohol, but contrasts are occasionally provided in the *Veda*s and *Brāhmaṇa*s between the 'base' intoxication from alcohol (*surā*),[195] and the 'elevated' intoxication of *soma.*[196] A

---

194. This term is used 279 times in the *Ṛgveda*; *c.* 400 times if other compound and variant forms like *madira* are included (Thompson 2003n.16).

195. For further references on this point, see Brough (1971:331); Malamoud (1996b:22). See also *Śatapatha Brāhmaṇa* 12.7.3.14: "separate, indeed, are the Soma-juice and the Surā-liquor" (trans. Eggeling). The *Viṣṇusmṛti* (51.30) prescribes penances for a Soma sacrificer who (even unaware) "has smelt the breath of a man who had been drinking spirituous liquor" (trans. Jolly). Similarly, *Manusmṛti* (11.150) states, "If a Brahmin who has drunk Soma, however, smells the odour coming from a man who has drunk liquor, he is purified by controlling his breath three times while submerged in water and then consuming ghee" (trans. Olivelle).

196. "Soma is truth, prosperity, light; and Surā untruth, misery darkness" (*ŚB* 5.1.2.10). In this regard O'Flaherty (1969:96) also cites the *Taittirīya Brāhmaṇa* (1.3.3.2): '*Soma* is male and *surā* [alcohol] is female: the two make a pair'. Hillebrandt (1980, Vol. 1:320–327) notes the vacillation in Vedic texts between praise and censure of *surā*, which is frequently paired with *soma. Soma* and *surā* are compared in the *Āpastambaśrautasūtra*; *surā* is prepared by fermenting cooked rice or barley, which is mixed with vegetable juice, milk, and the hair of a lion, tiger, and a wolf (Smith 2006:183). There is a description in the *Śatapatha Brāhmaṇa* (12.7.3.5–6) of the preparation, cooking (and apparent fermentation) of *surā* (which comprises rice, malted barley, nutmeg, areca-nut, cloves, hog-weed, and the bark of the *śāl* tree, *Vatica/Shorea robusta*), which is then mixed with *soma.* See also Oort (1995) for a summary of ancient references to *surā.* There were several kinds. It was drunk by women at festivals and weddings. In Tamil *surā* refers to strong liquor, in Kannada to toddy. It was also associated with chaos/mischief/darkness. The term *surā* is most probably a loan-word in Sanskrit, deriving from **sur*, which went from Proto-Aryan to Uralic languages; thus *surā* ('beer') in Sanskrit, and *hurā* (fermented mare's milk, *kermiss*), in Avestan (Parpola 2015:63). In Naggar (Himachal Pradesh) *surā* is drunk at an annual festival in March. It is prepared from around a dozen plants and is highly intoxicating, much more than ordinary alcohol (personal communication from Desh Raj, who kindly sent me photographs of the plants used). The names Raj supplied for some of these plants (mostly in

similar distinction is made in the *Avesta*, between the 'fury' that all other intoxicants produce, and 'gladdening Truth', which only *haoma* reveals (GERSHEVITCH 1974:48).[197] Commenting on the effect of *haoma*,[198] SKJÆRVØ remarks (2004:264) that, "the intoxication of the *haoma* is the only one that has the effect of re-establishing the cosmic Order; all the others have the opposite effect of bringing back Wrath and the forces of chaos". MALANDRA (1983:151) comments that also in the *Ṛgveda* an oft-repeated theme is of *soma* having the ability to bring one into a relationship with Truth. He also points out that *haoma/soma* is characteristically found as the subject of the verb *mad-* or with one of its nominal derivatives; and that *mad-*, when applied to *haoma/soma*, is a state that is "far from drunkenness".

The term *mada/madha* is difficult to translate adequately. BROUGH (1971:339) suggests something like 'possession by a divinity', which stimulates poetic creativity; STAAL (2001:752) notes its range of meanings, including delight, intoxication, inspiration, rapture and elation. BOYCE (1975:158) comments that the drink, "exhilarated and gave heightened powers; and this was the only intoxicant (*madha*) which produced no harmful effects…the *madha* of *haoma* is accompanied by its own rightfulness (*aśa*)". *Haoma* can produce ecstasy of all kinds and the ability to overcome every foe. The god Haoma was revered as a healer, able to bestow health and strength (BOYCE 1975:161).

Kului language) are: cannabis, *matosh* or *jata mashi* (*Nardostachys jatamansi* [Caprifoliaceae]), *tathi magdn* (*Cremanthodium* sp. [Asteraceae]), white *maura* (an orchid, possibly *Dactylorhiza* [Orchidaceae]), *gudil* (*Pedicularis bicornata* [Orobanchaceae]), *gil mill* (*Pedicularis* sp. [Orobanchaceae]), and *bakar shingi* (*Spiranthes* sp. [Orchidaceae]). Kate ARMSTRONG kindly provided the tentative identifications (in brackets).

197. "Indeed all other [forms of] intoxication are accompanied by Aēšma of the bloody club but Haoma's intoxication is accompanied by joyful truth" (*Y* 10.8, trans. JOSEPHSON). "[H]omage to Haoma, since all other intoxicants are accompanied by Wrath with the bloody cudgel; but the intoxication which is Haoma's is accompanied by Truth itself" (*Yasht* 17.2.5, trans. MALANDRA 1983:132).

198. *Y* 9.17–18; *Y* 10.8, 19; *Yašt* 17.5.

In the *Hōm Yasht*, the Avestan term *dūraoša* occurs ten times,[199] in all instances as a qualifier of *haoma*;[200] it is translated by Josephson as "death-destroying".[201] However, Bailey (1985:60–61) proposes on linguistic grounds that the Vedic term *duróṣa* (Avestan *dūraoša*), which occurs three times in the *Ṛgveda*, most probably means strong intoxication (i.e. not just mild stimulation).[202] If indeed *haoma/soma* can induce strong intoxication, then sense can be made of references that it was possible to drink too much *soma*, as there are mantras in the *Yajurveda* (19–21) for the *sautrāmaṇī*, a ceremony recommended to expiate and counteract the effects of excessive *soma* drinking. Winternitz (1981:161) comments briefly on this passage, in which are the recitations for what he describes as the "peculiar" *sautrāmaṇī* rite, in which *surā* is used instead of *soma*.[203] This ceremony is recommended for someone who has either drunk too much *soma* or who cannot endure it, when the *soma* drinker suffers from vomiting or diarrhoea,[204] and who, having not

199. *Y* 9.2, 4, 7, 10, 13, 19, 20, 21; 10.21; 11.10.

200. Hutter (1996:199ff.) also interprets other occurrences of the term *dūraoša* in the *Avesta* (for example, *Y* 32.14) as an epithet (Beiwort) for *haoma*.

201. Other translations are generally similar: Bleeck (1864:50–61), "far from death"; Mills (1887:230–247), "drives death afar"; Sethna (1976:385–405), "death-dispeller"; Malandra (1983:151–158), "keeps death far away". Khanizadeh (2016:3), however, translates the term as, "one whose destruction is difficult".

202. *ṚV* 4.21.6 (*duróṣas* – of the *hotar*, pouring the libation as the one "associated with the *duróṣa* plant"); 8.1.13–14 (*duróṣāso ámanmahi* – "we thought ourselves *duróṣa*"; followed by *ámanmahi anāśávo 'nugrāsaś ca*, "we thought ourselves slow and weak"); 9.101.3 (*duróṣa* – of the intoxicating plant *soma*).

203. Papopla (2015:302) proposes that rites such as the *sautrāmaṇī* in which *surā* is used stem from cultic practices of the worship of the horse-riding twin deities, the *Aśvins/Nāsatyas*, who are minor deities in Vedic religion. It is suggested that these deities were more important before the *Vedas* were consolidated; that their rites entailed drinking honey-beer (*madhu-surā*); and that these rites were eventually fused with the *soma* cult of Indra.

204. See also Gonda (1975:329), Oort (1995:223) and Malamoud (1996b) for discussions of this rite, its mythology and the use of *surā*. The *sautrāmaṇī* rite is also a possible addition to royal consecration rites, in the *vājapeya* and *rājasūya* ceremonies.

drunk (or held down) *soma*, could be denied the attainment of heaven.

One of the most frequently discussed passages regarding the effects of *soma* is the so-called *Labasūkta* (*ṚV* 10.119) ('song of the lapwing'), which is the only hymn in the *Ṛgveda* to describe in detail the effects of drinking *soma* (STAAL 2002:52). Here the poet describes how he has been 'inspired' and swiftly 'lifted up' after drinking *soma*, as though by raging winds, impelled upwards to the clouds.[205] Commenting on this passage, GONDA (1975:149–150) remarks that, "It would seem...that the poet describes his own ecstatic drunkenness in which he has reached a supernormal state of being, a sort of bliss and omnipotence: in this state he deems himself able to fly or soar, to dominate nature, to create or destroy, his 'soul' becoming released from the clog of earth".[206] This description is "to a great extent similar in aim and tendency" to *ṚV* 10.136, the so-called *keśin* (long-haired) hymn. This *sūkta* portrays a kind of shaman or perhaps 'medicine man', the precursor of the doctor as well as the priest, who in a state of ecstasy can soar in the sky and become united with the gods.[207]

Another oft-cited verse of the *Ṛgveda* in support of the possibly hallucinogenic properties of *soma* is *ṚV* 8.48.3–4: "We have drunk the *soma*, we have become immortal, we have attained the light, we have found the gods. What (trouble) can now enviousness cause us, what injury devised by a mortal, O thou that art immortal!...the mighty *soma* has entered us; we have come (there), where one prolongs one's lifetime".[208] In the verse *ṚV* 9.113.9, the poet expresses the desire to reach, through *soma*, the immortal, resplendent

205. "Forth like raging winds the drinks have lifted me up. Have I drunk of the soma? Yes! The drinks have lifted me up, as swift horses lift up the chariot. Have I drunk of the soma? Yes!" (*ṚV* 10.119.2–3, trans. THOMPSON). THOMPSON (2003) argues, *contra* FALK (1989) and others (see below), that this passage, being an *ātmastuti*, is describing the poet's own experience.

206. GONDA also mentions the glorification of *soma* in *ṚV* 8.48, as a producer of ecstasy, and as giving "room, freedom, comfort".

207. WERNER (1989) discusses this hymn at length in regard to shamanic practices and ecstatic experience.

208. Trans. GONDA (1975:149); see also KEITH (1925:168).

world in heaven.[209] The world of immortality is where there is the indestructible light.[210] *Soma* makes bright light (*ṚV* 9.64.4);[211] like the sun (Sūrya) above all the worlds (*ṚV* 9.54.3).[212] Soma is the light of the *yajña* (*ṚV* 9.86.10). Commenting on *ṚV* 9.107.20, ELIZARENKOVA (1996:26) maintains that *soma* clearly causes visions:[213] "We have flown away like birds, to the other side of the sun, shining with ardour, beyond" (trans. ELIZARENKOVA). Numerous times *soma* is said to produce *vipra* (inspiration/trembling). *Soma*, enhanced through the recitation of mantras, is said to 'possess' the drinker,[214] in the same way that a spirit/deity/entity may possess (*āveśa*) someone.[215] Entering someone, Soma gives strength and leads the singer to the heavenly light (*svar*), bestowing prosperity and striking down enemies. Unlike other deities (except Bṛhaspati), Soma is invasive; he takes hold of the supplicant like no other (SMITH 2006:184). Another aspect of *soma* is that it is described as 'furthering the power of action' (*dakṣasādhana*).[216] All of the aforementioned connotations are consistent with a plant-induced entheogenic experience.[217]

---

209. "Make me immortal in that realm, in the third region, the third heaven of heavens, where movement is accordant to wish, where the worlds are resplendent. O delight, flow to the mind". (*ṚV* 9.113.9) (trans. KASHYAP).
210. "O pure-flowing (Soma), establish me in that inexhaustible world of immortality where is the Indestructible Light" (*ṚV* 9.113.7) (trans. KASHYAP).
211. "Soma, the master of plenitude, brilliant in light, is pressed out" (trans. KASHYAP).
212. "Like the Divine Sun, the purified Soma abides above all the worlds" (trans. KASHYAP).
213. This point is also disputed by FALK (1989): see below.
214. "O Soma...being of divine vision, may you enter us" (*ṚV* 8.48.15; trans. KASHYAP).
215. SMITH (2006:179) comments that the majority of occurrences of *ā√viś* (possession) in the *ṚV* appear in the context of descriptions of the relations between the *soma* drink, the deity Soma, and various other deities and sages.
216. Five times in *ṚV* 9: for an interpretation see ELIZARENKOVA (1996:17).
217. A passage in the *Bhagavadgītā* (9.20–21) could readily be interpreted as referring to a temporary, visionary experience of 'heaven' under the influence of *soma*, which, being temporary, is inferior to the permanent liberation available to those who understand Kṛṣṇa's nature or recommendations: "The purified Vedic drinkers of Soma seek me with oblations to win their heaven; and on reaching the blessed domain of Indra enjoy the celestial joys of the

There are also indications that *soma* could cause vomiting; it is a purgative. In the *Taittirīya Saṃhitā* (2.3.2.6) it states that, "he who vomits Soma is deprived of power, of Soma drinking".[218] On a similar note, in the *Śatapatha Brāhmaṇa* (5.5.4.8–13), when Indra has not been invited to drink *soma*, he turns up anyway and drinks what remains of the pure *soma* in the tub. "It hurt him: it flowed in all directions from (the openings of) his vital airs; only from his mouth it did not flow";[219] in other words, a possible explanation, amongst others, of this mythological event is that the *soma* churned painfully throughout his system, but he did not vomit. The passage continues to explain that none of the four castes vomits *soma* but were anyone to do so, then there would be atonement. After drinking *soma* "wild animals" sprang from Indra's orifices and he spat three times, emptying out everything. "Being thus purged by Soma, he [Indra] walked about as one tottering. The Aśvins cured him...and he indeed became better".[220] "Let him also cure by this (ceremony) one purged by Soma; he whom Soma purges is indeed emptied out of everything, for Soma is everything". In the same *Brāhmaṇa* (12.7.2.1–2), the possible effects of *soma* are again mentioned: "Verily, his fiery spirit, his energy, or vital power, depart from him whom Soma purges either upwards or downwards. As to this they say, 'Truly, the Soma juice is the Brāhmaṇa's food; and, indeed, it is not owing to Soma when a Brāhmaṇa vomits Soma; and he who vomits Soma is one who, while being fit to (gain) prosperity, does not gain prosperity...'".[221] *Soma* is also occasionally identified as

Gods. But upon enjoying the vast world of heaven, their merit exhausted, they rejoin the mortals; thus following devoutly the Law of the Vedas and craving desires they come and go" (trans. VAN BUITENEN).

218. Trans. KEITH. It also states that, "for him who vomits Soma, he should offer this oblation of panic seeds". The identity of these seeds remains unclear.

219. Trans. EGGELING.

220. It seems that there could have been different kinds of *soma*, perhaps with additives. Tvaṣṭrī brought to a sacrifice *soma* juice, "suitable for witchery, and withheld [it] from Indra. Indra by force drank off his Soma-juice, thereby committing a desecration of the sacrifice. He went asunder in every direction, and his energy, or vital power, flowed away from every limb" (*ŚB* 12.7.1.1).

221. See also *ŚB* 12.7.3.9–10: "purged by Soma"; "he purifies (the liquor) in the case of one who has vomited Soma".

Vṛtra, the cosmic snake of resistance.[222] According to the *Taittirīya Saṃhitā* (6.5.11.4), the rice cake (*puroḍāśa*), which is offered after each pressing of *soma*, is a 'stay' or a 'rest' for the sacrificer (i.e. settles the stomach), preventing the purgative *soma* juice from flowing straight through him (Gonda 1982:46).

It appears that the juice of what could have been a vine, a creeper or another concoction is a purgative that can transport the imbiber to the realm of the gods and provide visions of light.

Regarding the effects of *haoma*, Flattery (Flattery and Schwarz 1989:19–23) observes that in ancient Iranian religion there are two worlds: the (usual) visible (*gētīg*) realm; and the invisible/intangible (*mēnōg*) realm. The only way that one can see into the *mēnōg* realm before death is through drinking *haoma.* It rendered the consumer of this "liquid, omniscient wisdom" *stard*, meaning as if stunned or dazed by a blow, or as being "sprawled on the ground"; in which condition, resembling sleep, visions of what is believed to be a spirit existence could be seen.

Flattery (pp.108–113) also discusses the blissful and visionary nature of the *haoma* experience,[223] and the request of the drinker for 'straightness' of mind when confronted with an 'ordeal' of encountering truth or justice. Flattery provides a translation (pp.15–16) of a section of the *Ardā Wirāz Nāmag*, an Iranian text (in Pahlavi) probably from the 9th or 10th century CE, which is popular among Zoroastrians. The account is of a theologian named Wirāz who takes a drug, the effects of which last seven days, in response to a challenge in times of doubts about 'true religion' (of Zarathustra). Wirāz drinks three cups of the preparation, passes over the bridge of the dead and arrives in the spirit world, where he is welcomed by two spirits, Srōš (Sraoša)[224] and Ādur, who interpret what he sees. He passes briefly through a kind of heaven and then through a tormented realm of 'hell', where the denizens are tortured and punished for their moral turpitude; he finally arrives in a place of

222. *ŚB* 3.4.3.13; 4.1.3.5.

223. Interpreting *Y* 11.10; 34.4; 46.7.

224. Sraoša is very prominent in Zoroastrian funerary rites; he records the deeds of people and reports them to Ahura Mazda. Along with Mithra and Rašnu, he is one of the three judges of the soul after death and has the responsibility of guarding the soul before its journey to heaven (Russell 1987:304).

everlasting light, in the presence of Ohrmazd (the Creator, Ahura Mazda) and the Archangels. This account, FLATTERY believes, is of an experience of *haoma*.[225]

VAHMAN (1986:193), who provides a translation of this text, interprets the drink (*may ud mang*) as a mixture of wine and henbane.[226] GNOLI (1988) observes that *mang* (= *bang*, Middle Persian) is described sometimes as a lethal and sometimes as a hallucinogenic drug.

> *Bang* was also an ingredient of the 'illuminating drink' that allowed Wīštāsp to see…the 'great mystery'.[227] This *mang ī wīštāspān* (Pahlavi *Vīdēvdād*. 15.14;[228] *Ardā Wirāz Nāmag* 2.15) was mixed with *hōm*. It

---

225. Death and rebirth experiences are common with high-dose psychedelics. See GROF (1975) for his seminal account of such experiences of patients under the influence of LSD. GROF developed the theory of four Basic Perinatal Matrices: (1) in the womb, (2) the period of initial birth contractions, (3) being under force in the birth canal, (4) the breakthrough of birth. These experiences can be relived under psychedelics. GROF's theory is one way (amongst several) of explaining the death-rebirth experiences that can happen on psychedelics.

226. Henbane (*Hyoscyamos niger*) is strongly psychoactive, beyond small doses causing hallucinations and loss of motor function, and is highly toxic, potentially causing death. Small doses induce a dry mouth, light sensitivity, headache and sexual arousal. Henbane is one of the approximately 2,500 species in the *solanaceae* (nightshade) family of plants, which also includes mandrake and belladonna. The psychoactive alkaloids in *solanaceae* are atropine, scopolamine (= hyoscine) and hyoscamine. Mandrake has the highest level of scopolamine amongst these plants. Henbane and other *solanaceae* were used as additives to 'magic' potions not only in Asia but also in ancient Greece and mediaeval Europe (see MÜLLER-EBELING *et al.* 2003:93–96; HATSIS 2014). In antiquity, it was one of the main plants used for divination. PLINY (*Natural History* 25.17) remarks that all kinds of henbane cause insanity and are dangerous medicine in any form, "yet the ancients used to take [the leaves] in wine under the impression that fever was so brought down".

227. In the 9th/10th century Pahlavi *Rivāyat* (Ch. 47.15–19: WILLIAMS 1990, II:78), Wīštāsp only accepts the religion of Zarathustra—even after death threats—after drinking a potion of wine and *mang* and falling unconscious, which showed him the value of accepting the religion. WILLIAMS (p.225) comments that, "This is similar to the episode in *Dk.* VII.4.85; *mang* seems to be a narcotic or hallucinogenic drug, not a lethal poison".

228. This reference to the *Vēndīdād* (15.14) is to a passage where a maiden asks

> was an integral part of the ecstatic practice aimed at opening the 'eye of the soul'...and was drunk by Ardā Wirāz before his journey into the other world.

GNOLI maintains that *bang* must be etymologically related to Avestan *baṇha/bangha* and one of the Sanskrit terms for cannabis, *bhaṅgā*.[229] He adds that in older Arabian and Persian sources the term is applied to three different plants: cannabis, henbane and datura.[230] In the case of Ardā Wirāz, it seems he was drinking a powerful, entheogenic 'mixed potion'.

BOYCE (1975, Vol. 1:280) discusses the "illuminating" mixed potion drunk by Wīštāsp, which is referred to in the *Dēnkard* (7.4.85). Wīštāsp asks four favours from Zarathustra and is granted one of them, which is to see his final fate and to see his place in the hereafter. Wīštāsp drank a bowl of *hōm* juice mixed with *mang*, lost consciousness and saw in a vision the glories of heaven that awaited him in the hereafter. On recovering his senses, he fully accepted the new teachings of Zarathustra.

THOMPSON (2003), one of so many scholars in a long line that have addressed the Vedic *soma* issue, admits at the outset that he has no adequate alternative to the currently popular theory that *soma* was the ephedra plant, when it comes to the identification of the ur-plant from which the sacred drink *soma* was extracted (see below); nor is he necessarily endorsing the idea of a psychedelic substance. However, after considering the passages of the *Ṛgveda* referred to above, he concludes that an adequate interpretation of these passages

---

for a drug to assist an abortion she wishes to perform. She is given "*baṅha* or *shaēta*". DARMESTETER (1960:223n.19) interprets *baṅha* (as *mang* or *bang*) as cannabis; and *shaēta* (*shēt*) similarly: "le *Bang* (de Vishtāsp) ou le Shēt (de Zoroastre)". This interpretation is probably correct as cannabis (and also hemlock) feature in several ancient, polyherbal recipes for aborifacience (PENNACCHIO *et al.* 2010:4). *Shēt* is still a slang word for hashish in that region; French hippies on the trail to India in the late 1960s adopted the term as a French slang word for hashish (though the term could possibly have an alternative derivation), which is still *courant* (personal observation).

229. However, the interpretation of the Avestan term *baŋha* as the Sanskrit *baṅghā/bhang* (i.e. cannabis) is not accepted by all scholars (see HUTTER 1996:189ff.).

230. On the properties and effects of datura, see below.

must surely recognize the visionary and ecstatic nature of the poets' descriptions of their own experiences, whatever the cause.[231]

A point of disagreement amongst some scholars is whether or not these hymns really depict visionary intoxication as a result of taking a psychedelic drug of some kind; alternatively, that these hymns are poetically inspired by a mild stimulant; or that fasting, sleep-deprivation or meditation practices may be sufficient for the poetic inspiration of the hymns. All these ideas have their proponents, whose arguments are now considered.

231. See also STURHMAN (1985) and (2006), who similarly emphasizes the visionary aspect of the poets' experiences.

CHAPTER 6

The botanical identification of *soma/haoma*: an overview

Since scholarly interest in the botanical identity of *soma/haoma* first properly began, around 250 years ago, scores of researchers have applied themselves to the topic, producing theories for over fifty potential candidates for *soma.* Some have concluded that proper botanical identification is impossible due to the paucity of available botanical information.[232] The three most currently influential and endorsed theories are that *soma/haoma* was/is: 1. ephedra; 2. fly-agaric (originally proposed by R. Gordon WASSON); 3. Syrian/mountain rue (more recently proposed by FLATTERY and SCHWARZ). These three theories will be considered in greater detail in subsequent chapters.

Two of the most comprehensive summaries of the published theories to date are those of O'FLAHERTY (1969) and HOUBEN (2003).[233] O'FLAHERTY (1969:102) notes that the first descriptions in any European language of the characteristics of *soma/haoma* were those of A. H. ANQUETIL-DUPERRON[234] (who brought out the first translation of the *Avesta* in 1771), Charles WILKINS (who produced a translation of the *Bhagavad Gītā* in 1784), and William JONES, who remarked on the issue in 1794 in his translation of the 'Laws of

---

232. TAILLIEU (1995:191), for example, who is a relatively recent contributor to this debate, echoes the conclusion of several previous researchers, who date back to 1882 (SWAMY 1976:22), that, "textual evidence seems inadequate to prove consistently one claim or another".
233. See also SWAMY (1976:12–16) for a useful summary of historical candidates.
234. He remarked that the plant resembled heather, with knots close together, and leaves like those of jasmine.

Manu' (*Manusmṛti*). WILKINS notes that, "*sōm* is the name of a creeper", whose juice is drunk at the conclusion of a sacrifice; JONES identifies the plant as a species of mountain rue. Subsequently, amongst numerous other propositions, rue (*Ruta graveolens* = harmala = garden rue), in various forms, has been periodically proposed as a candidate for *soma* and to this day, as mentioned above, is still one of the prevalent theories, which are discussed below.

Many of the proposed botanical identifications of the 19th century focused on a vine that has for centuries been used as a substitute in Vedic rituals in parts of India,[235] namely *Sarcostemma brevistigma*[236] (referred to as the 'moon plant' by some researchers). This vine produces a milky sap but has little (if any) effect when consumed.[237] It was also pointed out by some commentators, such as Friedrich Max MÜLLER in 1855, that the *Sarcostemma* vines are common to parts of India, such as Mumbai, which would not fit the textual descriptions of a rare mountain plant. O'FLAHERTY (1969:98n.7) also comments that nowhere in the *Veda*s is the *soma*

---

235. Some earlier researchers (for example, JOUVEAU DUBREUIL 1926) maintained that *soma* is an *Asclepiad* vine. *Periploca aphylla* is also mentioned as a substitute by several commentators (see O'FLAHERTY 1969:119–121; HOUBEN 2003:2.4). This is an erect, branched shrub of the *Asclepiadaceae* family that produces a milky sap, which eventually hardens and which is used in chewing gum. It is common in Rajasthan and Punjab. However, KASHIKAR (1990:24) claims that it is not used as a substitute. All species of *Asclepiadaceae* are more or less poisonous. The three species most used in medicine are *Caltropis procera, Asclepias tuberosa* (pleurisy root), and *Asclepias incarnata* (swamp milkweed). *Asclepias curassavica* is used as an emetic in the West Indies (GRIEVE 1995/2014).

236. = *Asclepias acida* = *Sarcostemma acidum* = *Sarcostemma viminale* = *Cyanchium viminale.* The identification of *Sarcostemma* was first made by William CAREY in his publication *Hortus Bengalensis* in 1814 (O'FLAHERTY 1969:103). The various kinds of *Sarcostemma*, in relation to *soma*, are discussed by ROTH (1881). *Sarcostemma brevistigma* and *Periploca aphylla* have again both been proposed more recently as possible candidates, by KARNICK (1980/81). *Asclepias acida* is still currently used in *soma* rites in coastal Andhra Pradesh, is referred to as *soma-lātā* or *soma-tīga*, but has no psychoactive effect at all (KNIPE 2015:213).

237. Martin HAUG drank a small quantity of a brew prepared from the *Sarcostemma* vine and felt nauseous and slightly intoxicated (O'FLAHERTY 1969:108).

plant itself said to have a milky sap, though milk is later added to the extraction. As noted previously, the colour of the extracted liquid is said to be brown, yellow, tawny or red.

Several commentators have proposed a distinction between two plants: *somarāja* and *somavallī* (or *somalatā*; i.e. *soma* 'vine' or 'creeper'), as in some regions, such as Nepal, a common vine is called *somalatā* (which was also identified by some commentators as a species of rue, *Ruta graveolens*).[238] However, few of the proposed identifications[239] support the descriptions, geographical habitat, and effects of *soma* alluded to in the *Veda*s and *Avesta*. Commenting on the voluminous research on *soma/haoma* O'FLAHERTY (1969:144) remarks that, "Handicapped by a rudimentary knowledge of the vernacular and ancient languages of India and by inadequate communication in the academic world, scholars covered the same ground over and over again. Time and again the same ideas reappear, are disproved, and reappear as if they were proven theories".[240] Since O'FLAHERTY's review (1969) there have been several other suggestions, none of which has yet gained any substantial scholarly endorsement or support.

---

238. Some, such as A. C. BURNELL, suggested in 1874 that different plants may have been used in different regions of India: he observed that on the Coromandel coast *Sarcostemma brevistigma* is used; while on the Malabar coast it is *Ceropegia decaisneana*.

239. Amongst the forty or so candidates proposed (some with reservations)—and assessed by O'FLAHERTY (1969)—were: alcohol, in various forms (numerous suggestions), including, by HAVELL (1920), who proposes a fermented alcoholic drink (from millet, *rāgī*); *Vernonia anthelmintica* (= *Conyza anthelmintica*) (H. T. COLEBROOK, 1808; J. O. VOIGT, 1845; K. L. BHISHAGRATNA, 1907); *Menispermum glabrum* or *Serratula anthelmintica* (H. H. WILSON, 1819); *Calonyction muricatum* (= *Ipomoea muricata* = morning glory) (H. DRURY, 1873); *Periploca aphylla* (J. G. BAKER, 1884); *Setaria glauca* (yellow foxtail) (J. F. DUTHIE, 1888); *Tinospora cordifolia* (R. N. KHORY, 1903); *Laserpitium [latifolium?]* (W. W. WILSON, 1906); *Vitex negundo* (C. HARTWICH, 1911); *bhāṃg* (cannabis) (B. L. MUKHERJEE, 1921; J. C. ROY, 1939); *Paederia foetida* (NADKARNI, 1954); *Crinum latifolium* (P. V. SHARMA, 1956).

240. Research on this topic continues to be voluminous; to the degree that even this particular quotation from O'FLAHERTY has now also been often repeated by commentators.

CHAPTER 7

Cannabis/hemp

Although a proposition for *soma/haoma* being cannabis (*bhāṃg* or *hashish*)[241] was first (?) made by George W. BROWN in 1890 (p.84), it was an article by B. L. MUKHERJEE in 1921 that attracted wider attention amongst scholars;[242] this proposition has yet again

241. *Bhāṃg* (Hindi) refers to the pounded lower leaves of the female plant, which (usually pounded together with spices and milk products) are formed into small pellets, a preparation for eating or drinking (dissolved in plain water or in water and yoghurt). *Hashish* (a term derived from the Persian) used to refer to the whole plant or to the leaves or buds but nowadays usually refers specifically to the preparation of the powdery resin that falls from mature female buds, which, after passing through sieves, is pressed into blocks. This is a technique currently employed almost exclusively by Muslim populations. *Caras* (charas) is prepared by rubbing the matured buds of the female plant in October. This (probably ancient) technique, which was refined in Himachal Pradesh primarily by French hippies in the mid to late 1960s, is employed primarily in the Indian and Nepalese Himalayas. In the last thirty years this technique has spread to other cannabis-producing countries, including Colombia and Jamaica.

242. Amongst the errors in MUKHERJEE's article, which is still being cited by some of those who endorse the cannabis thesis, is that *Satapatha Brāhmaṇa* 5.1.1.12 states that Soma is *uśānā*, which is *śaṇa*, which is cannabis. This reference is incorrect: however, as O'FLAHERTY (1969:128n.3) noticed—and as previously discussed in Chapter 4—verses 3.4.3.13 and 4.2.5.15 (of the Mādhyandinda recension) do refer to a plant called *uśānā* from which *soma* is made; but this has no relation to cannabis (or hemp). Further, although *śaṇa* (*san* in Hindi) may refer to cannabis, it usually refers to *Crotalaria juncea* Linn. (= Indian hemp), which is a plant with yellow flowers used for fodder, fibre and manure (HOERNLE 2011:80, v.23; KAMAL 1988:27; MEULENBELD 1989:62).

more recently been reiterated by SWAMY (1976),[243] WARADPANDE (1995),[244] and PENDELL (2010a:183),[245] and treated extensively by BENNETT (2010).

The use of hemp/cannabis[246] by humans for cloth, fibre, food, medicine and intoxication (in some instances), is indeterminately

---

243. BASHAM (1972:18) believes that, "soma may well have been hemp".

244. *Soma* is identified as *bhāṃg* (cannabis) by WARADPANDE (1995), who maintains that cannabis was also smoked in Vedic times, but his evidence (e.g. p.8: *ṚV* 9.1.8; p.10: *ṚV* 9.5.1) is unreliable. Even though smoking plants for remedies is to be found in early Ayurvedic texts, such as in *Caraka Saṃhitā* (*c.* 2nd century CE), smoking cannabis only began after the Portuguese introduced tobacco (with which it is usually mixed in South Asia) to India at the beginning of the 17th century (*Indian Tobacco: A Monograph* 1960:1). CARAKA (*Sūtrasthāna* 5.20–55 [SHARMA and DASH 1983:112–119]) prescribes mixing around two dozen dried and powdered plants (including *nyagrodha, udumbara, aśvattha* and *plakṣa*) into a cigar, which is then smoked (three puffs) eight times daily via a pipe. This is said to relieve numerous ailments in the neck and head, including excess *kapha*. Excess smoking is said to lead to deafness, blindness, dumbness, giddiness and bleeding from different parts of the body.

245. However, in a later publication (2010b:133–141) PENDELL shifts in favour of ephedra being *soma*, and suggests that *soma/haoma* may not necessarily have been 'psychedelic' but, rather, stimulant. As previously noted, he also suggests that *Peganum harmala* may have been an additive to an ephedra concoction. See below for further discussion of this suggestion.

246. There are many strains of cannabis, which grows on all continents (the exact extent of its historical ubiquity is uncertain). The polytypic classification of cannabis began with Jean-Baptiste LAMARCK (1744–1829) in 1783 (SCHULTES and HOFMANN 1980:88). It is currently classified in three main taxa: as *Cannabis sativa, Cannabis indica* and *Cannabis ruderalis* (though this rudimentary classification has been often challenged). In this classificatory scheme numerous sub-species of cannabis are accommodated. Even in the Himalayas there are many distinct varieties, ranging from kinds that attain only one metre in height to those that may attain seven metres in height. The plants exhibit a range of colours, from green/yellow to dark green to purple, and with different leaf and bud formations. Some varieties, even in a localized geographical region, are potently psychoactive while others are weak, sometimes with virtually no psychoactive effect. Similarly, some strains are better than others for cloth and fibre production. In general, the higher the altitude, the more psychoactively potent are the buds of the plant (owing to more resin being produced in buds to protect them from higher levels of ultra-violet light); but this does not hold for all strains.

ancient.[247] Some of the earliest certain evidence of its use, probably as an intoxicant, is from two burial sites, one near Bucharest and the other in north Caucasus, both dating from the early Bronze Age in the late 3rd millennium BCE. Braziers or censers that may have been used for smoke inhalation date to the 5th millennium BCE (SHERRATT 1991). The so-called Yamnaya culture, which flourished between from about 3500 to 2500 BCE in the Pontic region of the Black Sea and on the Caspian steppes, and which eventually spanned 3,000 kilometers, from the Danube to the Urals, used censers, probably to inhale cannabis smoke (PARPOLA 2015:53). Further south, cannabis has been in continuous use in the Mediterranean region since the late 2nd millennium BCE (SHERRATT 1995:21). Cannabis is mentioned in ancient Egyptian texts[248] in connection with rope making in the middle of the 3rd millennium BCE; a thousand years later its use is attested in several medical texts (MANNICHE 1999:82). (Evidence for the use of the opium poppy is similarly ancient.) The use of cannabis in the Iron Age, from western Europe to China, is attested to by abundant finds. Cannabis was probably known to ancient Iranians, as it is mentioned in the *Avesta*.[249]

Suggestions from the archaeological record lead SHERRATT (1991:52–54) to believe that the earliest manner of intoxication by cannabis was through burning the plant and inhaling the smoke. In the 5th century BCE, HERODOTUS (1968:265–266) famously described Scythians—in an account derived from an in informant in Olbia, on the north coast of the Black Sea—inhaling the smoke of cannabis buds (which he refers to as “seeds”) in small, enclosed tents; and howling with pleasure.[250] The plant is said by HERODOTUS

247. In a recent, comprehensive study, the general consensus on the complex issue of the most ancient natural habitat, cultivation and propagation of cannabis is that it originated in Central Asia, probably in the upland valleys of the Tian Shan or Altai mountains. Evidence for its use in China dates from between 3500 and 2500 BCE (CLARKE and MERLIN 2013:20ff, 201).

248. It is called *šmšmt* in Ancient Egyptian.

249. In the *Fravaši Yašt* (v. 124) the *fravaši* (guardian spirit) of someone called Pouru-baṅha (posessor of much cannabis) is listed.

250. This report was confirmed by excavations of burial mounds in 1947 at Pazyryk in the Altai mountains in Siberia, dating to the 5th century BCE. Tent-like structures containing stones and cannabis seeds were found (SHERRATT 1995:27).

to be both wild and cultivated.[251] Further east, in the Xinjiang region of China, there is firm evidence of the use of cannabis from the 6th century BCE: wooden bowls or leather baskets of cannabis were placed in tombs next to the head of the dead. Cannabis was here likely used for intoxication or medicinally as no hemp textiles have been found; nor at this site is there any evidence for its use as food or oil (JIANG *et al.* 2006).

In the South Asian region, the concise report by GRIERSON (1894) on references to hemp in Sanskrit and Hindi literature is still one of the most useful surveys of the historical use of cannabis on the subcontinent. He notes the following: that the principal names used in literature for the plant are *bhaṅga, indrāsana, vijayā* and *jayā*; the earliest reference to the name *gāñjā*—which these days refers to the buds of the female plant—dates from around 1300 CE; *vijayā* also refers to yellow myrobalan.[252]

Several surveys have been made by opponents of the *soma* as cannabis thesis, one of the most useful short summaries being by NYBERG (1997:386–387). *Soma* was improbably cannabis alone, for several reasons. Firstly, the stalks of the cannabis plant are not psychoactive at all and the most potent part of the plant is the buds of the female plant. Preparation of *bhāṃg* entails the pounding of the leaves or buds of the plant, but not the stalks or stems.

Secondly, there is little, if any evidence, of the use of cannabis in a religious, ritual or even medical context in South Asia before the 11th century CE,[253] though acquaintance with cannabis in Asia

---

251. PLINY (*Natural History* 20.97) knew cannabis, which originally grew in the woods (i.e. uncultivated) only as a medicine. Its seeds are said to cause impotence; it kills parasites, numbs the pain of cramped joints, and settles the stomachs of domestic animals.

252. = *Terminalia chebula* = *harītakī* (Hindi); a deciduous tree, which provides nut-like fruits that are used to alleviate cough.

253. Cannabis is now (again) widely recognized for its manifold medicinal properties (see, for example, GRINSPOON and BAKALAR 1997; RUSSO 2005). The first reports in a European language of the medicinal properties of cannabis were from India, by Cristoval ACOSTA in 1578; and then by Garcia D'ORTA in 1616. ACOSTA was a medical man from Burgos in Spain who wrote a treatise on medicines and drugs. D'ORTA was a doctor from Portugal, who ACOSTA met in India, and who was the first European to compile an Indian *materia medica*: *Coloquios dos simples e drogas he cousas medicinais da*

is nevertheless ancient. WITZEL (2003:52) notes that **bhanga* is one of the BMAC/Central Asian loan-words that subsequently appears in the later Vedic and Old Iranian languages; and that *śaṇa/ kana* is also likely a BMAC loan word (WITZEL 1999:65). This is supported by claims by SARIANIDI (1994; 2003) that there is evidence of the religious use of cannabis in the Turkmenistan before 1500 BCE (for more on this point, see below).

Supporters of the cannabis thesis usually cite references to it in the *Veda*s in support of the cannabis-as-*soma* hypothesis, one example being the occurrence of the term *bhaṅga* in the *Ṛgveda* at 9.61.13: "The gods approach Soma of perfect birth, he is the destroyer (*bhaṅgaṃ*) who speeds the waters, and (is accompanied) by the knowledge rays" (trans. KASHYAP).[254] In Sanskrit, besides referring to cannabis, *bhaṅga* also means 'breaking' or 'destroying'. It is apparent that in this verse the term is used as an epithet for *soma*, and does not indicate cannabis. Another oft-cited reference by supporters of the *bhaṅgā* thesis is in the *Atharvaveda* (11.6.15) (*c.* 1200 BCE) where it is stated: "To the five kingdoms of the plants, of which *soma* is chief (*śreṣṭha*), we speak. *Dharba*, hemp [*bhaṅga*],[255] barley [*yava*], *saha* ['mighty power']:[256] let them free us from distress" (trans. WHITNEY). It is difficult to know how to interpret this reference.[257] GRIERSON (1894:260) interprets this verse as a

India. There was no interest in the British medical world in the intoxicating properties of cannabis until the 19th century (MILLS 2012:27–32); then in its heyday, between 1840 and 1900, there were more than a hundred publications in western medical literature on the use of cannabis for various illnesses (GRINSPOON and BALAKAR 1997:4).

254. *Upo ṣu jātamapturaṃ gobhiḥ bhaṅgaṃ /.*

255. KASHYAP and SHASTRI likewise interpret *bhaṅga* in this verse as hemp.

256. The commentary to WHITNEY's translation calls *saha* simply, "a kind of herb". MONIER-WILLIAMS (p.1193) merely records this as a name of a plant. KASHYAP translates *saha* as, "mighty wheat".

257. MEULENBELD (1989:61n.2) comments that this, "may mean hemp"; and that SĀYAṆA regards it as *śaṇa* (which sometimes refers to cannabis). It was mentioned in Chapter 2 that barley was one of the ingredients of a *soma* concoction (to settle the stomach); and in Chapter 4 the association of *darbha* grass with *soma* was discussed (more on this below). As what appears to be cannabis is mentioned in the same context in this hymn of the *Atharvaveda* it seems possible that this plant may have been used as an additive in some forms of the preparation of *soma*; though this is purely speculative.

reference to *bhaṅgā* as a sacred grass, used with the other grasses mentioned as an oblation. However, the use of grasses as oblations is improbable. Cannabis (*śaṇa*) is also referred to in another verse of the *Atharvaveda* (2.4.5), where it is said that *śaṇa* is brought from the wilderness (*araṇya*) and used as a protective device (*maṇi*) against evil and poison, together with a *jaṅgiḍa maṇi* (a protective amulet made from various agricultural crops). There is another reference to *bhaṅga* in the *Atharvaveda* (8.8.3), where *bhaṅga* is used as a simile: "...let them be suddenly (*tājad*) broken (*bhañj*) like hemp (*bhaṅga*)" (trans. WHITNEY).[258]

WUJASTYK (2002:55) points out that a distinction needs to be made between the terms *bhaṅga*, which is masculine and means, as noted, 'break' or 'rupture'; and *bhaṅgā*, which is feminine and refers to hemp or cannabis.[259] Nevertheless, several references in the *Atharvaveda* (2.4.5; 8.8.3; 11.6.15) seem to be referring to the cannabis plant, but whether as an intoxicant, as merely a wild plant, or as a vital agricultural crop is unclear. However, MEULENBELD (1989:61n.2) maintains that, "the word *bhaṅgā* does not occur in Vedic texts".

KĀTYĀYANA (3rd century BCE), in his commentary (*Vārttika*) on PĀṆINI (5th–4th century BCE) 5.2.29—in this verse discussing the affix *kaṭac*—refers to *bhaṅgākaṭa* among agricultural crops that produce dust (or pollen), the others being bottle-gourd (*alābū*), sesame (*tila*) and flax (*umā*).[260] RENOU interprets *bhaṅgā* here as hemp (MEULENBELD 1989:61n.2), indicating KĀTYĀYANA's acquaintance with the pollen of *bhaṅgā*. If the 'dust' mentioned here is not pollen (from the male plant) but rather the psychoactive, resinous dust that falls from the mature buds of the female plant, then the produce that KĀTYĀYANA refers to is hashish. This seems to suggest, possibly, that the intoxicating properties of *bhaṅgā* may have been known about in South Asia in the early centuries BCE, but

---

258. *tājadbhaṅga iva bhajantām*.

259. NYBERG (1997:386) also notes the association of the Sanskrit term *bhaṅga* with some words in Uralic languages referring to mushrooms.

260. However, cannabis is not mentioned in the Black *Yajurveda saṃhitās* as one of the 'seven cultivated plants' (which are specified in other texts), used by the early 'Āryan' migrants and settlers in South Asia (RAU 1997:205). Though cannabis could have been collected from the 'wilderness'.

to what extent, or if it was used as an intoxicant or a medicine or merely as a useful plant, remains uncertain; scholars disagree.

There is a reference by VARĀHAMIHIRA (505–587 CE) in his *Bṛhatsaṃhitā* (XLVIII.39) to *vijayā* and other grasses used in the rites of a bathing festival; this is probably a reference to hemp, as the wording in this passage is similar to that of passage referred to above in the *Atharvaveda* (11.6.15) (GRIERSON 1894:260). In the 7th/8th century Buddhist *Cakrasamvaratantra* (ch. 50),[261] *śaṇa* (cannabis) is mentioned as one of several ingredients[262] to be used in a rite for an abundant life for a yogi.[263] These references indicate that cannabis was known about and used around the middle of the 1st millennium CE in South Asia. However, MEULENBELD (1989:61n.3, 64–66) disputes claims that cannabis is mentioned in early medical texts, such as SUŚRUTA's, as is claimed by several commentators.[264] The earliest unequivocal reference to cannabis in medical texts is in the *Cikitsāsārasaṃgraha* ('Compendium of the essence of medicine') of VAṄGASENA, who flourished between approximately 1050–1100 CE. He refers to cannabis as *bhaṅgā* and also as *indrāśana* and *tribhavanavijaya*,[265] and notes some similarity with opium. GRIERSON (1894:260) comments on the 11th-century work *Śabdacandrikā* by CAKRAPĀṆIDATTA, in which the names *vijayā, trailokyavijayā, bhaṅgā, indrāśana* and *jayā* are provided as synonyms for cannabis, which by this time is clearly understood as an intoxicant and a medicine. Other references to it subsequently occur in several other medical texts dating from 1100–1250 CE. In the 13th century ŚĀRṄGADHARA mentions *bhaṅgā* as an

261. (GRAY 2007:373–374).

262. These are wax gourd, gram, beeswax, Indian mustard, and the leaves of a household *tamāla* tree.

263. ALDRICH (1977) details the use of cannabis (*bhāṃg*) in sexual rites in the *Mahānirvaṇatantra*, at text that he dates to the 11th century. However, this text—famously translated by John WOODROFFE (= Arthur AVALON) and published in 1913—may possibly date to as late as the 18th century.

264. This claim is persistent: RUSSO (2005:2), for example, claims that SUŚRUTA (who he dates too early, from the 3rd to 8th centuries BCE; see WUJASTYK 1998:105) prescribes cannabis as an anti-phlegmatic. RUSSO (p.3) also maintains that, "it is likely about this time" that the more potent properties of *gāñjā* (i.e. female buds) were medically recognized.

265. DASH (1989:152) lists forty-three synonyms for cannabis.

intoxicating (*mada*) drug, which may be used for treating several medical problems, including cough, loss of appetite, anaemia and diarrhoea;[266] in the following centuries references to cannabis proliferate (GRIERSON 1894:261; MEULENBELD 1989:64; WUJASTYK 2002:46).

SANDERSON (2003:365–366n.43) notes the new appearance in the 16th century in some Tantric rites, particularly in the north-east of India, of an intoxicating cannabis drink known as *saṃvit/saṃvidā* or *vijayā*[267] (= *bhaṅgā*). SANDERSON comments that the use of cannabis for spiritual intoxication was probably adopted from Sūfī ascetics, such as those of the Madāriyya order, founded by Badī‘ ad-dīn Shāh MADĀRĪ (d.*c.*1440). This sect was one of several sects of radical, antinomian Sūfīs, known more generally (amongst other sectarian designations) as Qalandars or Haydarīs (who were referred to earlier in the context of a living *haoma* tradition in Iran), who used *bhāṃg* to excess and who first started settling in north India in large numbers towards the end of the 13th century. This large migration of Sūfīs from Afghanistan into India was most probably the main cause of the spread of the 'recreational' use of cannabis in the subcontinent, particularly in the northern regions.[268]

However, as mentioned previously, the Scythians, who were widespread in Central Asia in the 1st millennium BCE, were renowned for cannabis intoxication;[269] and members of at least one of their tribes were also *haomavarga* (*soma* drinkers). Between *c.* 200 BCE and 400 CE the Śakās (Scythians) were a dominant force in north-western India (from Gujarat to southern Uttar Pradesh), Pakistan and eastern and southern Afghanistan. It is conceivable (or even probable) that cannabis was cultivated and used by the Scythians in South Asia during that period; though there is no evidence for this

---

266. The most comprehensive, early account of the effects and uses of cannabis, and its mythology and cultivation, are in a chapter devoted to it in the *Ānandakanda*, a voluminous text on tantric alchemy and yoga, dating from the 12th or 13th centuries (WUJASTYK 2002:59–60).

267. *Vijayā*, meaning 'conquerer' or 'victor' is one of the common Sanskrit terms for cannabis; but it can also refer to other plants (MEULENBELD 1989:62n.4).

268. For further details, see CLARK (2016).

269. The English term cannabis derives from the Greek word *kánnabis*, which, in turn, is a loan word from the Scythians (WITZEL 1999:65).

as far as I am aware. It seems that the use of cannabis as an intoxicant or medicine was either limited or possibly even non-existent in South Asia before the 11th century, as religious texts barely refer to it, and medical texts not at all, despite contrary claims.

The third objection to cannabis (alone) as *soma/haoma*, which to me seems to be the most important, is its effect. Cannabis has a wide range of possible effects. In particular circumstances—such as after fasting or in very high doses in some individuals, particularly novices—it may produce strong psychedelic effects. Most people who have experimented with cannabis report occasions, though usually rare, of psychedelic kinds of effects. The vivid, flamboyant, mid-19th century account of hallucinatory hashish intoxication by Théophile GAUTIER is sometimes cited in this respect. GAUTIER was introduced to hashish by the dilettante painter Ferdinand Boissard DE BOISDENIER at the Hôtel Pimodan on the Île Sainte-Louis in the centre of Paris (DAVENPORT-HINES 2001:63) in one of the sessions of the Club des Hashischins.[270] He described how the meat he was eating turned to raspberries in his mouth, and how his neighbours' noses lengthened into probosces. The walls of the house heaved and palpitated like a human diaphragm. Amongst numerous apparitions, monks with wheels for feet and cauldrons for bellies appeared (GAUTIER 1969:205ff.). GAUTIER's account was first published in *Revue des deux mondes* in 1846, but he later admitted that his account had indulged in the gothic and fantastical fashion of the day, and that his account of his experience was wildly mythologized (JAY 2010:88).

BELL's (1857:212) description of his first experience of cannabis (in a large dose) is also quite typical of descriptions of extreme intoxication. Some time after the effects began he reports:

> These singular attacks of mental disturbance recurred oftener, and lasted longer...All ideas of time and space were especially bewildered, and I realized completely for the first time the ideas of some

270. GAUTIER—together with Charles BAUDELAIRE, Victor HUGO, Honoré de BALZAC, Alexandre DUMAS, the caricaturist Honoré DAUMIER, the painter Paul CHENAVARD, the writer Gérard DE NERVAL, and the sculptor Jean-Jacques PRADIER and his wife—was among the frequenters of the club, which usually convened every month at the hotel from around 1844 to 1849.

> metaphysicians, that time properly speaking, has no existence except in connection with a succession of mental operations or sensation… the whole physical nature surrendered itself, without further struggle, to the fullest and most complete belief in the actual existence of a thousand hallucinations.

BELL recovered fully after a few hours and believed that hashish could be a useful tool to understand insanity. BAUDELAIRE (1969:221), who also ate hashish in the club with GAUTIER, and also experienced hallucinations, remarks that, whether or not someone is sophisticated or ignorant, "they will find in hashish nothing miraculous, absolutely nothing but an extension of the natural…hashish will be a mirror of his impressions and private thoughts – a magnifying mirror, it is true, but only a mirror…there was nothing positively supernatural about the intoxication of hashish" (p.230).

It needs to be emphasized that cannabis does not on its own usually engender properly entheogenic experience, and only rarely hallucinogenic effects; one only has to observe people in cultures where cannabis is used regularly, and sometimes in large quantities, to observe that cannabis is not a 'visionary' drug,[271] even though there are instances of cannabis being revered in a religious sense in cultures that use it.[272] Cannabis, in anything other than 'heroic doses', is usually mildly soporific, though it can be simultaneously mentally stimulating, and it could be argued that it can come close to being an entheogen. Its most universal characteristic, observed by

---

271. There is abundant historical evidence for cannabis use that clearly demonstrates the usual range of effects produced in regular users. See, for example, ROSENTHAL (1971) for accounts of Qalandar Sūfīs' use of cannabis in the Muslim world in the 12th to 15th century. For a contemporary, general summary of the effects of cannabis, see EARLEYWINE (2005). It is also important to note the relative complexity of the effects of cannabis. Different species of the plant contain numerous psychoactive alkaloids in varying proportions, including around sixty cannabinoids, a hundred terpenoids, and twenty flavonoids (EARLEYWINE 2005:242). The marked variation in constituent molecules in different species of the plant produces a wide range of potential experiences; some kinds of cannabis engender more drowsiness, while others are more stimulatory. This, however, is greatly simplifying the subtle variation in subjective effects, which is still poorly understood from a pharmacological perspective.
272. For example, reverence for cannabis amongst Rastafarians, by some sects of *sādhus* in South Asia, and Qalandar Sūfīs in Central Asia.

numerous commentators, is the quality of exaggerating or amplifying the current sentiments and inclinations of the consumer, whereby pleasant or sensuous experience or sexual tendencies may be greatly enhanced; or, conversely, nervous, paranoid or anxious inclinations may be provoked. A good book, film, music (particularly), a landscape or physical exercise may become completely absorbing, while someone who is tired may simply fall into a deep sleep. However, at doses sufficiently large to produce almost entheogenic effects, by eating several grammes, the consumer is usually left practically incapacitated and 'pinned to the ground'[273] for several hours, which is usually not too pleasant, unless sleep ensues. Also, importantly, cannabis—however consumed and even in high doses—is not a purgative; and we have seen that *soma/haoma* appears to have been a purgative, similarly to ayahuasca.

It needs to be emphasized in this discussion that what is being assessed is to be understood as the usual or general effects of plants or substances. There are people who are particularly sensitive to the effects of drugs, stimulants or narcotics who may have an entheogenic or a frightening experience as a result of consuming almost anything. Arguments for or against the entheogenic properties of drugs or plants may rely on genuine but unusual reports of entheogenic experiences; however, what is being emphasized in this discussion is the normal range of effects in experiencers.[274] Another important consideration is that although the engendering of entheogenic states of consciousness is of course largely dependent on the dose and kind of drug consumed, as is frequently reiterated by commentators, the 'set and setting' of the experience is crucially influential: the appropriate environment and the intention and expectations of the consumer are very important factors governing the kind of experience undergone.[275]

---

273. BRAID (1850:33) cites an anecdotal report from Morocco that under an "intense dose" of hashish operations such as amputations may be performed, the narcotic state rendering the patient temporarily immune to the pain.

274. When at university in Wales in the late 1970s a friend of mine gave a French visitor a mug of 'British Rail' tea. The Frenchman had never previously drunk tea, only coffee. His heart-rate increased dramatically, he had a panic reaction, and he was then hospitalized so that his condition could be monitored.

275. Building on the published observations of Sydney COHEN and others, Timothy LEARY and his colleagues at Harvard famously popularized the

In conclusion, if, as is being suggested in this investigation, we are looking for an entheogen that was *soma/haoma*, then cannabis on its own can be ruled out, besides other reasons, because the effects are, essentially, too weak when used habitually.[276] Nevertheless, it seems entirely feasible that cannabis, along with other plants (possibly including ephedra), was used as an additive to or a component of a 'mixed' brew containing other chemical compounds provided by other plants. Despite his opposition to the cannabis thesis, NYBERG (1997:387) suggests that cannabis, "might have been an ingredient, in some preparations derived from the use of the original *soma/haoma*". This seems very probable. In Chapter 13 of this book, there is a reference to cannabis being an additive (or a main ingredient) to a *hōm* juice drunk in Syria. However, before moving on to a consideration of other plant candidates for *soma/ haoma*, the next chapter will explore altered states of consciousness, the parameters of entheogens in general, and how stronger entheogens might be distinguished from cannabis.

---

importance and influence of 'set' (mind-set) and 'setting' (environment) on psychedelic experience in a series of publications (first by LEARY *et al.*, 1963), which challenged a previously-held medical view that psychedelics mimic mental psychosis. Interestingly, nearly two millennia ago CARAKA (*Sūtrasthāna* 36.13) made similar observations on set and setting: "It is not that the various drugs and diets act only by virtue of their qualities. In fact they act by virtue of their own nature or qualities or both on a proper occasion, in a given location, in [an] appropriate condition and situation" (trans. SHARMA and DASH 1983:454).

276. METZNER (2005a:31; 2009:64) presents a scheme of various states of consciousness (see Appendix 5), onto which different kinds of psychoactive drugs and their effects can be usefully positioned. Properly entheogenic or psychedelic plants or substances can be categorized as 'high arousal', with the potential for inducing both strongly 'hellish' and 'heavenly' experiences. Opiates are tranquilizers (i.e. low arousal), ephedra (in its natural form) is a mild stimulant (i.e. high arousal), while cannabis can act as both a mild soporific (usually) and also as stimulatory (occasionally), depending on set and setting. Prototypical expansion of consciousness, as engendered by psychedelics such as LSD, usually entails a heightened sense of (and interest in) the complexity of phenomena; while prototypical contraction of consciousness, as in opiate use, addictions and compulsions, is associated with a narrowing of focussed interest in general phenomena, fixation on particular objects, and a simplification of awareness.

CHAPTER 8

Altered states of consciousness and demarcation criteria

In contrast with cannabis, plants potentially capable of regularly producing properly entheogenic/psychedelic effects, such as the peyote (*Lophophora williamsii*) and San Pedro (*Trichocereus/ Echinopsis pachanoi*) cacti,[277] iboga (*Tabernanthe iboga*),[278] *Salvia*

277. Both of these cacti contain mescaline, as do many of the twenty-five species of *Trichocereus* (SCHULTES and HOFMANN (1980:228). For the traditional use and effects of these cacti, see FURST (1972); SHARON (1972); SCHULTES *et al.* (2001:144–156, 166–169); BENCIOLINI and GUTIÉRREZ DEL ÁNGEL (2016:171–190). For personal testimonials of peyote experience by native, North American Indians, see SMITH (2000:116–125). For an account of an academic's experience of peyote (in eleven sessions) see ABERLE (1982:5–11), who summarises the most significant elements of a peyote session as: a feeling of personal significance of external and internal stimuli; the feeling of medical benefit; experiencing the power of peyote.

278. For examples of testimonials of experience with the iboga/eboga plant, which contains the strongly psychoactive alkaloid ibogaine, see RAVALEC *et al.* (2007); see SCHULTES and HOFMANN (1980:235–239) for the botany and chemistry of iboga. A full dose of ibogaine (from the macerated root of the iboga plant) is the basis of initiation into the Bwiti cult of Gabon and Cameroon, inducing a near-death experience (and occasionally actual death) referred to as 'breaking open of heads' (*abwing nlo*). For an account of a typical, native initiation and the visions (often of deceased relatives) reported by several local informants, see FERNANDEZ (1982:470ff.); for a foreigner's account of initiation, see PINCHBECK (2003:20–43). In the last twenty years or so, programmes of treatment with iboga (or ibogaine extract from the plant) for drug addicts and alcoholics have proved to be successful in some cases (PERRINE 1996:287–288; DICKINSON 2014).

divinorum,[279] psilocybin mushrooms,[280] or ayahuasca,[281] can produce intense experiences, often of a visionary nature in most people even when used frequently for many years. It needs to be mentioned that different kinds of entheogenic/psychedelic drugs and plants subtly engender qualitatively different kinds of experience and distinct structural singularities of consciousness, which are quite specific to the substance. However, even though there are subtle differences of effects between these plants, all of them usually induce a broadly similar scope of experiences and general neurophysiological activity.[282] Indeed, the reason these plants are called entheogenic is that consumption in anything but light doses can propel the consumer into what might be called 'the spirit world', where the consumer becomes vividly aware of not only being in a mentally or sensually enhanced or altered world, but has broken though a kind of invisible veil, which is perhaps more like a spectrum of effects and experience rather than a specific point of change, to what is beyond doubt—to the consumer—another kind of what seems to be a more real 'reality'.[283]

---

279. This plant, which is in the sage family of plants, is indigenous only in Mexico. It can be exceptionally visionary; see TURNER (1996) for his own extraordinary experiments with salvinorin, which he extracted from the plant, which had never been done before.
280. See METZNER (2005b:192–293); LETCHER (2006).
281. See below.
282. PERRINE (1996:258) classifies psychedelic (i.e. entheogenic/hallucinogenic/psychomimetic) drugs to the extent that the effects on the psyche resemble those of LSD: "Using this somewhat arbitrary but simple definition, the only drugs that are genuine psychedelics as ordinarily used are LSD, psilocybin and mescaline—and a dozen or so less common drugs whose chemical structures (lysergic acids, tryptamines, and phenethyl amines) are very closely based on this classic trinity". In one double-blind study participants were unable to distinguish between the effects of LSD and mescaline.
283. A point elaborated by the British philosopher J. L. AUSTIN (1962:62–77) is perhaps pertinent here: strictly speaking, we cannot meaningfully talk of a 'reality'; but there are real things, such as real cream and real ducks, which can be distinguished from synthetic cream and decoy ducks. 'Reality' has effectively no substance, as what it comprises in its totality is only 'real' things; there is no 'reality' other than the sum of real things. What is being alluded to in the discussion above is the perception of other kinds of entities and dimensions than are normally apprehended in sober, waking consciousness appearing to be real.

Strong mystical experience, however induced, entails passing through what PARTIDGE (2003) refers to as the 'epistemic boundary' to other realms of cognition, perhaps into a blissful Buddhist void, into knowledge of *brahman*, into an encounter with the *mysterium tremendum et fascinans*,[284] or in other instances to encounters with forces or entities which appear capable of being communicated with—whether those be God, bird-deities, spirits, demons, jewel-encrusted lizards, aliens, ghosts of deceased relatives or any other kind of non-material entity—which are not ordinarily experienced in sober, waking consciousness. Any of these entities may appear to function as potentially active, interventionist, causative forces or powers. Their interventionist capacity would of course be contrary to a contemporary scientific account of causation. To a modern, consensus scientist—and quite rationally from a common sense point of view—these would be mere phantoms or delusions.[285] It is not being proposed here that what has been referred to as 'the spirit world' has some kind of discrete, veridical, ontological existence, which psychedelic drugs and other mystical practices may permit access to; the phrase 'spirit world' is simply employed here in this discussion as a familiar shorthand for and traditional description of

284. This expression and also the term 'numinous' (from the Latin *numen* = an inherent spirit or divine power) are the hallmarks of Rudolph OTTO's influential study of mysticism (1978 [1923]:12–30).

285. The issue of the 'reality' of hallucinations in this regard is tricky. At what point does someone's conception become 'false'? When does artistic or spiritual imagination, conception or experience cross over a thin line of possible 'reality'? Some apparitions are plainly false to an observer: for example, someone might be having a conversation with an entity, a god, a ghost or whatever, who is invisible to an observer. Yet we have conversations with 'people' in our heads all the time; that such internal 'people' do not have, for example, wings, three eyes, or insect heads, is perhaps beside the point: I can have imaginary conversations with a person I know and also with someone with three eyes. For a comprehensive review of the various kinds, causes and phenomenology of hallucinations, see SACKS (2012). See also LETCHER (2016) for a useful analysis, *à la* Michel FOUCAULT, of what might be called the politics of description of the use of psychedelics. Non-users' (usually negative) descriptions of effects use a kind of terminology and discourse, i.e. 'scientific', that is usually different and in direct contrast with users' (usually positive) discourse and terminology of experience, which may employ various kinds of entities in accounts of experiences.

some people's explanation of experience. In the discussion that follows what is being pursued is not the reality or otherwise of non-material entities but rather the function of apparitions in the mind.

This brings us to a general consideration of 'altered states of consciousness'—using this phrase in the most general of applications—and what this really means,[286] in order perhaps to be better able to distinguish between properly entheogenic and non-entheogenic drugs. This will slightly extend the discussion beyond merely the effects of plants and substances into a surface exploration of altered states of consciousness, and whether or not demarcation criteria can be defined that are sufficient to distinguish between 'properly' entheogenic and non-entheogenic states of consciousness. It is hoped that when later in this chapter we arrive at a purview of the role of causation in experience, after an admittedly exiguous survey of the vast extant literature on the subject of altered states of consciousness, we will be able to establish at least some general criteria for demarcation of experiences, albeit to a limited degree. However, this brief survey of non-ordinary states of consciousness should be regarded more as an overview of the topography of possible states rather than an aim at strict definitions.

There are, of course, numerous ways of inducing significantly altered or non-ordinary states of consciousness: through fasting, dancing, intense drumming, meditating, prayer, sweat lodge, self-flagellation, sensory-deprivation, sleep-deprivation, ritual sex, hypnosis, extreme exertion, forced or restrained breathing, the touch of a guru,[287] drugs, or other means. Depending on the social context, the various kinds of altered states that people experience have widely divergent interpretations. One way of engaging with this issue might be firstly to distinguish the contexts of interpretation of altered states, namely (1) mystical, (2) indigenous spirit possession, (3) hypnosis,

---

286. Metzner (2009:4) pertinently comments on his "lingering discomfort with the concept of 'altered state'", and reminds us that consciousness is continually being 'altered': when we wake up in the morning, watch television, or engage in numerous other activities.

287. Muktananda (1974:20–21) claims that a disciple experienced *śaktipāt* (the transmission of 'divine' energy) when the disciple massaged his head. Svāmī Vivekānanda had a profound mystical experience after being touched by his guru Rāmakṛṣṇa Paramahaṃsa (Budhananda 1974:65–66).

and (4) contemporary medical.[288] This is, of course, just one of several possible ways of categorizing altered states of consciousness. The experience of a person undergoing a particular kind of altered state will naturally be understood quite differently in the four domains that have been specified: each has its own discourse and specific explanatory terminology, as a consequence of the different disciplines of inquiry. However, these four categories of experience often overlap. Mystical experience, for example, may be indistinguishable from possession in some instances; a hypnotic state may have the character of a mystical experience. We will now consider the four domains of altered states of consciousness, beginning with mysticism.

Regarding mystical experience in general, the dominant themes have traditionally been framed in terms of religious terminology, and there are three significant issues that have been tackled by numerous scholars with diverse opinions, which could be summarized, albeit briefly: (1) whether or not mystical experience is rare; (2) whether or not mystical experiences derive from a core reality or, alternatively, are quite different; (3) whether or not plant-based mystical experience is the same as naturally arising or religious mysticism. We will consider these issues in turn.

On the first issue, there are some commentators who claim that mystical experience is rare and not easily repeatable (see STAAL 1975:57ff.). However, such experiences are relatively common even in modern industrial societies,[289] even though in most instances the

---

288. Out-of-the body experiences (OBE) are also altered or non-ordinary states of consciousness, which may occur in mystical, possession or hypnotic states, during near-death experiences in accidents, during surgical operations, or more commonly as vivid extensions of dream states (see MONROE 1974).

289. SAUNDERS *et al.* (2000:36) refer to the national UK survey conducted by Alister HARDY at the Religious Experience Research Unit in Oxford in 1975. HARDY founded the Unit in Manchester College in 1966; it was renamed as The Alister Hardy Research Centre in 1985. Participants in the 1975 survey were asked: "Have you ever been aware of or influenced by a presence or power, whether you call it God or not, which is different from your everyday self". Over one third of the population aged sixteen or over answered 'yes' to the question. Continuing HARDY's research, HAY (1990) conducted several surveys, in one of which (pp.54–56), out of 100 students studying education at Nottingham University (of whom fourteen claimed

experiences are not particularly strong or overwhelming; and the world's anthropological and medical literature is replete with historical and contemporary examples. Also, spirit possession is a global phenomenon that still manifests to a greater or lesser degree in most human societies.

Regarding the second issue, concerning the source of mystical experience, the first point that needs addressing is the question of what mystical experience really is. It is not straightforward: there are dozens of definitions of mysticism and mystical experience,[290] which in commentarial literature is often synonymous with religious experience.[291] Already by the end of the 19th century the Anglican priest Dean William R. INGE had listed twenty-five

a religious affiliation, while twenty-one felt they were loosely Christian), sixty-five claimed to have had a religious experience. Two-thirds 'knew' the experience was religious; twenty-one felt they had been guided by a power; twenty-two had felt the direct presence of God; nineteen had felt a numinous presence; ten had experienced unity with nature; ten had had out-of-the-body or extra-sensory experiences; seven had felt the presence of an evil power. The most common age for religious experiences, which typically last a few seconds or minutes, is during the mid-teens. Such experiences are slightly more common (in a ratio of 4:3) among women. Another survey in 1986 (HAY 1990:58) revealed that prior to the survey around forty percent of respondents had never previously talked about their experience. Around a dozen collated surveys from Britain, the USA and Australia (HAY 1990:79–85) indicate that an average of around a third of the population of these countries report having had religious experiences; a relatively small number of people who have such experiences are church attenders (p.104). There is an empirical link between religious experience and ethical behaviour; one study illustrated a heightened concern for the welfare of other people after a religious experience (pp.76–77).

290. The term 'mysticism' derives from the Greek *mysteria* (not-seeing/secrecy/silence/initiation/ineffability). On the initiates (*mystes*) of the mystery rites (*mysteria*) of the ancient Greco-Roman world, see Ch. 15.

291. William JAMES was responsible for popularizing the phrase 'religious experience', a phrase which first appeared in print in 1809 (HAY 1990:10). *The Varieties of Religious Experience*, published in 1902, was the first widely read account of mysticism that included substance-induced experiences. In this work JAMES (1985:380–382) defines four marks of mystical experience: (1) ineffability, (2) noetic quality (of revelations/hidden truths), (3) transiency, and (4) passivity. These criteria are still among the most commonly accepted (DUPRÉ 2005:6341).

definitions of mysticism; the list would now be considerably longer (HUGHES 2003:306). Some commentators would even question the validity of a category of 'mysticism', seeing it as a post-Enlightenment attempt at universalizing diverse cultural and personal experiences (MOORE 2005:6355). However, strong mystical experience, in whatever culture, is generally reported as being either 'heavenly' or 'hellish' and as an immersion in a religious reality of some kind, rather than just as confusing, weird or hallucinatory.

There are ongoing debates, which attracted the most comment in the 1960s and 1970s, as to whether or not there are different kinds of mysticism that can be adequately distinguished; and more contentiously whether or not reports of mystical experience are referring to different kinds of 'realities' (many mysticisms) or to the same 'reality'. Concerning the latter issue, there are eloquent supporters of both opinions. KATZ (1978), for example, cogently argues in a well-known article for a diversity of mystical experiences and against a single underlying reality that mystics may believe they have experienced: "There is no *philosophia perennis*,[292] Huxley and many others notwithstanding" (p.24). However, KATZ focuses exclusively on religious mysticism and consequently the incompatible truth-claims by mystics of different religious traditions, sidestepping whatever might be the neurological processes underlying such kinds of experiences. According to KATZ's reasoning, we cannot know

292. As famously articulated in *The Perennial Philosophy* by HUXLEY (2009) [1945]. The core of this theory (see BRONKHORST 2001:176n.3) is that there is an unmanifest Godhead or Ground 'behind' the manifest world, which is both transcendent and immanent. Humans can know, love and become identified with this Godhead/Ground, the attaining of which is the final end-purpose of human life. This attainment is conditional on following a Law/Dharma/Way/Tao. The more there is of 'I' the less there is of the Godhead/Ground. BRONKHORST comments (p.175n.1) that HUXLEY incorrectly attributes the coining of the phrase '*philosophia perennis*' to LEIBNIZ; it was first used, but in another context, by Augustinus STEUCHUS in 1540. BRONKHORST also challenges HUXLEY's general universalism regarding religions: HUXLEY scarcely mentions Judaism or Confucianism; Confucianism, in particular, does not bear the *philosophia perennis* thesis. BRONKHORST suggests that perhaps a more universal religio-mystic practice (but not necessarily a philosophy) is inactivity.

what mystics of different religious traditions experience. Not only is there the notorious ineffability of mystical experiences, expressed by many mystics, but there is an additional opaqueness to mystical experiences, as without a common core that would be the source of experience we cannot ever really know what the reality is that is being claimed to be experienced by mystics; whence KATZ's presentation of incompatibilities. KATZ claims that all experience is mediated and shaped by culture and language and that there cannot be an experience of 'pure' consciousness, unmediated or conditioned in any way. The visions and experiences of mystics are essentially personal and social constructs within variant traditions and cultures.

KATZ's arguments against mystical 'perennialists', of which there are many,[293] have been challenged by FORMAN (1990), who

---

293. On the side of the perennialists, *Mysticism and Philosophy* by W. T. STACE, first published in 1960, is one of the most cited publications on mysticism. STACE proposes that the source of mysticism, which is not necessarily connected with religion, lies in a kind of pantheism ("pantheism is the correct statement of mystics", p.243). He maintains that there are two basic kinds of mysticism: (1) introvert (the most important kind), in which the self becomes identified with a featureless Self; there is no imagery. This Self is not exactly an ontological 'thing' (it is said [p.152] to be 'transsubjective'), and (2) extrovert, in which objects such as a deity may feature; all things become one in a sensory transfiguring of the external world. According to STACE (p.280) mystical experience results in intense conviction with minimal intellectual content. STACE excludes trances, visions, voices, raptures and violent emotionalism, as not being strictly mystical, and summarises (pp.131–132) seven features of mystical experience, in which the introvert and the extrovert experiences are almost the same (apart from the first two features in the following list), as the inner One is essentially the same as the outside One: (1) unifying vision/unitary consciousness; (2) the 'One' in all things/non-spacial; (3) sense of objectivity or reality; (4) blessedness, peace; (5) feeling of the holy, sacred, divine; (6) paradoxicality; (7) ineffability. STACE also maintains (pp.29–31) that, phenomenologically, drug-induced mystical experiences appear to be the same as those gained through great effort or religiously, though more research is needed on this topic. In a more recent, brief, introductory survey of around a dozen mystical paths GOLEMAN (1977) similarly reduces the goal of meditation (p.xix) to either 'One' (the path of concentration: leading to union with God) or 'Zero' (the path of mindfulness: leading to emptiness), but sees the 'awakened state' as homogenous (p.117). RANADE (1988) assesses mysticism primarily in central India; he assumes that God or *brahman* is the source of all mystical

labels the position of KATZ *et al.* as 'constructivism'. FORMAN (1990:4) comments that when KATZ was writing (in the mid-1970s) 'constructivism' was very much in vogue in the humanities and social sciences in general,[294] and that KATZ's arguments against 'perennialism', which had hitherto been the dominant thrust in studies of mysticism up to that time, were very much in line with this approach. FORMAN and other contributors to his book (1990) argue for the existence of what FORMAN describes as a 'pure consciousness event' (PCE), an innate capacity within everyone, which is not necessarily culturally determined, and which is the locus of many of the mystical experiences reported in different religious traditions. FORMAN is not wholly 'perennialist', as not all mystical experiences are PCEs, but nevertheless he and other contributors to his 1990 volume provide copious support for the claim that more or less identical PCEs are reported by mystics in different religious traditions. This formulation of a PCE avoids some of the difficulties inherent in the presentations of different kinds of mysticism by more religiously inclined commentators who believe that there is a common core to mysticism, and that some kinds of mystical experience derive from an encounter with God.[295]

---

experience. RANADE distinguishes intellectual, devotional, synthetic and personalistic kinds of mysticism, citing numerous exponents of each kind.

294. However, ALMOND (1990:212) notes that 'constructivism' or the 'many mysticisms' thesis can be found as early as 1909, in *Studies in Mystical Religion* by Rufus M. JONES.

295. In several influential publications ZAEHNER distinguishes between theistic and non-theistic mysticism. In *Hindu and Muslim Mysticism* ZAEHNER (1972:19) presents the notion of three basic kinds of mysticism, which he explores in this book: (1) pantheistic, (2) undifferentiated unity, and (3) a loving dialogue with god (see STAAL 1975:73–75; SMART 1978:13–14 for substantial critiques of ZAEHNER's position). Opponents of ZAEHNER are particularly critical of the way he positions a Christian love of God as a higher form of mysticism than, for example, found in India in the *Upaniṣads* in the identity of *ātman* and *brahman.* PARRINDER (1976), similarly to ZAEHNER, sees different types of mysticism in broadly similar categories: "Theistic mysticism seeks union with God but not identity. Monistic mysticism seeks identity with a universal principle which may be called divine though that would imply a difference from the human. Non-religious mysticism also seeks union with something, or everything, rather than monism" (p.15). "The theistic mystical experience is different from pantheist or pan-en-henic because it seeks a union with God in a relation of love. There can hardly be love for the negative Absolute

FORMAN's two main arguments against KATZ are, firstly, that there can be experiences 'unmediated'—whatever that really means—by language or culture. Consider, for example, pain states or PCEs: how are these events in any way 'mediated' by language or culture during the experience? It is perhaps relevant to consider that vast swathes of society's legal frameworks of ethics are built upon the tacit understanding that pain states in other people are real and similar to our own, even though, like mystical experience, they cannot usually be verified. How do we know when people are in pain except for the fact that they say they are? Secondly, echoing an observation by STACE (1960), it is a mistake to confuse an experience with its description by mystics. FORMAN (1990:17) maintains that KATZ provides no firm evidence that, for example, Jewish *devekuth* is different from Buddhist experience of *nirvāṇa.* Even though there may be a contingent link between the religious culture of the mystic and the report of experience, that link, it is argued, is not a necessary link, as KATZ maintains. Religious experiences may go beyond the religious structures that inform them. Currently, the views of KATZ and FORMAN represent the two most widely held positions on mysticism.

As LASKI (1980:9) points out, there are obviously only two possible sources of ecstatic experiences: they derive either from an extra-human source (supernatural, preternatural, other-worldly or divine) or are purely human. Pursuing the view of a purely human source of ecstatic experience, the psychologist Abraham MASLOW, through one of his popular books, *Religions, Values and Peak Experiences*, first published in 1964, was, alongside several other theorists of the time, influential in the development of post-theological explanatory paradigms, which widened the discussion of mystical experience beyond the religious domain. The book was published in the wake of many reports of mystical experience under LSD and psilocybin, which MASLOW occasionally but neutrally refers to. MASLOW's belief is that 'peak experience' (i.e. transcendent

---

or for chair legs [referring to HUXLEY's experience on mescaline recounted in *The Doors of Perception*]...Between the different traditions of theistic or personalistic mysticisms there are differences again" (p.193). However, ZAEHNER also comments (1972:7)—I believe accurately—that eradication of time is the lowest common denominator of almost all forms of mysticism. In other words, at least some similar physiological processes seem to be involved in almost all kinds of mystical experience.

experience) is not only highly valuable to the individual and society,[296] but is something uniquely individual and is, in a polarity that he invokes, at odds with the 'wooden', 'legalistic' formulas and precepts of established religion, the true essence or core of which is peak experience, according to MASLOW.[297] He maintains that the commonalities of peak experiences go beyond the confines of religion;[298] there are theistic and non-theistic peak experiences. However, one of the difficulties inherent in this framework is determining when an ordinary religious experience—such as during a regular church or temple service—crosses the threshold into a properly mystical experience. Similarly, at what point does a natural high or peak experience—such as winning a gruelling sports competition or becoming engrossed in the natural environment (nature mysticism)—become apt for definition as a mystical experience?

The third issue is whether or not mystical experiences that arise spontaneously or through religious meditation, penance or prayer are different from chemical- or plant-induced mystical experiences. There are supporters of both positions.[299] However, DUPRÉ

296. MASLOW's main theory, which is little considered in mainstream psychology these days, is that humans have a hierarchy of needs, the 'highest' being the need for self-actualization.

297. BHARATI (1976:201) comments that organized religion usually opposes mystical experience (particularly drug-induced mysticism) and 'free' sex because such intimate experiences are autonomous, solitary, anti-collective and threatening to the social control exercised by organizations.

298. "Whatever is *different* about these illuminations can fairly be taken to be the localisms, both in time and space, and are, therefore peripheral, expendable, not essential" (MASLOW 1970:20). See MASLOW (1970:59–68) for his twenty-five features of peak experience in the Appendix entitled 'Religious Aspects of Peak Experience'.

299. See WALSH (2015) for a short summary. PARRINDER (1976:186) believes the psychedelic and non-psychedelic experiences to be quite different. After a single, unsatisfactory experience with mescaline, ZAEHNER was prompted to write *Mysticism, Sacred and Profane* (1969 [1957]) to argue, as he states in his Introduction, against the validity of chemical- or plant-based mystical experience espoused by HUXLEY. ZAEHNER then devotes the first two chapters to the topic of mescaline, and an Appendix (B) to his own experience. However, he confesses that, "…*The Doors of Perception* leaves one with a sense of confusion; for unless one happens to have had an experience similar to that described by Mr. Huxley, it is very difficult to understand what the intense excitement is due to" (ZAEHNER 1969:4).

(2005:6342) comments on what he calls the 'genetic fallacy' in regard to drug-induced mystical experience: we are mistaken if we focus on causes of experience instead of describing the phenomenon itself. The discussion and understanding of mystical experience was significantly influenced by popular publications on psychedelics from the 1950s and 1960s—particularly in the English-speaking world by Aldous HUXLEY,[300] Alan WATTS, Timothy LEARY, Richard ALPERT and Ralph METZNER, amongst others—which contained both personal testaments and witness of hundreds of psychedelic sessions, mostly on LSD, peyote and psilocybin,[301] in which many participants experienced classic mystical states: visions of God, entities, angels and demons, *nirvāṇa*, cosmic unity, personal and social insights, etc.[302] In many instances these experiences were of deep and lasting significance for participants.[303] Of course, the

300. PARTRIDGE comments (2003:100) that *The Doors of Perception* and *Heaven and Hell*, first published in 1954, is probably the most famous book on psychedelics; and (p.104) that HUXLEY was the most influential author in the emergence of psychedelic spirituality in the West.

301. Frequently cited are MASTERS and HOUSTON (2000) [1966], who provide extensive accounts of experiences of peyote and LSD based on 206 sessions and interviews with another 214 people; see p.5 for a summary of effects. In *The Ecstatic Adventure* METZNER (1968) assembles twenty-four accounts of psychedelic experience from people with widely divergent backgrounds and lifestyles. *The Psychedelic Experience* (1992) [1964] by LEARY *et al.* was popular in the counter-culture among people attempting to find a frame for psychedelic experience outside a clinical or psychiatric environment. This publication—which seems quite naïve from a contemporary perspective, assuming as it does that ego-loss and consequent personality change are easy—was the first to propose a quasi-shamanic (Tibetan Buddhist) interpretation of psychedelic experience; hitherto the main framework, following HUXLEY and others, had been Asian, mostly in the form of Buddhist or Advaita Vedānta interpretations.

302. Although written in 1962, Alan WATT's *Joyous Cosmology* remains one of the most articulate accounts and interpretation of psychedelic-induced mystical experience, despite the many hundreds of reports that have been published since then. See also his useful, succinct résumé of the four main characteristics of transcendent experience (WATTS 2011 [1968]): a slowing down of time; awareness of polarity; awareness of relativity; awareness of eternal energy, often in the form of intense white light.

303. See, for example, CLARK (1969:77–91), who comments (p.126) that he followed up in a professional capacity as a psychologist approximately 300 users of psychedelics. Of these, well over half felt the main impact of the drugs to have been 'religious' and of lasting significance. MASTERS and

effects of psychedelics wear off after some time. However, naturally arising mystical experiences also usually evaporate, though there are well-documented cases of extended deep-trance states (such as

---

HOUSTON (2000:149) comment that, in their opinion, psychedelic experiences can be more effective than MASLOW's non-drug peak experiences. They refer (pp.254–255) to three LSD studies, one by Oscar JANNIGER and William MCGLOTHLIN (unpublished) of 194 subjects in a non-religious setting. Ten months later fifty-eight percent reported an experience of lasting benefit, twenty-four percent a religious experience. In a non-religious setting, forty percent of DITMAN *et al.*'s (1962) seventy-four subjects reported a greater awareness of God/a Higher Power/Ultimate Reality, while ninety percent of the ninety-six subjects in an experiment by C. SAVAGE, W. W. HARMAN, J. FADIMAN and E. SAVAGE in 1963 (unpublished) reported this greater awareness in a religious setting. MASTERS and HOUSTON (2000:302) conclude that psychedelics can produce both major and minor mystical experiences, but that many significant psychedelic phenomena should not necessarily be classed as mystical. Of 206 participants in LSD sessions, six had what they call 'introvertive mystical experience' of dissolving into ecstasy and light (p.307). The analysis of BARBER (1970:38–39) indicates that around five to six percent of people in monitored LSD sessions have a transcendent, light-filled experience.

The famous Good Friday, double-blind, psilocybin experiment with divinity students conducted in Marsh Chapel in Boston in 1962 by Walter PAHNKE, which was supervised by Timothy LEARY (see LEARY 1964 for the philosophical heuristic underpinning this experiment), was followed up by PAHNKE six months later. The twenty participants who had actually taken psilocybin showed significant elevations on the Pahnke Mystical Experience Questionnaire (which was based on STACE's seven-point scheme) and reported positive changes in attitudes and behaviour in the subsequent assessments. Between twenty-four and twenty-seven years later Rick DOBLIN (1991) did another assessment of seventeen of the twenty original participants. Although finding some defects in PAHNKE's study, particularly PAHNKE's inadequate reporting of psychological struggle, and that one participant needed to be tranquilized (which PAHNKE had omitted to report), DOBLIN largely corroborated the lasting positive effects and valid mystical experience of participants. Several studies conducted by FADIMAN (2011:103–113, 282–295) between 1962 and 1965 of the effects of single high-dose psychedelic sessions on several hundred healthy participants also found, in general, lasting, positive outcomes. More recently, Roland GRIFFITHS and his team have for several years been conducting controlled psilocybin experiments at Johns Hopkins University. Around seventy percent of participants have had profound mystical experiences, which in most instances have had lasting positive effects. Subjects were subsequently re-evaluated after a week, five months and fourteen months (GRIFFITHS *et al.* 2006; 2011).

nirvikalpa samādhi).[304] However, deep trance is not conducive to ordinary social activity, and remaining in a particularly heightened state of awareness while at the same time being relatively socially functional is the condition that some mystics, having undergone a profound experience,[305] appear to remain in,[306] unlike most of those whose access to 'higher states' is via psychedelics.

---

304. One of the most famous examples is the Bengali mystic Rāmakṛṣṇa Paramahaṃsa (1836–1886), who regularly entered *samādhi* for hours at a time and once remained in *samādhi* for six months, until contaminated drops of water placed in his mouth by a disciple caused movement in his stomach and a return to his body (Nikhilananda 1977:32). Braid (1850:10–15; also Paul 1882:54–57) describes in detail the voluntary internment in an underground cavern in Lahore for six weeks in 1837 of a *yogi/fakīr*, who through *prāṇāyāma* induced in himself a trance. After the sealed cavern and the box in which the *yogi* was interred were opened, the *yogi* appeared dead. His teeth were prized open with a knife, his upturned tongue (in *khecarī mudrā*) was straightened and *ghī* was put on it, and his limbs and head were massaged and plied with warm water. After half an hour the *yogi* twitched and then revived. Braid—who, incidentally, coined the term 'hypnosis' (Temple 1989:82)—also describes several other similar yogic internment feats, including the burial of a *yogi* in Jaissalmer in 1835 (pp.18–20) for a month, as well as cases of catalepsy, all of which he compares to animal hibernation, in which the pulse is one-tenth of its usual rate, and respiration one-thirtieth (p.45). It is but a speculation, but perhaps profound mystical states, such as the deep trance of *samādhi*, is a facility acquired by humans during an ice-age in order to survive. (The references to Braid and Paul were kindly provided by Suzanne Newcombe.)
305. In the Indian tradition, dating back to the *Upaniṣads* (early centuries BCE), four conditions of consciousness are specified: *jāgrata* (waking), *svapna* (dreaming), *suśupti* (sleeping), and *turīya* (the 'fourth'), which generally means *samādhi* (see, for example, *Māṇḍūkya Upaniṣad*). These days, as discussed, altered states have become more finely articulated. However, it is interesting to note that the mystic state has a long history of veneration in South Asia.
306. Consider, as a couple of the dozens of relatively recent possible examples, the well-documented life and teachings—in around ninety English-language publications; see, for example Jacobs (2010)—of one of the most famous of Indian saints, the Tamil mystic Rāmana Mahārshi (1879–1950); or of another famous saint, the Bengali mystic Ānandamayī Mā (1896–1982); see Bhaiji (1983); Lipski (1993). Rāmana Mahārshi, for example, distinguishes between a trance state (*samādhi*) and an 'active-aware' state, which he refers to as *sahaj samādhi* (*sahaj* meaning 'naturally arising' or 'innate').

On these issues BHARATI (1976) makes some apposite if provocative observations. Firstly, he claims to have had three profound mystical experiences[307] (which he terms 'zero-experiences') himself (pp.40–43), prior to taking LSD for the first time in 1958. He found his naturally occurring and LSD experiences to be very similar. Zero-experiences may be the result of great effort or long training but they can also arise easily by chance or grace. BHARATI (p.65) estimates—though with no corroborative data—that about half of all reported mystical experiences arose easily. Secondly, he doubts that many people called 'saints' in religious traditions ever had a zero-experience. Some were theologians, others just ordinary people who ended up being called saints due to the performance of miracles or other circumstances of fame or recognition.

Thirdly, zero-experiences, however induced, can—as observed above—wear off. BHARATI met the saint RĀMANA Mahārshi in 1951, two months before he died, and maintains (p.46) that he was clearly down from his 'high' (RĀMANA had been in trance for weeks when he was young; vermin ate his legs). At the time BHARATI met him he was walking, talking (but only occasionally), writing, arranging things and tending his cow. RĀMANA is contrasted with another saint, RĀMAKṚṢṆA Paramahaṃsa (see n.304), who was always coming and going from *samādhi* and often unable to function socially due to his ecstasies.

Fourthly, and perhaps more contentiously, BHARATI claims (p.91) that a zero-experience does not necessarily make someone a better person; ethical behaviour and mystical experience are not necessarily connected. A knave or a king or a dentist will most probably remain a knave or a king or a dentist after a zero-experience; a mystical experience does not necessarily make someone a better citizen, thinker or spouse; though it might do so. A zero-experience invades a person's ego and causes unpredictable changes but may have little lasting effect on the person's interactional pattern with other people; though, of course, it might improve someone. BHARATI (1976:63) comments that some erudite scholars find it difficult to accept that a genuine mystic may be neither a saint, nor a theologian,

---

307. BHARATI (1976:25) defines mysticism simply: (1) a person is a mystic if they say they are; (2) the person has had an intuition of mystic 'oneness'.

nor a humanist, just a person who has had a zero-experience; and that a mystical experience is just one of many possible, great life experiences (p.71). It may inure one to the vicissitudes of life, but not much more. However, regarding BHARATI's general evaluation of mystical experience, it perhaps needs to be countered with the observation that most people who have had a profound mystical experience rate it as the most important and significant experience of their life; they would not usually rate it as just a great experience on a par with other possible life experiences.

Perhaps an important starting point in unraveling the divergences of opinion about mysticism, which has been developed by some analysts, is to distinguish between (1) mystical doctrines, comprising 'mystic' ontologies and in some instances a theology, which are plainly diverse, (2) the various kinds of mysticism that some scholars have sought to distinguish, and (3) mystical experience.[308] Notwithstanding diverse terminology used in accounts of mystical experience, differences in explanations of mysticism, and divisions of opinion concerning genuine and non-genuine (i.e. plant- or chemical-induced) mystical experience, it has been proposed by JAMES, STACE, SMART and numerous other commentators (*contra* KATZ) that phenomenologically there appears to be a fundamental core to mysticism in general. Although it is abundantly apparent that reports of mystical experience are of numerous varieties and flavours, diversely affecting sensory awareness, emotions and thinking in various ways, an analysis of the neurological basis of experience—were it to be sufficiently mapped and understood—would, I believe, indicate commonalities of physiological processes. It cannot to my mind be an accident that reports of naturally occurring mystically religious experience, sensory deprivation[309] and the effects of psychedelic drugs are often so similar.

---

308. STACE (1960:32) argues for the need to distinguish mystical experience and interpretation.
309. For a brief summary and a personal account of the potentially psychedelic effects of sensory deprivation, see STEPAN (2016). John C. LILLY was the pioneer in the development of sensory deprivation tanks, beginning in 1954 in the USA. He soon combined sensory deprivation with LSD (see LILLY 1997: 98–108). These experiments refined his theory about the brain being a biocomputer, which was published in a seminal and popular book, *The Human Biocomputer*, first published in 1967.

This is an approach also adopted by HULIN (2014), who explores the broad commonalities of mystical experience, whether induced through austerities, nature, religious devotion or drugs; and proposes a primordial *mystique sauvage*, conceived independently of either a religious or a psychoanalytic framework.[310] HULIN comments (p.191n.1) that specific receptor sites and neurotransmitter chemicals seem to underlie both mystical experience and various forms of psychosis, even though there is still an epistemological gap between the phenomenology of mysticism and neurophysiology.[311] This seems to be increasingly borne out by neurological research, such as, for example, presented by SACKS (2012) in his work on various kinds of hallucinations.

HULIN's approach to mystical states accords with my own view: that the full spectrum of mystical experiences, particularly at the level of strong experience, however conceived,[312] are specific neurological states that are more or less identical, or certainly similar, in everyone, similar to how states or degrees of sleep or pain are more or less identical in nearly everyone, even though descriptions of experiences and the terminology used are of course widely disparate. That said, this conjecture about mystical experiences does not underestimate both the diversity and gradients of possible experiences, nor the singularities of experience undergone by particular individuals. Although mysticism is essentially a strand within religion, there are what appear to be multiple webs of connection between mystical experiences, shamanism, spirit possession, and yogic *samādhi*. Nevertheless, even though there are apparent similarities between various kinds of altered states, it is

---

310. "...toutes ses occurrences [de l'expérience mystique] concrètes paraissent se conformer à un même scénario de base..." (p.293).

311. "Reste que nous ne disposent pas actuellement des outils conceptuels nécessaires pour penser cette double réalité, phénomenologique et neurophysiologique, des états extatiques et des états de conscience en général".

312. In the realm of religion as, for example, possession by the Holy Spirit, the attainment of the higher Buddhist *jhānas*/*dhyānas* (levels of spiritual attainment), Sūfī dissolution in *fanā-al-fanā* (extinction of extinction of the self), or immersion in various kinds of yogic *samādhi*.

appropriate also to acknowledge the differences between them; comparisons need to be undertaken cautiously.

The second category of altered states that I categorized, indigenous spirit possession, refers to the globally ubiquitous and usually normative cultural phenomena of spirit possession, trance states and mediumship, in which people enter into communication with entities of various kinds through different means.[313] However, as discussed by LEWIS (1995:25, 40), people who are possessed are not necessarily in a trance state; possession—which occurs in various degrees—has a wider range of meanings than trance.[314] In general, accounts by participants in these kinds of altered states have a far more practical interpretation by the experiencer, usually having a specific functionality within the community within which the experience takes place, in particular healing various kinds of social rifts and personal ailments.[315] The anthropological studies by both BOURGUIGNON (1973) and LEWIS (1995) indicate that possession

313. BEYER (2010:166), in the context of Amazonian shamanism (but which has wider applications to anyone who claims to encounter spirits or other such entities), remarks that there seem to be three modes of interaction with spirits: the shaman can travel to where spirits are (the classic 'flight of the soul'); the shaman can summon spirits to where the shaman is; or spirits can enter and take possession of the shaman's body. Concerning cases of spirits taking possession of someone, OESTERRIECH (1974), in his extensive study of this global phenomenon, documents many dozens of reports going back to Biblical times. He categorizes five kinds of possessing agents: a benign spirit, an evil spirit, the spirit of someone deceased, the spirit of someone living, and the spirit of an animal. Possession may be either voluntary or involuntary, and may be either somnambulistic or lucid. In somnambulistic possession the person has no recollection of being possessed, while in lucid possession the person remains fully conscious of what is happening.

314. LEWIS (1995:44) also takes issue with ELIADE (1974), who tries to drive a wedge between spirit possession and shamanism; this, LEWIS maintains, is untenable if we go back to source material. The shaman's body is also a receptacle for spirits, the control over which he gains over time, allowing him to treat others.

315. See, for example, BOURGUIGNON (1973) for case studies of spirit possession in Sub-Saharan Africa, South Africa, Palau (Pacific Caroline Islands), Yukatán (Mexico), St. Vincent (West Indies), and São Paulo (Brazil). See SMITH (2006) for the South Asian context. See DAVIS (1985) for possession in the context of Haitian voodoo and zombies.

occurs in far greater frequency in social situations of oppression, such as when people are in slavery or where women feel oppressed[316] within the family structure.[317] However, although in some ways different from mystical experiences, there seem to be similar kinds of processes at work in both possession states and mystical experience. If someone is possessed there is a simultaneous 'emptying out' of the personality of the person being occupied. Similarly, in mystical states, whether the experience is of a void or of being engulfed by a presence or a spirit, it is the void or the presence that usurps the person's self-reflecting, incumbent personality.

The third category I have invoked concerns hypnosis, where a part of the subject's active mind is put to sleep or controlled by a hypnotist. Such a condition is usually referred to as a trance. However, this kind of trance experience is in most respects quite different from a 'standard' mystic trance, the difference being that the hypnotized subject may be quite unaware at the time of the condition he or she is in,[318] unlike the mystic who is generally hyper-aware of his or her condition. Further, the comprehensive review of dozens of studies of hypnotism by BARBER (1970:115–318) indicates that in many instances it is not necessarily a trance state that facilitates a response to the hypnotist in the performance of instructions or suggestions by the person hynotized, but rather—similarly to the placebo effect—it is simply the susceptibility of the hypnotized person to commands or suggestions that causes hypnotic behaviour.[319]

---

316. SMITH (2006:231) comments that in South Asia possession of women is more common than of men.

317. LEWIS (1995:110) outlines three contexts of possession: (1) afflictions (involuntary possession by an evil spirit); (2) voluntary, controlled possession (as in quasi-religious devotion; or as when realized by a shaman); and (3) afflictions that are sent by a shaman (as in witchcraft), the cure for which is exorcism, not by taming or domesticating the invading spirit.

318. TEMPLE (1989:76–106), in his extensive study of hypnosis—which is not at all the same as sleep—examines cases of people in a trance yet still wide-awake.

319. BARBER delineates (p.284) eleven antecedent, variable factors that contribute to this kind of suggestibility in a person being hypnotized, and trance is not the main factor. These include the words used in instruction, the relationship of the person to the hypnotist, and the expectations of the person hypnotized. GRINSPOON and BAKALAR (1998:254) note that hypnosis can have many

In some experiments on hypnosis and pain (pp.237–239) subjects in a light trance or not in a trance responded less acutely to suggestions of pain than subjects in deep trance. BARBER comments (p.136) that an inherent problem in defining hypnotic trance is that a trance is usually defined by the manifest responses to suggestions by a hypnotized subject, yet—entirely circularly—the explanation of subjects responding to hypnotic suggestions is that they must be in a trance.

The fourth category of altered states referred to is the modern medical. Even though altered states or non-ordinary consciousness may be expressed by people undergoing them in mystical or religious terms, when they manifest they are usually labelled by the medical profession as mania, psychosis or schizophrenia and are not considered to be either divine or useful. These days, if someone reports to a doctor in the USA that they are 'hearing voices', even if no other unusual or deleterious symptoms are apparent or reported, the person is automatically diagnosed as schizophrenic (SACKS 2012:53–54). HAY (1990:67) also notes that anyone who reports just two of eight of the classic 'symptoms' of religious experience is classified in the 1987 edition of the *Diagnostic and Statistical Manual of Mental Disorders*, published by the American Psychiatric Association, as being in the prodromal or the residual phase of a schizophrenic disorder.

Having all too briefly considered these four broad categories of altered states, it remains to be asked if there is any way of providing adequate demarcation criteria for properly entheogenic experience, however that arises or is interpreted. Besides the notion of a *philosophia perennis*, Aldous HUXLEY also famously popularised the idea of the mind as a 'reducing-valve',[320] a mechanism that is necessary to screen out what would be an overwhelming mass of

---

of the same effects as psychedelic drugs, particularly in the suggestibility of the hypnotized or intoxicated subject. Feelings of elation, depression, fear, anger, catatonic or paranoid states, changes in body image, and sensory enhancement are easily induced; and the alleged healing powers of hypnotic and psychedelic states are similar.

320. An idea originally developed by the French philosopher Henri BERGSON. HUXLEY fused this idea with the notion of 'Mind at Large', proposed by the British philosopher Charles D. BROAD.

sensation, which would inhibit ordinary social interaction and activity. If the reducing-valve is bypassed, we pass into another realm of cognition. Perhaps another way of describing one of the most significant aspects of what are essentially ineffable experiences beyond the epistemic barrier is to consider such experiences of the spirit world as comprising an immersion in, what seems to the person experiencing it, a different realm of causation, of both external events and in the connectivity of mental processes. The notion of associative causation or 'magical' thinking as a meta-mechanism that functions 'above' or alongside our ordinary, explanatory and functionally-necessary ideas of causation is not of course a novel proposal; over the last 150 years influential anthropological theorists have similarly postulated mechanisms of 'associative' or 'magical' thinking to account for the animistic and correlative beliefs of primitive societies.[321] Many psychologists—the most influential being Sigmund FREUD—have also explored the role of 'magical' thinking in both childhood development and adult understanding.[322]

Amongst traditional cultures and in nearly every human society until relatively recently, alternative, relational kinds of 'causal' structures are generally explained in terms of spirits, powers, deities or entities. They may heal, warn, punish, grace, instruct, tell of distant happenings, or predict future events. They are usually but not always culturally specific and operate outside the ordinary domains of time and cause and effect.[323] They inhabit the experiencer's mental

321. 'Associative thinking' (characterised as 'pre-logical') is a phrase that was coined by Edward Burnett TYLOR (1832–1917), the founder of cultural anthropology, in *Primitive Culture* (1871). This trope was further explored by James FRAZER in *The Golden Bough: A Study in Magic and Religion* (1911), Lucien LÉVY-BRUHL in *How Natives Think* (1925), and E. E. EVANS-PRICHARD in *Witchcraft, Magic, and Oracles Among the Azande* (1937). The detailed study by THOMAS (1978) explores how magical thinking and perceived natural 'signs' were deeply embedded in both ordinary life and religious categories in all levels of society in the 16th and 17th centuries in England.

322. See, for example, FREUD (1960:83ff.).

323. In what is now a well-known and provocative (and disputed) thesis, JAYNES (1976), exploring the functions of the two hemispheres of the brain, suggests that hearing voices and receiving instructions from deities or

museum and their agency may appear to be personally validated in people who have such experiences. Recent work in neurology demonstrates that visualizations can significantly affect the firing and organization of neurons in the brain (DOIDGE 2016:6–11, 59–61); chronic pain, for example, can be alleviated. These findings clearly have implications for understanding the efficacy of 'religious' imagination, particularly concerning healing from illness or disease.

I would like to suggest—perhaps obviously and somewhat tautologically—that a 'properly' entheogenic experience might perhaps be defined, albeit in one of several ways, as being in a state in which the experiencer is aware of being in a universe that appears to function according to a different set of overriding causal principles. As David HUME, in *An Enquiry concerning Human Understanding* (2007 [1748]:20–21), so provocatively suggested in his analogy of the billiard balls,[324] ordinary notions of causation might be considered

---

spirits was a universal mode of mentation (which survives in trace form in contemporary societies amongst schizophrenics, occult mediums and others) in human cultures prior to about 1800–1500 BCE. Although aspects of his 'bicameral' thesis are problematic (one aspect being current societies, such as in India, where such communication is still a feature of religious life), JAYNES nevertheless provides compelling evidence of 'hearing voices' and communication with deities in pre-literate cultures. For some contemporary accounts of communing with spirits, see HUNTER and LUKE (2014). For a summary of experience of 'encounters' under the influence of DMT with entities of various kinds (a relatively common experience), and how to assess the veridicality of such experiences, see LUKE (2011). The functions of the two hemispheres of the brain in consciousness, a topic first widely popularized by ORNSTEIN (1975), is also deeply explored by MCGILCHIST (2010), who maintains that in different periods of history either the right or the left hemisphere was dominant. Currently, he argues, we are in danger of depersonalization due to the dominance of the left hemisphere: we are losing empathy in the pursuit of certainty and definition.

324. Section IV.7–10: "...causes and effects are discoverable, not by reason, but by experience...all the laws of nature, and all the operations of bodies without exception, are known only by experience...The mind can never possibly find the effect in the supposed cause, by the most accurate scrutiny and examination. For the effect is totally different from the cause, and consequently can never be discovered in it. Motion in the second Billiard-ball is a quite distinct event from motion in the first; nor is there anything in the one to suggest the smallest hint of the other...When I see, for instance, a Billiard-ball moving in a straight line towards another, even suppose motion

as a mere habit of mind, rather than an objectively real state of affairs. When our ordinary habits of mind are disrupted or overridden, whether by psychedelic or other means, besides the well-known and oft-referred to experiences of manifold sensory alterations—sometimes including synesthesia—and the progressive blurring of the boundaries and content of the person's inner and outer world, it is also the experiencer's grip on time and ordinary causation that is most noticeably affected; and connections between events, thoughts and perceptions are comprehended differently. Building on the research of Alister HARDY at the Religious Experience Research Unit in Oxford[325] and also of Edward ROBINSON, HAY (1990:41–43) notices that among all of the hundreds of reports of mystical or religious experience by ordinary people the most commonly reported experiences were of synchronicity and the patterning of events; not in a trivial sense, such as discussed by JUNG,[326] for example, but that somehow one's life has an unfolding pattern to it. These experiences do not necessarily, though they often will, involve a direct awareness of a sacred or transcendent presence.

These observations on the significance of causation in non-ordinary states of consciousness finds further support in recent studies of brain imaging of subjects under the influence of LSD. The Integrated Information Theory (IIT) of consciousness[327] is explored by GALLIMORE (2015) in relation to psychedelic states.

> Overall, this model [IIT] suggests that the expanded awareness and enhancement of cognitive flexibility afforded by the psychedelic drugs comes at a functional cost: increasing the entropy of the cause-effect

---

in the second ball should by accident be suggested to me, as the result of their contact or impulse, may I not conceive that a hundred different events might as well follow from that cause? May not both these balls remain at absolute rest? May not the first ball return in a straight line, or leap off from the second in any line or direction? All these suppositions are consistent and conceivable. Why then should we give the preference to one, which is no more consistent or conceivable than the rest? All our reasonings *à priori* will never be able to shew us any foundation for this preference".

325. See HAY (1990:1–39) for an account of HARDY's research.

326. See the classic monograph by JUNG (2008) for further details.

327. See OIZUMI *et al.* (2014) and TONONI and KOCH (2015) for an introduction to this exceptionally dense theory.

> repertoire of mechanisms within a complex expands the characteristics and meaning of concepts and produces a richer, more flexible state of consciousness (a greater range of brain states can be explored), but this is at the expense of the cause-effect information associated with each concept (p.9).

GALLIMORE (2015:14) concludes that psychedelic drugs can increase cognitive flexibility—enhancing creativity, novel thinking and imagination—owing to the attenuation of cause and effect mechanisms in the brain. Regarding a further utility of psychedelic states, it is perhaps as a consequence of 'associative' thinking that what seem to be psychological insights may arise in a psychedelic session; previously unnoticed connections between past events and/or people can present themselves. STOLAROFF (2015:198) comments:

> After forty years of careful study, it is my observation that one of the outstanding actions of psychedelics is the dissolving of habitual patterns within the mind. One of the most powerful mental habits that humans employ is the hiding of undesirable material from consciousness. Thus, a very important function of psychedelic substances is to permit access to the unconscious mind.[328]

Beyond 'alternatively causational' altered states that have been mentioned, in what SHULGIN describes as a +4 experience, "a rare and precious transcendental state",[329] all causation dissolves as all

---

328. Such experiences are typically regarded as an expansion of consciousness. However, in such experiences, what is being expanded, and what, in the process, is being simultaneously contracted (regarding conscious experience of other domains of the individual's awareness) is inherently complex. For a useful discussion of this issue and for the introduction of a novel explanatory concept (termed 'epilogenesis') for the functioning of consciousness, see KING (2014). Epilogenesis (which means something like 'conscious choice') is the process whereby what may previously have been unconscious thoughts, memories, activities or actions are brought into consciousness. Psychedelic agents may, it is argued, facilitate the bringing to awareness of what was otherwise unconscious. The awareness of previously unconscious process or personal events is, of course, the first and necessary step towards changing attitudes or behaviour.
329. SHULGIN's basic classificatory scheme (1997:607–608) for the range of possible psychedelic (and other kinds of drug) experiences (The Shulgin Scale) has now become commonly employed in commentarial literature. SHULGIN does not, strictly speaking, consider the +4 state as really

experiences and perceptions become merged in a timeless, ecstatic condition, in a total or comprehensive simultaneity, in which everything is perceived as being simultaneous and connected;[330] there is no sense of sequential causation (or sequential agency), as time has ceased to be functionally apparent.[331] This is the zero-experience

---

connected to +1, +2 or +3 states (of relative strength of a drug's effect): +4 is in a category apart. See also STRASSMAN (1995) for a historical summary of various schemes devised for measuring the effects of psychedelic drugs, and for the questionnaire he used in his research into DMT experiences. Since the late 1990s, A. DITTICH's evaluations of altered states of consciousness, published (originally in German) in a series of versions (known, successively, as the APZ, OAV and 5D-ASC scales), have become the most widely used scales. Only two other measuring scales have gained similar acceptance in applied research, namely the Phenomenology of Consciousness Inventory (PCI) devised by R. J. PEKALA, J. STEINBERG and V. K. KUMAR, and the Hallucinogen Rating Scale devised by STRASSMAN *et al.* (STUDERUS *et al.* 2015:3). See STUDERUS *et al.* (2015) for an evaluation of these scales of measurement and for suggested modifications of the evaluation process. Another questionnaire, designed by MACLEAN *et al.* (2012), the Mystical Experience Questionnaire (MEQ), is another evaluative tool, currently being used at Johns Hopkins University by Roland GRIFFITHS and his team in their current research on mystic states induced by psilocybin.

330. Although the 'ultimate' state is considered by many mystics to be formless, some theologians place forms beyond the formless. For example, in his *Gītā Bhāṣya* (3.15, 3.30 etc.) the 13th-century Vedāntist RĀMĀNUJA places Kṛṣṇa beyond the formless *brahman*. Similarly, the 11th-century Muslim theologian AL-GHAZALI maintains that after the soul has realized its identity with God, beyond that, "the comely forms of the spiritual world reveal themselves, comprising the souls of angels and prophets" (ZAEHNER 1972:169). The 'ultimate' is an experience of a profound 'living process', which is more like a personality than a 'thing'; hence the natural tendency to characterize the 'ultimate' as a 'person'—who necessarily has characteristics (*saguṇa*) that distinguish whatever it is from anything else—rather than as characterless 'thing' (*nirguṇa*). Or it could be that RĀMĀNUJA and AL-GHAZALI are merely privileging speculative philosophy over experience.

331. At the heart of this discussion is the very nature of consciousness itself, which is one of the historically most persistent problems in philosophy and psychology. JAYNES (1976:1–18) provides a useful summary of eight of the most-widely held theories of consciousness. At one end of the spectrum of theories, behaviourism, which dominated psychology from around 1920 to 1960, maintains that consciousness does not really 'exist'. At the other end of the spectrum there is the view that the universe is 'conscious'. Panpsychism

of ego-death, which is near physical death. It is being suggested that whatever *soma/haoma* was, it was capable of engendering such kinds of experience. At the beginning of this chapter several psychedelic plants were mentioned, most of which have this potential capacity. In the chapters that follow we will explore various suggestions for the botanical identity of *soma/haoma* and it will be argued that none of them, apart from ayahuasca, are sufficiently potent regularly to induce properly entheogenic effects or the zero-experience.

---

has a long, noble and philosophically problematic history, maintained in various forms by theorists and philosophers including PLATO, LEIBNIZ, SCHOPENHAUER, and more recently by JAMES, WHITEHEAD, RUSSELL and STRAWSON. Besides these two positions are various forms of dualism and notions of consciousness as 'emergent'. SHELDRAKE (2013), alternatively, proposes that any organism capable of self-regulation could be considered as conscious. On this view the sun and our planet would be conscious but the moon would be unconscious. JAYNES (1976) understands consciousness to be a process, rather than a thing. It seems probable that theories of consciousness may in some instances have been significantly impelled either by authors' own mystical experience or the reports of others. Some theories of consciousness (and theology) may, it is suggested, have arisen as a direct response to resolving the conceptual paradox between consensus, causal reality and timeless states of alternative causation.

CHAPTER 9

Diverse theories about *soma/haoma*

Since the comprehensive review of candidates for *soma* was published by Wendy DONIGER [O'FLAHERTY] in WASSON's book on *soma* in 1968, several other plants have been proposed as *soma/ haoma*, which are now briefly surveyed.

MULHOLLAND (1976) does not propose an identification of the plant but argues that the extracted *soma* juice was an oil of some kind. KHLOPIN (1980) argues for Turkish mandrake (*Mandragora turcomanica*), which is improbable, even though there is considerable evidence of the use of this plant in ancient Egypt and Greece (MANNICHE 1999:117–119; SCHULTES *et al.* 2001:90–91); and one species, *Mandragora caulescens*, is native to India in Sikkim (SINGH 2006:191). The root or the bark of the root was traditionally used as an aphrodisiac and as a soporific (SCHULTES and HOFMANN 1980:296; GRIEVE 1995/2014), but owing to the severe toxicity of the plant there is risk of overdose and even death.

SINGH (1981) proposes sugarcane, while RAUSING (1988) suggests fermented sugarcane cane juice. WINDFUHR (1985) proposes ginseng, a suggestion improbable for several reasons, but primarily because the effects of ginseng are so mild.[332] RAMANATHAN (1995) argues rather eccentrically that *soma* not a plant at all but a 'mere concept'. Similarly, SHARMA (1996) argues that originally *soma* was non-intoxicating; it was, essentially, only rain or water.

---

332. A species of ginseng, *Panax pseudo-ginseng* Wall., is native to parts of Nepal, the Indian Himalayas, south-east Tibet, Bhutan, north Myanmar, Thailand and western China (MANANDHAR 1989:64). It has mild aphrodisiac and stimulant effects, similar to better-known species of ginseng. The variety in Sikkim is anecdotally reported to be more effective than Korean ginseng (BURMAN 2003:68).

JONES (1995)[333] maintains that *soma* is datura/thorn-apple (*Brugmansia*).[334] This also seems improbable, firstly because it is the seeds that are the most potent part of the datura plant, but much more importantly, datura is toxic and can cause a complete disorientation of the consumer for up to eight months (personal observation).[335] SHANON (2010:47) comments: "unlike Ayahuasca, datura is seriously dangerous—its consumption can result in madness, irreversible physiological damage, and even death".[336] JAY (1999:19–20) remarks that, "Datura does have visionary properties but is more accurately described as a toxic deliriant...the effects are highly unpleasant". JAY also provides anecdotal accounts of its

---

333. This publication is cited by several commentators but I have been unable to locate it anywhere, so I am unable to make any detailed comment on this work.
334. There are many varieties of datura (*Stramonium*) in both the Old and New Worlds. *Brugmansia* is, essentially, a domesticated South American species. See SCHULTES and HOFMANN (1980:264–278) for clarification of the botanical identity of various species.
335. The main alkaloids causing intoxication from datura are the tropane alkaloids atropine and scopolamine.
336. It has been known to be dangerous since antiquity. THEOPHRASTUS (*c.* 371–287 BCE), one of ARISTOTLE's pupils, remarks in his *Enquiry* (9.11.5–6) that thorn-apple can cause madness: if 3/20ths of an ounce are given, the patient becomes, "merely sportive and [thinks] himself a fine fellow; twice the dose if he is to go mad outright and have delusions; thrice the dose if he is to be permanently insane". RUSH (1771), a doctor in Philadelphia, reports on a child who had severe symptoms of accidental datura poisoning, who he successfully treated, primarily by inducing the vomiting of the consumed seeds. COOPER (1797:43) cites BEVERLEY's *History of the Present State of Virginia* (1705:24), which contains a report on a group of soldiers who ate datura leaves—also known in North America as Jimson weed, from the following incident in James-Town (PENNACCHIO *et al.* 2010:6)—and endured a mania that lasted eleven days: "one would blow up a feather in the air; another would dart straws at it with much fury; and another stark naked was sitting up in a corner like a monkey, grinning and making mouths at them...In this frantic condition they were confined, lest they should in their folly destroy themselves". COOPER (p.45) also mentions that there are many instances of death from consuming stramonium (datura/thorn-apple). VON BIBRA (1995:79) comments (in 1855) on incidents in Goa (India) of thieves poisoning victims, and wives rendering their husbands insensible with thorn-apple seeds.

dangers, including coma and death. He adds that despite the almost global ubiquity of the plant, nowhere is it illegal: it is too unpleasant. However, datura is used by some Amazonian groups as a medicine in a broad range of therapeutic applications,[337] and ceremonially for rites of passage and for divinatory purposes by several native groups of North and South America[338] (SCHULTES 1972:46–49; SCHULTES and HOFMANN 1980:270–272; DAVIS 1985:39–40; DEVEREUX 2008:131–132).[339] Datura also is also occasionally mentioned in the context of 'black' sorcery in South Asia and Tibet in some Tantric Buddhist rites (SIKLÓS 1993; PARKER and LUX 2008:7–11).[340]

---

337. It is used for childbirth and in an external plaster for broken bones and is considered to be the most intoxicating and strongest of all medicines by the Matsigenka of the Peruvian Amazon. Datura is dangerous and has caused fatalities (SHEPARD 2005:3.4.2). It is usually taken alone and is used only very rarely (SHEPARD 2014:23). In Kashmir and Ladakh it is used as an antiseptic. Its leaves are applied to boils and sores, and flower juice is applied for earache. In Russia it has applications for asthma, bronchitis and epilepsy, among other uses (KAUL 1997:114). Datura has a long, global history of use for the treatment of asthma and other respiratory ailments (PENNACCHIO *et al.* 2010:5, 82).
338. SCHULTES and RAFFAUT (2004:48–51) provide notes on three kinds of *Brugmansia* (datura) used for medicine and divination in Colombian Amazonia: *Brugmansia aurea* (= *Datura candida*), *Kinde borrachera* (a highly atrophied form of *Brugmansia*), and *Munchiro borrachero* (a highly-prized, rare atrophied clone of *Brugmansia aurea*).
339. For a personal account of a datura trip in a quasi-shamanic context, see RYMLAND (1999).
340. SIKLÓS comments on the use of datura in the *Vajramahābairava Tantra*. It can be used to cause madness and death. SIKLÓS argues convincingly that *Datura metel* is indigenous to South Asia, and was not an import from the New World, which some commentators have maintained. In a black magic 'six *yogini* rite' detailed in the *c.* 8th century *Cakrasaṃvara Tantra*, the roots, stem, leaves, flower and fruit of a plant—identified by the commentator Bu-ston (1290–1364 CE) as datura (GRAY 2007:352n.12)— and other items are bound with charnel ground cloth. Mantras are recited and the name of one's enemy is written down; the victim will become insane. A recipe in the 14th-century *Nyingtik Yabtsi* (an eleven-volume compendium on Dzogchen meditation) prescribes a concoction made from the seeds of *Datura metel* for opening the body's subtle energy channels and cultivating visions. The distillate is to be dropped into the eyes through the hollow shaft of a vulture's quill (BAKER 2004:194).

A suggestion is made by GREENE (1992:106–137)[341] in a chapter entitled 'The True Identity of Soma' that *soma* was made from an ergot fungus (*Claviceps* = 'club-headed'),[342] which, famously, is the main precursor in the manufacture of LSD, the properties of which were accidentally discovered by Albert HOFMANN at the Sandoz laboratories in Basel, Switzerland, in 1943.[343] The ergot fungus, which contains around thirty different indole alkaloids, grows on grains, particularly rye, and is usually highly toxic.[344] Consumption of contaminated flour or bread can result in madness, gangrene, convulsions and death, a condition known as ergotism or Saint Anthony's fire.[345] GREENE suggests that a dissolution of grain in

---

341. This proposition is also made independently by SHELLEY (1995), who, however, provides no convincing evidence. Also, inconsistently, he suggests (p.25) on the basis of passages in the *Ṛgveda* that *soma* is a harvested fungus that has a cap that can be severed from its stalk, which would not be feasible for the relatively tiny ergot fungus. Even more unfeasible is the proposition (p.11) that, "This perfect metal [gold] of the alchemists was the sacred fungus".
342. The ergot fungus hypothesis was also proposed by WASSON, HOFMANN and RUCK (1978) as the basis of the *kykeōn* of the Eleusian mysteries (see Chapter 17).
343. LSD was first synthesized in 1938: see HOFMANN (2005:46ff.); HINTZEN and PASSIE (2010:3ff.).
344. For all aspects of ergot, including pharmacology and the history of discovery, see BOVÉ (1970).
345. The last of the many historical outbreaks of poisoning through consumption of contaminated bread was in southern Russia in 1926–27. Several sources state that in Europe the last occurrence of this phenomenon was in France in the village Pont-Saint-Esprit in August 1951, resulting in five deaths. However, OTT (HOFMANN 2005:39) maintains that this latter incident was not due to ergot poisoning but to seeds disinfected using an organic mercury compound. SAMORINI (1997) notes that another cause of the food-poisoning has been suggested, namely *Aspergillus funigatus*, a fungus containing alkaloids that infects wheat. For the history of outbreaks of ergotism, and how it became associated with Saint Anthony, see BOVÉ (1970:144–160). Ergot had a limited use medicinally as an ecbolic (stimulating uterine contraction to induce childbirth). It was first recorded as a remedy in 1582 by the German physician Adam LONITZER (or LONICER) and then in 1808 by the American physician John STEARNS. It entered the United States Pharmocopoeia as an official drug in 1820 but was subsequently abandoned due to its toxicity. However, it is still used for postpartum hemorrhage (BOVÉ 1970:275; HOFMANN in RUCK 2006:154).

water and then in fat (in the form of milk or curds) could have been filtered through a woollen fleece, which could remove the ergot toxins, leaving free lysergic amides to produce a psychedelic trip.[346] His favoured candidates for the grain used are finger millet[347] (*Eleusine coracana*) and *kodrava* (*Paspalum scrobiculatum*). Although interesting as a hypothesis, it seems very doubtful that such a potentially hazardous and imprecise preparation could ever have been used to concoct *soma*: mistakes could have been lethal, or, at the least, highly debilitating.

However, SHEPARD (2005:3.2.2) suggests that although the kind of ergot fungus (*Claviceps purpurea*) that grows on rye is highly toxic, owing to its ergoline alkaloids, another kind of ergot fungus (*Claviceps paspali*) which grows on grasses does not contain debilitating ergoline alkaloids, though as in *Claviceps purpurea*, it does contain the psychoactive indole alkaloid, lysergic acid amide.[348] However, as discussed in Chapter 17 of this book, the only kinds of grass that become infected with *Claviceps paspali* did not grow in ancient Greece. Also, as OTT (1998:27) points out, there are currently no data at all available on alkaloid content of Indian mountain-grown ergot of the species favoured by GREENE.[349] The idea of ergot as a

346. The effects of lysergic acid amide (LSA/ergine) are discussed in Chapter 17 of this book.

347. It was noted in Chapter 4 of this book, on 'substitutes' for *soma*, that cultivated millet (*śyāmāka*) was listed as a substitute in the *Brāhmaṇas*.

348. SHEPARD (2005:3.4.7) also discusses the use by indigenous peoples of lowland Amazonia (of Brazil, Venezuela, Colombia, Ecuador, Peru and Bolivia) of cultivated sedges infected with an ergot fungus (*Balansia cyperi* of the *Claviceptacae* family) for a wide variety of visionary, social, psychological and medicinal purposes. Each sedge variety has a highly specific magical or medicinal use. Some are used to cure insanity or to control passions, others cause temporary or permanent insanity. Nine novel ergot alkaloids were found in extracts from a single sedge variety from Ecuador. The use of sedges infected with *Balansia cyperi* is further discussed in Chapter 17.

349. OTT (1998:28) also cites the report by the Indian ethnobotanists PAL and JAIN (1989), who collected information on the use of forty medicinal plants in the Midnapur district of West Bengal by the Lodha, Santal, Oraon and other tribal people. The Lodhas are reported (p.468) to ingest the outer covering of dehusked grains of *Paspalum scrobiculatum* (kodo millet) for hallucinations, which could indicate ergot intoxication, even though, according to OTT, the grain is known to be poisonous, especially after

ritual intoxicant first gained widespread attention with the publication in 1978 of *The Road to Eleusis: Unveiling the Secrets of the Mysteries* by WASSON, HOFMANN, and RUCK, where it was proposed that a preparation of ergot was the basis of *kykeōn*, the ritual drink of the Greek mystery rites at Eleusis. This theory is further explored in Chapter 17.

Reviving a proposition first made in 1919 by C. COHEN (SWAMY 1976:15), SPESS (2000) proposes water-lily (*Nymphaea lotus*) and lotus (*Nelumbium speciosum*), which are related plants. SPESS maintains (p.28) that, "the Indian varieties of lotus and many water-lilies…are entheogenic".[350] The proposal for the lotus plant *Nelumbo nucifera* is endorsed and further elaborated by MCDONALD (2004), who similarly claims (p.152) that the lotus plant has entheogenic properties. The lotus plant is certainly important in the mythology and iconography of South Asia, in both Buddhist and Hindu traditions, and the lotus plant (particularly the Egyptian blue variety) is well known to have mild psychoactive properties, but nowhere, as far as I am aware, is there any substantiated report that either lotus or water-lily has properly entheogenic effects.

In support of the entheogenic properties of the water-lily (*Nymphaea caerulea*), MCDONALD (2004:152) cites DÍAZ (1975) and EMBODEN (1981). However, although in several articles EMBODEN has usefully drawn attention to the narcotic properties of the water-lily and its use and veneration in ancient Mayan[351] and

---

rain, causing delirium and violent tremors. PAL and JAIN (p.466) also note the use of other plants for "hallucinations". Smoking the dried roots of the abundant weed *Amaranthus spinosus* (prickly/spiny amaranth) is said to cause hallucinations (eating a paste of roots is said to cause temporary insanity). Oraons smoke the dry leaves of *Artemisia nilagirica* (Indian wormwood) for hallucinations; and Lodhas are said to eat the dry kernels of *Terminalia bellirica* (Beleric/bastard myrobalan = [Sanskrit] *vibhitaka*) for hallucinations. However, it should be noted that neither Indian wormwood nor Beleric myrobolan are reported anywhere else to have hallucinogenic properties.

350. There are about fifty species of *Nymphaea* in temperate and tropical areas, all of which are aquatic (SCHULTES and HOFMANN 1980:330).

351. See also DÍAZ (1997:651), who believes that several Mayan references to an aquatic plant that inebriates refer to *Nymphea ampla*, which was probably used as a sacred psychotropic during the time of classic Mayan civilization.

Egyptian societies, no substantive evidence is provided for entheogenic properties. EMBODEN (1979:396ff.), in turn, cites DÍAZ (1975), who is said to have found contemporary recreational use of the crude rhizomes of the water-lily in Chiapas, Mexico:[352]

> It was asserted [by DÍAZ] that these [rhizomes] provoked 'prolonged and powerful hallucinatory effects'. Following this lead with chemical analyses, Diaz isolated aporphine alkaloids from the plants.[353] These compounds differ from apomorphine by two hydroxyl groupings. Apomorphine is a synthetic derivative of morphine and both are classified in the United States as narcotics.

EMBODEN also mentions that the analysis undertaken by DÍAZ (1975:179–180) identified in the water-lily nuciferine and nornuciferine, which, apart from medical uses, particularly in China, can act as mild, sedative intoxicants. EMBODEN also cites several studies undertaken since 1882,[354] when opium substitutes were being sought, which confirm the narcotic and sedative effects of various species of *Nymphaea* on not only humans, but also on mice, dogs and eels.[355] Apart from the anecdotal evidence of 'hallucinatory effects'[356] provided by DÍAZ, the chemical analysis

352. The report by DÍAZ (1975:176–181) on the use of water-lily as a hallucinogenic ("alucinogena") contains the claim (p.176) made by an informant ("un informante directo nos relató") in Chiapas that the consumption particularly of the raw, fresh bulb of the plant (*Nymphaea ampla*) can cause hallucinations. This is the single anecdotal report that is used as the basis for the assertion that water-lily can be hallucinogenic. DÍAZ also mentions the possibly 'sacred' ("sagrada") use of this plant by the Mayans and Egyptians, comparing it to "soma" or "bhang". Is this perhaps the historical root of subsequent claims by EMBODEN, MCDONALD and SPESS that either water-lily or lotus was *soma*?
353. Aporphine and morphine alkaloids are closely related (ROBINSON 1968:63ff.).
354. See also EMBODEN (1981:53–54).
355. Numerous anecdotal reports on the internet generally endorse the mildly narcotic properties of the plant. See, for example https://www.erowid.org/experiences/exp.php?ID=15372 (accessed 29/05/2014).
356. EMBODEN (1981:61) also claims that, "on his own physiological constitution, [EMBODEN] found the floral extract to be a visual and auditory hallucinogen". This report of the effects of *Nymphaea ampla* are exceptional, and not, as far as I am aware, reported anywhere else—apart from the anecdotal report by DÍAZ, mentioned above—in accounts of the effects of this plant.

points unequivocally to narcotic properties of the water-lily and lotus, instead of the stimulatory effect of an entheogen. SCHULTES and HOFMANN (1980:331) note the suggestion that has been made that an aquatic lily was employed as a narcotic by the Mayans, but comment that, "Recent Mexican ethnobotanical investigations have failed to uncover an instance of hallucinogenic use of the lily". However, that said, some evidence will be presented in Chapter 13 that a species of *Nymphaea* may have been one of many ingredients of a *soma* potion.

On the assumption that *soma* was entheogenic, there is a strand of thought in R. Gordon WASSON's later (1986) contribution to the debate (see Chapter 11) that the specific identity of *soma* is not of paramount importance, that it was the transformation or expansion of consciousness engendered by *soma* that is the important issue: "I think I am the first to call attention to this tabu [about mushrooms] that leaves Soma without a name in English, and certainly the first to suggest that we call it 'Soma' out of respect for what it has represented for the human race, in the Old World and the New" (1986:74). This more generalized concept of a 'universal *soma*' as a transformer of consciousness may have been influenced by the notion of *soma* as *amṛta*, the 'nectar of immortality', which was referred to in Chapter 2. However, the notion of a '*soma* function' as a mechanism involved in the general dynamics of consciousness had already surfaced around the beginning of the 20th century in psychoanalytic circles in Vienna, though I do not know whether or not WASSON was aware of this. The idea was explored by Sigmund FREUD, Karl ABRAHAM in an article entitled 'Myths and Dreams' in 1908, and later by Carl G. JUNG in several talks and publications, though the workings of the '*soma* function' was variously conceived by these three psychoanalysts (MERCUR 2013:538–546).[357]

---

357. In correspondence in May 1908 FREUD had suggested to ABRAHAM that he include a discussion of *soma* in his article. FREUD believed that *soma* is a psychoactive substance that occurs naturally in the body, which is one's libido, the chemical composition of which remained unidentified. In his article, ABRAHAM connects nectar, ambrosia, amrita, soma and haoma: it vitalizes, inspires, and confers immortality. He also links NIETZSCHE's Dionysian principle to sexual desire and *soma*. JUNG refers to *soma* in two passages in *Wandlungen und Symbole der Libido* (1912), in which he

The idea of a '*soma* function' is again taken up by WILSON (1999), who sees parallels in Indian and Irish mythology (between Indra and Fionn, for example) and looks for entheogens in ancient Irish culture (but with little firm evidence). WILSON is more concerned to demonstrate what he calls the '*soma* function' (of transforming consciousness) in Irish mythology, rather than attempting to establish a proof of the use of particular plants, particularly entheogenic mushrooms, which he believes lie at the heart of ancient Irish and brahmanical religion.[358] In a similar vein of 'universalism', FRAWLEY (2013:42) contends that *soma* was never regarded as a single plant or species: "Soma appears to refer to the juice or essence of any plant. Soma is ultimately the healing essence of all the plants and beyond that even the essence of all healing, joy and well-being"; it is, essentially, "a plant metaphor" (p.326); "the real Soma is a secretion in the brain from spiritual practices of Yoga, pranayama, mantra and meditation" (p.333).

DI MAIO (2013a; 2013b) has recently discovered the San Pedro cactus (*Echinopsis pachanoi*), or a very close relative, growing (it is claimed) wild in the Kamand valley, in Mandi district, Himachal Pradesh state. It is usually assumed that this plant was only native to the Americas. This cactus and another, more common, tall, cactus-like plant, *Euphorbia royleana*, which contains a toxic (and medicinal) sap, are proposed as possible candidates for *soma.* San Pedro, which, like the peyote cactus, contains mescaline, is well known in South and Central America as a powerful entheogen; it is used religiously in rituals and has a long history of use. However, descriptions in the *Veda*s of *soma*'s stalks and the like, and the pressing for its juice seems to make it unlikely that San Pedro was ever identified as *soma.* More importantly, botanists are generally unanimous that the *pachanoi* species is only to be found in the

---

equates *soma* with nectar (which makes the soul drunk with the Logos); and also, similarly to FREUD, associates *soma* with libido. JUNG subsequently, in 1929, discussed *soma* as both a mythological symbol and as something psychoactive. He also interpreted 'immortality' psychologically and not metaphysically: it is an experience of the timelessness of the unconscious.

358. WILSON also extends this concept of '*soma* function' globally. For example (p.134): "...if all mushroom cults are descended from Arctic shamanism—then Maria Sabina's psilocybe mushrooms may be Soma plants, not only typologically, but historically".

Americas.[359] No examples (apart from those in this report) have ever been found in Asia, except as imported specimens.[360]

Finally, regarding recent propositions for *soma*, probably one of the most unfeasible theses to date is KALYANARAMAN's (2004) proposition that *soma* in the *Ṛgveda* is neither a plant nor a drink but is electrum (or "gold-silver pyrite") ore; and that the *Ṛgveda* is a secretly-coded alchemical text.[361]

---

359. See ROHAS-ARÉCHIGA and FLORES (2016:21–25) for an overview of the global distribution of the cactus family (*Cactaceae*). Only one kind of cactus, the epiphytic genus *Rhipsalis*, is found outside the Americas. This kind has spread, undoubtedly by birds, to tropical Africa and Madagascar, and across to Sri Lanka and southern India.
360. However, remaining open-minded to all possibilities (even if highly improbable), see Appendix 6.
361. Referring to *ṚV* 9.70.7 and 9.97.9 (p.82) the author states that, "*soma* is not a plant with thorns; it was a lump of ore with pointed metallic protrusions (sharpened horns)". In support of this extraordinary thesis KALYANARAMAN (pp.67–102) argues (quite untenably) that *oṣadhi* does not refer to a plant or a herb (the usual meaning), and (p.79) that *aṃśu*, "can also denote metallic protrusions and veins of an ore-block". SPESS (2000) also, bizarrely, finds evidence of alchemy in the *Ṛgveda*.

CHAPTER 10

Ephedra

Towards the end of the 19th century, for the first time it was speculated that *soma/haoma* might have been a kind of 'narcotic'.[362] The ephedra plant, of which there are around forty kinds[363] (NYBERG 1997:394), and known as *mā huāng* ('yellow hemp')[364] in China—where it is used medicinally—then began to gain ground[365] as a possible candidate for *soma/haoma.*[366] It is still probably the foremost

---

362. O'FLAHERTY (1969:113) cites a publication from 1884 in Russian by D. N. OVSIANIKO-KULIKOVSKI on this point. A textbook of psychoactive substances by Louis LEWIN (*Phantastica: die betaubenden und erregenden Genußmittel*), first published in 1924, provided four potential identifications for *soma*: *Periploca aphylla, Sarcostemma brevistigma, Setaria glauca* and *Ephedra vulgaris.* LEWIN (1998:279) doubted the suitability of any of them and believed (p.135) that *soma* was a strong alcoholic preparation. The English translation (from German) of this book (*Phantastica: Narcotics and Stimulants, for Medical Doctors and Non-Doctors*), published in 1931, inspired Aldous HUXLEY to write *Brave New World* (1932) (HALBFASS 2001:221; HOUBEN 2003:2.4), which features *soma* as a kind of 'perfect' chemical compound, with all the advantages of Christianity and alcohol but with none of their defects; a trope subsequently expanded in *Island* (1952) and *Brave New World Revisited* (1958). In small doses it brought a sense of bliss; in larger doses it produced visions; three tablets elicited deep, refreshing sleep (see WEZLER 2001:195). However, HUXLEY believed (1999:11) that, practically, three different effects (euphoric, hallucinant and sedative) from one drug would be, "an impossible combination".
363. Including *Ephedra vulgaris, Ephedra intermedia, Ephedra pachyclada.*
364. The bush is dark green when growing but when dry is yellow.
365. The ephedra plant was first identified as containing a drug—isolated in 1885 by YAMANASHI from *Ephedra sinica*—which was subsequently called ephedrine in 1887 (BROUGH 1971:361; HOUBEN 2003:2.3).
366. This theory was considered by STEIN (1931) but rejected in favour of an alcoholic preparation of wild rhubarb (a theory also endorsed by

proposition, endorsed by researchers including SRIVASTAVA (1966; 1970), MADHIHASSAN (1986; 1987a), FALK (1989; 2002/3) in detailed articles, KASHIKAR (1990) in a short monograph, and more recently by NYBERG (1997). Also, as noted previously, it is a widely held view among Zoroastrian scholars that ephedra is *haoma*: it has been used as *haoma* up until recent times and it is assumed by some scholars that this was the case in antiquity.

The Russian archaeologist Victor SARIANIDI published many articles and books on research he undertook for around forty years, beginning in the mid-1970s,[367] in Afghanistan and also in Bactria and Margiana,[368] in eastern Turkmenistan, for which he coined the acronym BMAC (Bactria Margiana Archeological Complex). The principal ancient, monumental temple complexes of a civilization that flourished between *c.* 2200 and 1700 BCE in Turkmenistan that he excavated are known as Togolok-1, Togolok-21, and Gonur 'Temenos', which is the largest. Many other Bronze Age sites have also been discovered in this region, mostly in the region bordering the Murghab river, which is a tributary of the Āmu Daryā (Oxus) river. This civilization is also called the Oxus civilization.

The main complexes excavated by SARIANIDI had rooms with white, gypsum plaster walls (which he interprets as having been for religious rituals), fireplaces and large storage vessels (SARIANIDI 2003). He reports finds in vessels of the remains of cannabis, papaver (poppy) and ephedra at all three temple complexes (SARIANIDI 2007:174). Pressing stones, mortars, special grinders, ceramic strainers and vessels with perforated bottoms were also discovered.[369]

R. C. ZAEHNER in 1961). However, the great Sanskritist Karl GELDNER, in his translation of the *Ṛgveda* (the full text of which was finally published in 1951), endorsed the case for ephedra. Another supporter of the ephedra theory is N. A. QASILBASH (1960) (O'FLAHERTY 1969:138–143).

367. He died in Gonur in 2013.

368. Bactria and Margiana were the names used by the Greeks for those territories in Turkmenistan.

369. These findings lead WATSON (2012:177) to believe that *soma* was a mix of ephedra, cannabis and papaver and "perhaps" also Syrian rue. However, this assertion does not fully take into account whether or not this concoction would be sufficient to induce entheogenic experience, which, it is argued in this book, *soma/haoma* was. WATSON inaccurately states that both ephedra and rue are "hallucinogenic", which neither is.

SARIANIDI (2007:175ff.) also finds, in the specific forms of altars and burials in the Margiana temple complexes, evidence which he interprets as constituting proto-Zoroastrian rites. However, the interpretation of evidence as 'proto-Zoroastrian' has been challenged (LAMBERG-KARLOVSKY 2013); SARIANIDI retro-fits all the evidence into a pre-conceived proto-Zoroastrian mould.[370]

SARIANIDI sees the finding of ephedra as further proof that this was *haoma* (or an ingredient of *haoma*), which, he maintains (1994:388) was a hallucinogenic concoction. However, SARIANIDI's specimens of traces of these plants (including ephedra) were not validated in subsequent analysis (NYBERG 1997:400; BAKELS 2003). SARIANIDI's response (1999:309–310) to these negative results—which were originally found to be positive when samples of the scrapings of a vessel were tested at Moscow University and published by MEYER-MELIKYAN in 1998—is that subsequent tests, which were negative, were undertaken five years later, during which time the vessels had been exposed to the rain and wind of the desert, which, SARIANIDI claims, eroded the remains.

Further east, small bundles of ephedra twigs in cloth pouches have been found beside nearly every one of the excavated mummies, most of which date from 2000–1000 BCE, in the Tarim basin, in Xinjiang province, China (STEIN 1932:502ff.; BARBER 1999:159ff.).[371] These mummies are of Caucasian-looking

---

370. Also, with very little supporting evidence and a great deal of speculation, SARIANIDI proposes that 'Aryan' ancestors from Anatolia established the Oxus civilization. LAMBERG-KARLOVSKI (2013) argues that there is no substantial evidence for this hypothesis and that the archeological indications point rather to an indigenous development of the Oxus civilization.

371. It is sometimes reported that pollen samples of ephedra that are 60,000 years old have been found at Neanderthal burial sites (for example, NYBERG 1997:400). This claim derives from excavations at the Shanidar caves in northern Iraq conducted by Ralph SOLECKI between 1951 and 1960. In his book, *The First Flower People* (1971), SOLECKI claims that Neanderthal burials included varieties of ephedra, daisy, yarrow, hollyhock, Saint Barnabus thistle, groundsel and other plants (EDULJEE 2014). However, doubt about this has been expressed by TATTERSALL (1995:170), who suggests burying rodents may have been responsible for pollen deposits. More recently, the claim about Neanderthal pollen samples has been challenged by FIACCONI and HUNT (2015), who maintain it is more likely that pollen samples were far more recently introduced to the site.

humans,[372] some of whom are wearing pointed felt hats in the style of European witches. BARBER (1999:159–166) suggests links and similarities—but without any substantial corroboration—between the discoveries of SARIANIDI in Turkmenistan, the cult of *soma/ haoma*, and the ayahuasca cults of the Amazon.

The ephedra bush grows widely in the Mediterranean region, the Middle East and China.[373] Its branches can be easily cut into stalks. The usual effects of consumption are as a mild stimulant, similar to the effects of caffeine or adrenaline. When the Mormons arrived in Utah in the mid-19th century, they made tea from ephedra stalks (*Ephedra nevadensis*) because, ironically, stimulants such as the use of tea and coffee were prohibited by Mormon law (SPINELLA 2001:114). In the Khyber Pass region of Afghanistan, Pathans use ephedra twigs in a decoction as a household remedy for illness and as a tonic (MADHIHASSAN 1987a:10); in Sikkim it is used as a folk remedy to treat asthma (BURMAN 2003:68). However, in higher doses, particularly of the refined product, ephedrine can be as stimulating (and as dangerous) as an excessive dose of amphetamine.[374]

---

372. Referred to as 'Loulan/Qäwrighal people' by BARBER, named after the sites of discovery. Some, if not all, of these people were most probably what have been called 'epi-Scythians', a branch of Scythians who may have first reached this region in *c.* 800 BCE (LITTLETON 1998).

373. It is hardy enough to grow in Britain. I collected a few stalks from a specimen of *Ephedra tweediana* growing in the Royal Botanical Gardens at Kew in London. Sprinkling and then immersing a stalk in water did not cause it to swell, as is described in the *Veda*s for *soma*; though it is not impossible that stalks of other species of ephedra would swell if sprinkled with (or immersed in) water, though I have come not come across any experiments concerning this phenomenon.

374. Ephedrine has several medical uses: it can improve muscle strength and alleviate fatigue; and can be used for asthma and low blood-pressure. As with most stimulants, ephedrine is dose-critical: the normal dose-range is from 15–30mg of the actual (pure) alkaloid (ephedrine); 1–2gm can be lethal. The consumption of too much ephedrine, which is used both medically and recreationally, can cause palpitations, heart problems, nausea, dizziness and other symptoms. Long-term use or over-consumption of ephedrine can lead to stroke or heart attack. Side-effects include headache, irritability, restlessness, anxiety, insomnia, tachycardia, urinary disorders and vomiting. Several deaths from cardiac toxicity have been reported (SPINELLA 2001:115–117). See also http://www.bodyactive-online.co.uk/ supplements/ingredients/ephedrine.asp http://www.erowid.org/chemicals/ ephedrine/ephedrine_dose.shtml (accessed 13/12/2013).

FALK's (1989; 2002/3) case for ephedra includes the local identifications in Afghanistan, Balochistan and northern Pakistan of the ephedra plant as '*hōm*' (or *hum/huma/sum* or the like);[375] that it is used as both a medicine and as a stimulant (which would fit Vedic descriptions of the *soma* plant being *jāgṛvi* 'keeping alert');[376] its extracted juice is bitter (or 'sharp')[377] and reddish; it has a stem, roots and branches; it can be aphrodisiac;[378] and it can cause vomiting. It is used by Zoroastrians in Iran and India, and until recently (1975) by Nambudiri brahmans of Kerala in their *soma* rituals. NYBERG (1997:396) adds that the variety with the highest ephedrine content (*Ephedra equistina*) grows mainly in mountainous regions.

Although the stimulating effects and many of the other properties of *soma/haoma* are widely agreed upon, what remains as contentious is whether or not *soma/haoma* had psychedelic or entheogenic properties. Both FALK and NYBERG see no evidence that *soma/haoma* was necessarily psychedelic or 'visionary'. FALK (1989:79) maintains that, "there is nothing shamanistic or visionary in early Vedic or in old Iranian texts";[379] in a more recent article FALK (2002/3:148) reiterates his scepticism that Vedic hymns

375. PRANAVANANDA (1983:148) notes that *Ephedra vulgaris* is referred to as *soma* or *soma-kalpa* by villagers at Nagaling, where it grows abundantly (this village is in Tibet on the way to Mount Kailās from Almora, which is in the Kumaun district of Uttaranchal State, in India). The plant is used to treat asthma. Syrian rue and henbane also grow in the Kailās region (MCKAY 2016:105).

376. However, a doubt about this point has been raised by THOMPSON (2003), who sees the *jāgṛvi* epithet as more associated with Agni in the *Ṛgveda*. STUHRMAN (2006:16) is more critical, maintaining that although many times *soma* is said to inspire, causing trembling (Zitternder = *vipra*), nowhere in the *Ṛgveda* is it said that *soma* keeps one awake ('wachmacht'). However, ELIZARENAKOVA (1996:19) notices three occurrences of the transitive use *jāgṛvi* ('making awake') in the *ṚV*, all of them connected to *soma*. FALK (2002/3:148) adds that there are also twenty occurrences of the intransitive use of *jāgṛvi* in the *ṚV*.

377. *Tīvra*, which is said to be the strongest kind: *ṚV* 1.23.1.

378. This does not seem to be entirely supported by FALK's reference to *ṚV* 8.91.1.

379. WEZLER (2001:207) similarly remarks that, "it is possible that the use of *soma* had certain visionary effects, but there is no evidence that it led to mystical experiences".

(specifically the *Labasūkta, ṚV* 10.119) describe hallucinogenic experience. NYBERG (1997:398) maintains that the stimulatory properties of ephedra are sufficient for it to be *soma.* However, FLATTERY (FLATTERY and SCHWARZ 1989:72–73) argues that the pharmacological intensity of ephedra is too weak for it to have been the plant used in ancient Iran.[380] He points out that Zoroastrian priests have been drinking ephedra extracts for centuries without noticing its intoxicating effects; that ephedra is unknown in Indic or Iranian folk medicine; and that it is not regarded as intoxicating in China. I would add that there is nothing like 'reverence' for ephedra in any culture that currently uses it; and neither FALK nor NYBERG take into consideration what *madha/mada* would seem to indicate in Zoroastrian and Vedic texts; a point that we will return to.

Another possible objection to the 'solo' ephedra thesis is that during the longer Vedic *soma* rituals the drinking of *soma* may periodically continue throughout the night or over successive days, when *soma* is often drunk by the sacrificer (*yajamāna*) and the priests every few hours; up to twenty-nine times (see STAAL 1996:81ff.). The *ahīna* rite entails, according to one commentator, the repeated drinking of *soma* juice, lasting from two to twelve days (*Viṣṇusmṛti* 54.25n.25). Sustained use of entheogens over several days is practised by some ayahuasca groups (see below), but ephedra being a stimulant, there is a threshold beyond which it is unpleasant to consume more (as noted above); as, for example, after drinking too much coffee: "like caffeine…[Mormon Tea/ephedra] can make the user very "edgy" and have an adverse effect on the nerves" (ANDREWS and RINDSBERG 2010:79). OTT (1998:11) comments that, "Moreover, nobody who has tried the wretched *Ephedra* species, sources of the adrenaline-like alkaloid ephedrine, would ever imagine such could inspire rapture and ecstasy". However, given the prevalence of ephedra in Zoroastrian religious practice and the discovery of its ancient use in central Asia, it seems probable that ephedra may have been used as an additive to an entheogenic concoction.

---

380. STAAL (2001a:759) also believes that ephedra is one of the least likely among the many candidates. NADKARNI (1954:489), from an informed medical perspective, is highly sceptical that *soma* was ephedra.

CHAPTER 11

Fly-agaric mushrooms (*Amanita muscaria*)

In 1968 the debate over *soma* took a dramatic turn with the publication of R. Gordon WASSON's *Soma: Divine Mushroom of Immortality*. WASSON, an American banker-turned-scholar, together with his Russian wife Valentina Pavlovna WASSON (formerly GUERCKEN), had become fascinated with psychedelic mushrooms; they were pioneers of ethnomycology. Experience of psilocybin mushrooms,[381] first in Mexico on 29th–30th June 1955,[382] had been profound. WASSON had 'experienced God' and came to believe that psychedelic mushrooms were the catalyst behind divine revelation in many of the world's religious traditions. Research into the *Veda*s led WASSON to believe that the *soma* used in ancient India was the

---

381. For the various kinds of mushroom containing psilocybin/psilocin (magic mushrooms), see STAMETS (2005:69–75); LETCHER (2006:13–17). By 1995 the known global distribution of psilocybin mushrooms was of 172 varieties and species (GUZMÁN 1995:137); Mexico has the highest number (44) of hallucinogenic psilocybin species in the world (GUZMÁN 2002:5). For the pharmacology of psilocybin/psilocin and its relation to other potentially psychedelic tryptamines, see PRESTI and NICHOLS (2005). The tryptamine alkaloids found in psilocybin mushrooms and DMT are chemically similar to serotonin and similarly effect the brain through the 5-HT2A receptor, which is also implicated in cognition, mental states, degenerative disorders and working memory.
382. This was with Maria SABINA, who asked him why he wanted to have the mushrooms. WASSON replied that he wanted to "find God", which SABINA could not understand: to find God people usually go to church; mushrooms are for sick people, and WASSON wasn't sick (BEYER (2010:43).

red, speckled fly-agaric[383] mushroom (*Amanita muscaria*),[384] even though WASSON himself had failed to have an ecstatic experience on fly-agaric. On numerous occasions during 1965 and 1966 he ingested the mushrooms but usually felt nauseous and fell asleep: "The results were disappointing" (WASSON 1969:75).[385]

The most psychoactive compounds amongst many others in *Amanita muscaria* are muscarine[386] (which is present only in very low concentrations) and ibotenic acid (both of which are quite toxic),[387]

---

383. So called because flies that settle on the mushroom become intoxicated and swoon, as though dead; usually they subsequently revive. Agari is a region north of the Sea of Azov (north-east of Crimea), which was inhabited by a tribe of Scythians called Agari, whose shamans used the mushroom (MAYOR 2010:101).
384. This mushroom only grows in a mychorrizal relationship with particular trees: usually under birch but also (more rarely) under aspen, beech, fir, larch, oak and pine trees. *Amanita muscaria* grows in many countries; also in the Indian Himalayas and Kodaikanal in Tamil Nadu (RAWALA *et al.* 2002). It is unclear whether or not WASSON knew about fly-agaric growing in India. SAMORINI (1995) discusses megalithic structures, called *kudo-kallo* ('umbrella stones'), in Tamil Nadu and Kerala, which have been variously dated between 1400 BCE and 100 CE. He suggests that they most probably represent fly-agaric mushrooms.
385. [DONIGER] O'FLAHERTY, a Sanskritist who contributed the substantial summary of the history of research on *soma* to WASSON's book (O'FLAHERTY 1969), and who inadvertently first interested WASSON in the idea that fly-agaric mushrooms could be *soma*, was herself always doubtful of the thesis that WASSON developed (DONIGER 1997); though she endorses the view that *soma* was, nevertheless, a hallucinogenic drug (O'FLAHERTY 1981:133). GERSHEVITCH (1974:47) maintains that WASSON was aware of what seemed to be a potential difficulty with his thesis; that he had read DARMESTETER's rendering (translated into English) of *Yasna* 10.5 ("Oh Haoma, do thy grow in all thy trunks, in all thy branches, in all thy stems"), which would have excluded *Amanita muscaria.* However, a more accurate reading of this particular passage in the *Avesta* is not, according to GERSHEVITCH, entirely unsupportive of *Amanita* (though other passages are).
386. First identified as a toxin in 1869, and eventually isolated in 1950 (HUMMEL 1997:84). The effects of muscarine poisoning include excessive perspiration and salivation, abdominal pain, nausea, vomiting and diarrhoea (FEENEY 2013:282). Muscarine does not cross the blood-brain barrier, so it does not affect the brain (PRESTI and NICHOLS 2005:108).
387. Digestion, cooking or drying the mushroom transforms ibotenic acid (which is a GABA-A agonist) into muscimol; hence the preference in Siberia for dried

and muscimol[388] (which is the compound most responsible for the 'high' produced by the mushroom).[389] Apart from a few exceptions, most experimenters do not have an experience on fly-agaric mushrooms that is particularly insightful, visionary or ecstatic.[390] MCKENNA (1992:108) comments: "Instead of realizing that *Amanita*

---

rather than fresh mushrooms. The highest concentration of these compounds is in the skin of the cap and the yellow tissue immediately beneath it. For further details of the chemical compounds—and their effects—in fly-agaric, see OTT (1975:208–212); SCHULTES and HOFMANN 1980:44–55; FEENEY (2013:281–282). See also FURST (1988:33–66) for a useful summary of *Amanita muscaria*'s discovery and use in Siberia.

388. Muscimol, ibotenic acid and muscazone are three related isoxazole alkaloids found in fly-agaric mushrooms, muscimol being the main alkaloid.

389. *Amanita* can cause a notable motor dysfunction in both animals and humans; other effects include twitching, visual disturbances, trembling and convulsive-like movements of the extremities. General effects include fatigue and sedation, followed by sleep (SPINELLA 2001:389). Besides humans, only deer and ravens are known to consume the mushrooms wittingly (BEDROSIAN 2000:2). At high doses delirium, coma and amnesia have been reported (GRINSPOON and BAKALAR 1998:29).

390. On one occasion, WASSON's Japanese friend, who had first dried the mushrooms over a fire before eating them, had a euphoric experience. MCKENNA (1992:109) reports twice consuming fly-agaric himself; he felt nauseous and experienced stomach cramps and blurred vision. BEYER (2010:287) remarks that although small doses of *Amanita* can produce euphoria, "doses large enough to cause hallucinations—which appear to occur only rarely and sporadically—are physically incapacitating, with effects including drowsiness, confusion, muscle twitches, loss of muscular coordination, and stupor". FALK (2002/3:146) also cites anecdotal reports of its effects, which include restlessness, dizziness, disturbance of visions and speaking, and hallucinations. However, HEINRICH (1995:191–198) ate the mushrooms every day for a month in 1977. After initial experiences of nausea and discomfort, he (and his friend) finally attained a magnificent, revelatory euphoria; HEINRICH was absorbed into the unsurpassable light of the Godhead. Attempting to repeat the experience, he eagerly ate the mushrooms a few days later, only to be plunged into hell. Such entheogenic reports of fly-agaric experience are nevertheless very rare, despite the widespread availability of the mushrooms in Asia, Mesoamerica, North America, Asia and Russia. PENDELL (2010c:284) comments: "For the Queen of Entheogens, it's all pretty muted. One would expect more. (I mean, compare it to say, mandrake.) From a distance, the silence in the hall is louder than the one or two who are clapping. The only people shouting are the Siberians".

muscaria was an unlikely candidate for Vedic Soma, WASSON became convinced that some method of preparation must have been involved. But no ingredient or procedure has ever been found that reliably transforms the often uncomfortable subtoxic experience of *Amanita* into visionary journeying to a magical paradise".

MCKENNA (1992:110–111) comments that WASSON eventually, but inconsistently and obliquely, endorsed psilocybin mushrooms instead. Indeed, in *Persephone's Quest*, published in 1986, WASSON remarks (p.135): "But the possible role of *Stropharia cubensis* [psilocybin] growing in the dung of cattle in the lives of the lower orders remains to this day wholly unexplored. Is *S. cubensis* responsible for the elevation of the cow to a sacred status?". Other comments by WASSON in this publication lead one to wonder if he had become aware that his fly-agaric mushroom thesis was untenable. In another instance, having just stated that (p.89), "these hints may point towards *Stropharia cubensis*", WASSON, remarkably, adds, "We may recall [though readers were not informed previously about this important point] that in India Hindus of the three upper castes are forbidden by their religion to eat mushrooms of any kind". WASSON (1986:119–120) later quotes MANU (5.5, 19; 6.14; 11.156) on the consumption of mushrooms by the twice-born being expressly forbidden. He also quotes William JONES (who quotes YAMA commenting on MANU): "the ancient Hindus held the fungus in such detestation...This is the most extravagant outburst of mycophobia that we have found anywhere, surely the most extravagant to be found in the Indo-European world").[391]

After his publication in 1968 of *Soma: Divine Mushroom of Immortality*, it seems that WASSON had discovered unequivocal evidence that the consumption of any kind of mushroom was forbidden to Hindus: *soma* could not have been a mushroom. Yet, inconsistently, he maintains in *Persephone's Quest* (p.33) that, "*Amanita muscaria* was *the* entheogen of the ancient world. The citations of Soma in the

391. MANU's prohibition on mushrooms was framed around 1,500 years after the composition of the *Ṛgveda*, and it has been suggested by some commentators that it is possible that this prohibition was not endorsed in earlier Vedic culture. However, the general conservatism of brahmanical culture would seem to rule out the possibility that a plant that was supposedly once so revered could become so reviled.

Rig Veda are all consistent with this reading". If this is the case, why propose *Stropharia cubensis* (on several occasions); or even more bizarrely, what do we make of the quoted brahmanical prohibitions on mushrooms?[392] Nevertheless, according to OTT (1998b:17), WASSON remained convinced of his fly-agaric thesis to the end of his life.[393]

Although the hypothesis in WASSON's book received a few favourable reactions from Indologists,[394] some reviewers were adversely critical. John BROUGH, a Sanskritist, published a detailed review (BROUGH 1971) of WASSON's thesis in the *Bulletin of the School of Oriental and African Studies*.[395] While praising WASSON's research into the use of fly-agaric in eastern Siberian Russia by Koryaks and shamans in the Kamchatka Peninsula, and by others in Siberia[396]—which comprises a section of WASSON's book—BROUGH could not accept that this information in any way supported

392. See RIEDLINGER (1993) for a comprehensive analysis of the problems WASSON had with his *Amanita* thesis (including his personal correspondence with MCKENNA about it), his ambivalence concerning psilocybin mushrooms, and his candidates prior to *Amanita*, which included morning glory (see below), *Lagochillus inebriens* (Turkish mint) and the ergot fungus. WASSON was initially under the impression that psilocybin does not grown in South Asia (or had become extinct), though he was subsequently introduced to it in 1967 in the Simlipal Hills of Orissa. Psilocybin mushrooms are also to be found abundantly in the Kodaikanal hills of Tamil Nadu. According to *Economic Microfungi of Tibet*, a Chinese publication, *Psilocybe coprophilia, Psilocybe cubensis* and *Psilocybe merdaria* can all be found in Tibet (BAKER 2004:460n.24). In September 1987 I found a potent variety (of uncertain classification) growing at over 4,000 metres on a pass to the Khām valley in eastern Tibet.

393. For details of how WASSON's enthusiasm for mushrooms developed and intimations of how he occasionally 'adjusted' the evidence to fit his thesis, see LETCHER (2006:142ff.); and how WASSON sometimes chose to ignore evidence that was contrary to his 'universal' mushroom hypothesis, see also EMBODEN (1982:145–146).

394. From Stella KRAMRISCH (1975), André BAREAU and Daniel INGALLS (see OTT 1998b); see also HOUBEN 2003:3.1).

395. KUIPER (1969) also, while acknowledging WASSON's contribution to the debate, found several faults in the WASSON's interpretation of the material from the *Ṛgveda*.

396. FALK (2002/3:145–146) mentions that fly-agaric is also used in the Schetul valley in Eastern Afghanistan.

a case for the identification of *soma* with fly-agaric in the *Veda*s. Among the objections raised were several important arguments. Probably the strongest objection (pp.336–338) to WASSON's thesis is that in Siberia the mushrooms are either consumed whole or, more commonly, only the caps are eaten.[397] WASSON's textual evidence is almost entirely from passages in the *Ṛgveda* and he ignores the detailed descriptions, particularly in the *Yajurveda* and *Śatapatha Brāhmaṇa*, of the elaborate pounding with stones of the *soma* plant (a point first made by BROUGH's wife). The dried mushrooms could be sprinkled with water to inflate them, but why would they need to be extensively pounded? [398] Also, unlike *soma* juice, extracted fly-agaric juice would not need to have been filtered through a woollen fleece sieve, because the mushrooms can be consumed whole, as is the practice in Siberia. Besides other reasons, the pounding of the *soma* stalks with stones seems to rule out the use of fly-agaric.[399]

BROUGH also found fault with some of WASSON's translation of Vedic passages. BROUGH (pp.343–348) criticized WASSON over his interpretation of *ṚV* 9.74.4, which WASSON interpreted as priests urinating *soma* juice,[400] which, purified through prior consumption, is then drunk by others,[401] as is sometimes the practice in Siberia.

---

397. See also NYBERG (1997:341).

398. This point has been reiterated by several other critics, including FALK (1989) and NYBERG (1997).

399. WEZLER (2001:198n.30) tried pounding between stones three fly-agaric mushrooms in Austria, and, predictably, only produced wet stones.

400. *ṚV* 9.74.4 states that, "The *swollen* men/heroes (= the Maruts) *piss* down (the fluid) set in motion" (trans. SKJÆRVØ 2004:266). Other passages in the *ṚV* (e.g. 1.64.5–6; 8.4.9–10) also refer to either Indra—who famously quaffs 'buckets' of *soma*—or his companions (the Maruts and their horses) pissing after drinking *soma* and releasing thundering streams of fertilizing rain. But there is no indication in any of these passages that the pissed *soma* is drunk, as is done in Siberia. WASSON (1971:177–178) also refers to two passages in the *Ṛgveda* (9.73.8; 9.97.55), which he interprets as indicating a "third filter" for the *soma* juice, that being someone who has drunk *soma* and pissed it out, which another person can then drink. However, 9.73.8 merely refers to *soma* being thrice purified (…*spaśaḥ svañcaḥ*); while 9.97.55 states that, "The three purifiers are spread out" (trans. KASHYAP) (*saṃ trī pavitrā vittāni eṣi*). There is no evidence in these two passages to indicate a human filter for *soma* juice.

401. WASSON (1972b:206) also speculated that the Indian medicinal practice of drinking urine may have originated in the drinking of Vedic priests' urine,

BROUGH argues that WASSON's interpretation of this and other passages is erroneous.[402] WASSON wrote an extensive rejoinder to BROUGH's review but WASSON's *ad hominem* attack on 'elite Vedists' did not go down well with the editors of the SOAS *Bulletin*, who refused to publish it. Undaunted, WASSON published his reply independently (WASSON 1972c).[403] However, WASSON's reply, in the view of most scholars, failed to address BROUGH's main arguments against the identity of fly-agaric and *soma*. FALK (2002/3:146–147) points to several passages in the *Dharmasūtras* that expressly prohibit the consumption of mushrooms:[404] "Not a single reference leaves room to doubt this". Nevertheless, as OTT (1998b:33), HOUBEN (2003:3.1) and STAAL (2001a:762–763) note, WASSON's lasting contribution to the debate over *soma* is that he introduced the idea of it being a psychedelic.

WASSON's mushroom theory has been so influential that it is probably still currently the most widely-held general belief about *soma*,[405] maintained by many people, despite the objections that

---

which would be psychoactive, being infused with active ingredients of fly-agaric.

402. In a subsequent article, BROUGH (1973) provided several further objections (some of which were made in his 1971 publication) to the 'urine' theory; and also that the colour of *soma* is described as *hari* (yellow/golden/green) in the *Ṛgveda* (fly-agaric is red); and that the wool-like tufts of the fly-agaric are mistakenly confused by WASSON with the woollen filter used to strain the *soma*.

403. WASSON sent a signed copy to the SOAS library, which I accessed in the course of research for this book.

404. *Manusmṛti* (5.5), for example, as mentioned in the footnote above, states that, along with garlic, leeks and onions, mushrooms are a prohibited (*abhaksya*) food. DANDEKAR (1995:22) comments that although the term 'mushroom' (*kṣumpa*) occurs (once) in the *Ṛgveda* (1.84.8) (see also BAILEY 1984), *soma* is never referred to as such; and also points out that the Vedic poets (as noted above) had a great aversion to mushrooms.

405. An art exhibition entitled 'Soma' was held in Berlin by Carsten HÖLLER in 2010; reindeer and fly-agaric mushrooms were displayed. The book on the exhibition featured the artwork and extracts of several of the most influential publications about *soma* (HÖLLER 2011), including the rejoinder by BROUGH (1989) to WASSON (1968), and articles by FALK (1989) on ephedra, and by McDONALD (2004) on the lily/lotus plant; however, the majority of the articles in the book (which depicted a fly-agaric mushroom on the front cover) were devoted to these mushrooms.

have been raised;[406] and it periodically reemerges.[407] STUHRMAN (1985) supports the proposition for *Amanita muscaria*, arguing for the 'hallucinatory' and 'light-filled' nature of the visions. Or, if it is not *Amanita*, then, "es müßte sich ein anderes alkaloidhaltiges Gewächs handeln" (p.91).[408] HOUBEN (2003:3.1), however, is sceptical: he points out that William BLAKE's visions, which did not depend on any drug, could similarly be described as 'psychedelic'; and that such effects may also be induced by fasting and sleep-deprivation. More recently, STUHRMAN (2006) has extended his argument for the use of fly-agaric in the early period of Vedic composition. He replies (p.20) that HOUBEN's argument about fasting and sleep-deprivation as methods for producing the visions of mystics are irrelevant in the context of the *Ṛgveda soma* songs, as the authors clearly state, "Wir haben *soma* getrunken" [we have drunk *soma*]. However, the objections to the *Amanita* thesis, outlined above, still seem to rule out this proposition.

It is interesting to observe that WASSON's fly-agaric thesis has been so influential that some commentators have suggested that this mushroom appears in other religious contexts as well.[409] HAJICEK-

---

406. SMITH (2000:45–63), in a review of WASSON's book ('Historical Evidence: India's Sacred Soma'), originally published in 1972, also maintains that WASSON's fly-agaric theory is correct; as does ESCOHOTADO (2010:156ff.); however, no discussion is presented in this latter publication of the several possible counter-arguments. GRINSPOON and BAKALAR (1998:39–40) also endorse WASSON's thesis.
407. OBERLIES (1998:166n.96), in his monumental study of the *Ṛgveda*, remains generally agnostic, commenting that although the botanical identity of *soma* may be of interest for historians of culture, for understanding Vedic religion it is practically irrelevant ("faktisch irrelevant"); though he refers (p.279) to *soma* as "ein (halluzinogener) Rauschtrank" [a (hallucinogenic) intoxicating drink]. In an earlier publication he mentions *soma* as a "halluzinogene Droge" (OBERLIES 1989:74), which he maintains (p.85n.60) *soma* doubtless [kein Zweifel] is; he subsequently endorsed the fly-agaric mushroom thesis (OBERLIES 1995:237).
408. It must be another plant with alkaloids that is involved.
409. HEINRICH (1995) not only endorses the fly-agaric thesis for *soma* (pp.8–17), but also finds 'clues' indicating fly-agaric use in the *Purāṇas*, in grail mythology and in the Bible. Besides HEINRICH, 'evidence' for fly-agaric use in the Bible is (famously) presented by John Marco ALLEGRO (*The Sacred Mushroom and the Cross*, 1970), and more recently by Jan IRVIN and Andrew RUTAJIT (*Astrotheology and Shamanism*, 2009), and John RUSH

DOBBERSTEIN (1995) maintains that some Buddhist *siddha*s used it for 'enlightenment'; but the largely allusive evidence he provides from the 11th/12th century Tibetan Buddhist text, *The Stories of the Eighty-Four Siddhas*, is questionable. A central example is the supposition that a pancake on which is piled delicious food and balanced by the *siddha* Karnaripa (who has been sent out to beg) on the tip of a needle 'represents' a fly-agaric mushroom. His case rests largely on WASSON's erroneous thesis that *Amanita muscaria* was used in religious rituals in South Asia. WASSON's fallacious idea that South Asian brahmans drank urine containing psychoactive muscimol is also interpreted, via allusive 'evidence' by HAJICEK-DOBBERSTEIN, to have been practised in a Buddhist context.[410]

Similarly, WOHLBERG (1990), in another religious context, that of classical Greek civilization in the early centuries BCE, suggests that the cult of the deity Sabazios had an antecedent cult, which it superseded, which was the cult of *soma-haoma*, which, following WASSON, he maintains was prepared from fly-agaric mushrooms.[411]

(*The Mushroom in Christian Art*, 2011). See HASTIS (2016) for a criticism of these theories, particularly concerning these authors' erroneous use of 'evidence' in the Gospels. BROWN and BROWN (2016) further perpetuate the belief in the role of psychedelic mushrooms in early Christianity.

410. CROWLEY (1996) generally endorses not only the thesis that *soma* was fly-agaric in ancient India, but also maintains that the *amṛta* of some Tibetan Vajrayāna rituals was the intoxicating urine of Buddhist monks who had consumed the mushrooms. Neither proposition is, in my view, adequately supported. CROWLEY also suggests that *soma* (which he specifically identifies as Buddhist *amṛta*, which these days comprises mostly coloured water or only mildly psychoactive plants) may previously have also been cannabis, camphor, or psychoactive plants in general.

411. Apart from the speculative comparisons of similarities between the Greek and Indian cults, a substantial part of WOHLBERG's argument rests on 'allusive' evidence in the Greek religious world to fly-agaric mushrooms: for example, that Sabazios was once a mushroom; that people in the cult of Dionysos (who, it is argued, was originally Sabazios) wore a covering which was not deerskin (as some have supposed) but a representation of the fly-agaric colours; and the emergence of the prominence of the fir and white poplar trees in Greek culture was because of the memory of the symbiosis of these trees with the mushroom. In a similar vein, RUCK (2008) suggests that several plants, animals, motifs and myths in classical Greek culture are substitutes for or 'represented' *Amanita muscaria*, which, he claims, was formerly venerated in that world. These include crocus and violet, the leopard sacred to Dionysos, the antlered hind sacred to Apollo's sister,

Intoxication from fly-agaric mushrooms is, according to WOHLBERG, found in the mystery cults of the classical Greco-Roman world. (In Chapter 17 of this book an alternative theory of what was consumed in mystery cults is presented.) If, however, WASSON's thesis is incorrect, as has been argued, then allusions to fly-agaric mushrooms in other religious traditions appear to be quite unfounded.

Jason's golden fleece, apples plucked by Heracles and Perseus, the Cyclopes who built Mycenae and Athens, and Persephone's abduction, which was ritually enacted in the lesser mysteries, and interpreted by RUCK as the ritualized hunt for *Amanita muscaria*. RUCK's analysis depends primarily on the notion that fly-agaric was the 'original' *soma* of the Āryans, which, it has been argued, is, to this author, improbable.

CHAPTER 12

Syrian rue (*Peganum harmala*)

By the 1980s it was generally agreed amongst researchers that whatever *soma/haoma* might have been in the ancient world, some of the previous identifications could be ruled out with reasonable confidence. It was improbably cannabis alone, for reasons explained previously. Nor was *soma* any form of alcohol, which requires fermentation; and *soma* is pressed and drunk shortly afterwards, which would not have allowed enough time for fermentation.[412] Also, as previously discussed, alcohol (*surā*) is sometimes viewed disparagingly in the *Veda*s, and clearly distinguished from *soma*. *Soma* appears to have had an effect as an entheogenic drug (though this is still occasionally disputed),[413] which eliminated as candidates *Sarcostemma brevistigma, Periploca aphylla* and other similar non-psychoactive vines used on their own.[414] In its natural form ephedra

---

412. "La preparation du soma exclut toute utilisation de ferment" MALAMOUD (1996b:21).
413. NICHOLSON (2002), although generally endorsing a 'shamanic' interpretation of the relevant Vedic passages, examines the similarity between his own (and other mystics') experience of visual imagery—primarily in terms of light and specific patterns (phosphenes) induced through meditation—and imagery induced by *soma* that is depicted in the *Veda*s. If such visions can be produced through meditation, sleep-deprivation and fasting, then *soma* does not necessarily have to be a psychoactive plant; though this bypasses the issue of the extensive preoccupation with the pressing of *soma*, particularly in the *Yajurveda*.
414. NYBERG (1997) analyses the most espoused candidates for *soma* and provides cogent arguments against the possibility of it being: cannabis, opium poppies, *Sarcostemma brevistigma, Periploca aphylla, Panax ginseng,* fly-agaric, *Rheum [palimatum]* (wild rhubarb), *Lagochilus inebrians* (a plant used as an intoxicant—prepared as a tea—by Uzbeks, Turkmens, Tajiks and Tartars, but

seems to be too weak to be *soma/haoma* and sustained use of it is debilitating. The case for *Amanita muscaria* also seems untenable.

Reviving a proposition, noted previously, first made in 1794 by William JONES for *soma* being 'mountain rue' (known as *esphand/isphand/isfand/spand/sipand* throughout the Middle-East and Asia), a sophisticated argument is made for Syrian rue (*Peganum harmala*) by FLATTERY and SCHWARZ (1989).[415] This learned publication provides a great deal of information on the history of the use of rue as a medicine and an intoxicant in Iran and neighbouring regions;[416] its seeds are still used for apotropaic purposes (p.42);[417] and it is used as an aphrodisiac by Turks and others (p.92).[418] There is archaeological evidence from the Caucasus region of its use—probably as an intoxicant that was burnt and inhaled—that dates from the 5th millennium BCE (SHERRATT 1995:30).[419] PLINY (23–79 CE) considered rue (*ruta*) to be among the chief medicinal plants,[420] with numerous applications, and also

---

hitherto not suggested to be *soma*), and *Peganum harmala*.

415. This proposition was also revived by NARANJO (1997:178) in 1967. It is also endorsed, following FLATTERY and SCHWARZ, by RUDGLEY (1998:53) and MYERS (2011:138–141).

416. GNOLI (1989; 1993) is unconvinced of the thesis in general and also of several propositions made in this publication: among them, although acknowledging the possible connection of the Avestan term *spə̄nta* ('sacred') with *sepand*, a Persian term for rue, he sees no necessary connection between *sepand* and *haoma*; nor is he convinced by the authors' arguments for the evolution from the original sauma rite to what is historically known as the *haoma* rite, and the consequent change to the use of non-psychoactive substances.

417. FLATTERY and SCHWARZ (1989:117) maintain that the seeded pomegranate, currently used in Zoroastrian ritual, has replaced rue, as a substitute.

418. Jewish brides in Israel put rue in their hair and bridegrooms put it in their clothes to ward off evil spirits (DROWER 1956:86). The ancient Egyptians and Assyrians probably used rue; certainly, later, the Copts, around 2,000 years ago, used it as a medicine, primarily to treat skin diseases, worms and "sick testicles" (MANNICHE 1999:145).

419. Detailed in several publications, SHERRATT maintains that globally and for specific reasons 'smoking' culture generally preceded 'drinking' culture (mostly of alcohol but also of opium and other psychoactive plants); the switch occurred during or after the late Bronze Age.

420. DIOSCORIDES (3.51–54) (2000:423–428) records several, similar medical applications for rue. The mountain or wild varieties are said to be referred to as *moly* by Cappadocians and others.

as one of the main ingredients of antidotes (*Natural History* 20.153).[421]

Concerning the effects of Syrian rue (*Peganum harmala*), FURST (1976:44) remarks that although known to Arab physicians since antiquity for its intoxicating potential,[422] and despite its wide geographical spread[423]—in the Mediterranean and central Asia, and having several close relatives in the south-western United States and Mexico—so far as is known it has never been employed hallucinogenically.[424] Syrian rue contains almost equal quantities of the alkaloids harmine and harmaline, and tetrahyrdroharmine (THH), which are β-carboline derivatives, belonging to a class of compounds that act as monoamine oxidase inhibitors (MAOIs: see below).[425]

In a pioneering study, NARANJO (1973:119–169) conducted psychotherapeutic sessions with thirty volunteers in 1964 to test the effects of harmaline. The drug is described by NARANJO as

---

421. As with many other medicinal plants used in Greek and Roman society, rue was often infused in wine.

422. PLINY (*Natural History* 20.51) remarks that: "An overdose of this juice [from rue] possesses poisonous qualities... Strangely enough, it is neutralized by the juice of hemlock... whether given in food or in drink [rue also works] against poisonous fungi". In these observations, PLINY may be correct, as atropine (which is in hemlock) works as an antidote to muscarine poisoning (SHEPARD 2005:3.2.3).

423. Rue is a relatively common plant in South Asia (NYBERG 1997:389). Also, it was introduced into Texas and quickly, by 1938, had become established in the region (DEKORNE *et al.* 2002:14). It is now native not only in New Mexico but also further north in southern Arizona and parts of Nevada (MOORE 1989:120). It is a hardy plant that can take over other vegetation if planted in the same area (TURNER 1994:60). This is an objection that has been raised against it being *soma*: the texts say that *soma* is rare and from the mountains; and when unavailable, substitutes were used. STAAL (2001:764) sees the abundance of mountain rue as the most serious objection to this plant being *soma*.

424. Commenting on the rue thesis of FLATTERY and SCHWARZ, OTT (1996a:203–204) remarks: "The reader of the... book finishes with an empty feeling... where is the evidence, from the authors' own experimentation (if necessary), that *Peganum harmala* is a visionary plant?"

425. See OTT (1996a:204–206, 223–231) for a history of the discovery and chemistry of harmine and harmaline; see BEYER (2010:216) for a summary. R. H. F. MANSKE and associates were the first to synthesize harmine and harmaline, in 1927 (STAFFORD 1977:263).

'oneirophrenic' (dream-inducing):[426] "[The] effect on most subjects is that of eliciting vivid, dream-like sequences, which may be contemplated while awake with closed eyes, without loss of contact with the environment or alterations of thinking" (p.3). Harmaline induces a state of relaxation and a tendency to withdraw from the environment, to keep eyes closed, and to want all noises and sounds to be kept to a minimum (p.120). It lowers blood pressure and may also induce sleep.[427] NARANJO found the benefit of harmaline to lie primarily in allowing psychotherapeutic access to unconscious processes and imagery. Although most studies have concluded that harmine and harmaline do not elicit psychedelic experience,[428] there is, however, some evidence that large doses of harmaline, even though liable to cause nausea and vomiting, can produce visionary experience that could almost be classified as psychedelic (BEYER 2010:209, 217).[429]

---

426. For more information on oneirogenic/oneirophrenic plants and compounds, and the subtle distinction, in effect, between these and psychedelic/ entheogenic agents, see TORO and THOMAS (2007).
427. See also GRINSPOON and BAKALAR (1998:15) for a summary of the effects of harmala alkaloids.
428. Reports of the effects of self-administration of harmine (the effects of which are not consistent) are of relaxation and withdrawal, dizziness, nausea, ataxia, an increase in belligerence, fleeting sensations of lightness, mild sedation at low doses and unpleasant neurological effects at higher doses (BEYER 2010:215). OTT (2011:107) remarks that plants containing harmine find ethnomedical use on three or four continents, and always as sedatives or hypnotics. DEKORNE (2011:146) comments: "Harmine/harmaline is said to effect hallucinosis at highly toxic levels, but in less heroic quantities is at best a tranquilizer, at worst an emetic". In the context of around 4,000 psychedelic therapy sessions that he conducted, Leo ZEFF similarly remarks (STOLAROFF 2004:86) that, "It takes a helluva lot to turn on [with harmaline] and you get so God-damned sick if you took enough to turn on that it's horrible. We take it with acid or psilocybin and it puts a new dimension on the acid trip". TURNER (1994:61) comments: "the Harmala experience by itself is quite mild, although some acquaintances of mine have obtained full psychedelic effects from Syrian Rue by consuming small amounts over the course of a day to circumvent the nausea". TURNER also provides accounts (pp.62–72) of the significant potentiating effect of rue when used with other psychedelics.
429. See also JAY (1999:85ff.) for personal accounts of psychedelic bioassays with rue.

For intoxication with *Peganum harmala*,[430] it is usually the angular, red/brown seeds that are used[431] as they have the highest content of harmaline and harmine. These are usually boiled before being crushed, producing a reddish extrusion.[432] A problem with the mountain rue thesis is that neither in the *Avesta* or the *Veda*s is *soma/haoma* mentioned as being seeds: rather, it is consistently referred to in both sets of texts as what seems to be fibrous twigs or stalks or stems.[433] Nor is any mention made of 'cooking' *soma/haoma*; and in Vedic rites *soma* is the only oblation that is specifically not cooked, burnt or boiled (HILLEBRANDT 1980, Vol. 1:327; STAAL 2001:764). Nevertheless, it is well-known to anyone who has investigated ayahuasca that if *Peganum harmala*—which is rich in harmine and harmaline (which are monoamine oxidase inhibitors)—is mixed with any of the dozens of plants now known to contain *N,N*-dimethyl-tryptamine (DMT),[434] then a powerful ayahuasca-like psychedelic agent can be produced.[435]

Given the references referred to earlier of *soma/haoma* probably being a stalk or vine of some kind, then it might seem improbable that the 'original' *soma* described in the *Veda*s and *Avesta* used was rue (if indeed there ever was an 'original' *soma*). However, it seems

---

430. See SHULGIN and SHULGIN (1997:302ff.) for a detailed account of the effects of different doses of *Peganum harmala* (also in combination with DMT and other substances). See FLATTERY and SCHWARZ (1989:31ff., 148) on dosages, the geographical distribution, the preparation and the strength of the various parts of the rue plant, and its varieties, including *Peganum nigellastrum* and *Ruta graveolens* (garden rue). *Ruta graveolens* is native to India (NADKARNI 1998:344) and is the partially cultivated variety of the wild *Peganum harmala*, which was introduced into the near-East from Greek territory.

431. Also, thick smoke from burning seeds is inhaled; this is also mentioned in classical Persian poetry (FLATTERY and SCHWARZ 1989:47).

432. This red liquid is used as dye in the Middle East, particularly for carpets.

433. This point is also made by NYBERG (1997:390).

434. FLATTERY also comments (p.100n.5) that an admixture with other plants is particularly efficacious with harmel; and that several *Desmodium* species are rich in DMT, which is confirmed independently by several investigators (see also below; accessed 13/12/2013): http://wiki.dmt-nexus.me/w/index.php?title=Desmodium_gangeticum&oldid=5376, http://www.psychonaut.com/dmt/42497-plantes-et-dmt.html, http://www.drugs-forum.com/forum/showthread.php?t=33229

435. See DEKORNE *et al.* (2002) and OTT (2006) for copious information on this topic.

possible that rue was effectively used either as a main or an alternative source of MAOI in the ancient world,[436] as rue is one of the plants called *hōm* in Central Asia, and it has related names in India.[437] Also, earlier in this book the manufacture and consumption of a rue-based form of ayahuasca in current use by Qalandar Sūfīs in Iran was reported, illustrating the possibility that this formula was in use in ancient times, as far back as the Bronze Age. However, the practicality and effectiveness of the 'cold pressing' of rue and a plant containing DMT needs further investigation.

Ephedra is also referred to as *hōm* in Central Asia, and, as previously discussed, there is considerable evidence of its ancient use and veneration; it has been found present besides numerous Bronze Age mummies. Ephedra is apparently synergistic with rue (DEKORNE *et al.* 2002:18), though I have been unable to determine whether or not a combination of ephedra and rue is potentially entheogenic;[438] it may be, but it seems unlikely in my view that ephedra was a primary ingredient in an ancient formula for *soma/haoma.* PENDELL (2010b:129) comments:

> Nor should *Ephedra* be combined with MAOIs…Tests combining ephedrine with moclobemide, a reversible monoamine oxidase-A inhibitor, found a two to four-fold potentiation of ephedrine's effect on blood pressure, and a 0.6 potentiation of ephedrine's effect on heart rate. The most common adverse reactions were palpitations and headache.

However, PENDELL later suggests (2010b:133–141) that, specifically because of the stimulatory effects of ephedra, the combination of ephedra and rue may have been a formula for *soma/haoma.* I am doubtful; nevertheless, it seems amply conceivable that relatively small amounts of ephedra could have been one of the plants added to entheogenic concoctions, to boost the wakefulness of consumers.

---

436. BARBER (1990:164) endorses a suggestion by FLATTERY and SCHWARZ that *haoma* may have been rue, mixed with ephedra to keep the consumer awake.

437. NANDKARNI (1954:1081) lists *somarayen* as one of the names for *Ruta graveolens* in Malayali; and *somalatā* in Sanskrit.

438. There are claims that ephedrine can act as an MAOI (see below); however, although ephedra can potentiate DMT and other psychedelics (having MAOI-like effects), it is not an MAOI *per se* (DEKORNE *et al.* 2002:25). ROBINSON (1968:132) also comments that compounds such as cocaine and ephedrine inhibit MAO *in vitro*, but their familiar pharmacological properties probably have nothing to do with this.

CHAPTER 13

Many plants are *soma/haoma*

Perhaps there have been clues to the botanical identity of *soma/haoma* since research and investigation first began. Consider taking botanical terms in the languages of local people in Asia, both now and historically, at face value. A number of the propositions for plants being *soma* discussed so far are called *soma/haoma/hum/hom* and the like by local people. Indeed it is the linguistic evidence that has in some publications been an element in several of the cases that have been made for *soma* being: ephedra (by FALK and others); Syrian rue (by FLATTERY and SCHWARZ); and cannabis, by some supporters of this thesis. BENNETT (2010:542–548; SILVER 1979:258–259) reprints an article from an edition of the *New York Herald* from March 15th 1895, entitled 'Orgies of the Hemp Eaters',[439] which describes the revelries of "Nosairiyeh tribesmen" (sic)[440] in the small town of Latakieh in north-western Syria. Significantly, they refer to the *bhāṃg* that they ritually consume (together with alcohol) every full moon as *hom.* I would suggest that none of the propositions for ephedra, rue or cannabis is wrong; nor, in a way, is the proposition of those who see a '*soma* function' and not even a specific plant.

As noted previously, the root √*su/hu* indicates 'something pressed'. It seems feasible that ephedra, rue and cannabis, which have been discussed, and several other plants (some of which have been mentioned) were all pressed at one time or another as constituents of a *soma* concoction, in different recipes and combinations that varied over time and location, depending on the local (or possibly very distant) availability of psychoactive plants.

---

439. Chris BENNETT kindly supplied me with publication details for this article.
440. At a guess, this refers to a sect of Nasiriyya Sūfīs.

Perhaps proponents of the ephedra, rue and cannabis propositions are all correct to an extent. I suggest that *soma* was, in most instances, a mixture of plants that was always sufficiently potent to produce an entheogenic trip; that's **the** reason for the superlative praise and adoration for its deific and salvic properties. The designation of the name *soma* to a plant may indicate that the plant (or a part or an infusion of it) can indeed be (and was historically) used in the production of an entheogenic concoction; that's how so many plants acquired the same name *soma/haoma*. Perhaps a suitable translation of *soma/haoma* might simply be (a potential) 'entheogen'.

Even the identifications as *soma* of the non-psychoactive *Asclepiad* vines such as *Sarcostemma brevistigma*, which is referred to, amongst other names, as *soma* (NADKARNI 1954:1106), may possibly not be incorrect; though this is pure speculation. *Vernonia anthelmintica* (purple fleabane), which has several medicinal applications (HUA *et al.* 2012), is called *somarāja*, amongst other names (NADKARNI 1954:1267);[441] and several other plants with medicinal uses are also called *soma* or the like in Sanskrit or other South Asian languages.[442] *Sarcostemma brevistigma* and other plants

441. It was noted previously that this plant was proposed to be *soma* by both COLEBROOK and VOIGT.

442. A Sanskrit name of the rare tree *Ficus dalhousiae* (Dalhousi's ficus) is *somavalkhom* (NADKARNI 1954:548). This tree has many medicinal properties and contains alkaloids (PRANUTHI *et al.* 2014:58). The Sanskrit names of the creeper *Cocculus cordifolius* include *somavallī* and *amṛta*. Among the many medicinal properties of *Cocculus cordifolius* are its effect as an aphrodisiac and a tonic (NADKARNI 1954:356). SRIVASTAVA (1966:812–816) provides a list of plants called *soma, somavallī, somalatā, sum, hum* and the like in Indian medical texts, including (besides the plants already discussed) *Ipomoea muricata* (a species of the morning glory creeper, which contains lysergic acid amide: see below), *Centella asiatica, Cocculus hirsutus, Crinum latifolium, Fraxinus floribunda, Paederia foetida, Polyalthia cerasoides, Psoralea corylifolia, Sarcopetalum tomentosum [?], Setaria glauca, Caesalpinia crista, Piper chaba, Thespesia lampas,* and *Vitis vinifera.* Relatively little is known about the medicinal (and possibly psychoactive) properties of about half of these plants. VALIATHAN (2003:596) records, perhaps mistakenly, *somavalka* as *Acacia polyantha* Willd. *Acacia polyantha* A. Spreng, of the *Mimosaceae* family, is synonymous with *Albizia inundata* Mart. (= *Cathormion polyanthum* A. Spreng) (IPNI). However, this tree is native to South America. Interestingly, its leaves contain DMT.

not so far recorded as having psychoactive properties have in recent times been pressed on their own by brahmans to make *soma*, but known, however, to be without effect by those who drink these concoctions.[443] Nevertheless, I would suggest that it behoves us to be open-minded to the possibility that any plant referred to in Asian languages as *soma/haoma* may at one time or another have been an additive to (or even a prime constituent of) a *soma* concoction; though it is also probable that some plants called *soma* have no connection to an original entheogenic preparation, as local misidentifications and naming of plants may well have been erroneous; and, of course, that particular plants have medicinal properties or contain one or several of the approximately 5,000 known alkaloids[444]—which are best known for their pharmacological effects, and which occur in between approximately ten to twenty percent of all plants—provides no evidence *per se* that they are potentially psychoactive, as practically every plant has some medicinal uses, and some contain alkaloids that are not evidently psychoactive. However, even though the individual plants or trees themselves may have little or no psychoactive effect when consumed on their own, the potential psychoactive synergy of plants mentioned here that are called *soma* with other psychoactive plants remains largely unexplored in many instances. It is worth recalling that research into the presence of DMT in many species of reed and grass only properly began in the 1990s, resulting in surprises for both chemists and botanists.

Looking at the *soma/haoma* discussion from a purely linguistic perspective, it is also apparent that some of the other plants proposed to be *soma* are not referred to as *soma* in local languages, in the regions where the plant grows, or in wider language communities: it is only modern researchers who have thought that one or another of the dozens of proposed plants is '*soma*', even if it is not called that

443. See KUMAR *et al.* (2007) for the alkaloid content and biological effects of extractions of *Sarcostemma brevistigma.*

444. Alkaloids nearly always contain nitrogen and are usually but not always colourless, crystalline solids. Higher plants are the chief sources of alkaloids, but they also occur in club mosses, horsetails and some fungi. Around 7,000 species of plants are known to contain alkaloids (SCHULTES and HOFMANN 1980:21).

in any Asian language. This could count as evidence against some of these propositions.

If we are seeking an entheogenic concoction in ancient Asia, it seems most probably to have depended, as a main base, on plant concoctions similar in chemistry to that of ayahuasca, but with many possible additives. OTT (2006:25–28) categorizes 100 additives to native Amazonian ayahuasca concoctions; it could have been similar in Asia. OTT (2006:18–19) also discusses stimulants such as *guaraná* and coca that are added by some groups to their ayahuasca concoctions. It could have been similar in Asia, where ephedra stalks or other plants containing ephedrine could have been added to an ayahuasca analogue. In a similar comparison, in recent times, while one branch of the Santo Daime church in Brazil (see below and Appendix 4) approves the use of cannabis during ayahuasca rituals as an additive to the experience, another branch of the same church disapproves of its use. It seems entirely feasible that such kinds of variation obtained in the ancient world, particularly considering that the use of *soma* may have continued for a thousand years or more across much of central Asia. *Soma/haoma* was never a single plant or we would have found it by now. It was many plants, some of which are yet to be definitively analyzed for potentially psychoactive properties.

There seems to be a hint of the multiplicity of *soma*s in the *Ṛgveda* (9.65.23): "(May the Somas) which are in Ārjīka, Kṛtva or in the middle of rivers (or homesteads), or among the five peoples (be beneficial to us)".[445] Also in the *Veda*s there are other seemingly incompatible references to *soma* if *soma* was but a single plant. For example, *ṚV* 10.94.3.3 refers to, "chewing the twig of the red (Soma) tree". "Soma is released from all woods even dry" (10.89.5.4). *Soma* is even said to be in all plants/herbs (*sarvā oṣadhīḥ*) (10.97.7). As noted previously, in the *Atharvaveda* (19.39.5–6, 8) *soma* is mentioned in connection with the *aśvattha* (peepal) tree and the *kuṣṭha* plant.[446] The *kuṣṭha* plant is revered in the highest terms in the *Atharvaveda* (5.4): it is from the hills and is a remedy against *takman* (v.1);[447] it is descended from the gods, as *soma*'s benign

445. Trans. KASHYAP (also below).

446. Referred to in Chapter 4, being either a kind of ginger or snow lotus.

447. A disease that is accompanied by skin problems, probably leprosy.

friend (v.7); it is a powerful healing plant (v.10); it comes from the snowy mountains. The gods won the *kuṣṭha* plant in the third heaven—at their seat, the *aśvattha* (peepal)—and brought it in a golden ship (6.95); it is the flower of immortality (v.2);[448] it is the best of plants (19.39.4);[449] it cures all maladies and stands by the side of *soma* (19.39.5–8). Could *kuṣṭha* have been an additive plant to a *soma* concoction?[450]

---

448. *tatrāmṛtasya puṣpaṃ devāḥ kuṣṭhamavanvata.*

449. The *kuṣṭha* plant is also said to have two other names: *nadyamāra* and *nadyāriśaḥ* (*AV* 19.39.2), which both MONIER-WILLIAMS (p.525) and KAMAL (1988:16) interpret as *Costus speciosus* (wild ginger). However, HOERNLE (1893:22 [part I, v.97]) translates *kuṣṭha* as *Saussurea auriculate* (snow lotus). Perhaps there is a possibility (though this is speculation) that instead of wild ginger *kuṣṭha* is aromatic ginger, *Kaempferia galanga*, also of the ginger family (*Zingiberaceae*), as *kuṣṭha* is said to be aromatic (KAMAL 1988:17). *K. galanga* is a particularly fragrant plant that is more common in south-east Asia, but which also grows in India, where it is known as *candramūlika/candramūla* (SINGH 2006:185). It is used in Papua New Guinea to induce visions and dreams (THOMAS 2000:39–40) and is also reported to be used in the Fore region as a hallucinogen (RUDGLEY 1999:175). However, the psychoactive properties of this plant are generally weak (it is sold as a cooking ingredient in some Chinese food shops in the UK and elsewhere); perhaps some indigenous varieties are more potent. SCHULTES and HOFMANN (1980:323) comment that, "Phytochemical corroboration of any hallucinogenic or other properties of *Kaempferia galanga* is wholly lacking, but few if any investigations have been carried out on this species". Subsequent to this publication, *K. galanga* was tested and found to have strong MAOI properties (NORO *et al.* 1983), comparable to pharmaceutical drugs formerly used in the treatment of depression: isocarboxazid, phenelzine, and tranylcypromine (TORO and THOMAS 2007:46). This adds a slight probability to the notion that the plant may possibly have been an additive to (or, in some preparations, an essential ingredient of) *soma* concoctions.

450. Also praised similarly in the *Atharvaveda* (5.5), as a powerful healing plant, is the *silācī* plant (also referred to as Arundhatī and Kānīna), which seems to be a creeper (v.3). Interestingly (but I am uncertain whether or not this is of any significance), *silācī* is said (v.5) to spring from the *plakṣa, aśvattha, parṇa, nyagrodha, dhava* and *khadira*. As discussed in Chapter 4, the first four of these trees are stated in the *Brāhmaṇas* to be *soma* substitutes. *Khadira* (Hindi *khair*) is *Acacia catechu* (which has several medicinal uses and is also used for gum); *dhava* is the shrub *Grislea tomentosa*. KAMAL (1988:29) identifies *silācī* as *Boswellia glabra/serrata* (Indian frankincense), but this seems to be unlikely because *Boswellia glabra* is a medium-sized

FLATTERY and SCHWARZ (1989:73–75) do not believe ephedra to be the original *haoma*, though claim, as suggested above, that it may well have been an archaic additive to the extract. As mentioned previously, in the *Avesta* (*Y* 10.12, 17) *haoma* is said to be "of many kinds"[451] (BOYCE 1975:158); the word *haoma* frequently appears in the *Avesta* in the plural.[452] Concerning the constituents of *haoma*, BOYCE (2001:5) remarks that, "The ritual offering to the waters at the end of the *yasna* was prepared from milk, the leaves of one plant and the juice obtained from pounding the stems of another. The pounded plant was called in Sanskrit 'soma', in Avestan 'haoma', a name which means simply 'that which is pressed'".

In Chapter 4 were discussed several substitute plants that are referred to in the *Brāhmaṇa*s, and also the *uśānā* plant and *dharba/ kuśa* grass, which are all identified as *soma*. If the suggestion of linguistic clues is correct, then these plants may contain the requisite chemicals to produce, in combination with other plants, an ayahuasca analogue concoction.

Relevant to the foregoing proposition about *soma* being an ayahuasca-like concoction—with plants containing DMT and MAOI as 'basic' ingredients, to which other plants could have been added, to enhance, boost or modify the concoction—an article on the preparation of two kinds of *amṛta* concoctions, detailed in a 6th-century CE Kashmiri text,[453] is quite apposite. LEONTI and CASU (2014) discuss the so-called 'Bower Manuscript',[454] which was

---

deciduous tree. I have been unable to identify *silācī*, but could it possibly also have been a *soma* additive plant?

451. "There on those mountains you grow up, Haoma of many kinds, with milk, golden" (*Y* 10.12); "I praise all the Haomas which are on the mountain tops, which are in the depths of the valleys" (*Y* 10.17, trans. JOSEPHSON). There are also other references to (plural) *haoma*s in the *Avesta*: *Y* 3.3; *Y* 4.1, 3, *Y* 27.6; and in the *Visparad* (MILLS 1887): 9.1; 11.1, 2; 12.1, 2.

452. STAAL (2001:763) comments that he was baffled to learn that there were many *haoma*s in Iran. WEZLER (2001:198) remarks that it is perhaps necessary to assume that, "the term *soma* denoted different plants at different periods in the history, and the prehistory, of the Aryans after and before their migration to Iran or the Punjab".

453. HOERNLE (1909:887), however, who translated this text, dates it to the third quarter of the 4th century CE.

454. The manuscript, a collection of seven texts (by four authors) on separate leaves, is in one of the several variants of the Gupta script. It is the oldest-

discovered by Lieutenant Hamilton BOWER in 1890 in an ancient Buddhist *stūpa* by the river Kashgar on the Silk Road near the town of Kuchar in Eastern Turkestan (China), north of Takla Makan. It comprises texts in partly ungrammatical Sanskrit written on birch-bark leaves. Amongst the many recipes in the texts there are two of particular interest in the context of elixirs. One is for '*amṛta* (immortality) *prāśa* (food) *ghī* (clarified butter)'[455] and the other is for '*amṛta* oil', which are specified as panaceas and also as medicines to treat nervous disorders; together they contain around 100 herbal ingredients.

LEONTI and CASU observe that exhilarating effects are not described but believe that the presence of both DMT and MAOIs (the basis of ayahuasca; see below) in several of the constituent plants of the concoctions would, nevertheless, produce exhilarating effects. They propose that this formula, probably in a stronger form (or dose), was the basis of the *soma* of the *Veda*s, but comment (p.378) that, "Notably, the recipes do not contain any clear indication regarding the dose at which the mixtures should be applied for the treatment of the various health conditions and purposes for which they are recommended". Perhaps it needs no mention, but even potentially potent psychedelic agents can, of course, be taken in light doses for a variety of medicinal or recreational purposes.

Having detailed the dozens of plant ingredients for these two *amṛta* potions (a few of which remain botanically unidentified), LEONTI and CASU provide the botanical details and chemistry of six kinds of plants, which occur in both formulas for *amṛta*. All plants are native to South Asia and known to have psychoactive properties: 1. *Desmodium gangeticum (Fabaceae),* 2. *Mucuna pruriens (Fabaceae),* 3. *Nelumbo nucifera (Nelumbonaceae),* 4. *Sida rhombifolia, Sida spinosa* and *Sida cordifolia (Malvaceae),* 5. *Tabernaemontana divaricata (Apoynaceae),* and 6. *Tinospora cordifolia (Menispermaceae)*. LEONTI and CASU comment (p.382) that for many of the other species of plants mentioned in the *amṛta*

---

known, original medical treatise, translated into English by Rudolph HOERNLE (1841–1918) in the early 20th century.

455. HOERNLE (2011:90n.55) states that this particular formula appears also in *Caraka Saṃhitā* (VI, 16, l.22ff.), in *Aṣṭāṅga Hṛdaya* (IV, 3, vv.93b–100) in a somewhat expanded form, and in contracted form in *Vaṅgasena* (XI, vv.38–43) and *Bhāva Prakāśa* (II, 2). In the latter the minor ingredients are altered.

recipes, no or only scarce phytochemical and pharmacological data exist.

Desmodium gangeticum is commonly known as *śālaparṇī* (in Sanskrit); it is also referred to as *amśumatī*,[456] which can mean 'rich in *soma* juice' (ROTH 1881:684n.1). Besides other local names, it is also called '*soma*' and is associated with *soma* rites. Another of its names (in Ayurveda) is *saumya* (TROUT 2004a:11), which may (or may not) simply refer to its 'cooling' capacity. The Indian variety of *Desmodium gangeticum* (= *Hedysarum gangeticum*) is rich in both DMT and 5-MeO-DMT,[457] the significance of which lies in the manufacture of ayahuasca,[458] which is further explored in the following chapter. There are many plant sources of DMT and 5-MeO-DMT, which are powerfully psychedelic, but these chemicals, even if consumed in large quantities, remain ineffective, as previously mentioned, unless combined with a monoamine-oxidase inhibitor (MAOI), which allows DMT to flood the brain for several hours.

Mucuna pruriens (Bengal velvet bean/cowhage) is another plant that contains, besides other alkaloids, both DMT and 5-MeO-DMT (in trace amounts),[459] which are found in the seeds, leaves and roots (GHOSAL *et al.* 1971; TROUT 2002:122). This annual plant, which grows throughout the Indian plains, is known in Sanskrit as *kappicacchu* or *ātmaguptā*. Besides other uses, it is used in Ayurvedic

456. Another synonym is *dīrgamūlā* (several other plants are known by this name: MW:482).

457. SHULGIN and SHULGIN (1997:268) describe *Desmodium gangeticum* as, "the classic model, with DMT and 5-MeO-DMT and their two N-oxides as the defining components of the leaf, the stem, and the root". Assays were also conducted by TROUT (2004a:9) with identical results. *Śālaparṇī* is a plant used widely in Ayurvedic medicine for treatment as an anti-asthmatic, anti-oxidant, anthelmintic, anti-inflammatory, for diarrhoea, fever, and as an analgesic (KIRTIKAR and BASU 1984, Vol. 1:758–759). Without being combined with an MAO inhibitor, no effect from DMT would be noticed (see below); however, *D. gangeticum* also contains traces of β-carbolines (LEONTI and CASU 2014:378). Harmine and harmaline are β-carbolines and function as MAOIs in ayahuasca (see below). TROUT (2004a:9) remarks (without a reference) that FLATTERY has suggested that *soma* could have been an analogue of ayahuasca made from *śālaparṇī* and *Peganum harmala* (Syrian rue).

458. *Aya huasca* means 'vine of the soul'/'vine of the dead'.

459. It also contains, in small amounts, nicotine, serotonin, bufotenin, and β-carboline.

medicine to treat Parkinson's disease.[460] This is effective owing to the presence in the plant of L-DOPA,[461] a psychoactive chemical, which is nowadays manufactured in pure form as a drug to treat the disease.

Regarding *Nelumbo nucifera* (the lotus plant), the chemistry of this plant was referred to in Chapter 9. The main psychoactive properties of this plant are more opiate-like than stimulant. However, there may be beneficial effects from adding this plant to an entheogenic (or ayahuasca-like) concoction.

The three *Sida* species considered by LEONTI and CASU have a worldwide distribution. *Sida/Sidona rhombifolia* (arrowleaf sida) and *Sida cordifolia* (flannel weed/country mallow) are known, respectively, as *atibala* and *mahābala* in Sanskrit.[462] *Sida rhombifolia* has a variety of medicinal uses, primarily for nervous, urinary and venereal diseases. Significantly, all three *Sida* species (*rhombifolia, spinosa,* and *cordifolia*) contain the stimulant ephedrine, besides other alkaloids (including tryptamines).

The fifth plant detailed by LEONTI and CASU is *Tabernaemontana divaricata* (pinwheel flower/crape jasmine/East India rosebay), the roots of which are used in Ayurvedic medicine as an anthelmintic, for eye diseases, as an analgesic, and as a treatment for scabies. Known as *cāndnī* or *tagar* in Hindi, in Sanskrit it is called *nandīvṛkṣa*[463] or *nata*. A total of forty-two different alkaloids have been identified in this plant. Interestingly, one of these is ibogaine. In

460. It is used in Indian folk medicine against snakebites. The hairs of the seed pods cause extreme itching.

461. = L-3-4-dihydroxyphenylalanine. This chemical is a precursor for neurotransmitters in the brain, namely adrenaline, noradrenaline and dopamine. Too large a dose can result in toxic psychosis, palpitations and headache (LEONTI and CASU 2014:382). Use of this drug, which works by increasing the brain's depleted levels of dopamine, was initially pioneered by the British neurologist Andrew LEES in the 1970s. Initial enthusiasm was tempered by subsequent instances of unwanted symptoms of delusions and hallucinations in some patients (LEES 2016:23–27, 48–49).

462. *Pandanus Database of Indian Plants* records for this plant the Hindi names *barelā* or *lālbarelā*; LEONTI and CASU (2014:379) also provide the Hindi names *bariara, kareta* and *bhundli*, none of which is attested in any dictionary consulted. However, *balā* is attested, in Hindi (WAGENAAR 1996), for *Sida acuta.*

463. This name also refers to several other plants (MW:527).

one assay by BAU *et al.* (2013), from 42 grams of alkaloidal fraction 50 mgs of ibogaine were obtained, as were a number of other ibogaine-type alkaloids. It may be recalled that the iboga plant was referred to in Chapter 8 as an entheogenic plant with religious use in West Africa.

Tinospora cordifolia (heart-leaved moonseed) grows throughout India. Known usually as *giloy* in Hindi, it contains several alkaloids and has a number of medicinal uses (SINHA *et al.* 2004), including for diabetes, peptic ulcer and hepatitis. In Sanskrit, amongst other names, it is referred to as *maduparṇi* (HOERNLE 2011:73), *guḍūcī*, *somavallī* and *amṛta* (NADKARNI 1954:1220;); in Ayurvedic medicine its most common name is *amṛta* (DASH and KASHYAP 1980:67). Significantly, present in *Tinospora cordifolia* are jatrorrhizine, berberine and palmatine,[464] all of which, individually, have been demonstrated to be MAO-inhibitors (both MAO-A and MAO-B):[465] "Therefore, synergistic MAOI-I effects can be expected [from] a protoberberine-rich *Tinospora cordifolia* extract" (LEONTI and CASU 2014:283).

LEONTI and CASU conclude, in Section 8.4 (The MAO-I 'Ayahusca-hypothesis') that, taking into account both the qualitative

464. Two aporphine glycocides have also been isolated from the plant. Apomorphine, which can be derived from aporphine, is used to treat Parkinson's disease. LEONTI and CASU (2014:382) note that aporphine is chemically closely related to magnoflorine, which is present in *Tinospora cordifolia*, and that aporphine has considerable affinity with the neurotransmitters dopamine and serotonin. The alkaloids berberine and palmatine have been found to interact with the 5-HT_2 receptor. The specific effects of some of the alkaloids in this plant on the brain (and mind) are currently uncertain.

465. Monoamine oxidases are a family of enzymes found in the brain, gut, liver and other tissues; they catalyze the oxidation and inactivation of monoamine neurotransmitters, including serotonin, noradrenaline and dopamine, which are important in the regulation of mood. There are two kinds of MAO: MAO-A and MAO-B. MAO-A is found primarily in the intestine and in the regions of the brain that have serotonin, norepinephrine, dopamine and tyramine substrates; MAO-B is found primarily in platelets and in the regions of the brain that are rich in dopaminergic neurons. Drugs that suppress MAO-A in the brain have been used as anti-depressants since the 1950s, though these drugs remain far longer in the system than plant-based sources. MAO inhibitors inhibit the MAO enzyme, thereby allowing serotonin, norepinephrine and dopamine to accumulate in the synapse (CULPEPPER 2013:3).

and phytochemical profiles of the plants discussed, a psychoactive potion could most probably be obtained by making a concentrated MAOI juice of *Tinospora cordifolia* with either *Desmodium gangeticum* (which contains DMT) and/or a *Sida* sp. extract, which in a high dose could engender psychedelic visions. They comment that the alkaloid content of particularly *Tinospora cordifolia* and *Desmodium gangeticum* is considerable. The combination of *Tinospora cordifolia* with a species of *Sida* would produce more of a stimulant, amphetamine-like effect, owing to the presence of ephedrine; whereas a combination of *Tinospora cordifolia* with *Desmodium gangeticum,* with less of a *Sida* species, would also be psychedelic but less stimulant.[466] The combination of these plants with the others containing alkaloids including ibogaine (in *Tabernaemontana divaricata*) and nuciferine (in *Nelumbo nucifera*) would produce a concoction with heightened effects. However, the interactive and cumulative effect of the combination of all these alkaloids together in the concoctions detailed by LEONTI and CASU remains to be explored.

LEONTI and CASU also remark (p.384) that besides the plants specified above, other plants specified in the recipes for the *amṛta* potions may have as yet unidentified psychoactive properties.[467] In

466. LEONTI and CASU (p.384) also warn of the potentially dangerous toxicity of MAOIs, when taken in combination with particular foods or other substances.

467. BHAVABHAṬṬA (9th century), who comments on the *Cakrasamvaratantra* (ch.1), an 8th-century Tantric Buddhist text, remarks (GRAY 2007:160n.20) that the *soma* beverage of the brahmans, which is placed on a tawny cowhide at the time of sacrifice, is the sap of the *kāliṅga* creeper (*kāliṅgalatārasaṃ*). *Kāliṅga* is usually identified as the Conessi tree or as Tellicherry bark, also known as *kuṭaja* in Sanskrit (*kurcī/kuḍā* in Hindi), which is *Holarrhena antidysenterica* (Wall.), a deciduous shrub or tree with white flowers, which grows all over India. Other Sanskrit synonyms include *mallikā puṣpa, giri mallikā, vatsaka, koṭī vṛkṣaka,* and *śakra bhūraha* (DASH and KASHYAP 1980:465). Particularly the bark and the seeds of this tree have aphrodisiac and also numerous medicinal properties (it enjoyed a period of repute in Europe), but it is not a creeper or a vine (*latā*), so it may be that BHAVABHAṬṬA is referring to another plant. *Kāliṅga* is also known as 'Indra's tree/food' and is fabled to have sprung from drops of *amṛta,* which fell to the ground from the bodies of Rāma's monkeys, which were restored to life by Indra (*Pandanus Database of Plants*). My hunch is that it may contain either DMT or an MAOI, as *kuṭaja* is one of the plants used in this formula for *amṛta*

this regard it is interesting to see that included in the recipe for *amṛta* oil,[468] besides the plants detailed above and numerous others in the two recipes (some unidentified), are *udumbara* (*Ficus racemosa/glomerata*), *nyagrodha* (*Ficus indica*), *aśvattha* (*Ficus religiosa*), *plakṣa* (*Ficus infectoria*), the roots of *kuśa* (*Desmostachya bipinnata*) and several other kinds of common grasses.[469] It may be recalled that in Chapter 4 these four species of *Ficus* (*udumbara, nyagrodha, aśvattha* and *plakṣa*)[470] are all referred to in various *Brāhmana*s as *soma* 'substitutes'. The possibility that *kuśa* and other grasses are potential sources of DMT is explored in the next chapter. As far as I have been able to discover, no assays on these species of *Ficus* have been conducted specifically to determine whether or not they contain alkaloids that could act as MAOIs. Tests that were conducted at the Royal Botanical Gardens at Kew in London[471] on samples of peepal and banyan failed to reveal either harmine or harmaline; though tests for general MAOI potential have not yet been conducted.

The significance of the Bower Manuscript and its recipes for *amṛta* is that it demonstrates that 1,500 years ago in India there was sufficient botanical knowledge to combine plants containing MAOIs and DMT into an entheogenic concoction, even though in the current state of knowledge we cannot precisely determine the synergic effect of all of the ingredients specified in these texts, nor, as already mentioned, the intended doses. However, the *amṛta* recipes add considerable weight to the thesis being proposed in this book that *soma* was never a single plant, but a combination of plants, based on an ayahuasca-like formula, sufficient to produce an entheogenic effect; and that this combination most probably varied over time and depended on the availability of plants known to be potentially psychoactive.

(HOERNLE 2011:106). However, I have not yet found any report of analysis of this plant for potentially psychoactive properties.

468. Interestingly, in the recipe for the *ghī* kind of *amṛta* is included *kṣīravidārī/vidārī* (*Ipomoea digitata*). Several *Ipomoea* species contain lysergic acid amide (LSA: see below). I have been unable to find out whether or not this species of *Ipomoea* also contains LSA, which would be significant if that were the case.

469. *Kāsa* (*Saccharum spontaneum*, wild sugarcane), *ikṣu* (*Saccharum officinarum*, sugarcane), and *sara* (*Saccharum sara/bengalense*, tall cane).

470. These are, respectively, Indian/cluster fig, banyan, peepal, and wavy-leaf fig.

471. Melanie-Jayne HOWES very kindly arranged this test for me in January 2016.

CHAPTER 14

A renewed case for a psychedelic: ayahuasca

It is to the ayahuasca thesis for *soma/haoma* that we now turn. An endorsement by THOMPSON (2003) for the visionary nature of the Vedic passages was referred to in Chapter 5 of this book. He points out that FALK (1989) avoids the close association of *soma* with *mada* that is made in the *Veda*s. In the same vein, in relation to early Iranian religion, FLATTERY remarks (FLATTERY and SCHWARZ 1989:13–15, 113) that *Yasna*s 9–11 in the *Avesta* refer to *haoma* inducing *madha.* Although not at all conclusive, if *mada/madha* is taken to mean 'divine' (or entheogen) intoxication—and not just stimulation—then what must be considered is the possibility of psychedelic experience; though, as noted earlier, not all scholars agree with this. However, the only suggestion so far made for a 'properly' psychedelic plant was that of WASSON, a thesis found to be unsatisfactory for several reasons, which have been discussed.

FLATTERY (FLATTERY and SCHWARZ (1989:96–98, 145–147), commenting on *Yasna*s 8 and 11, maintains that the drinking of *haoma* was an 'ordeal'. *Yasna* 11 gives a warning that woeful consequences will befall anyone who attempts to resist the effect of the drug,[472] advice that is all too familiar to anyone experienced in the use of strong psychedelics. The priest (*zōt/zaotar*), following Zarathustra, should surrender his body to *haoma* and show himself to be a follower of Truth. *Haoma* was not taken casually to induce visions but used to gain information about the spiritual world. What could it be that produces visions of another realm through an ordeal of some kind after consuming a bitter drink?

---

472. "Quickly cut a share of the meat for the rapid Haoma so that Haoma will not bind you like he bound the scoundrel, Frangrasyan the Tur, in the middle third of the earth, encircled by iron [chains]" (*Y* 11.7, trans. JOSEPHSON).

TAILLIEU (2012) notices an indication[473] that *haoma* was pressed together with a plant called *hadhānaēpata*, which is a word of disputed meaning. He comments that, "In the known Zoroastrian rite a pomegranate twig is used, but this must be a substitute for the original plant". In the *Avesta* there are several references to the *hadhānaēpata*, nearly always in association with *haoma*, and propitiated with the same reverence.[474] The several Zoroastrian specialists who I have asked about this plant have no idea what *hadhānaēpata* is, apart from being "possibly" pomegranate, as these days pomegranate twig, leaf or root is used in the Avestan *yasna* liturgy when *hadhānaēpata* is called for. However, this identification is not accepted by FLATTERY and SCHWARZ (1989:76ff.). They point out that although *haδāna* means 'with seeds' or 'seedy', it cannot be pomegranate because *haδānaēpātā* (sic) is said in the *Avesta* to be not only an intoxicant but also incense, and pomegranate cannot be used for either of those purposes; nor is there any apparent reason why pomegranate should enjoy such an elevated status. *Haδānaēpātā* is apparently a soft wood (*Vīdēvdād* 14.2–3), unlike pomegranate, which is a hard, close-grained wood that is good for a slow-burning fire. *Haδānaēpātā* is left undefined and untranslated in the Pahlavi textual tradition and has no surviving cognates in later languages; its meaning was probably confined to the priestly class. FLATTERY and SCHWARZ do not venture an identification for this plant, but it seems likely to me is that it may have been a leafy plant containing DMT that was used in the preparation of *haoma*, a proposition that is further explored below. It was mentioned in Chapter 3 that the giant, leafy reed *Arundo donax*, some varieties of which are rich in DMT,[475] could be the plant used currently in the preparation of an ayahuasca analogue in Iran.[476] This plant is very seedy (having a plume of seeds rather like Pampas grass: see Appendix 2), has soft wood, and smells pleasant when burned. Is this *hadhānaēpata*?

---

473. *Y* 68.1. "...let this Zaothra [priest] then attain for thee (for satisfaction), for it is thine with its Haoma, and its milk, and its Hadhānaēpata" (trans. MILLS).

474. *Y* 3.3: "And I desire to approach the Haoma-water, and the fresh milk with my praise, and the plant Hadhānaēpata" (trans. MILLS); similarly *Y* 22.1; *Y* 52.9; *Y* 66.1; *Y* 68.1; and also *Visperad* 11.2.

475. And also 5-MeO-DMT, bufotenin, and bufotenidine (the latter is toxic).

476. The tryptamine content of *Arundo donax* can be potently activated with an MAOI (see below) to a 'psychedelic' level even when smoked: see LEPRECHAUN (2008).

In Chapter 4 of this book (on 'substitutes'), it may be recalled that *kuśa* or *darbha* grass is frequently mentioned in connection with *soma* and Vedic ritual.[477] This common grass extensively pervades the Vedic world: it is strewn in the ritual enclosure and on the *vedi* (the Vedic sacrificial altar); it is sat upon for meditation and during rituals; it provides a 'seat' for deities;[478] it has protective and purificatory properties; and it is used in numerous brahmanical rites, such as for 'life-rituals' (*saṃskāra*s).[479] It is an essential component of Vedic ritual, elevated to a very high status in many contexts (see a photograph of *kuś* grass in Appendix 3). GONDA (1985:45) remarks that, "Occasionally the use of *kuśa* grass is prescribed almost to excess". In the *Atharvaveda* there are several references to the holiness of *darbha* grass. It has a numinous power and can turn enemies away; it is of divine birth (19.32.6–7); wearing an amulet made of *darbha* grass destroys rivals (10.28.1); the power of *darbha* can make us luminous (19.32.9); the healing remedies are *aśvattha* (the peepal tree), *darbha* and *soma* (8.7.20).[480] In the *Pāśupatasūtra* it states that, "The act of drinking Soma-juice with the top-end of

477. See GONDA (1985) for a comprehensive review of all aspects of *kuśa* grass (ch.3), *darbha* (ch.4) grass, and other grasses used in Vedic ritual.

478. *Kuśa* grass also features in some *tantra* rites. For example, in the *Svacchandatantra* (2.183ff.), Śiva is born from the Goddess of Speech (Vāgīśvarī), for whom a small house is symbolically created from *kuśa* grass (TÖRZÖK 2007:463). In TIRUMULAR's (*c.* 11th–13th century) Tamil text, the *Tirumantiram*, a work on *tantra* and yoga, an offering of rice and *kuśa* grass is prescribed (vs. 1324–1325) for *arcana* (worship/adoration); *kuśa* is one of the substances to be used in funeral rites for a yogi (v.1921). *Dūrvā/dūb* grass is said to be of great importance in Āyurveda, Tantra and spiritual practices. In *Dūrvā Tantra* rites pieces of the grass are offered to Gaṇeśa, which is said to be a 'strange' key to power (SARASVATĪ n.d.:133).

479. Such as during pregnancy (*garbhasaṃskāra*); for the first shaving of a child's hair (*cūḍākaraṇa*); and in funeral rites (PANDEY 1994:66, 100, 266–272).

480. It is the remover of fury and wrath (6.43); *darbha* is one of the five plants that can deliver us from woe (the others being *soma*, hemp, barley and *saha*) (11.6.15); its thousand branches increase our life span (19.32.3); through *darbha*, "I can pierce through the tongue of [a] foe and his speech" (19.32.4); *darbha* is to be worshipped in a thousand ways, as it can protect us (19.33.1); "O darbha, ascend (to the great states of consciousness) with the Indriya powers" (19.33.2); "May you purify and protect us in our calamities" (19.33.3); *darbha* is the killer of demons, the strength of the gods (19.34.4) (trans. KASHYAP 2011–2012).

kuśa-grass by a Brāhmaṇa every month may or may not be equal to begging (alms)".[481]

GONDA (1985:26) comments that when a *soma* sacrifice draws to a close, the adherents of several schools throw grass in the remains of the water that is mixed with *soma*; the grass is squeezed and makes the water sharp of taste; the mixture is distributed among those who are entitled to receive a cup filled with *soma*; they partake of the mixture, each of them from his own cup, by smelling it [?]. After discussing several similar references to grasses, GONDA remarks: "The conclusion seems legitimate that here the grass represents *soma,* or gives the drink at least the character of *soma*, and that, according to the tradition as a whole, several grasses may fulfill that function". The *Kauṣītaki Brāhmaṇa* (8.8) appears to discuss mixing *soma* with *darbha* grass;[482] and similarly, the *Taittirīya Saṃhitā* (2.5.3.5) seems to be alluding to a mixture of grass and *soma*;[483] later in this text (5.6.4.2) the *darbha*s are described as, "ambrosia [the drink of immortality], the strength (*vīrya*) of the (earth); he offers on it". GONDA (1982:62) comments that, "*dūrvā* grass is often used in lustrations and other auspicious rites, believed to cause happiness, prosperity and longevity and even to be akin to *soma*".[484] *Darbha* is

---

481. Trans. CHAKRABORTY (1970:75). This remark is in the commentary on the text by KAUṆḌINYA, who may be dated between around 4th–6th centuries CE (CHAKRABORTY 1970:14).

482. "Then turning to the left, they approach the Somas in the waters; they place them here within the altar, for that is the abode of the Soma; they distribute the branches of Darbha grass; when the waters and the plants come together, then the Soma is complete" (trans. KEITH). However, it could be that it is the 'magical' power of purification of *darbha* that is being referred to, rather than to a substantial mixture of plants; as in *Aitareya Brāhmaṇa* (7.33), where, in the *rājasūya*, into the [*soma*] cup of the sacrificer have been cast two shoots of *darbha.* Similarly, in the performance of the standard form of the *soma* ceremony, the *adhvaryu* priest begins the *pṛṣṭhastotra* ('hymn of praise') using water in which *dūrvā* had been placed (*Śatapatha Brāhmaṇa* 4.3.3.17; GONDA 1985:119). Two blades of grass are often handed from one priest to another during Vedic rituals (GONDA 1985:175ff.).

483. "[Milk] places power and strength in him and later impels him by curds; and he proceeds in order (of production). If he curdles it with Putika plants or with bark, that is fit for Soma" (trans. KEITH). *Darbha* is also added to sacrificial milk and butter (GONDA 1985:61). (It was previously suggested that 'Putika' most probably refers to a kind or clump of grass.)

484. *ŚB* 4.5.10.5; 7.4.2.12.

not infrequently mentioned in the same ritual context as the branches or twigs of several important trees, among them the *plakṣa* (*Ficus infectoria*) tree, which, as noted previously, may possibly have psychoactive properties.

In Chapter 4 of this book, on *soma* substitutes, it was observed that nearly all of the 'substitute' plants mentioned in the brahmanical commentarial literature were either one or another of several species of *Ficus* or appeared to be various kinds of grasses. The frequent mention of kinds of common grass, particularly *kuśa* or *darbha*, as substitutes for, or in connection with, *soma* is distinctly curious.[485] DEEG (1993:100ff.) maintains that in older Vedic literature *darbha* is regarded as an intoxicant, and that the effect of *darbha* resulted in its being referred to in the *Ṛgveda* (10.136) as *viṣa* (poison), as a consequence of it being used incorrectly. Although DEEG presents considerable evidence that *darbha* was regarded as an intoxicant or a drug, maintaining that references, for example, to *darbha* as a drink of immortality (*TS* 5.6.4.2) are only entirely explicable if *darbha* was intoxicating, he does not explain how this common grass could have produced such a powerful effect.

Kuśa/darbha grass has several therapeutic applications in Ayurvedic medicine.[486] It also has a special status as a plant in mythology and in religious rituals.[487] But why is it so revered, apart

485. FRAWLEY (2013:329) also comments that one kind of *soma* grows in marshy or aquatic areas and is some sort of reed grass; and that in the *Atharvaveda* (11.6.15) *soma* is connected to *darbha* or *kuśa* grass.

486. Including for diarrhoea, menorrhagia, jaundice, skin disease, excessive perspiration, heliobacter pylori, and ulcers (PANDEY 2013). It has properties that are antidiarrhoeal (HEGDE *et al.* 2010), antimicrobial (KUMAR *et al.* 2010), antioxidant (GOLLA and BHIMATHATI 2014), and antibacterial (PACKIALAKSHMI and ALWIN 2014).

487. In the Hindu myth of the 'churning of the ocean of milk' (referred to in Chapter 2) Viṣṇu assumed the form of a tortoise/turtle (*kūrma*), on whose shell rested Mount Manthara/Mandara. As the mountain rotated, churning the ocean, in one version of the myth several hairs were rubbed from the shell of the tortoise; these washed ashore and became *kuśa* grass. One of the objects produced by the churning of the ocean of milk was a pot (*kamaṇḍalu*) held by Dhanvantari (the physician of the gods) of *amṛta* (nectar), which, at one point in the story, was placed on *kuśa* grass. The children of Kadrū (Garuḍa's stepmother) attempted to get the pot but Garuḍa snatched it away. The snakes (*nāgas*) licked the sharp leaves of the grass hoping to taste some drops; this caused their tongues to fork (MANI 1989:32). The hairs of the

from its multiple, practical uses: for seats, baskets, ropes, girdles, amulets, clothes, fodder, straining water, and igniting sacred fires? If the 'original' *soma* was indeed psychoactive, and known to have been so, what sense can be made of the various kinds of grasses recommended in the *Brāhmaṇa*s as substitutes for *soma*?

A possible explanation could be in the pharmacology of the plant. *Kuśa/darbha* grass is a species of *Phalaris* grass (in the family of *Graminaceae/Gramineae/Poaceae*), and there is a growing body of discussion worldwide about extracting *N,N*-dimethyl-tryptamine (DMT) from this grass (a relatively simple process),[488] which

---

boar (*varāha*) incarnation of Viṣṇu are said to be *kuśa* (*Bhāgavata Purāṇa* 3.13.35). Kuśa is the name of one of Rāma's two sons (the other being Lava) in the *Rāmayāna*. *Darbha* (*kuśa*) grass is worshipped by *vaiṣṇava*s on *darbhaṣṭami*, which falls on the eighth day of the moon in the month of *bhadra* (*c.* 23rd September to 22nd October). In South India stalks of *kuśa* grass are put in water pots and tanks at the time of eclipses (personal communication from Chandra VISHVANATH).

Kuśa also appears in Buddhist mythology and rites. The Buddha was offered eight handfuls of *kuśa* grass by Maṅgala (a grass-cutter) to make a seat under the Bodhi (peepal) tree, where he attained enlightenment. In the Tibetan Buddhist Kālacakra rite participants receive two stalks of *kuśa* grass to reveal clear dreams on the night prior to initiation. Buddhist ascetics, yogis and *siddha*s are often depicted seated on *kuśa* grass. According to tradition, the Buddha was cremated at Kushinagar ('town of *kuśa*') (BEER 2003:21–23).

488. On this Japanese website (http://mitibatasure.tripod.com/kusayosi.html) (accessed 13/12/2013). there is information about extracting DMT from this grass (known as *kusa yosi*) and anecdotal reports of the effects from smoking it. Similarly, in the USA, the ubiquitous *Phalaris aquatica* (bulbous canary grass) contains DMT. see, for example https://mycotopia.net/forums/botanicals/82666-phun-phineas-phalaris.html; http://www.drugs-forum.com/forum/showthread.php?t=76577; http://www.ehow.co.uk/info_8059409_hallucinogenic-plants-native-united-states.html (accessed 13/12/2013).

On this latter website, it is also noted that DMT is to be found in prairie bundleflower (*Desmanthus illinoensis*), an erect plant with clusters of white flowers which grows in many areas including Pennsylvania, Florida, Texas and North Dakota. The root bark contains a "whopping 25%" DMT (SHULGIN and SHULGIN 1997:268). *Phalaris* DMT, which can be smoked, and which can be extracted from several plants, including reed canary grass (*Phalaris arundinacea*), is discussed on the website (http://deoxy.org/smokedmt.htm) (accessed 13/12/2013). It is also claimed that *Phalaris aquatica*

appears to be more concentrated in the tips or the leaf blades.[489] However, there are around twenty varieties of *Phalaris*,[490] and different strains of grasses vary widely in their alkaloid content, depending on their specific locality, soil constituents, season, humidity, available light, and other factors. Some varieties contain no psychoactive alkaloids at all.[491] Interestingly, some species of

---

(Italian Strain AQ-1) has a higher DMT content than *Phalaris arundinacea* and supposedly higher than any other plant discovered thus far. Recipes for making DMT from grasses appeared in DEKORNE's original (1994) Loopmanics publication, but not in the updated 2011 edition. SHULGIN and SHULGIN (1997:261, 418) provide confirmation of relatively high amounts of DMT in these and other grasses and reeds. The best-known genera for sources of DMT are: *Arundo donax* (giant reed, reported to have been originally imported from India: DEKORNE 2011:156), which was mentioned in Chapter 3 as a possible component of Iranian *haoma*; *Arundo phragmites* or *Phragmites communis* or *Phragmites australis* (common reed); and *Phyllostachys* spp. (bamboo). Some species of *Arundo donax* contain a range of alkaloids similar to those found in *Phalaris*, including DMT, 5-OH-DMT, 5-MeO-MMT, and 5-MeO-DMT (FESTI and SAMORINI 1993:264). ANONYMOUS (2005) has published a method for extracting DMT from *Phragmitis australis*, a common reed. OTT (1996a:246) also confirms DMT in these and other grasses, in five species of acacia, and in five species of *Desmodium*, including *Desmodium gangeticum* (= *śālaparṇī*, referred to in the previous chapter). See also SMITH (1977) for a list of plants containing DMT and other tryptamines.

489. "The DMT in *Phalaris* grass… is concentrated in its leaves and stalks. Potent extractions can be made from what are no more than 'grass clippings'". More accurately, some varieties of *Phalaris* contain higher concentrations of 5-MeO-DMT (DEKORNE 2011:158, 171), which is stronger in effect than DMT, and about four times more potent relative to extracted weight. See OROC (2009) for a comprehensive account of experiences with pure 5-MeO-DMT; see also BALL (2016). See DEKORNE (2011:159ff.) and DEKORNE *et al.* (2002:85–123) for accounts of experience of an ayahuasca analogue made from rue and various species of *Phalaris* grass. Not only in India, but also in Europe and classical Roman literature, there is an ancient custom of holding (or biting on) a blade or stalk of grass in one's mouth as a sign of submission (JAIN 1983). Could this be a distant folk memory of the ritual, entheogenic use of psychoactive grasses?

490. There are nine species in the USA, four of them introduced from Europe (DEKORNE *et al.* (2002:94).

491. One of the species, reed canarygrass (*Phalaris arundinacea*), contains at least nine alkaloids (including DMT and 5-MeO-DMT), grouped as either phenols, indoles or β-carblines (DEKORNE *et al.* 2002:95). For the alkaloid

Phalaris are sufficiently rich in DMT and 5-MeO-DMT to provide an ayahuasca-like experience, when combined with a plant containing an MAOI (see below) (FESTI and SAMORINI 2004).[492]

In August 2016 Professor Simon GIBBONS at the School of Pharmacy (UCL) very kindly arranged for a test for DMT in a sample of *kuśa* grass that had been brought from India. As mentioned in the Introduction, this test proved negative. This could mean that *kuśa* grass does not ever contain DMT, or it could be merely that the particular sample tested was without DMT, due possibly to the season, time, soil conditions, or it being a slightly variant sub-species of the grass. However, some alkaloids seemed to be present and further tests on larger samples of *kuśa* grass are now being arranged, which might possibly be more fruitful, given the significance of *kuśa* in Brahmanical rites and the references that have been provided for the associations of *kuśa* and other grasses with *soma.* If indeed, as is being proposed, *soma/haoma* was probably based on analogues of ayahuasca, then it seems sensible to explore the potential psychoactive properties of any plant that may have been used, as it was primarily through the analysis of plants used in ayahuasca rites in South America that the synergistic chemistry of DMT and MAOIs was revealed.

A consideration of the ritual use of ayahuasca by South American congregations also reveals the way that the use of ayahuasca-like analogues could have similarly developed into religious ritual in ancient Asia. Ayahuasca is used ritually by around seventy indigenous

---

content of different varieties of *Phalaris*, its global distribution, and for the most comprehensive of bibliographies to date on these grasses, see FESTI and SAMORINI (1993:265–287; 2004).

492. Consumption of *Phalaris* grass or *Arundo donax* by cows and sheep, it is claimed, can cause staggers, the symptoms of which include muscular tremors, difficulty digesting, excessive salivation, and malfunction of the tongue and lips (FESTI and SAMORINI (1993:247, 252). However, SHULGIN (1997:260–261) and TROUT (2002:126–127) maintain, with considerable evidence, that staggers is probably not caused by either the DMT or the 5-MeO-DMT in these plants but rather is due to a fungus within the grass. SAMORINI (2002:18–26) presents widespread reports of cows and horses who deliberately intoxicate themselves on several species of grass and 'locoweed' and appear to relish the experience.

groups (OTT 2006:12)[493] in western Amazonia,[494] and increasingly in the wider world. Besides its use among South American shamans,[495] ayahuasca is the sacrament used by several Brazilian Christian organizations in their services, the three largest being the churches of the União do Vegetal (UDV), the Santo Daime, and the Barquinha. Over the last three decades, the UDV and Santo Daime have increased their congregations not only in cities in Brazil and other countries in South America, but also in North America, Japan and Europe.[496] Simultaneously, there has been a considerable increase in the number of independent shamans conducting ayahuasca rituals in many countries.[497] Apart from isolated occurrences, ayahuasca is nearly always consumed in a prescribed ritual, the form depending on the shaman or the particular group that conducts the sessions. Music, singing or hymns[498] are central in nearly all of the rituals that involve ayahuasca. In some ways contemporary ayahuasca cults that have become established in recent decades in North

---

493. See OTT (2006:31ff.) for the history of the discovery of the chemistry of ayahuasca, which properly began in 1905.

494. BEYER (2009:208–209) comments that: "The ritual use of ayahuasca is a common thread linking the religion and spirituality of almost all the indigenous peoples of the Upper Amazon, including the mestizo population; it seems probable that the shamanic practices of most of western Amazonia—Brazil, Venezuela, Colombia, Ecuador, Peru, Bolivia—form a single religious cultural area. Ayahuasca use is found as far west as the Pacific coastal areas of Panama, Colombia, and Ecuador; southward into the Peruvian and Bolivian Amazon; among the Indians of Colombia, among the Quechua, Waoroni, Shuar, and other peoples of Ecuador; and in Amazonian Brazil".

495. Besides ayahuasca, the most important plants used by Amazonian shamans are tobacco and datura (*toé*), which was referred to previously.

496. For histories of the three main ayahuasca religions of Brazil, see CEMIN (2010), LABATE and PACHECO (2011) for Santo Daime; ARAÚJO (2010) for Barquinha; GOULART (2010) for UDV. For concise summaries, see also BEYER (2010:288–292). For a summary of the three churches, see Appendix 4.

497. The legal situation in regard to the use and possession of ayahuasca is complex internationally, with different statutes currently applicable in different countries. See the articles in Section 3 of LABATE and JUNGABERIE (2011) for further information.

498. On this topic, see LABATE and PACHECO (2010). The UDV refer to their hymns as *chamadas*, while the Santo Daime refer to theirs as *hinos*, and to the hymnbooks as *hinários*. The term *icaro* is also used for 'hymn' among many indigenous groups.

America and Europe embody an ethos and function somewhat similarly to the mystery cults of the classical Greco-Roman world (mystery cults are discussed in Chapter 16).

As mentioned in the introduction to this book, the plants usually used to manufacture ayahuasca[499] in South America are the vine *Banisteriopsis caapi*[500] and the leaves of *Psychotria viridis.*[501] The term '*ayahuasca*'—as with *soma*—may refer both to the vine from which it is made, and also to the drink that is produced from it. The vine contains a monoamine-oxidase (MAO)-inhibitor in the form of three primary alkaloids: the β-carboline derivatives harmine, tetrahydroharmine (THH) and harmaline[502] (it also contains small amounts of DMT and other tryptamines). The *chacrona* leaf contains DMT. Other plants are sometimes added to this combination.[503] DMT, which is a very powerful entheogen,[504] is widely distributed

---

499. The vine has many names amongst the various groups that use it in South America, including *cipó, chichipu, nishi, oni, yajé, hoasca, daime, vegetal, caapi, kamarampi, supay, shitana, banku, natem* and *shori.* FLATTERY and SCHWARZ (1989:24) note that an Amazonian tribe, the Guarani Indians, call *caapi 'jaoma'* (i.e. *haoma*).
500. Also called *jagube.*
501. The most common name for which is *chacrona/chacruna,* a bush that is related to the coffee plant, in the plant family *Rubiaceae*. It is also called *raína* ('queen'). It is sometimes replaced by the leaves of *Diplopterys cabrerana,* a South American rainforest vine that is usually referred to as *chagropanga* or *chalipanga,* which is from the same plant family (*Malpighiaceae*) as the *Banisteriopsis caapi* vine. It is believed in Amazonia that besides increasing the length and strength of the trip produced by the *caapi* vine it causes the occasional bluish aureole of the visions (SCHULTES and RAFFAOUF 2004:30).
502. These harmala alkaloids are also present in the bark of *B. inebrians, B. quitensis* and in another vine belonging to the same family, *Tetrapterys methystica* (GRINSPON and BAKALAR 1998:15).
503. For details of additives, see BIANCHI and SAMORINI (1993); OTT (1996a:206ff.). The most common additive is tobacco juice; not uncommon is the addition of datura (*toé, huanto* = species of *Brugmansia*). See also BEYER (2010:277) and SAÉS (2011:133) for concise summaries. OTT (2006:19) categorizes four groups of entheogenic additives: 1. *Nicotiana*, 2. *Brugmansia*, 3. *Brunfelsia*, 4. *Psychotria/Diplopterys.*
504. See STRASSMAN (2001) for a comprehensive (and now widely-cited) report on the effects of injecting DMT (produced in a laboratory) on sixty volunteers, an experiment conducted in a hospital environment in Albuquerque, New Mexico, in the 1990s.

not only in plants in the natural world but also in small amounts in our brains.[505] As mentioned in the previous chapter, if DMT is ingested orally it is rapidly broken down by enzymes in the gut, which renders it ineffective. However, the simultaneous ingestion of an MAO-inhibitor allows DMT to flood the brain, resulting in a psychedelic experience, if sufficient quantities of both agents are consumed together. The formula works for any two plants containing DMT and an MAO inhibitor:[506] this is the 'royal alchemy'[507] that if properly prepared and appropriately consumed permits access to 'the spirit world', for want of a better description.[508]

Leaving aside the obvious and variable effect of any psychedelic brew owing to the relative density and concentration of the plant

---

505. On the widespread presence of DMT in the natural world, see SHULGIN and SHULGIN (1997:247–284, 'DMT is Everywhere'); see also BEYER (2010:264–265) for the Amazonian context. Tryptamines (including DMT and 5-MeO-DMT) and also some β-carbolines occur naturally in small quantities in the tissues and fluids of mammals and in the blood, spinal fluid and urine of humans (CALLAWAY 1993; PERRINE 1996:284).

506. The discovery of the specific chemistry of this entheogenic effect is usually attributed to HOLMSTEDT and LINDGREN, which was published in 1967 (OTT 1996b; 1997). However, in 1955 William BURROUGHS had already alerted Richard SCHULTES to the importance of the combination of *Banisteriopsis caapi* and *Psychotria viridis* (to produce the 'fireworks' of the *yagé* experience: see BURROUGHS and GINSBERG 1971), which information SCHULTES presented at a conference in Los Angeles in 1967 (LEES 2016:108–112).

507. The interaction of these two chemical compounds is complex, and it is not always or necessarily the case that an MAOI potentiates DMT; the reverse effect (of blocking DMT) may occur with some MAOI treatments (OTT 1996b).

508. It needs to be emphasized that a very wide spectrum of experiences is possible on all psychedelic drugs—particularly on ayahuasca—ranging from mild to overwhelming (depending on dosage); ecstatic to infernal (depending on set and setting and the psychological disposition of the person), even in the same session; and revelatory to confused. For some few people, even large doses of ayahuasca may have no effect at all. It also needs to be cautioned that psychedelic drugs of all kinds can induce psychosis (usually temporary) in people with an unstable mind or who have a history of mental illness in the family. However, over the last half a century it has been conclusively demonstrated that there are very few adverse reactions to psychedelics when the session is properly planned and conducted in a congenial environment.

material in the mixture in relation, by volume, to water content, there is also a range of possible effects due to the relative amounts of the DMT and MAOIs[509] in the mixture. As discussed previously in the chapter on Syrian rue, harmine and harmaline are psychoactive on their own; and, as also just mentioned, pure DMT is powerfully entheogenic. The relative proportions in a concoction of not only DMT and MAOIs, but also other alkaloids in the plants, cause a wide spectrum of possible effects; of course, also compounded with the individual's general disposition, both generally and on the specific day of consuming a concoction. The effects of any drug are complex and are not apt for uniform reduction, particularly in regard to psychedelics or entheogens, which at different dose-levels can have widely different effects, almost like different drugs. ROBINSON (1968:126) remarks: "An important adage of pharmacology is that no drug has a single effect even though one effect may predominate or, by adjustment of concentration, one effect may be favored over others"; and that, "[T]he interpretation of a drug action as due primarily to MAO inhibition is extraordinarily difficult" (p.132).

A few common sources of DMT have been already been mentioned: others are *Mimosa hostilis*[510] (known as *vinho da jurema* in South America) and some species of acacia;[511] new sources are

---

509. CALLAWAY (1999:266–267) discusses two Brazilian varieties of the *Banisteriopsis caapi* vine (referred to by the UDV as *tucunaca* and *caupurí*), which are chemically and morphologically distinct. They have different β-carboline constituents, producing slightly different experiences.

510. From which plant source DMT was first isolated in 1946 by Gonçalves DE LIMA (SHULGIN and SHULGIN (1997:248).

511. CHRISTIE (2014) maintains, in a brief article, that an Egyptian species of acacia (*Acacia nilotica*) is the fabled Egyptian 'Tree of Life' and contains DMT; he proposes that the ancient Egyptians used to prepare an ayahuasca concoction from it. However, neither ancient nor more modern (Coptic) Egyptian texts record entheogenic properties of this tree; though several practical and medicinal uses, such as for skin diseases, are reported (MANNICHE 1999:65–67). MYERS (2011:162ff.) goes further and hypothesizes that not only the Egyptians but also Gnostics made an ayahuasca analogue from acacia and Syrian rue. Another species of acacia, *Acacia catechu* (= *khadira*, Sanskrit), has several uses in Ayurvedic medicine; CARAKA (*Sūtrasthāna* 25.42) notes its use for skin diseases and leprosy.

continually being discovered.[512] The best-known sources of MAO inhibitors are *Banisteriopsis caapi*[513] and Syrian (mountain) rue (*Peganum harmala*).[514] However, more than sixty plants containing harmine, and more than seventy plants containing DMT have so far been identified, which in any of the possible combinations—of which there are around 4,200—have been found to produce very similar effects (OTT 1997; 2011:109ff.);[515] and other plants containing these psychoactive ingredients are being continually discovered every year (OTT 2001).

How the traditional combination of plants used in South America was originally discovered is unknown. Shamans and religious groups generally endorse 'mythical' explanations (usually involving teachings from spirits in the forest). BEYER (2010:211) speculates that the combination of plants may have been discovered accidentally by medicine-people combining two purgative plants, as purging is a feature of healing in many Amazonian cultures.[516] There is evidence

---

512. OTT (2006:79–81) lists seventy-four plants (in fourteen different botanical families) that contain DMT and other tryptamines.
513. Which also contains small quantities of DMT and other tryptamines.
514. GRACIE and ZARKOV (1985) published simple methods for extracting MAOI from *Banisteriopsis caapi*, Syrian rue, and passion flower (*Passiflora incarnata*), and compare the effects of different combinations. OTT (2006:71–73) lists sixty-seven plants (in nineteen different botanical families) containing MAOI β-carbolines. More plants containing β-carbolines are discovered every year.
515. OTT (2006:49–68) gives detailed accounts of bioassays (on himself) of various doses of pharmahuasca preparations, which were extracted from several different plants.
516. SAMORINI (2002) and SIEGAL (2005) provide abundant evidence of animals, birds and insects intoxicating themselves with plants. SIEGAL hypothesizes that humans may have discovered many plant intoxicants from observing the behavior of animals. In the Amazon region it has been reported (SIEGAL 2005:64) that jaguars, uncharacteristically for carnivores, chew the bark and leaves of the *Banisteriopsis caapi* vine, presumably to intoxicate themselves. This hypothesis is supported by footage shown on British television in August 2008—in an episode entitled 'Peculiar Potions' from the BBC documentary series 'Weird Nature'—of a jaguar becoming intoxicated after chewing the vine. Ritual/religious intoxication by humans through psychoactive plants is indeterminately ancient. Throughout later Neolithic Europe, from *c.*4200 BCE, it is apparent that there was widespread ritual/religious use of

that the use of ayahuasca has spread to various indigenous groups in South America in the last three hundred years,[517] but although there are claims of ancient use by the Inca royal family and others, the evidence for this is uncertain (LABATE and PACHECO 2011:79).

Amongst the South American groups that use ayahuasca, the *Banisteriopsis caapi* vine is sometimes said to provide the 'force', while the *chacrona* leaf provides the light. Some Amazonian groups describe the vine as male and the leaf as female (FOTIOU 2014:175). In the tradition of the ayahuasca religions the vine is cut and collected from the jungle by men and the leaves are collected by women. The vine—of which there are many kinds with slightly different qualities[518]—must be arduously pounded by wooden mallets (in the 'making', *feitio*),[519] after which the stalks are cooked with the leaves in large pots, a process that requires much experience and expertise to produce an excellent brew. Although boiling the ingredients is the usual method of preparing ayahuasca, 'cold' preparation and consumption of the vine, which is mashed up, strained and mixed with water, is also practised by some South American groups (STAFFORD 1977:262; OTT 1996:208; OTT 2006:15–16;[520] BEYER 2010:221).[521]

The duration of the effects of a typical dose is around two to four hours. Some *mestres* administer ayahuasca in a single dose, others in two or three (or more doses), which are usually administered in glasses containing 150–200 millilitres of the liquid. The colour of

---

intoxicants, in particular cannabis and opium (SHERRATT 1991); and there is no reason to assume that the ritual use of intoxicants was not practised also in Asia.

517 Some indigenous Amazonian groups appear to have only adopted the use of ayahuasca in the last 150 years; some only in the last sixty or seventy years (see SHEPARD 2014).

518. See OTT (1996a:207) for details.

519. For a brief description of this, see SHANON (2010:23).

520. OTT (2006:16) comments that heating harmaline may degrade it (even though many indigenous groups cook the prepared vine to make ayahuasca).

521. OTT (1997) reports on the effective preparation in cold water, by several groups in Brazil, of the root-bark of *vinho da jurema*, which is rich in DMT, and which on its own is potently visionary. A potent concoction can be made from uncooked, ground-up *Phalaris* grass leaves (*Phalaris aquatica* (Italian strain AQ-1) and the seeds of *Peganum harmala* (DEKORNE *et al.* 2002:115).

ayahuasca is usually dark 'muddy' brown, though it is sometimes more red or more yellow; the range of colours is the same as found in the *Veda*s for *soma*. In general, the thicker and more dense the liquid, the stronger is the dose. The strongest preparations have a thick, viscous consistency (these preparations are usually administered in much smaller doses). Although the taste is particularly bitter or 'sharp', freshly produced ayahuasca sometimes has a taste that could almost be described as having a sweet edge.

Ayahuasca is a purgative (*purga*): vomiting and diarrhoea are common; it is called the 'vomiting medicine' by some Amazonian groups. Preparation through fasting (or, at the minimum, a light clean diet free of toxins), is required to facilitate an easier passage through what can be an ordeal; for which reason ayahuasca is also referred to indigenously as a 'diet' (*dieta*). Celibacy is also often recommended both prior to and following an ayahuasca session.[522] Ayahuasca is regarded by its *aficionados* as both a teacher and a medicine; it is also referred to as a 'doctor' (*el doctore*).[523] It can show latent ailments or the cause of them and can inspire the person to give up bad or compulsive habits.[524] Amongst indigenous Amazonian peoples it is used for a variety of purposes: as a divinatory

522. Dietary restrictions are important to avoid potentially unpleasant or even lethal interactions between MAOIs and particular foods, notably fermented foods, cheese, alcohol and sauerkraut (there are also other restricted foods). Tyramine, found in cheese and other restricted foods, is the main chemical responsible for potentially antagonistic reactions. Pharmaceutical medications that affect MAOI are also potentially very dangerous. Amazonian groups often restrict the use of salt, sugar and spices prior to ayahuasca sessions. OTT (2006:68) comments that dietary restrictions are pharmacological, while sexual restrictions are spiritual.
523. For a perspective on the therapeutic and healing use of ayahuasca within the Santo Daime, see DE ALVERGA (2011).
524. Several programmes of rehabilitation from drug-dependence through treatment with ayahuasca have been running since the mid-1990s in both Holland and South America. For further information on ayahuasca and drug-rehabilitation, see LABATE, SANTOS, ANDERSON *et al.* (2010). See FRECSKA *et al.* (2016) for the chemical mechanisms in the brain that are believed to be partly responsible for the healing (from common diseases) and de-addictive potentialities of ayahuasca; of particular interest is Sig-1R receptor activity. Social factors also play a role in healing.

tool, to counter witchcraft, as an aid for hunting and warfare,[525] for religio-social purposes, for divine guidance, for contact with the spirit world, and for achieving ecstatic states.[526] The ayahuasca churches are considered by members to be schools that impart teachings, with a progression of knowledge that results from attending sessions (or rituals).

Ayahuasca produces visions, though not for everyone, that can be indescribably beautiful and also terrifying.[527] Visions of light are common,[528] generally following initial experiences of geometric patterns. In one compilation of reports of experience, over half of those who drank ayahuasca saw snakes.[529] The experience is, at its deepest level, an encounter with oneself, with the source of life. There is a sense of 'seeing' and 'knowing' in a more profound way than in ordinary waking consciousness, and an enhanced sense of connectedness to the natural world.[530] When the dose is strong, near-death experience is common: one faces oneself (or God/Gods) without any of the usual, external supports of consensual reality. After a session, there usually remains a sense of clarity and 'cleanness'; and after a strong experience, one of rebirth: everything usually seems more close, alive and real. This sensation can last for several days, or longer. However, there can, of course, be no adequate

---

525. The Amazonian Yaminawa tribe used occasionally to use ayahuasca as a catalyst for war, when 'visionary' confrontation with a rival tribe failed (SAÉS 2011:136). Some Amazonian groups use ayahuasca to strengthen group identity and to summon success for warfare and hunting (DE MORI 2011:28).

526. DOBKIN DE RIOS (1972:39–42) provides a useful schematic chart of the various uses of ayahuasca amongst Peruvian groups of the Amazon region.

527. The most common vision in the indigenous context is of large, brightly-coloured snakes. Felines and birds of prey are also common (SHANON 2010:118, 213); see also LUNA and AMARINGO (1999) for imagery. SHANON (2010), a professional psychologist, has compiled extensive data on the effects, experiences and visions produced by ayahuasca.

528. See SHANON (2010:272ff.).

529. The visions of a group of twenty-four participants are presented by METZNER (1999:46–186).

530. SAÉS (2011:137) remarks: "When you ask the Yaminawa users what they take ayahuasca for, the most common answer—I dare say that the same answer would be given throughout the indigenous Upper Amazon—is that they simply take it to *see*".

description of an experience of the 'other realm' that can result from the consumption of entheogens; by definition, a dimension which is not in 'human time' and which is in a different audio-visual realm of sensation and mentation.[531]

Having all-too-briefly outlined the use and practices of ayahuasca, I would like now to speculate on its possible use in Vedic and Zoroastrian religion in ancient times.

---

531. For a couple of the older 'classic' accounts of anthropologists who experienced ayahuasca visions, see HARNER (1973), who drank it for the first time in 1961 with Jivaro Indians of the Ecuadorian Amazon; and KENNSINGER (1973) who recounts the uses of ayahuasca by, and his experiences with, the Peruvian Cashinahua tribe.

CHAPTER 15

Vedic and ayahuasca rituals

The purpose of Vedic ritual is generally considered as explicable in terms of religious, metaphysical, material[532] or spiritual purposes.[533] As an example of one kind of current, popular interpretation: discussing the culmination of the *yajña* GYANSHRUTI and SRIVIDYANANDA (2006:80) remark that, "The host [*yajamāna*] is said to derive mental satisfaction, inward peace and general purification of actions from the process, which indicates spiritual advancement".[534] Commenting on the symbolism of the *Brāhmaṇa*s, RENOU (2004:128) remarks that, "The sacrificer leaves his body,

---

532. FALK (1997:86–87) summarises several theories that have been advanced concerning the purpose of the sacrificial procedures of the *Ṛgveda*: as (primarily) being a ritualized guest meal (THIEME); as serving to enact cosmological mythology at the winter solstice (KUIPER); or as representing strife between competing parties (HEESTERMAN). FALK prefers, alternatively, to interpret some of the details and mythological tropes of the *Ṛgveda* as indicating the importance of the economy, ecology and availability of water: "The ritual was possibly meant to effect the arrival of the spring floods initiating the rejuvenation of nature and man".
533. DANDEKAR (1958:6), for example, remarks that, "An important feature of the Vedic sacrificial ritual is that it is believed to aim at both the emancipation of the individual as well as the progress of society".
534. Other benefits of *yajña* are said to be that (p.15), "it cleanses the atmosphere [and] helps to restore the seasons and ecological balance. This could mean a reduction in pollution levels, adequate and timely rainfall, increased ground water levels and control over rising temperatures". Such views are not uncommon amongst modern, orthodox Hindu commentators; and at some venues *agnihotra* and Vedic *yajña* are performed for this purpose; for example http://www.agnihotra.org/ (accessed 13/13/2013).

'makes the journey to heaven'[535] and inverts the relations in which he stands. He is himself the object sacrificed". Observations such as these on the experience of Vedic sacrifice are of course intelligible as explanations of religious processes; but how much more significant would those experiences be if the participants had consumed a powerful entheogen? If the possibility is entertained that a form of ayahuasca was being manufactured in the ancient world, then I believe that an interesting perspective on the Vedic ritual world of the *somayajña* might be considered. That *soma* is just one of the deities addressed in Vedic recitation may perhaps have misled commentators into underestimating the central importance that the consumption of *soma* may have had in ancient Vedic practice:[536] though this is, admittedly, a bold proposition.

That said, I would like to draw attention to the structure and performance of a typical ritual of the Santo Daime church.[537] Shamans and religious groups perform various kinds of rituals, but as previously mentioned, apart from special cases of its use for healing or private purposes, ayahuasca is almost always consumed in a group ritual, usually involving chanting and singing, and conducted by a priest (or priests) or a shaman.

The rituals of the Santo Daime exhibit a number of striking similarities with Vedic rituals. That there are such similarities does not by itself provide logical support for the proposition that a form of ayahuasca may have been manufactured in ancient Asia. Other groups and churches that use ayahuasca have different rituals that are quite unlike Vedic ritual. However, a comparison of Vedic and Santo Daime rituals illustrates the possibility that the regular drinking

---

535. For example, "'We have come to the heaven: to the heaven we have come', he says; verily he goes to the world of heaven" (trans. KEITH, *TS* 1.7.6). Similarly, the eagle, in the myth of the eagle retrieving *soma* from heaven—referred to in Chapter 2—has been interpreted by brahmans as a vehicle taking the *yajamāna* to heaven (KNIPE 1967:337).

536. HEESTERMAN (2005), for example, who is a great authority on Vedic religion, in his encyclopedia entry on the *Brāhmaṇa*s, which are replete with references to the preparation and drinking of *soma*, does not once mention *soma*.

537. For an extensive personal account of the history, *mestres* and rituals of the Santo Daime church, and for the effects of 'Daime' (*ayahuasca*), see ALVERGA (1999).

of ayahuasca by a congregation is perfectly consistent with the notion that Vedic rituals were developed for that purpose. Every drug has an observable and usually quite predictable range of effects, and I would suggest that amongst all of the entheogenic/psychedelic drugs or intoxicants currently known, an ayahuasca analogue would seem to be the most apt to engender naturally the range of procedures—and to produce the effects—that are apparently embodied in Vedic ritual.[538]

Santo Daime rituals have a distinct form. They take place at fixed times in the annual religious calendar.[539] Rituals typically last between six and eight hours, but may extend for up to three days.[540] Participants who drink ayahuasca are enjoined to control their diet and to eliminate specific foods that may disturb the finely balanced equilibrium of the MAO inhibitor. *Daime* is usually drunk at the beginning of the ritual, with more doses administered at approximately two- or three-hour intervals. The first to drink are the priests, who know the hymns and their order, and who lead the ritual. There are occasions when a Santo Daime ritual is performed but when no

---

538. Although apparently unaware of the chemistry necessary to provide an entheogenic concoction, BARBER (1999:164)—who writes on the mummies of the Tarim Basin (referred to previously), who nearly all carry bunches of ephedra twigs—comments that ancient Zoroastrianism and the ayahuasca cults of the Amazon region are, "remarkably similar".

539. 7 Jan, Padrinho Alfredo's birthday; 19 Jan, demise of Padrinho Sebastião/ day of Saint Sebastian; 18 March, São José; Easter, Good Friday–Saturday; 1 May, Mayday; 2nd Sunday in May, Mother's Day; 12 June, São Antonio; 23 June, São João; 25 June, Madrinha Rita's birthday; 28 June, São Pedro; 6 July, *Mestre* Irineu's deathday; second Sunday in August, Father's Day; 6 Oct, Padrinho Sebastião's birthday; 1–2 Nov, All Souls Day; 7 Dec, Nossa Senhora de Conceciāo; 15 Dec, *Mestre* Irineu's birthday; 24 Dec, Jesus' birthday; 31 Dec, New Year; 5–6 Jan, Three Kings (Twelfth Night).

540. A session could be compared somewhat poetically to a boat journey, as the sacrifice is occasionally described in Vedic texts: from a familiar harbour onto the wide ocean, with both bright, calm weather and also wild storms; a diligent crew of priests directs the boat to its final destination, the harbour from which the ship set sail: "'Let us mount that ship fair crossing by which we may pass over all evils' (he says); the ship fair crossing is the sacrifice; the ship fair crossing is the black antelope skin; the ship fair crossing is speech; verily thus having mounted upon speech with it he crosses over to the world of heaven" (trans. KEITH, *Aitareya Brāhmāna* 1.3.1.13).

daime is drunk (or just water or another substitute).[541] Particular rituals are conducted largely in meditative silence, but nomally the rituals are accompanied by the singing (or chanting) of hymns (*hinos*). Particular *trabalhos* ('works', as Santo Daime rituals are called) involve a sometimes lengthy two-step dancing routine (*bailado*). Depending on the occasion, *hinos* for the ritual are selected typically in serial batches from among the thousand or so hymns contained in the dozen or so collections of hymns (*hinários*)[542] in separate books.[543] They are sung by the entire congregation, who are arranged in lines (men and women separately), the rhythm maintained by the shaking of *maracas*. At particular junctures in a *trabalho* there will be unison cries by all participants of '*viva*' (long live)[544] to particular people or entities.[545]

The hymns in each of the books were all 'received' from the 'astral plane' by one or another of the revered *mestres* in the Santo Daime tradition, similarly to the supposed reception of the collection of Vedic mantras by *ṛṣi*s (seers). These hymns[546] are primarily addressed to the Virgin Mary, God the Father, John the Baptist, Juramidam (an Amazonian entity),[547] *Mestres* such as Irineu (and his four accomplices), Sebastião and Alfredo, *Raínha* (Queen of the Forest), flowers and gardens, and to the sun, moon and stars. Amongst those also addressed (or merely mentioned) are 'spirit entities',[548]

---

541. See CEMIN (2010:56) for further information.

542. These number from approximately sixty to 150 per book (collection).

543. The recursive structure of the ceremonies, involving specific batches of hymns in different sequences, depending on the occasion, is similar to the recursive structure of Vedic rituals. STAAL (1996) has made intriguing analogies with bird-song and the 'deep structures' of some human religious activity.

544. Similar ejaculations to deities are made in Vedic performance.

545. Usually to: the Eternal Father, the Queen of the Forest, Jesus Christ the Redeemer, Patriarch Saint Joseph, Empire Chief (*Imperio*) Juramidam (see below), all Divine Beings, the Holy Cross, the Brotherhood, our President, and sometimes others too.

546. This analysis pertains to the CEFLURIS branch of the Santo Daime.

547. *Jura* = God; *midam* = soldiers. Juramidam, who may be likened to the head of an 'army', is sometimes personified as the nature of the 'work'; he was disclosed to Ireneu in visionary experience.

548. These include Tuperci, Ripi Yayá, Jaci, Tarumim, Equiôr, Papai Paxá, Curupipipiraguá, Barum, Marum, B.G, Soloína, and Papai Samuel, all of which appear in Irineu's *hinário*. These forest 'spirit-entities' (of which

the Three Kings[549] and Saint Joseph.[550] If the entire collection of hymns is considered, it is apparent that approximately five percent of the hymns are specifically addressed to *daime* (i.e. ayahuasca)[551] itself.[552]

Apart from the inclusion of women in the drinking of ayahuasca in rituals and the ritual dancing, practically all the other features of the Santo Daime ritual that have been mentioned have counterparts in the practices and performance of Vedic ritual, except, of course, the absence of the centrality of the sacred fire and of offerings to it. Particularly striking are the commonalities of visions, purgative effect, reverence for the plant preparation, and the sense of rebirth that the brew elicits.

The rituals of the Santo Daime church have been constructed (or 'received' from an emic point of view) primarily as a vehicle for the consumption of the ayahuasca sacrament. It is not as though the drinking of the holy tea is a mere adjunct to the ritual: the drinking of the tea is central, and the rituals are implemented for that purpose, as they provide a safe, controlled, defined kind of 'hologram' within which there is a sacred, circumscribed space for a powerful, healing, visionary, psychedelic experience to take place. If the Santo Daime rituals were to be analyzed solely from the contents of the hymnbooks

---

there are around thirty in the Santo Daime 'pantheon') have various characters, as chastisers, teasers, mischievous, etc. In all *hinários* there are also frequent references to *beija-flor* (the humming-bird), Archangel Saõ Miguel, Querubins, Anjos Serafins, Espirito Santo, and *Imperio* Juramidam. In Alfredo's *hinário* we find the *Princessas* Soloína and Janaína, and Cires Beija-Mar. From others contemporary with Irineu there is also Marachimbé. In total, there are perhaps sixty-four personages (including people and entities) addressed in the *hinários*.

549. Called Tintum, Agarrube and Titango.

550. The *hinos* of *Mestre* Irineu are central amongst the hymnal collections in the Santo Daime. In this collection, around 137 are addressed to the Virgin Mary (who has several epithets, including 'Divine Mother', 'Mother of Jesus', 'Mother of God', 'Virgin Conception'); 113 to God the Father; 52 to Jesus; 32 to 'flowers and gardens'; and 14 to *Raínha* ('Queen' [of the forest] = *chacrona*). Many of the references are allusive: such as 'flowers' referring to the flowers of the *Banisteriopsis caapi* vine.

551. Indirectly, there are other references to *daime*, as "I (*eu*)-me the singer", "I-me the donor of the *hino*", "I-me the *daime*", and "I-me, god".

552. Personal communication of an analysis kindly provided by a very experienced *daimista*.

or from the structure of the ritual, without an understanding of the effect or significance of the ayahuasca, the purpose of the ritual could be entirely missed. It is worth noting that the totality of the hymns is the only written teaching of the Santo Daime church. That prayers to particular deities are sung or recited; or that the paraphernalia of the rituals—such as the kind of crucifix exhibited,[553] the flowers used, or the number of candles lit, for example—may have a particular religious or mythological significance, is not the main function of the ritual: the main purpose is to drink ayahuasca.

What is easy to overlook is the relationship that the priests and his team of Vedic or ancient Iranian sacrificers may have had to *soma/haoma*, if indeed it was an entheogenic drug. In the context of ayahuasca cults throughout South America, it is the ceremonial reverence for the plant as a kind of deity that is evident; but as just mentioned, that could be misconstrued in some way if the effect of the plant is not adequately taken into account. What is being suggested is a different way of looking at ancient Vedic and Zoroastrian ritual: as developed *primarily* as vehicles for an entheogenic trip.

---

553. Santo Daime uses the Caravaca crucifix. It has a double cross-bar and was introduced by Fanciscan missionaries to America. This kind of cross is also used as a 'wishing cross' in some African-American communities, and is popular in north and north-eastern Brazil.

CHAPTER 16

Greek mystery rites

Related to this investigation into *soma/haoma,* I would like also to propose that in the Greek mystery rites, specifically the annual rites performed at the great temple of Eleusis (about twenty kilometres west of Athens) but probably also in other Greek and Greco-Roman mystery cults (*mysteria* = *initia* in Latin), kinds of 'wine' were used that contained ayahuasca analogues or possibly other mixtures of plants that could similarly induce entheogenic experience.[554] It is suggested that the 'wine' used as the ritual potion used for initiation, known as *kykeōn*, was a medium for an infusion of psychoactive plants rather than being effective alcoholically. Theories about the ingredients of *kykeōn* will be considered in the following chapter.

The famous mystery cult of Eleusis—which was the most important of several mystery cults of the classical Greek and Greco-Roman worlds—was of the goddess ('Mother Earth') Demeter/ Ceres (partnered with Zeus) and her daughter Persephone (or Korē, the maiden/virgin). In the myth of Eleusis[555] Persephone was with

---

554. RUCK (2006:58) suggests that in ancient Greece tryptamines from acacia-smilax together with beta-carbolines from the saffron plant could have been combined to produce an ayahuasca-like analogue, similar to the mixture of *Banisteriopsis caapi* and *Psychotria viridis* in South America. He maintains that the psychoactive properties of saffron, in sufficient quantities, are as strong as nutmeg (which has known psychoactive effects). I have been unable to determine which of the approximately 240 species of smilax RUCK is referring to; but smilax is not, as far as I am aware, known to contain tryptamines.

555. This myth has several variant components, notably in the Orphic and Sicilain versions.

friends picking flowers[556] at a place called Nyasa, on the slopes of Mount Ætna in Sicily, when she was spied by Aidoneus/Pluton (brother of Zeus and master of the underworld),[557] who happened to be driving along in his chariot drawn by four coal-black steeds. Persephone was abducted into the underworld and raped by Pluton.[558] She was eventually rescued as the earth had become barren and produced no food without her, owing to the anger of her mother Demeter; and the gods on Mount Olympus were deprived of sacrificial offerings until Zeus intervened and demanded her release. This was one of the best-known Greek myths. The Eleusian rites were believed to have civilized humanity through Demeter's two gifts to the world, of grain and the mysteries.[559]

---

556. Variously identified in different versions of the myth as roses, violets, crocus, iris, hyacinth or narcissus.
557. Demeter, Persephone and Plouton were the main deities at Eleusis; though Eubuleus (variously identified, usually as either the son of Demeter or of Zeus) and Triptolemus (who brought agriculture to the world, teaching the use of the plough, sickle and spade) were also worshipped there (BONNECHERE 2003:181). However, BURKERT (1987:46) maintains that initiates into the mysteries at Eleusis did not have any form of credo.
558. Before being taken into a crack in the earth leading to the underworld, Persephone flung her girdle into the Kyane river, calling on the water-nymphs to carry it to Demeter. In her search for her daughter Demeter saw Persephone's glittering girdle in a stream in Sicily. A fountain, who had once been a nymph called Arethusa, told Demeter that she had seen Persephone in the underworld with Pluton. Demeter entreated Zeus for her release, and Hermes, accompanied by Spring, descended to the underworld to petition Pluton; and he agreed to release Persephone. However, a spirit of darkness called Asclaphus revealed that Persephone had eaten four pomegranate seeds given to her by Pluton; so, subsequently, she had to spend a third of the year (four months) underground as his wife, though she was allowed to spend two thirds of the year on Mount Olympus with the gods. A common theme in the mythology of several of the mystery cults is the death and subsequent, seasonal revival of a spouse or child of a deity associated with the growth of nutritive plants.
559. The mystery cult of Demeter and Korē also took place in several other sanctuaries in the classical Greek and Greco-Roman worlds and was the most widespread of the mystery cults in Greece (BURKERT 1983:255). Other mystery cults included those of Dionysos, Mithras, Themis, Isis, Serapis, Artemis, Antinoos, Kabeiroi (on Samothrace), Hekate, Hera, the Phrygian (central Turkey) cult of Kybele and Attis (her abandoned son, whom Kybele

After examining the mythological and archeological evidence, MYLONAS (1974:14) concludes, despite slight discrepancies in chronology, that the Eleusian rites were most probably established in the second half of the 15th century BCE, in Mycenean or late Helladic times. (This is around the same time that it is believed that the Āryan migrations from Central Asia arrived in South Asia.) However, scholars are divided over the question of the historical origins of the mystery cult of Demeter and Persephone at Eleusis.[560] The rites at Eleusis, which in its latter phase accommodated up to 2,000 or 3,000 participants, were eventually prohibited during the reign of the Roman emperor THEODOSIUS (r. 379–395),[561] and in 395 CE Eleusis was destroyed by ALARIC I (370/375–410 CE), king

---

subsequently fell in love with), and the Phrygian/Thracian (Thrace borders Bulgaria, Turkey and northern Greece) cult of Sabazios, amongst others. The cults of Kybele and Sabazios were closely related with the cult of Dionysos, and were largely, or entirely, confined to women (SEAFORD 2006:35). Worship of Kybele goes back at at least to the time of the civilization of Çatal Huyuk (in Turkey) around 6000 BCE. She was a fat woman who gave birth seated on a throne, flanked by felines, and known as Kubaba to the Hittites. Bulls were sacrificed at her shrine (PARPOLA 2015:236–237). GRAF (2003:241) remarks that most scholars (following Franz CUMONT) classify three major mystery cults (of Demeter at Eleusis, of the Great Gods of Samothrace, and of Dionysos), and three younger 'oriental' cults (of Isis and the other Egyptian gods of her circle, of the Great Mother, and of Mithras). There were, however, several other mystery cults; some were indirectly related to Eleusis (which was the most important cult of antiquity), others arose independently.

560. BURKERT (1987:8) remarks that, "There is slight archaeological evidence, and great enthusiasm among scholars, for Mycenean antecedents of the Eleusian cult". However, MYLONAS (1974:15ff.) observes that although there are some indications of Cretan origins in the 'Homeric' Hymn to Demeter (*c.*7th/6th century BCE), wherein the goddess tells the daughters of Keleos—king of Eleusis—that she came from Crete to Eleusis, in an important inscription at the Cretan temple/palace of Knossos that lists the deities to receive offerings, neither Demeter nor Persephone are found. MYLONAS discusses three other places that scholars have suggested as places of origin: Egypt, Thessaly, and Thrace. MYLONAS favours Thrace, in the north. COSMOPOULOS (2015:150–159) argues against origins in Egypt, Crete, Thrace, Thessaly and south Greece, and favours origins in Eleusis itself.

561. The mysteries of Demeter may have continued secretly at Athens until the 8th century (WRIGHT 2011:8).

of the Visigoths,[562] thus ending the performance of annual initiation rites that had continued uninterrupted for around 1,800 years.[563]

Six elements were shared by all mystery cults: secrecy, preliminary purification, symbolic formulary, simulation of death, visual revelation, and a sacramental meal. Payment was required for participation.[564] It seems that initiation at Eleusis influenced all the subsequent mystery cults that developed (DELATTE 1954:700–702; CASSADIO and JOHNSTON 2009:6ff.). Most mystery rites entailed animal sacrifices and were performed annually, though some were biennial or triennial, and nearly always at night. The sanctuaries usually contained an underground room or cave where the rites were conducted. During the rites of the mystery cult of Dionysos, similarly to the reports of experience at Eleusis, initiates saw terrifying

---

562. General restrictions and prohibitions by Roman authorities on mystery cults continued in subsequent centuries. In one of the earliest Old Latin documents (on a brass tablet) dated to 186 BCE, Bacchic rites of Dionysos were decreed by the senate to be illegal without a licence. Roman citizens were forbidden participation. Secret mystery rites, which had become established in many cities, including Rome, were seen as a political threat; many adherents were imprisoned and 4,000 were put to death (ESCOHOTADO 2010:337–348; RUCK and LARNER 2013:432). *Bacchants* were the intoxicated, sexually licentious devotees of Dionysos, which was one of the most popular mystery cults of the Greco-Roman world. During frenzied rites 'wine' was drunk and a live animal (usually a goat) was dismembered (*spargmós*) and eaten raw by the *bacchants*. The most famous, classical, literary account of Bacchic rites is by EURIPIDES in *Bacchae*. In the *Phaedrus* (265) PLATO refers to four kinds of madness, one of them being the initiatory madness of the cult of Dionysos. The unveiling of a phallus in a winnowing fan is one of the central events in Dionysian rites (BURKERT 1983:271). BURKERT (1985:277) remarks that an, "undeniable aspect of the mysteries is the sexual aspect: genital symbols, exposures, and occasionally veritable orgies".

563. The only time that the procession to Eleusis was interrupted was when the news reached Athens (in 336 BCE) that ALEXANDER the Great had sacked Thebes (MYLONAS 1974:257). General restriction and prohibitions by Roman authorities on mystery cults continued in subsequent centuries.

564. At Eleusis the *hierophant* received one *obol* each day of the rites from each initiate, while the heralds (*spondopheroi*) received half an *obol*, and the priest of Demeter an *obol*. The sanctuary also received from Athens and her allies grains and oxen (FERGUSON 1989:107). Public slaves were occasionally admitted at public expense (WRIGHT 2011:13).

apparitions and light appearing in the darkness of the nocturnal ritual environment (SEAFORD 2006:82).

The initiation at Eleusis was initially restricted to the local citizens of Eleusis, was then extended to Athenians, and by around the 7th century BCE was available to all, including women, foreigners and slaves,[565] provided they spoke Greek and had not committed a heinous crime, such as murder. Treason and witchcraft were subsequently also included as constituting restrictions on participation. Officials known as *mystagogue*s were assigned single persons or groups of initiands to instruct them in the coming course of the rites and to assess whether or not they were sufficiently inwardly and outwardly pure enough to participate. Most Athenians were initiates (*mystes*), as were many Roman emperors, writers and philosophers. The mystery rites had two phases, the 'lesser' and the 'greater' rites. The annual 'great' rites,[566] which culminated in the drinking of *kykeōn* and a dramatic and musical performance at the temple of Eleusis, in which Demeter was ritually reunited with Korē (SOURVINOU-INWOOD 2003:30ff.), lasted for nine days in September/

565. Each year one child was also initiated. This is an enactment of an episode in the myth of Persephone. Before their reunification, her mother Demeter, disguised as a crone, was wandering in search of her daughter. At Eleusis, she was invited to look after Demophon (or, in some versions of the myth, Triptolemus), the son of the king Keleos and queen Metaneira of Eleusis. She anointed the child with ambrosia and put him in a fire, not to kill him but to purify him for immortality. However, Metaneira snatched the child from the fire, depriving him of immortality (GUERBER 1953:107–114; BURKERT 1983:280–281).

566. Two months before the full moon of the month of the rites heralds announced the great mysteries and requested an armistice for fifty-five days during times of the rites from those from Hellenic cities engaged in war (WRIGHT 2011:6; COSMOPOULOS 2015:17).

October (from 15th–23rd of the month of *boedromion*).[567] A special form of the event occurred every four years.[568]

The 'lesser' mysteries were conducted openly in February/ March (from 19th–21st of the month of *anthesterion*) at Agrai (a suburb of Athens) by the Illisos river, where initiands gathered at a temple dedicated to Demeter and Korē to begin purifications.[569] The 'lesser' and 'greater' rites were formally combined in the 7th century BCE. In the 'lesser' rites something special was eaten and drunk and one became *mystes*; this became an essential preliminary initiation before participation a year later in the 'great' rites, when one could

---

567. On the day preceding the festival (the 14th of the month *boedromion*) the sacred objects were brought in cylindrical containers (*cistai*) from Eleusis to a temple at Athens. The first day (the 15th) included a proclamation and invitation: only the 'pure' were eligible. No fancy clothes should be worn; cosmetics were not permitted for women, who had to let their hair down. The 16th (day 2) was known as 'Seawards, initiates', when initiates would purify themselves in the sea or in one of two salt lakes on the sacred way. The 17th (day 3) was a day of mourning (over Demeter's loss of Persephone) when initiands sacrificed a purified pig and fasted all day till nightfall, when seedcakes, parched corn, salt, pomegranate and sacred wine mixed with milk and honey were consumed. The 18th (day 4) was called *epidauria* or *asklepieia*, when the healing god was invoked (WRIGHT [2011:11] maintains that the *epidauria* was on 22nd); and in procession women carried baskets containing sesame, corded wool, pomegranate, reeds, corn, ivy boughs and poppyseed cakes. On the 19th (day 5) the *dadouchos* (torch bearer) led a torch-lit procession around the temple of Demeter. The 20th (day 6) was a day of fasting and when sacrifice took place; this was the day of Iakchos, when the initiands went in a nocturnal procession, singing and dancing along the sacred way (which was twenty-two kilometers), from the sanctuary of Iakchos at Athens to Eleusis, carrying a statue of the god and other ritual objects. At night and on the following day (and possibly also the next night: COSMOPOULOS 2015:21) initiation took place, on the 20th–21st (days 6–7); and the statue of Iakchos was returned to Athens. The 22nd (day 8) included libations to the dead. On the ninth day (the 23rd), the 'day of earthen vessels', fertility rites were performed and the initiates returned to Athens. On the 24th the council of Eleusis received a report on the ceremonies (FERGUSON 1989:106–107; BURKERT 1985:286; WRIGHT 2011:9–19).
568. Several other annual, agricultural and fertility festivals also took place at Eleusis: see COSMOPOULOS (2015:12–14).
569. Dionysos was also associated with these rites, but probably only from the 7th century BCE (SAMORINI 2000:23).

become *epoptes* (one who has 'seen').[570] Thus, participating in the rites were *mystai*, who were attending for the first time, and *epoptai*, who were participating for the second time. On the sixth night of the annual 'great' rites, prospective initiates, chanting "Iakchos, Iakchos",[571] arrived at Eleusis in procession from Athens. The procession represented the search for Persephon, followed by the eventual finding of her in a great light at the climax of the rites. Just before arriving at the sanctuary, when crossing a bridge, the people in procession were lewdly mocked by actors wearing masks. The 'great mysteries', during which the ritual potion *kykeōn* was drunk, were conducted in absolute secrecy during the final two days and night that initiates spent in the sanctuary; revealing what happened was punishable by death.[572]

The vision of light revealed at the Eleusian rites happened in the inner sanctum of the temple building (*telestērion*, the 'hall of completion') by the chief priest (known as the *hierophant*),[573] who since the institution of the performance of the rites, always came

---

570. *Mystai* has the sense of 'eyes closed' or 'blindfolded'. *Epopteia*, the 'seeing', is the highest grade of initiation (CLINTON 2003). Some scholars have proposed further grades or stages of initiation: see SAMORINI (2000:8) for further details. WRIGHT (2011:17–18) proposes three degrees of initiation. In the last centuries of the performance of the Eleusian rites the preliminary initiatory requirement to first become *mystes* was sometimes dropped (BURKERT 1983:265).
571. It seems that Iakchos was originally identified with Dionysos.
572. Some aristocratic Athenians, including PLATO's lover Alkybiades, stole *kykeōn* in 415 BCE and used it at home with his friends in Athens. They were arrested for profaning the mysteries (SAMORINI 2000:20). Alkybiades escaped death (but his property was seized) after the judge heard PLATO's plea for mitigation. This is one of several instances reported of people profaning the mysteries. FERGUSON (1989:105) notes LIVY's comment (31, 14) that two strangers, who were not initiates and who had wandered inadvertently into the sanctuary, were executed.
573. The *hierophant* was usually married and acquired a new name when elected to office. He was kept in purity, having no contact with the dead or unclean animals, and was accompanied in rites by two women, the *hierophantide*, also from the Eumolpos family, who could marry and were chosen for life. They attended as priestesses upon Demeter and Persephone and initiated women participants.

from the Eumolpos (good voice) clan/family.[574] The *hierophant* showed a blade of cut wheat to initiates, who remained in silence; but initiates were also 'shown' *hiera*, which, from some reports, seems to have been something in a box or basket. The *hiera* were carried in a procession along the twenty-kilometer road from Athens to Eluesis, accompanied by those to be initiated at the temple of Eleusis. Whatever was in the box was totally secret. There have been several hypotheses about what this could have been, including 'real' or 'mystical' grains of wheat, cakes, wool, glebe, and either male or female genital organs (Delatte 1954:691). Ruck (Wasson *et al.* 1978:79; 2006:17) provides reports by some initiates that indicate the revelation in the form of a vision or a ghostly apparition of phantoms or of Persephone herself, rather than material objects.[575]

Burkert (1987:11) remarks:

> Mysteries were initiation rituals of a voluntary, personal and secret character that aimed at a change of mind through experience of the sacred … Participation in mysteries was a special form of experience, a *pathos* in the soul, or *psyche*, of the candidate, [which] is clearly stated in several texts (p.89)[576] … in psychological terms, there must have been an experience of the 'other' in a change of consciousness, moving far beyond what is found in everyday life.

Burkert (1987:90) quotes a participant of the Eleusian rites who said: "I came out of the mystery hall feeling like a stranger to myself". Mylonas (1974:285) quotes Pindar (*fr.* 102): "Happy is he who, having seen these rites, goes below the hollow earth; for he knows the end of life and he knows its god-sent beginning". Marcus

---

574. The other temple officiants of high office who administered the rites came from the clan/family of Kerykes, who derived their ancestry from Eumolpos's son, Keryx. These included the torch-bearer, who also killed and skinned the sacrificed ram, and the *hierokeryx*, the herald. The *phaidantes* maintained custody of the sacred vessels. All officiants wore purple robes and myrtle crowns (Burkert 1983:282; Cosmopoulos 2015:16–17).

575. This is the view of Kerényi (1977) and also of Rudolph Otto (1978) [1925], who, similarly to Jaynes (1976), maintains that the Greeks really *saw* deities (Burkert 1983:286).

576. Burkert (1987:89) cites Aristotle (*fr.* 15) on mystery rites: "…at the final stage of mysteries there should be no more 'learning' (*mathein*) but 'experiencing' (*pathein*), and a change in the state of mind (*diatethenai*)".

AURELIUS described the experience of 'Mysteries' as being between revelatory dreams, divination, and miraculous cures (BONNECHERE 2003:176).

According to BURKERT, PLATO's *Phaedrus* clearly refers to the mystery rites at Eleusis, to the, "initiations that must be called the most blessed of all",[577] wherein the soul's chariot is described ascending to the highest summit in the realm of the gods, where a glance beyond heaven is possible and, "where resplendent beauty was to be seen". These divine visions may subsequently be resuscitated by images of beauty in the world. BURKERT (1987:92–93) comments that PLATO's use of the terms *mystai* (initiates) and *epoptai* (Eleusian initiates of the highest degree, who have 'seen') refer unequivocally to the Eleusian rites. BURKERT also observes that PLATO makes an oblique allusion to terrifying events, *deimata*, preceding the veneration of the divine; and remarks that the rites at Eleusis are, "both the most frightening and the most resplendent of all that is most divine"; the experience moving between terror and happiness, darkness and light.[578] SEAFORD (2004:229) comments that trembling (*tromos*) was a typical feature of mystic initiation, before the transition to calm or stillness (*hēsuchia*).

In an oft-cited passage, PLUTARCH (*fr.* 178)—probably here referring to the rites at Eleusis—describes the process of dying in terms of a mystery initiation:

> At the moment of death, the soul suffers an experience similar to those who celebrate great initiations...Wanderings astray in the beginning, tiresome walking in circles, some frightening paths in darkness that lead nowhere; then immediately before the end of all the terrible

577. See PLATO (1973:56–57): "But beauty was once ours to see in all its brightness, when in the company of the blessed we followed Zeus as others followed some other of the Olympians, to enjoy the beatific vision and to be initiated into that mystery which brings, we may say with reverence, supreme felicity. Whole were we who celebrated that festival, unspotted by all the evils which awaited us in time to come, and whole and unspotted and changeless and serene were the objects revealed to us in the light of that mystic vision".

578. CLARK (2009:200–201n.7, n.20) provides further references to the terrifying nature of the experience.

> things, panic and shivering and sweat, and amazement. And then some wonderful light comes to meet you…[579] (BURKERT 1987:91–92).

BURKERT comments (p.98) that, "It is left to our imagination how the 'frontier of death' was reached.[580] BERNABÉ (2009:105–106) remarks that PLUTARCH specifically compares initiation into 'great mysteries' with the experience of death. BERNABÉ also maintains that PLUTARCH's description refers to mystery rites in general, and that the highest level of initiation in mystery rites is very similar to a death experience. BONNECHERE (2003:178), referring to the mystery rites of Trophonius, but also commenting on mystery rites in general, remarks that, "The encounter with death is at the root of these rites".[581] Similarly, commenting on the mystery rites at Eleusis, FERGUSON (1989:104) comments that, "Parallel with the springing of new life from the ground [in spring] is the promise of new life from death for initiates". WRIGHT (2011:15) remarks that, "The epopte were supposed to have experienced a certain regeneration and to enter upon a new state of existence, and they were fantastically deemed to have acquired a great increase of light and knowledge".

---

579. "…pure regions and meadows are there to greet you, with sounds, dances and solemn, sacred words and holy views; and there the initiate, perfect by now, set free and loose from all bondage, walks about, crowned with a wreath, celebrating the festival together with the other sacred and pure people, and he looks down on the uninitiated, unpurified crowd in this world in mud and fog beneath his feet". However, this account may have been influenced by Orphism (MYLONAS 1974:265–269).
580. For a summary of the mythology, rites and reports of initiates at Eleusis, see HOFMANN in FIELDING (2008:25–29). For a more comprehensive account of the mythology of Eleusis, see also the useful study by SAMORINI (2000).
581. "Once in a black hole in the dead of night and overcome with fear, the consultant must often have lost consciousness in a sort of hallucinatory syncope combined with auditory sensations. The oracle seems to have functioned by provoking in certain consultants 'visionary trances', which they perceived as the passage of their souls into another world" (BONNECHERE 2003:178).

CHAPTER 17

Kykeōn and the ergot hypothesis

Perhaps the most intriguing question concerning the Eleusian and other mystery rites is what could cause a near-death experience or a profound 'change of mind'. In their book *The Road to Eleusis: Unveiling the Secret of the Mysteries*, WASSON, HOFMANN, and RUCK (1978) propose that the 'wine' of the mysteries that produced ecstasy, terror and visions, which was drunk during the rites, was a psychedelic concoction based on lysergic acid amide (LSA) as the main psychoactive chemical. Lysergic acid amide was referred to previously in relation to theories about *soma*. It has some of the effects of LSD and can be obtained—according to one of the two main hypotheses proposed by WASSON *et al.*—from a preparation of ergot fungus harvested from the wild grass host *Paspalum distichum*, which, according to *The Road to Eleusis*, was widely disseminated in the Mediterranean region (but see below). The ergot theory is still probably the most widely accepted proposal for the *kykeōn* amongst scholars who believe an entheogen was used, though some commentators are still of the opinion that no drug was involved.[582]

In *The Road to Eleusis*—and also in subsequent publications—RUCK further suggests (p.118ff.) that while the 'major' rites were based on the ergot fungus (represented by wheat), the 'minor mystery' rites were based on fly-agaric mushrooms (*Amanita muscaria*).[583] It is known that the participants in the minor mysteries ate and drank

582. BURKERT (1987:108–109) and COSMOPOULOS (2015:21) are sceptical that any kind of drug was necessarily used in any mystery rites.

583. RUCK *et al.* (2011:41ff.) also maintain that fly-agaric mushrooms were in a concoction drunk for initiation into the Greco-Roman cult of Mithras.

something.[584] Even though some of the classical Greco-Roman artistic evidence and RUCK's interesting exposition of classical mythology could provide support for this hypothesis, it seems debatable. As discussed previously, fly-agaric has what I believe are too many negative side-effects to be considered as the entheogen of mystery rites.[585] Further, as SAMORINI (2000:38) points out, harvesting sufficient quantities of mushrooms—of whatever kind—for mystery rites with up to 2,000 participants would have required elaborate organization, which does not appear to be mentioned in any classical source.[586]

In the culture of ancient Greece wine was always diluted with usually three or four (but up to twenty) parts water; drunk neat it could cause madness or death.[587] Wine was not ever distilled, as the

584. In a subsequent publication, RUCK (1997:132) maintains that, "the sacred mushroom of Zeus's people, as R. Gordon Wasson has shown, was the *Amanita muscaria*... The Persians... remembered it as *haoma.* Among the Hindus, it was *soma*". RUCK suggests (2006:52) that fly-agaric mushrooms appear to be depicted on a winnowing fan on the so-called Lovatelli urn (discovered in 1879), in what has been interpreted as representing the preparations for initiation at Eleusis (which is, however, contested by some scholars: see SAMORINI 2000:38). See also SAMORINI (2000:36ff.) for artistic classical Greco-Roman representations and a discussion of what could be fly-agaric mushrooms used in the 'lesser mysteries'. Of particular interest to most commentators on this topic is the 5th-century BCE Pharsalus (Thessaly, Greece) bas-relief, which shows what has been interpreted as two goddesses holding what appears to be a large mushroom (or a flower), which is also specifically discussed by SAMORINI (1998). SAMORINI (2000:50) believes that what was probably consumed in the minor mysteries was either fly-agaric or psilocybin mushrooms, despite his reservations concerning their harvest.

585. See also SAMORINI (2000:37), who also cites a concern over side-effects of fly-agaric.

586. WEBSTER (2000:60) also comments that, "Thousands of specimens of even the strongest *Psilocybin* mushrooms would have been needed, at a time of year when the climate of Greece was just barely subsiding from the summer heat and dryness... And as anyone who has collected wild mushrooms knows, they seldom appear on-schedule, in such dependable quantities, even when an area known to produce a certain variety has been identified".

587. HERODOTUS (6.84), commenting on the cause of the madness and eventual death of the monarch KLEOMENES, remarks that his madness was most probably due to his association with Scythians, who are in the habit of

technique of distilling alcohol was unknown until around 1000 CE, but it seems that 'wine' was invariably infused with other plants and drugs that rendered it more potent.[588] RUCK (2006:94–95) comments that in Greek every drink that induced 'drunkenness' was simply called 'wine'. He adds that, "The wines for sacral purposes were even more intoxicating than those for social situations, for according to Plato, they were intended to induce madness".[589]

As mentioned previously, the ritual drink of the 'great' mystery rites at Eleusis was called *kykeōn*,[590] which means 'mixed potion' in Greek. Several days of celibacy and purifications and fasting during the day before the ritual initiation preceded the drinking of *kykeōn* at Eleusis. Dietary restrictions pertained to the fast: on kinds of fish[591] (mullet,[592] dog-fish and black-tails), domestic birds (especially

---

drinking their 'wine' neat, without water, and that this was the cause of KLEOMENES losing his mind. It is apparent that this was no ordinary wine, perhaps being a kind of *haoma* administered by a sect of Scythians who were referred to earlier in this book: the *haomavarga*. An epigram of ERASIXENUS states that he died after drinking two cups of wine in straight succession (RUCK 2006:95).

588. Wine drunk at the theatre contained a special herbal additive (RUCK 2013:364).

589. See RUCK (WASSON *et al.* 1978: 89–93) for a useful overview of the various kinds of, strengths of, and additives to 'wine' in classical Greek and Greco-Roman culture.

590. There were many kinds of *kykeōn*, used in other religious rites, at funerals, magical rites, and in medicinal treatments. See DELATTE (1954) for one of the most thorough treatments of this topic. For various kinds of *kykeōn* (some of which contain very strange ingredients, such as the beating heart of a hoopoe), which appear in dramatic, poetic and other texts, see DELATTE (1954:722ff.).

591. Tablets in front of the temple listed prohibited foods. According to WRIGHT (2011:16) the forbidden fish were whistle-fish (probably *Sciaena aquila*), gurnet, crab and mullet. The whistle-fish and crab were believed to be impure. The gurnet may have been forbidden because of its eating of poisonous fish. WRIGHT offers no explanation of a restriction on mullet.

592. As mentioned previously, preliminary restrictions on specific foods whose chemistry (particularly foods with MAOI properties) could potentially adversely interfere with the finely-balanced chemistry of ayahuasca preparations are usually practised amongst indigenous groups in South America who consume it. Interestingly (though this is but speculative), several species of mullet (*Mugil cephalus, Mulloidichtythys samoensis,*

chicken and pigeon), wine, beans, pomegranate, apples, eggs and improperly killed animals; nor was it permitted to touch a dead body or a woman who had recently given birth (MYLONAS 1974:258). Preliminary preparations for initiation also included the sacrifice of a pig by every participating Athenian. Very similar (if not identical) preliminary dietary restrictions pertained to other mystery cults, including those of Trophonius, and of Demeter at Haloa (BONNECHERE 2003:179).

It seems that the *kykeōn* of the Eleusian mysteries was prepared in an exact dose KERÉNYI (1977:178), which was drunk at the conclusion of the fast from a small cup or bowl. It was dispensed from a vessel called a *kernos*, which was a circular holder containing small cups surrounding a larger central cup, in which the *kykeōn* was probably held, [593] having been decanted from a larger vessel. Consumed with *kykeōn* was what seems to have been a cake or small loaf taken from a basket,[594] a similar combination of a ritual drink consumed with a small cake or bread that we observed in connection with Vedic and Zoroastrian rites.

The ingredients of the *kykeōn* concoction used at Eleusis are obscure. One of the few certainties is that it consisted of barley groats (similarly to *soma*) that had been pulverized, usually in a mortar and pestle, and added to a liquid. In some preparations of *kykeōn* the grain was soaked either in 'wine', honey, milk or oil. The concoction was in many instances seasoned with an aromatic plant, such as *glechon*, which is usually identified as pennyroyal mint,[595] and

---

Neomyxus chaptalli, and *Upeneus arge*) are now known to have psychoactive, intoxicating properties (TORO and THOMAS 2007:87). Although these species of fish are currently Asian in habitat, could it be that the psychoactive properties of some kinds of mullet were known to the ancient Greeks potentially to cause adverse reactions if *kykeōn* is subsequently consumed?

593. The contents of the small bowls surrounding the *kykeōn* vessel is obscure: they seem to be connected to the *heira* (holy things), but also may have contained grains of corn, oats, rice, lentils, peas etc., perhaps to be consumed before or after the *kykeōn* (SAMORINI 2000:16).

594. See SAMORINI (2000:14–15) for the evidence behind the opinion that this was what was contained in the cylindrical wicker basket (*kiste*).

595. KERÉNYI (1977:179–180) believes that *glechon* (pennyroyal, *Mentha pulegium*, a kind of mint similar to spearmint), the tender leaves of which, besides roasted and ground barley groats, were an ingredient of the *kykeōn*,

which is often mentioned in connection with *kykeōn*, usually as an ingredient; it was sometimes used in the form of a twig to stir the *kykeōn*.[596] However, RUCK remarks (WASSON *et al.* 1978:100–101) that the identification of *glechon* (or *blechon*) with pennyroyal cannot be certain, as several plants were called *blechon* in the classical period, and that in ARISTOPHANES' *Peace* the plant is introduced as an aphrodisiac. RUCK also provides several references in classical sources that warn of the dangers of the profane use of *glechon/blechon*, which, he believes, indicates that the plant was improbably pennyroyal, because its effects are too mild.

WATKINS (1978:16–17), commenting on a passage in which there is one of the very few instances in the *Iliad*[597] where the term *kykeōn* is used,[598] draws attention to the similarity of *kykeōn* to the *soma* concoction of the *Veda*s. Nestor and Machaon participate in a ritual and drink *kykeōn*, the primary ingredient of which is 'Pramneian wine', the meaning of which, WATKINS remarks, was lost already in antiquity, and is without etymology: "But clearly it is no ordinary wine". In the ceremony described in the *Iliad* the *kykeōn* is mixed

may have been hallucinogenic. However, although this plant has folk medical applications, it is sufficiently mild to be used in regular cuisine. (Nevertheless, the concentrated oil can be used as an aborifacient and is toxic.) PLINY (*Natural History* 20.52–56) records the use of wild pennyroyal as an antidote for snake and scorpion bites, for inducing menstruation, and for spasms, cholic and cholera, amongst other applications. Besides KERÉNYI's supposition, there is no evidence for this plant being at all hallucinogenic. DELATTE (1954:732) also remarks that much is made by some commentators of the *glechon* causing nervous excitement among the *mystēs*, but without any reason. It has been reported (MAZZIO *et al.* 2013) that some of the herbs of the mint family (*Lamiaceae*) have weak MAOI properties; though it seems unlikely that weak inhibition in a kind of mint could account for any properly psychoactive effect. It was also suggested by HOFMANN in a personal communication with VALENCIC (1994:329) that mint might have been used to mitigate the nauseous effect of the ergot.

596. This 'old form' of *kykeōn* is referred to by PLINY in his *Natural Histories* (20.153) (DELATTE 1954:716).

597. At the beginning of Book 14, when Nestor and the wounded Machaon leave the battle and repair to Nestor's tent. This is the most ancient reference to *kykeōn* in Greek literature (DELATTE 1954:711).

598. The very first reference to *kykeōn* is in an inscription in pre-Greek characters on an amphora dated to 1200 BCE (SAMORINI 2000:16).

with a milk product (goat's cheese), honey and barley, just as in Vedic ritual. The same kind of *kykeōn* potion, to which a 'drug' is added, is made by Circe in the *Odyssey* (10.234) for Ulysses and his companions (DELATTE 1954:712). WATKINS also notes the semantic isomorphism between *kykeōn* and Vedic noun *āśír*[599] (mixed potion).

Similarly to historical research opinions on the identity of *soma/ haoma*, scholars have variously proposed the opium poppy,[600] Syrian rue, kinds of alcohol or entheogens in the form of either psilocybin or fly-agaric mushrooms[601] as the basis of *kykeōn.* Following DELATTE's (1954:731–732) analysis of the *Homeric Hymn to Demeter*, SAMORINI (2000:14) maintains that *kykeōn* could not have been ordinary alcoholic wine, as Demeter, when offered it, refuses it in favour of *kykeōn.*[602] As noted earlier in this chapter, SAMORINI also points out (p.15) that there were many kinds of *kykeōn* of varying consistencies (depending on water content), some being medicinal, and that the only common ingredient was barley. A further observation that SAMORINI makes is that, strictly speaking, *kykeōn* means 'that which is mixed again'; this is to stir up sediment that may have fallen to the bottom of the dispensing container, which makes sense of several passages by classical authors who refer to the mixing of *kykeōn* (p.17).[603]

It has been previously mentioned that among the epithets in the *Veda*s for *soma* is *amṛta*; *haoma* is referred to *dūraoša* in the *Avesta*; and *kykeōn* was known as *nektar* and *ambrosia.* All these epithets

---

599. KAPADIA (1959:21) comments that *āśir*, without an adjective, refers to *soma* to which milk is added.

600. SAMORINI (2000:31) cites an observation by M. D. MERLIN (*On the Trail of the Ancient Opium Poppy*, 1984), of which he is sceptical, that opium was used in the *kykeōn* as it can mitigate the effects of ergot poisoning; though this seems a highly improbable formula for ritual use. VALENCIC (1994:329) made several inquiries about the possibility of opium being added to a psychedelic *kykeōn* and concludes that the most probable effect would be the diminution rather than enhancement of any entheogenic effect.

601. Three different people have been proposed by scholars as being the first to suggest that *kykeōn* was an entheogen: WASSON in 1956, KERÉNYI in 1962, or Robert GRAVES in 1964. It was probably both GRAVES and WASSON together, who at different times proposed either psilocybin or fly-agaric mushrooms (SAMORINI 2000:24–27).

602. *Homeric Hymn to Demeter*, vs. 19–21 (trans. STAPLES in RUCK (2006:138).

603. The mixing was performed by women who had carried the *kykeōn* vessels on their heads in procession to Eleusis (RUCK 2006:64).

refer to overcoming death/non-death/immortality.[604] If we take these epithets at face value, then it seems feasible that the concoction in question could produce a near-death (and consequent rebirth) experience. In the timeless state of entheogenic trance, there is no time, and hence no birth or death. Scholars disagree on whether or not such kinds of experience were engendered by entheogenic/psychedelic wine or *kykeōn*, or, alternatively, arose as a consequence of 'natural' religious frenzy. I believe, however, that the evidence points almost incontrovertibly to an entheogenic concoction.

The hypothesis, originally proposed by WASSON *et al.* in 1978, that a kind of ergot fungus was the main hallucinogenic ingredient in the ritual drink *kykeōn* consumed during Greek mystery rites, is revisited and reviewed by VALENCIC (1994), WEBSTER *et al.* (2000), and SAMORINI (2000). While VALENCIC is sceptical of the ergot thesis and raises several pertinent objections, WEBSTER *et al.* and SAMORINI generally support it.

SAMORINI makes further observations, but also provides corrections to one of the hypotheses proposed by HOFMANN (in WASSON *et al.*, 1978), referred to earlier, concerning ergot as the main reagent of *kykeōn*. It is pointed out (FESTI and SAMORINI 1999:97; SAMORINI 2000:29–31) that the grass which grows on the Rarian plain near Eluesis, which was proposed by WASSON *et al.* (as one of two alternative hypotheses) to be the host for the ergot fungus *Claviceps paspali*, could not have been *Paspalum distichum*, as that species of grass did not grow in Greece at the time of the Eleusian rites. HOFMANN favoured *Claviceps paspali* as the kind of ergot fungus used in the *kykeōn* (rather than ergot growing on rye) because of the less toxic alkaloid content of *Claviceps paspali* in comparison with other species of ergot.[605] But *Claviceps paspali*,

---

604. A significant difference between the Greek concept of ambrosia (as a nectar of immortality) and the Indo-Iranian notion of *amṛta* is that only in the latter cultural sphere is the drink of immortality deified: there is no goddess or god of nectar or immortality in the Mediterranean world (THOMPSON 2007:67).

605. The main active alkaloids of this ergot fungus are ergine (D-lysergic acid amide = LSA) and ergonovine (D-lysergic acid-L-2-propaolamide = ergometrine = ergobasine = ergotocine), which occurs only in a small amount in the ergot fungus (SCHULTES and HOFMANN 1980:33–39; HOFMANN 2011:16–17). The reason for the multiple names for ergonovine is that the same alkaloid was almost simultaneously discovered in the mid-1930s by five separate teams

the kind of ergot fungus favoured by WASSON *et al.*, exclusively infects graminaceous plants of the *Paspalum* genus.[606] However,

---

of researchers, who all called it different names (BOVÉ 1970:108–110). As mentioned previously, more than thirty alkaloids—several of which have been developed for therapeutic applications—have been isolated from various kinds of ergot, the first being ergotamine by A. STOLL in 1918. Lysergic acid is the common nucleus of ergot alkaloids (HOFMANN in RUCK 2006:154–155). Five alkaloids are known to be psychoactive in humans: ergine (lysergic acid amide), isoergine, ergonovine (= ergometrine), elymoclavine, and lysergol.

Lysergic acid amides (LSA) occur naturally in several plants besides ergot, notably in the seeds of some of the many scores of varieties of the morning glory creeper, which is in the *Ipomoea* family. However, only some species of this genus (*Convolvulaceae*) are psychoactive, notably *Ipomoea violacea, Ipomoea tricolor,* and *Ipomoea sidaefolia/Rivea corymbosa/Turbina corymbosa* (see SCHULTES and HOFMANN (1980:256–257) for clarification of variant botanical classifications of this species). The alkaloid content of the seeds of different plants, even of the same species, varies considerably. The varieties of morning glory favoured for their LSA content are Pearly Gates and Heavenly Blue. The seeds of this plant, used and revered by the Aztecs and Mayans of Mexico and known as *ololiuqui*, were famously identified by the ethnobotanist Richard SCHULTES in the late 1930s; their chemistry was subsequently revealed by Albert HOFMANN. They are still used in shamanic rituals in Mexico by Chontal, Mazatec and Zapotec Indians.

The psychoactive alkaloids lysergic acid amide (LSA/ergine), isoergine and ergonovine, are also in the seeds of the perennial climbing vine, Hawaiian baby woodrose (*Argyreia nervosa*) (JORDAN 1994; *The Psychonaut.org* 2013), a plant also of the *Convolvulaceae* family, originally from South Asia, but now indigenous to Hawaii, parts of Africa and the Caribbean. Known as *vidhārā* and *adhoguḍa* in Sanskrit, it is used in Ayurvedic medicine. This plant has no known history of religious or shamanic use in South Asia, but in one report (*The Psychonaut.org* 2013) it is suggested as a candidate for *soma.* In comparison with the seeds of psychoactive varieties of morning glory, the seeds of Hawaiian baby woodrose contain between two and four times the amount of lysergic acid amide. A close relative of this vine (sometimes identified as the same plant and also native to South Asia) is *Argyreia speciosa* (elephant creeper/woolly morning glory; Sanskrit: *bastāntrī/chagalāntrikā/vṛdhadāra/vṛdhadāraka/vṛdhadāru*; Hindi: *samundar ka paṭ/samundarsokha*). Ergometrine (= ergonovine) is one of three alkaloids found in its seeds. It is used in India in various Ayurvedic treatments and as an ingredient of an aphrodisiac concoction (GILANI *et al.* 2010). (Some of the alternative Sanskrit names provide for this plant by GILANI *et al.* are uncertain.)

606. SAMORINI (2000:29) additionally comments that *Papsalum distichum* L. is an uncertain classification; the name does not refer with certainty to any single known species.

not one of the 250–450 species of the genus *Paspalum* is indigenous to Europe. Only recently, probably in the last century, have some species arrived in Europe. So the kind of ergot used for *kykeōn*—if indeed any kind of ergot was used—could not have been *Claviceps paspali*.[607]

As the first of HOFMANN's hypotheses (that the ergot of the *kykeōn* was hosted by *Paspalum distichum*) is, it seems, impossible due to the historic reason of the non-European geographic distribution of the host grass, another possible candidate as the entheogenic source of the *kykeōn* mixture is the ergot species *Claviceps purpurea.* The second of HOFMANN's hypotheses regarding the ancient Greeks' use of ergot fungus is that it was the more common species[608] of purple-coloured ergot *Claviceps purpurea* (which infests nearly all graminaceous plants), the psychoactive alkaloids of which, after grinding, are water soluble. According to HOFMANN, this variety of ergot does not always possess debilitating toxins, as are usually present in this and other species of ergot.

In ancient Greece, wild ryegrass (darnel, *Lolium temulentum* L. or *Lolium perenne* L.),[609] which is widely disseminated in the Mediterranean region, and also barley were well known to be occasional hosts to the ergot *Claviceps purpurea.* The ergot fungus was in Greek called *erysibe* (which was also one of the names of Demeter), meaning a kind of 'rust', so named after the appearance of the tiny red/orange ergot fungi. According to RUCK (WASSON, *et al.* 1978:115) both rye and barley were potential hosts of the ergot used in the Eleusian mystery rites.

RUCK (p.126) provides several references from classical sources, including ARISTOTLE, THEOPHRASTUS, OVID and PLINY, that wild ryegrass (*aira*) infected with ergot could cause, heaviness, vertigo

607. SAMORINI (2000:19) also points out that the *hierophant* at Eleusis displays an ear (or 'flower') of corn to the initiands and that the most likely interpretation of 'flower' is as sclerota of ergot. That the host of the fungus would have been a kind of corn rather than the grass *Paspalum distichum* is further supported—if this suggestion is accepted—by the fact that Greek artistic representations of the 'holy' cereal/grain/grass of Eleusis do not look like *Paspalum distichum*, which is visually distinctive, usually having two spikes above the stem.

608. Between twenty-six and forty species of *Claviceps* are currently identified; the taxonomy is not consistent (SAMORINI 2000:42).

609. Darnel has no psychoactive properties on its own.

and hallucinations; it was also called the 'plant of frenzy'.[610] However, SAMORINI (2000:41) maintains, in accord with HOFMANN, that although the alkaloid content varies extensively in *Claviceps purpurea* (some strains contain no alkaloids and others produce mainly toxic alkaloids), [611] this kind of ergot contains, in some instances only, non-debilitating psychoactive alkaloids. SAMORINI also maintains (p.48) that there are instances of ergot intoxication which are what he describes as "clean" and without negative physical effects. In this regard, he cites effects of ergot intoxication from the roots of *Securidaca longipedunculata* by the Balanta people of Guinea Bissau and the use of the *Balansia cyperi* ergot fungus in the Peruvian Amazon region.[612] These two suggestions are now considered.

For almost a century the plant *Securidaca longipedunculata* Fres., which is native to West and South-West Africa, has been of interest to chemists and pharmacologists. This plant (in the *Polygalaceae* family) is known locally as *tchúnfki* and is used by witch doctors against 'evil spirits' and for many medical purposes, including the treatment of rheumatism, fever, headache, cough, toothache, various inflammatory conditions, and snake-bite. Fresh roots have a pungent, disagreeable smell and are used to control pests of plants in storage. Aqueous extracts of the root are used in religious rites by the Balanta people of Guinea Bissau for psychotropic effects. These effects are almost certainly caused by ergot alkaloids, which include elymoclavine, dehydroelymoclavine and a newly

---

610. As noted previously, PAL and JAIN (1989) report the voluntary ingestion in India of the husks of grain of *Papsalum scrobiculatum* L. to engender hallucinations. The symptoms of poisoning from consuming the infected grain include trembling, vertigo, perspiration and the inability to swallow. No fatalities have been reported.

611. HOFMANN (in RUCK 2006:153) reports that tests on rye conducted in three regions of Switzerland found that ergot from the Midlands contained mostly ergotamine, from Valais mostly ergotoxine, and from Grisons no alkaloids at all.

612. See SAMORINI (2000:44ff.) for other worldwide reports of indigenous, voluntary use of ergot consumption for a variety of medicinal and divinatory purposes.

discovered ergoline alkaloid, which infest the roots of the plant, but only in the dry season (COSTA *et al.* 1992:1641; SCANDOLA *et al.* 1994; WRÓBEL *et al.* 1996:685; JAYASEKARA *et al.* 2002:577). SAMORINI (1996:40–41) suggests that this plant might be an African *kykeōn.* However, in this article he also observes that the roots of the plant are also considered to be toxic by those who use them: "These are used by different tribes to kill or commit suicide; they are usually inserted into the vagina, rectally, urethrally or even orally. The death usually occurs after 12 hours". The potential toxicity of this plant seems to weigh considerably against support for the thesis that this or a similar kind of ergot was the basis of the Greek *kykeōn.*

The report by PLOWMAN *et al.* (1990) on the use of sedges (*Cyperus articulatus* and *Cyperus prolixus*)[613] infected with a kind of ergot fungus (*Balansia cyperi*) describes uses in the Amazon region for several purposes: induction of labour, abortion, contraception, curing baldness, vascoconstriction (to stem bleeding), gastric complaints, calming angry people, as a stimulant, as an additive to ayahuasca brews, for magic (for success in hunting or to counter witchcraft), and as a hallucinogen (the rhizomes are dried and smoked to engender hallucinations). It is best known in the Peruvian Amazon as a contraceptive. PLOWMAN *et al.* also mention (p.459) that studies have shown that livestock grazing on *Balansia*-infected grasses have difficulty in conceiving and experience spontaneous abortion. This interesting report on the use of ergot in the Amazon seems to be very slim evidence (if any at all) for the notion that ergot could have been the main basis of the Greek *kykeōn.* Women participated in the mystery rites and there is no indication that they were screened for pregnancy before participation. Also, crucially, there is no report so far, as far as I am aware, of a bioassay by any ethnographer who has drunk a concoction containing sedges infected with the *Balansia cyperi* ergot fungus.

There are a few reports of experiments conducted in the western world with various other extracted ergot alkaloids, which are not

613. At least six species of *cyperus* are now known to be infected by *Balansia cyperi* in North and South America (PLOWMAN *et al.* 1990:455).

particularly favourable.[614] VALENCIC (1994:327–328) and also SAMORINI (2000:46–47) cite four reports of self-experimentation[615] with the ergot alkaloids ergonovine[616] and methylergonovine.[617] At large and more effective doses hallucinogenic (or LSD-like) experience was reported, but accompanied by strong and debilitating side-effects, including tiredness, leg cramps and uncoordinated motor skills, which overwhelmed and disturbed the psychic effects.

Reports of the effects of naturally occurring or extracted LSA (ergine), which is one of the alkaloids found in both ergot and morning glory seeds, while not always negative, also do not seem to provide for consumers the rapture reported at Eleusis. The effect of d-lysergic amide (ergine/LSA) is some ways similar but much less potent (fifty to a hundred times, by weight) than the diethyl-amide in LSD.[618] High doses of 200–500 seeds of morning glory produce effects that are reported to be not dissimilar to LSD. However, they are accompanied in most cases by initial nausea, drowsiness or

614. Ergot alkaloid derivatives are currently being explored for use in the treatment of Alzheimer's and Parkinson's disease (see HOUGHTON and HOWES 2005).
615. By HOFMANN (1978:31); BIGWOOD *et al.* (1979); OTT and NEELY (1980). VALENCIC also cites Michael RIPINSKY-NAXON, who, in *The Nature of Shamanism* (1993), reports ingesting with his co-workers 6 mg of ergonovine. They experienced unimpressive psychic changes (mostly slight perceptual alterations), accompanied by leg cramps.
616. VALENCIC (1994:328) provides a summary of the reports by HOFMANN, WASSON and RUCK on the consumption of 2.0 mg of ergonovine maleate (ergonovine is a water-soluble component of ergot), which is about six times the normal dose used for ceasing postpartum haemorrhaging. HOFMANN experienced slight nausea, a strong desire to dream, and some psychedelic activity that lasted for about five hours, while no effect was reported by WASSON and RUCK. BIGWOOD *et al.* (1979) report that at higher doses (10 mg) ergonovine had a mild entheogenic effect but accompanied by debilitating leg cramps and lassitude. All four experimenters had a mild hangover the next day and none wished to take more than 10 mg in another experiment, as the negative somatic effects greatly overshadowed the psychic effects.
617. OTT and NEELY (1980) report effects nearly identical to those of ergonovine from methylergonovine, though ergonovine is approximately fives times as potent per weight as methylergonovine.
618. The lysergic acid molecule, which is the basis for making LSD, occurs in ergine, ergonovine and ergotamine. These alkaloids are found (in varying proportions) in the ergot fungus, morning glory seeds and Hawaiian baby woodrose (FESTER 2006:4).

torpor, and coldness in the extremities, "suggesting that the ergine content of the seeds may be causing some vascular constriction. (If this is the case, there may be some danger of ergot poisoning resulting from excessive dosages of the seeds)" (SAVAGE *et al.* 1972:454).[619] For several reasons naturally occuring LSA can have some negative and unpleasant effects: "If repeated high doses are taken on a regular basis it can lead to long term cumulative negative effects on one's health as a result of blood vessel damage" (*The Psychonaut.org* 2013:4–5).

PERRINE (WEBSTER *et al.* 2000) summarises four reports of self-experimentation with lysergic acid amide (lysergamide/ergine/ LSA). Humphry OSMOND reported, in 1955, a state of apathy and listlessness, accompanied by increased visual sensitivity, followed by a relaxed feeling. HOFMANN (2005:136–137) compared *ololiuqui* (morning glory) rather unfavourably with LSD, describing a sensation of mental emptiness and the unreality and meaninglessness of the outer world, an enhanced sense of hearing and a not unpleasant physical lassitude.[620] HOFMANN also tested the effects of isoergine, the effect of which was very similar to his experience with *ololiuqui.* A report by H. SOLMS (1956) is broadly similar to that of HOFMANN.

Given the well-known and potentially debilitating effect of the consumption of raw ergot, an ingenious solution is proposed by WEBSTER, PERRINE and RUCK (2000). According to WEBSTER, HOFMANN had suggested that ergonovine and methylergonovine could be extracted from *Claviceps purpurea* by water; but that would

---

619. See SAVAGE *et al.* (1972) for a brief résumé of the effects of naturally occurring lysergic acid amide in the seeds of *Ipomoea purpurea* (morning glory, from the varieties Heavenly Blue and Pearly Gates). For LSA generally, see *The Psychonaut.org* (2013:4–5).

620. SCHULTES and HOFMANN (1980:250–252) note the experiments of HEIM *et al.* (1968), who concluded, "that ololiuqui and its main constituents (lysergic acid amide, isolysergic acid amide) did not produce typical psychotomimetic symptoms but rather effects more like those encountered in toxic psychosis resulting from the action of a drug such as scopolamine". SCHULTES and HOFMANN also comment that there is a qualitative difference between the principles of *Ipomoea violacea* and *Turbina corymbosa* and LSD, the latter being, "a very specific hallucinogen, whereas the psychic effects of lysergic acid amide and the total alkaloids of these two plants are characterized by a pronounced narcotic component".

not prevent the uptake of toxic ergopeptide alkaloids, specifically ergotoxine and ergotamine.[621] Several years previously WEBSTER had experimented with chemically extracting ergine and isoergine[622] from ergotamine, from boiled seeds of *ololiuqui*, using potassium hydroxide. He reports a powerful trip from consuming the extracted concoction. As both ergot and morning glory seeds contain lysergic acid amide (LSA/ergine), it was a significant discovery when he then found out that in the 1930s ergine extraction had been similarly successful with *Claviceps purpurea*, also using potassium hydroxide, using a method of partial hydrolysis, a process that crucially depends on reaction times and cooking temperatures.

As to how the *hierophant* and his team in ancient Greece could have extracted by non-chemical means the desired alkaloids from *Claviceps purpurea* without the *kykeōn* being infused with toxic alkaloids, WEBSTER and PERRINE propose that the Greeks used the ash, which contains potassium, of burnt hardwood. Left to stand, the liquid containing water, the ergot fungus and the ash would have become infused with potassium carbonate, which would (possibly also with heating and with the addition of wine containing 10% or so of ethanol to improve the solubility of the alkaloids) have effectively eliminated the toxic alkaloids, through a process of partial hydrolysis. PERRINE wonders whether such a potion would be too caustic to drink and suggests two possibilities: that the potassium carbonate in the potion, if left to stand for a few days, could absorb enough oxygen to turn into potassium bicarbonate, which is relatively harmless; or that either wine or vinegar could have neutralized the ashes.[623] These novel suggestions are followed by a technical description of how the chemical hydrolysis could work.[624]

---

621. These alkaloids are abortifacient and dangerously vasoconstrictive, sometimes leading to gangrene in cases of ergot poisoning.
622. Ergine is the simple amide of lysergic acid; isoergine is produced in small amounts, together with ergine, in the hydrolysis process.
623. WEBSTER also suggest (in RUCK 2006:174) that fruit juice, such as grape juice, containing citric, ascorbic and tartaric acids may have been used to neutralize the solution.
624. The chemistry of this process is further detailed by WEBSTER in RUCK (2006:179–182). The proposition of a satisfactory entheogenic compound hinges on a potential change in the molecular structure of ergine, which

Despite the ingenuity of the proposed solution to the problem of the toxicity of ergot, there seem to be two fundamental rejoinders to the thesis. Firstly, even if the chemistry were to work successfully, the reports of the effects of isolated ergine (LSA), or of ergine combined with isoergine (referred to previously), do not seem particularly favourable if we are looking for the kind of entheogenic experience reported by initiates at Eleusis. But more importantly, as far as I am aware, no one has yet tried following the chemical protocols described by these authors and simply boiled or soaked raw ergot with wood ash and wine (or vinegar) and then consumed the drink: perhaps for the simple reason that it could be fatal. If it is that easy to make *kykeōn* in this way, why has no one ever reported it or tried it?[625]

(hypothetically) would bond and work in parallel and in equilibrium with isoergine, producing an effect similar to that of *ololiuqui*. Other experiments (pp.182–184) with migraine tablets (called Gynergen, which contain ergotamine tartate), and using vodka as a solvent, were not particularly successful; there was some nausea and stomach cramp. A summary of the theory of ergine/isoergine extracted through wood ash is also presented by WEBSTER in DANNAWAY *et al.* (2006: part 2). This theory is summarized and several reports of preparation (without wood ash), ingestion and effects of both LSA and ergonovine are provided on a comprehensive blog by TREGAR (2010); useful comparisons are made with the chemical structure and effects of the rare psychedelic drug ALD-52, which is somewhat similar to LSD; and there are reports on the effects of and extractions from the migraine medication Sansert (methysergide maleate). Several people report good, strong trips with both extracted LSA and ergonovine, which could, potentially, support the ergot hypothesis. However, in most of the reports on this blog the adductions of ergonovine (which are undertaken primarily to remove the alkaloids in ergot or morning glory that cause vasoconstriction) require processes, materials or equipment that would not have been available to ancient Greeks.

625. VALENCIC (1994:331) comments that, "to my knowledge there has not been a single attempt to ingest water soaked ergot with other putative ingredients that would simulate the kykeon in a controlled environment. What can be found aplenty in some writings are explanations of ways, more or less complicated, of how raw ergot could be ingested safely. It is this discrepancy between theoretical discourse and the lack of experimental evidence that my criticism is aimed at in the first place".

Given the capacity of this common form of ergot, *Claviceps purpurea*, to be so debilitating and possibly even more dangerous,[626] this author remains sceptical that an unrefined dilution of the ergot fungus was the essential ingredient of *kykeōn*, despite the impressive array of visual and mythological allusion that has been corroboratively presented by supporters of the thesis.[627] The associations of imagery of sieves, ears of corn, ergot and Demeter with the rites of Eleusis are persuasive in support of the ergot hypothesis, and the reports of 'clean' ergot experience are important and certainly worthy of further exploration. However, on balance these considerations do not to my mind sufficiently weigh positively enough against the many negative historical reports of debilitation and unpleasant symptoms from ergot consumption. However, perhaps a possibility is that an ergot fungus was used as an additive to the *kykeōn*, as in Amazonia there are reports of it being added to an ayahuasca brew to add to the visionary effect (PLOWMAN *et al.* 1990:457).

If *kykeōn* was an entheogen, and if it was neither purely ergot, fly-agaric or psilocybin mushrooms, then perhaps another line of investigation might be to consider the notion that ayahuasca analogues of some kind might have been used, inherited perhaps from an earlier culture.

---

626. In one of the very few contemporary reports of self-experimentation with ergot, COLE (2007:ch. 17) describes how she became so intoxicated from a controlled dose of ergot wine, which had been prepared by an expert psychedelic chemist, Gordon Todd SKINNER, that she nearly died. SKINNER had to pound and massage her heart region to prevent heart failure and death.
627. SAMORINI surmises (pp.14–15, 45) that prominent depictions of the agricultural sieve (*liknon*) or another sieve-like tool (*airapinon*) in classical art associated with the mystery rites at Eleusis could be explained by the function of the sieve to separate the large sclerota of the ergot fungus from grain.

CHAPTER 18

Bronze Age origins of entheogenic cults

An aspect to the general hypothesis that has been developed in this inquiry is to suggest that the knowledge of plants was sufficiently developed by the Bronze Age for some societies in Asia and the Middle East to prepare ayahuasca-like analogues from a variety of plants, which could have provided entheogenic experience in a ritual environment.[628] This knowledge, orally preserved in ritual cults, could, I suggest, have found its way to Greece and the institution of the Eleusian rites at approximately 1600 BCE, when scholars are generally agreed the rites were initiated. BURKERT (1985:278) points to some evidence that the mystery rites may be even older than Eleusis.

As mentioned in Chapter 10, remains of cannabis, opium and ephedrine have, it seems, been found in late Bronze Age temple complexes in Turkmenistan (though, as noted previously, this has been disputed). The finding of these substances leads SARIANIDI to believe that there was religious use of (in his words) "hallucinogenic" drugs in the ancient world. Similarly, CASTLEDEN (1990:143) interprets the 'poppy goddess' found in late Bronze Age (Minoan) Crete as an indication of the ritual use of opium in that culture. He cites Thomas DE QUINCEY's *Confessions of an English Opium Eater* (1821) on the visionary nature of opium intoxication, and how this form of intoxication and consequent withdrawal symptoms may

628. KNIPE (1967:342–343) discusses Akkadian seals from the earliest (Uruk) period, one of which depicts a nude, bearded, cyclopic hero, drinking through tubes the contents of a vat, which KNIPE is tempted to interpret as the preparation of a ritual drink. This is a scene dominated by the hero Etana and an eagle, reminiscent of Indra and the eagle, referred to in Chapter 2.

have inspired some of the decorative art of Bronze Age Crete, such as in the form of daemons, some of which are, "fantastic composite monsters".[629]

An objection to these suggestions is that neither opium, cannabis or ephedra on its own is properly entheogenic, visionary or hallucinogenic. Vivid, dream-like experiences are usual with opium. Ephedra is well known as a stimulant; the more complex effects of cannabis were discussed Chapter 7. The objection to these propositions, also raised previously, is that none of these plants is properly entheogenic on its own; but it seems probable, owing to apparent evidence (though this is disputed in some instances) of use of these plants in the Bronze Age, that they may have been additives to a more potent 'base concoction' involving plant sources of DMT and MAOI. If we are looking for inspiration for artistic and religious motifs in the ancient world, or, more importantly, for plants that could feasibly engender the kinds of rituals performed in the Vedic and Zoroastrian worlds, then it seems more probable that they were inspired by an entheogenic concoction (visionary in the true sense of the word), rather than by either cannabis, opium or ephedra alone. There is no substantial evidence, either now or historically, of either cannabis, opium or ephedra (or, for that matter, fly-agaric mushrooms) engendering—or being the cult object of—the kind of ritual performed by the Santo Daime church and Vedic ritualists.

It is perhaps interesting to consider the possibility that both the Indo-Iranians and the Greeks may have acquired the **sauma* cult—if indeed it was a kind of *soma* concoction that the Greeks were using—in Central Asia in the late Bronze Age from a 'wider' Bronze Age culture. It was mentioned in Chapter 3 that THOMPSON (2007:67) believes that the linguistic evidence indicates that the term *aṃśu* (*anću*)—an earlier name for *soma*—was derived from the language of the *soma* cult's Indo-European ancestors. WITZEL (2003:36ff.) discusses a number of religious terms, including *anću*,[630] which he

629. Similar conclusions about Bronze Age artwork inspired by opium and cannabis are made by DEVEREUX (1997:151ff.).

630. WITZEL (2003:36) maintains that also **yātu* (black magic), **atharwan* (priest), **ṛši* (seer), **magha* (gift/offering/sacrifice), **ćarwa* (name of Rudra), *indra*, and *g(h)andharw/b(h)a* (demi-god/demon) are Central Asian loan-words into Old Iranian and Old Indo-Aryan. PARPOLA (2015:66) derives 'Indra' from the proto-Uralic god of weather/thunder/sky from **ilmar*/**inmar*.

maintains are Central-Asian loan-words derived from the language used in the wider BMAC area in Turkmenistan where the temple complexes investigated by SARIANIDI are to be found. Primarily on linguistic evidence, WITZEL (2003:31) maintains that there was an early, widespread network of cultural interactions between the populations of the Fertile Crescent, the Caucasus, the steppes, the Urals, Iran and India. SARIANIDI (1999) also postulates broad, if tentative, cultural links stretching between the Bronze Age temple complexes of Cyprus, Mycenean and Minoan Greece, Elam, Mesopotamia, the Indus valley and the BMAC area in Turkmenistan. Specific features of monumental architecture, styles of pottery and jewellery and particular decorative motifs all seem to indicate some kind of common linguistic and cultural heritage, at least minimally. Particular emblems, motifs and styles of architecture are common to Mediterranean, Mesopotamian and BMAC cultures (SARIANIDI 2007:156ff.). There is specific evidence of contact between BMAC and Mesopotamia (PARPOLA 2015:70), and between the Indus civilization and Mesopotamia (POSSEHL 2002).[631]

Excavations of Bronze Age sites in Central Asia at Sintashta, centered on tributaries of the Tobol and Ural rivers, have revealed that this culture shared at least some Indo-Iranian practices and beliefs with the cultures of those who composed the early parts of the *Avesta* and the *Ṛgveda*: in the hierarchical, ritual significance of the horse, the bull and the sheep in funeral rites, and in practising both cremation and burial (KORYAKOVA and EPIMAKHOV 2007:96).

LAMBERG-KARLOVSKI (2013) also discusses the evidence for the extent of possible contact between late Bronze Age civilizations of the Near-East, Central Asia and the Indus.[632] He remarks (p.24) that in the last centuries of the 3rd millennium BCE a restricted inventory of BMAC artifacts appears at a number of sites on the Iranian plateau and in the Indus valley and the Persian gulf. There is no doubt that BMAC exerted an influence on these distant cultures

631. Many more artifacts of Indus origin have been found in Mesopotamia than Mesopotamian artifacts found in the Indus region.

632. At its height in the 3rd millennium BCE, the Indus valley civilization comprised around a million inhabitants. It was known as Meluhha to the Sumerians (PARPOLA 2015:163).

and that there were "extensive relations" (p.48) in a region that has been described by Gregory POSSEHL as the 'Middle-Asian Interaction Sphere', encompassing north-south interactions between BMAC, the Indus valley, the Iranian plateau and the Arabian peninsular. Both Akkadian and Indus seals have been found at Gonur in BMAC, and although no BMAC artifact has been discovered so far in Mesopotamia, BMAC seals and statuary have been recovered in Mohenjo Daro and Harappa in the Indus valley. PARPOLA (2015:71) refers to what has been called 'Trans-Elamite' iconography. The art of BMAC has a lot in common with that of Kerman (Jiroft) and, further back, with the proto-Elamite art of western Iran and Uruk-period Mesopotamia.

The extent to which the Mesopotamians knew about BMAC (perhaps as Simashki or as Marhashi)[633] is nevertheless contested (LAMBERG-KARLOVSKI 2013:41–43). PARPOLA (2015:70), however, refers to finds at Gonur from the late 3rd millennium BCE, which include not only ivory pins and combs from the Indus valley and a large, square Harappan stamp seal with an image of an elephant and an inscription in the Indus script, but also a cylinder seal, which, according to its cuneiform inscription, belonged to the cup-bearer of a Mesopotamian king. This seems to be firm evidence of contact between BMAC and Mesopotamia.

WITZEL (2000:289) comments that BMAC influence is found all over the Central Asian plateau, from Hisar and Susa in the west, to Shahdad and Yahya in the south, and to Quetta, Mehrgarh, even at sites of the Indus civilization, such as Mohenjo Daro and Harappa.[634] WITZEL (2003:54n.200) also notes the "remarkable overlap between BMAC and Indus shamanic concepts", commenting on a BMAC cylinder seal and a terracotta tablet from Mohenjo Daro, which show

633. WITZEL (1999:67) places Simashki in the Kerman/Bandar Abbas area, in southern Iran, and Marhashi in west Balochistan, in the Bampur region, in south-eastern Iran. PARPOLA (2015:70), however, believes that the Mesopotamians referred to BMAC as Šimaški.

634. In a subsequent publication, WITZEL (2003:27) maintains that the spread of late (*c.*1500) BMAC influences into the Indus valley, Balochistan, Susiana, and other areas is now well documented; and that BMAC, which declined *c.*1500 BCE, influenced the late stage of the Indus civilization, though it is uncertain whether or not Harappan and BMAC languages were related.

similar scenes of processions of flag- and standard-bearers, the latter involving the carrying of animals on a pole, accompanied by a figure beating a typically shamanic, circular drum.

PARPOLA (2015:76) proposes that around 2000 BCE an early wave of Proto-Indo-Aryan speakers took charge of BMAC. In its late phase, the people of BMAC became very mobile (on horses) and spread widely in central Asia, coming into contact with the Indus valley civilization,[635] eastern and western Iran, the Gulf, Syria and Anatolia, and the steppes. Typical BMAC metal seals have been found as far east as the Ordos Plateau in the Inner Mongolia autonomous region of China. If the **sauma* cult was originally practised in Central Asia, in the BMAC region in Turkmenistan—and subsequently acquired by Indo-Aryans—it seems possible, given the tentative cultural links that have been outlined, that the **sauma* cult was practised more widely in other Bronze Age temple complexes in the Near East and Central Asia. Alternatively, perhaps the **sauma* cult was originally restricted to the BMAC area and only diffused with migrating Indo-Aryans around 1600 BCE when the BMAC complex declined, a time when many other Bronze Age Asian cultures declined. The rapid and seemingly non-violent demise of the Indus valley culture, also around 1600 BCE, has long puzzled scholars: various explanations of climate change, drought or deadly disease have been proposed. WITZEL (2000:290) notes that, "The sudden decline of all cultures of the area, from Mesopotamia to the Indus and from Bactria to Bahrain and Oman, at the beginning of the second millennium, cannot simply be explained by an 'invasion of Aryan hordes'".

The eruption of the volcano on the island of Santorini[636] (Thera/Thira/Stronghyle),[637] which lies 110km north of Crete, is now known to have occurred around 1613 BCE (± 13 years).[638] It has now been

635. BMAC seals have been found in late-phase Indus culture at Somnāth (Gujarat) and Gilund (Rajasthan) (PARPOLA 2015:79).

636. 'Santorini' also refers to the small group of islands, in the centre of which lies the volcano.

637. It was called Calliste (most beautiful) in the ancient Greek world.

638. See FRIEDRICH (2009:100–121) for detailed arguments and evidence. In more recent times, minor eruptions occurred in 1707, 1866, 1926, 1939–41, and 1950–51.

firmly established that this was the largest volcanic eruption in the history of the earth since the last Ice Age. PAGE (1970:13–18) calculates that the eruption was approximately four times as powerful as the eruption of Krakatao/Krakatoa (near Sumatra) in 1883. The eruption of Sanorini could be heard 3,000 miles away and seven inches of ash fell in South Africa, 4,500 miles away. More recently, FRIEDRICH (2009:80–81) estimates that the eruption may have been up to ten times the size of that of Krakatao. The resultant tsunami circled the earth twice. Significantly, winds carried the ash cloud from the volcano east from Santorini. The effects were reported even in China where, during the reign of King CHIEH, the sun went dim. Irregular weather, famine, drought, flooding and extensive crop failure continued for seven years (FRIEDRICH 2009:59, 97).

The volcano and a giant earthquake (or earthquakes) around the same time (or perhaps several years apart) were almost certainly the cause of the sudden collapse of the Minoan civilization on Crete. It seems feasible, amongst other possibilities, that the collapse of a loosely connected web of city-states,[639] or perhaps just the dire circumstances that followed the volcanic eruption, may have resulted in the migration of 'Āryan' people eastwards, towards India, looking for supplies of food or cattle, perhaps seeking a new homeland, in the form of the migrations that first arrived in South Asia around 1600 BCE (several other significant migrations of people in the Near East occurred around that time). The people migrating to South

639. It has been very contentiously suggested by MENZIES (2012)—an amateur and much-derided historian—that this cataclysmic event resulted in a tsunami that destroyed the fleet and the main administrative headquarters on Crete (or perhaps Santorini) of what was a widespread and loosely connected empire, which was Atlantis, a proposition that finds some evidential support in classical Greek sources, particularly in PLATO's works (see FRIEDRICH 2009:262–279). Although fault may be found with some of MENZIES' suppositions, perhaps the suggestion worthy of consideration is of an empire that loosely stretched far wider than the eastern Mediterranean, Libya and Egypt, regions that are now generally acknowledged to have had substantial connections at the end of the Bronze Age. With extensive crop failure, a consequent rapid decline in population, the virtual collapse of communication and sea-borne supply routes of this empire, the demise of the Indus valley towns of Harappa and Mohenjo Daro could perhaps be explained, as could the widespread movement of people in Asia around 1600 BCE.

Asia would have brought the entheogenic rituals—in the form of Vedic ritual—from Central Asia but may have lacked the original plants used for producing entheogenic concoctions; hence the need to obtain supplies of what appears to be stalks of a vine from the upper Oxus region in Turkmenestan. This would have been one of the ways—using a particular vine, as that is what it appears to be from the descriptions in the religious texts—among several ways to produce an entheogenic concoction. Substitute (or alternative) concoctions using different plants are mentioned in the *Brāhmaṇa*s; "many *haoma*s" are recorded in the *Avesta.* Could it be that the 'substitutes' for *soma* mentioned in the *Brāhmaṇa*s were already being used by the time Vedic ritualists arrived in South Asia? The migrations of people from Central Asia may also, it is suggested, have resulted in the bringing of the secret formula of the *kykeōn* to Greece, and the establishing of the cult of Eleusis, which is believed to have been founded around 1600 BCE.

The sophistication of many late Bronze Age cultures in architecture, metallurgy, handicrafts, ship-building and crop production is abundantly apparent in the extant remains in the Near-East, Central and South Asia. What is being speculatively postulated is that the people of either one or several of these cultures had developed, probably during hundreds of years of trial and error, sufficient and extensive botanical knowledge—which could have been widely shared between the cultures of the Near-East, Central and South Asia—to manufacture potent entheogenic libations from a wide variety of plants, libations that would have had different ingredients depending on the plants available in the locale of manufacture. Entheogenic libations would have been administered and consumed by priests in ceremonies conducted in an environment that would have been secure from exterior disturbance. This, essentially, is the thesis being proposed in this book.

CHAPTER 19

Rejoinders to the ayahuasca thesis

Five potential objections spring readily to mind to the main thesis being proposed, that in the ancient world *soma/haoma* may have been an ayahuasca-like concoction.

Firstly, why is there not more specific information in the *Vedas*, *Brāhmaṇas* or *Avesta* about how *soma/haoma* is made? That the specific method of the preparation of *soma* or *haoma* is not mentioned in either Vedic or Zoroastrian texts is not surprising. This is not a recipe that any manufacturer would wish to divulge, for two reasons. It would be dangerous if prepared incorrectly or used outside controlled ritual or therapeutic contexts, except by those with expertise. It takes great skill and experience to know how properly to prepare any psychoactive plant. As for all psychoactive drugs, knowledge of precise dosages and contraindications are crucial not only for the safety and well-being of the consumer but also to ensure effectiveness at a psychological level. Slightly less material can have little or no effect; a slightly higher than required dose can transform the experience in a significant order of magnitude. Whatever kind or kinds of psychoactive *soma/haoma* plants were being prepared in Asia, precise quantities of water and other additive ingredients would have had to be calculated, based on the psychoactive content of the particular type of vine, grass or plant that was being prepared. This kind of information must have been known about by the priests who dosed people with *soma/haoma*, whatever kind of drug it may have been.[640]

640. PADHY and DASH (2004:20) comment that detailed phytography of plants used for *soma* would have been generally restricted (orally) to a guru; and that still today there is a (false) belief amongst tribal physicians that revealing

mentioned in the *amṛta* formulas in the Bower Manuscript offer potentially fruitful lines of inquiry.

Thirdly, the foremost objection to the thesis being presented must be that the process discussed in relation to the making of ayahuasca in South America entails the use of the indigenous vine *Banisteriopsis caapi*, which, as far as I know, does not grow in Asia; nor have I been able to identify an Asian relative of that vine that might contain harmine, harmaline or another MAO-inhibitor.[646] And the evidence from the *Veda*s in particular seems to indicate specifically the pressing of sections of a robust vine, as stones are needed to crush it and (it seems noisily) extract the juice, as is required for *Banisteriopsis caapi* in the Amazon region. The lack of any definitive evidence of the specific use of a vine in the making of *soma* might seem to count against the thesis being presented. However, the process of making ayahuasca, its effects and ritual environment are sufficiently similar to Vedic beliefs and practices that I cannot see what other line of research might better contribute to the discovery of the identity of *soma/haoma*, considering that over sixty plants have now been found to contain an MAO inhibitor, and seventy others which contain DMT; and every few years other plants with these chemicals are identified. Nevertheless, it seems just possible (though perhaps remotely) that there once was growing in Central Asia a vine whose extracted juice alone could engender a psychedelic experience, and that this vine has become entirely extinct, maybe due to climate change or over-harvesting.

Fourthly, several of the plants proposed as components of an ayahuasca analogue concoction in ancient Asia may, it has been suggested, in some instances contain either DMT or an MAOI; though this is yet to be definitively determined for several of the

646. However, in the last few decades several studies have illustrated that there may have been more contact between cultures in the ancient world than had been previously recognized. Given that there seems to be some evidence of ancient transatlantic contact, it seems not entirely beyond the realms of possibility (though, nevertheless, highly unlikely) that a psychoactive vine or other plants containing MAOI could have found their way to Asia from either South America or Mesoamerica; or that knowledge of ayahuasca analogue combinations may have passed from Central or South America to Asia, or vice versa (see Appendix 6).

plants suggested as potential ingredients to a concoction. However, the amount of psychoactive material extractable through 'cold' pressing would, in many cases, be insufficient to be psychoactive without some kind of solvent extraction, which was clearly not what was undertaken in the ancient world. The only example I have found of sufficiently psychoactive 'cold' extraction was of DMT from *Arundo donax*; and that is but a single report, which was cited. Further, besides that one report (which nevertheless corroborates the possibility of the procedure being more widespread in Asia, rather than just being restricted to one location in Iran), I have not discovered any other contemporary or historical ethnographic account in Asia of the extraction, through cold pressing or otherwise, of psychoactive substances from the various grasses, reeds or trees that have been surveyed in this book.

The fifth and final rejoinder to the 'anahuasca' thesis that has been presented in this inquiry is that if there was sufficient botanical knowledge in ancient Asia to manufacture a form of ayahuasca from indigenous plants, then why did the preparation and use of a psychedelic concoction cease? For this question I have no answer, or indeed for a subsidiary question of why 'substitutes' for *soma*—whatever they were—are mentioned in the *Brāhmaṇa*s.

CHAPTER 20

Concluding remarks

Despite the cogent objections to the thesis that have been admitted (and there may be others too), it seems that in the absence of a **single** plant solution to the *soma/haoma* problem which has eluded some of the keenest researchers in the world for around 250 years, the ayahuasca proposition that has been presented seems to me to be the most viable line of inquiry to pursue (notwithstanding the possibility mentioned above that a single entheogenic plant has become extinct). The starting point has been to try and identify plants that could possibly have been used. Other suggestions may or may not arise as a result of further investigation.

If it is accepted that *soma/haoma* was indeed a plant (or plants) that was/were used in the ancient world, then another step is to try to determine the effects produced by it. If, as THOMPSON (2003) maintains (which I believe is almost indisputable), the accounts of the Vedic poets describe their own experiences, then *soma/hoama* appears to have all the hallmarks of an entheogen; this is what the texts seem to describe (though it is readily acknowledged that this is still disputed by some scholars). Although fasting and sleep-deprivation may produce altered states of consciousness, the visions of the Vedic poets, according to their own accounts, were as a result of consuming the juice of a plant (or plants) that they had pounded with stones. In the current climate of interest in psychoactive plants—so many of which have now been identified—it is very curious indeed that a **single** plant with ayahuasca-like or entheogenic properties has not yet been discovered in central Asia; though this is not to say that such a discovery is impossible in the future. Evidence has been presented that none of the three main candidates endorsed by various researchers in the last twenty-five years for *soma/*

haoma—namely fly-agaric, Syrian rue and ephedra—has all the properties that appear to pertain to *soma/haoma*. Of all the currently known psychedelic preparations, ayahuasca is not only powerfully entheogenic but is also purgative, as is *soma* according to the *Brāhmaṇa*s, which is primarily due to the MAO inhibitor. Vomiting may occur with other entheogens, but that is unusual;[647] while it is common with ayahuasca.

Also, as mentioned in the introduction, a vital consideration in the research for this book has been an attempt to assess the probability of the numerous candidates that have been proposed as apt for consumption in a Vedic or Zoroastrian ritual environment. *Soma/haoma* needs to be strong enough both to keep participants awake and (it has been argued) to be reliably visionary, not only throughout the course of the ritual, but also over many centuries of use. Further, even though visionary, the consumption of strong doses of *soma/haoma* needs nevertheless to be entirely suitable for ritualists who need to continue precise recitation of mantras throughout ceremonies over a long period of time; and not be so debilitating that the ritualist is unable to concentrate on the required recitation. *Soma/haoma* also needs to be a kind of drug that can be consumed every few hours for several days without side-effects or diminished efficacy; and to be genuinely considered as a 'spiritual' medicine (which it was) it cannot be a drug that leaves any undesirable hang-over or negative after-effects. Of all known candidates, ayahuasca fits all these requirements, as the parallels with its use in the Santo Daime church have hopefully illustrated.

If, as seems to be case, *soma/haoma* does have entheogenic (or psychedelic) properties, and if there is no other single plant that could be a candidate, then it seems that the only logical conclusion would be that in the ancient world there might have been the requisite knowledge of how to prepare ayahuasca-like preparations from a variety of plants. Such a discovery was made in the upper-Amazon, whenever that was, and illustrates that a similar discovery could, in theory, have been made in ancient Asia; after all, humans must have been forever experimenting with plants.

647. Vomiting is unusual from the consumption of LSD, psilocybin or DMT, but is more common with peyote and San Pedro cacti.

The living psychedelic tradition of the Amazonian region has led, particularly in the last thirty years or so, to the discovery of numerous psychoactive plants that grow there, as documented by OTT (1996a) and others. However, as a consequence of the absence of a living psychedelic culture in Asia (apart from the local use of fly-agaric in a few places, and the *hōm* cult in Iran, referred to earlier), there has not been a degree of pursuit by scientists and ethnobotanists similar to that which has been undertaken in South America in the last few decades of analysis of numerous plants that may have psychoactive properties, particularly in the form of DMT or MAO-inhibitors. My belief is that an analysis of plants associated with Vedic and Zoroastrian rituals, a few of which have been mentioned in this book, may lead to the discovery of other plants with psychoactive or potentially psychedelic properties.

What I have been unable to ignore—as irrelevant to the discussion—is the religious use of ayahuasca in South America; this seemed worth drawing attention to. As mentioned earlier, the use of ayahuasca in South America in rituals that have striking parallels with Vedic kinds provides no proof that a form of ayahuasca was used in ancient Asia, but does illustrate that regular use of this powerful psychedelic concoction is entirely consistent with the development of rituals such as manifest in Vedic culture, which provide a secure psychological framework for entheogen experiences.

Amongst some groups of the upper-Amazon, people go to the jungle, cut sections of a twisted vine, bring it to a ritual enclosure and beat it rhythmically with wooden mallets in a spirit of great reverence. The extract is mixed with water (and usually boiled), and leaves containing DMT are added. The bitter, 'sharp', brownish-reddish-yellowish, tawny-coloured sacred brew is strained and served ceremonially by priests to participants in regularly performed rituals. The church-based rituals are orderly events, following a strict protocol, comprising respectful people who have either fasted or restricted their diet. In the Santo Daime church the ritual entails the chanting from a collection of hymnbooks of mantra-like hymns throughout most of the session. The tawny brew causes vomiting, visions, encounters with spirit entities, and reveals the light of the spirit world. It is as powerful as a bull, as swift as a steed; it can be an ordeal; it can give the impression of flight, of soaring in the heavens; it can produce ecstasy; it can take one to the edge of death and consequent rebirth; and at the conclusion of the ritual session the participants may feel cleansed by truth, and reborn; they return to their daily householder lives, maybe wondering how they might internalize the sacrifice.

References

Abaev, Vassilij Ivanovitch (trans. Jacques Veyrenc) (1975). 'Contribution à l'histoire des mots: 1. Vieil-iranien hauma- et le nom eurasien du houblon'. In *Mélanges linguistiques offerts à Émile Benveniste*, pp.1–3. Paris: Société de Linguistique de Paris.

Aberle, David F. (1982) [1966]. *The Peyote Religion among the Navaho.* Chicago/London: The University of Chicago Press.

Aldrich, Michael R. (1977). 'Tantric Cannabis Use in India'. *Journal of Psychoactive Drugs*, Vol. 9, no. 3 (July–September), pp.227–233.

Almond, Philip (1990). 'Mysticism and Its Contexts'. In Forman (ed.), pp.211–219.

Alper, Harvey P. (ed.) (2002) [1989]. *Understanding Mantras.* Delhi: Motilal Banarsidass Publishers.

Al-Snafi, Ali Esmail (2015). 'The Constituents and Biological Effects of *Arundo Donax* – A Review'. *International Journal of Phytopharmacy Research*, Vol. 6, Issue 1, pp.34–40.

de Alverga, Alex Polari (trans. Rosana Workman) (1999). *Forest of Visions: Ayahuasca, Amazonian Spirituality, and the Santo Daime Tradition.* Rochester, Vermont: Park Street Press.

——— (2011). '"Mr. Chico, please heal yourself!" – Spiritual Healing in the Santo Daime Doctrine and its Interface with Medical-Scientific Knowledge'. In Labate and Jungaberie (eds), pp.201–221.

Andrews, Steve, and Katrinia Rindsberg (2010) [2000]. *Herbs of the Northern Shaman: A Guide to Mind-Altering Plants of the Northern Hemisphere*, 2nd edn. Winchester (UK)/Washington (USA): O-Books.

Anonymous (2005). *DMT from Phragmites australis - the common reed.* Shaman Underground Publications.

Apte, Vaman Shivram (1998) [1965]. *The Practical Sanskrit-English Dictionary.* Delhi: Motilal Banarsidass.

Araújo, Wladimyr Sena (2010). 'The Barquinha: Symbolic Space of a Cosmology in the Making'. In Labate and MacRae (eds), pp.73–82.

Austin, J. L. (1962). *Sense and Sensibilia* (reconstructed from the manuscript notes of G. J. Warnock). Oxford: Clarendon Press/Oxford University Press.

Avesta: Avesta: The Religious Books of the Parsees (from Professor Spiegel's German Translation of the Original Manuscripts, in three Volumes), trans. Arthur Henry Bleeck (2005) [1864]. Elibron/[Hertford: Muncherjee Hormusjee Cama].

Le Zend-Avesta (trans. James Darmesteter). Vol. 1: *La Liturgie* (*Yasna et Vispéred*) (1960) [1892]; Vol. 2: *La Loi (Vendidad), L'Épopée (Yashts), Le Livre de Prière (Khorda Avesta)* (1960) [1893]. Paris: Adrien-Maisonneuve.

The Zend-Avesta, Part III: *The Yasna, Visparad, Âfrînagân, Gâhs, and Miscellaneous Fragments* (trans. L. H. Mills) (1887) (*Sacred Books of the East*, Vol. XXXI, ed. F. Max Müller). Oxford: Clarendon Press.

Hōm Yasht: based on translation by Karl F. GELDNER: *Avesta, Sacred Books of the Parsis* (1886). Stuttgart: W. Kohlhammer. www.avesta.org/yasna/y9to11.htm (accessed 15/04/2014).

Hōm Yašt: see JOSEPHSON (1997).

BADINER, Allan (ed.) (2015). *Zig Zag Zen: Buddhism and Psychedelics*. Santa Fe/London: Synergetic Press.

BAILEY, H. W. (1984). 'Vedic *kṣúmpa* - and Connected Data'. In S. D. JOSHI (ed.), *Amṛtadhārā: Professor R. N. Dandekar Felicitation Volume*, pp.17–20. Delhi: Ajanta Publications (India).

——— (1985). 'Durauzha the drink exhilarant'. *South Asian Studies*, Vol. 1, pp.57–61.

BAKELS, C. C. (2003). 'Report concerning the contents of a ceramic vessel found in the "white room" of the Gonur Temenos, Merv Oasis, Turkmenistan'. *Electronic Journal of Vedic Studies [EJVS]*, Vol. 9, Issue 1c (May 5).

BAKER, Ian (2004). *The Heart of the World: A Journey to the Last Secret Place*. New York: The Penguin Press.

BALABANOVA, S., F. PARSCHE, and W. PIRSIG (1992). 'First Identification of Drugs in Egyptian Mummies'. *Naturwissenschaften*, Vol. 79, p.358.

BALL, Martin W. (2016). '5-MeO-DMT: The Ego, Energy, and Nonduality'. In Robert DICKENS and Nikki WYRD (eds), *Psychedelic Press*, Vol. XIX (Breaking Convention Special Edition), pp.21–30. London: Psychedelic Press.

BAO, M. F., J. M. YAN, G. G. CHENG, X. Y. LI, Y. P. LIU, X. H. CAI, and X. D. LUO (2013). 'Cytotoxic indole alkaloids from Tabernaemontana divaricata'. *Journal of Natural Products*, August 23, Vol. 76 (8), pp.1406–1412.

BARBER, Elizabeth Wayland (1999). *The Mummies of Ürümchi*. London: Macmillan.

BARBER, Theodore Xenophon (1970). *LSD, Marihuana, Yoga, and Hypnosis*. Chicago: Aldine Publishing Company.

BARFOOT, C. C. (ed.) (2001). *Aldous Huxley between East and West*. Amsterdam/ New York: Rodopi.

BARNABÉ, Alberto (2009). '*Imago Inferorum Orphica*'. In CASSADIO and JOHNSTON (eds), pp.95–130.

BARTHOLOMAE, Christian (1904). *Altiranisches Wörtebuch*. Strassburg: Verlag von Karl J. Trübner.

BASHAM, A. L. (1972) [1967]. 'Soma'. In George ANDREWS and Simon VINKENOOG (eds), *The Book of Grass: An Anthology of Indian Hemp*, pp.17–24. Harmondsworth, Middlesex, UK/Ringwood, Victoria, Australia: Penguin Books.

BAUDELAIRE, Charles (trans. Norman CANNON) (1969) [1860]. 'An Excerpt from the Seraphic Theatre'. In SOLOMON (ed.), pp.219–231.

BEDROSIAN, Robert (2000). 'Soma among the Armenians'. http://rbedrosian.com/soma.htm (accessed 28/02/15).

BEER, Robert (2003). *The Handbook of Tibetan Buddhist Symbols*. Chicago/London: Serindia Publications Inc.

BELL, John (1857). 'On the Haschish or Cannabis Indica'. *The Boston Medical and Surgical Journal*, Vol. LVI, no. 11, April 16th, pp.209–216; Vol. LVI, no. 12, April 23rd, pp.229–236.

BENCIOLINI, Maria, and Arturo GUTIÉRREZ DEL ÁNGEL (2016). 'From Solid to Frothy: Use of Peyote in the Cora and Huichol Easter in Western Mexico'. In LABATE and CAVNAR (eds), pp.171–190.

BENNETT, Chris (2010). *Cannabis and the Soma Solution*. Walterville, Oregon: TrineDay.

BEYER, Stephan V. (2010) [2009]. *Singing to the Plants: A Guide to Mestizo Shamanism in the Upper Amazon*. Albuquerque: University of New Mexico Press.

Bhagavadgītā (trans. and ed. J. A. B. VAN BUITENEN) (1983). *The Bhagavadgītā in the Mahābhārata*. London/Chicago: The University of Chicago Press.

Bhāgavata Purāṇa [Śrīmad Bhāgavatam] (trans. and ed. A. C. Bhaktivedanta Swami PRABHUPADA), Vols 1–41. (1976). New York/Los Angeles/London/Bombay: The Bhaktivedanta Book Trust.

BHAIJI (trans. G. DAS GUPTA) (1983). *Mother as Revealed to Me*. Calcutta: Shree Shree Anandamayee Charitable Society.

BHARATI, Agehananda (1976). *The Light at the Centre: Context and Pretext of Modern Mysticism*. London/The Hague: East-West Publications.

BHATTACHARYA, Pradip (1984). *The Secret of the Mahabharata*. Aurangabad: Parimal Prakashan.

BHATTACHARYYA, N. N. (ed.) (2007). *A Cultural Index to Vedic Literature*. New Delhi: Manohar.

BHAWE, S. S. (1957, 1960, 1962). *The Soma Hymns of the Ṛgveda: A Fresh Interpretation* (Part 1: RV 9.1–15; Part 2: RV 9.16–50; Part 3: RV 9.51–70). Baroda: Oriental Institute.

BIANCHI, Antonio, and Georgio SAMORINI (1993). 'Plants in Association with Ayahuasca'. *Jahrbuch für Ethnomedizin und Bewußtseinforschung/Yearbook for Ethnomedicine and the Study of Consciousness*, Issue 2, pp.21–42. Berlin: Verlag für Wissenschaft und Bildung Berlin.

VON BIBRA, Baron Ernst (trans. Hedwig SCHLEIFFER) (1995) [1855]. *Plant Intoxicants: A Classic Text on the Use of Mind-Altering Plants*. Rochester, Vermont: Healing Arts Press.

BIGWOOD, Jeremy, Jonathan OTT, Catherine THOMPSON, and Patricia NEELY (1979). 'Entheogenic Effects of Ergovine'. *Journal of Psychedelic Drugs*, Vol. 11 (1–2), January–June, pp.147–149.

BLATTER, Ethelbert, and Walter Samuel MILLARD (1954) [1937]. *Some Beautiful Indian Trees*. Bombay: The Bombay Natural History Society.

BOCK, M. P., and D. G. PARBERRY (n. d.). 'LSA: The Psychoactive Ergot Alkaloids and their occurrence in the Microfungi'. http://www.tacethno.com/info/claviceps/ergotalkfungi.txt (accessed 21/08/2015).

BONNECHERE, Pierre (2003). 'Trophonius of Lebadea: mystery aspects of an oracular cult in Boetia'. In COSMOPOULOS (ed.), pp.169–192.

BOURGUIGNON, Erika (ed.) (1973). *Religion, Altered States of Consciousness, and Social Change*. Columbus: Ohio State University Press.

BOVÉ, Frank James (1970). *The Story of Ergot*. New York/Basel: S. Karger.

BOWMAN, Raymond A. (1970). *Aramaic Ritual Texts from Persepolis* (The University of Chicago Oriental Institute Publications, Vol. XCI). Chicago/Illinois: The University of Chicago Press.

BOYCE, Mary (1975–1982). *A History of Zoroastrianism*, Vols 1–2. Leiden/Köln. E.J. Brill.

——— (trans. and ed.) (1990) [1984]. *Textual Sources for the Study of Zoroastrianism*. Chicago: University of Chicago Press.

——— (2001) [1979]. *Zoroastrians: Their Religious Beliefs and Practices*. London/New York: Routledge.

——— (2012) [1998]. 'Haoma ii. The Rituals'. In *Encyclopædia Iranica*, Vol. XI, pp.662–667. http://www.iranicaonline.org/articles/haoma-ii (accessed 27/02/2015).

Brāhmaṇas: *The Gopatha Brāhmaṇa of the Atharva Veda* (eds Rajendralāla MITRA and Harachandra VIDYĀBUSHAṆA) (2012) [1872], (Bibliotheca Indica, New Series, nos. 215 and 252). Forgotten Books/[Calcutta: Asiatic Society of Bengal].

Pravargya Brāhmaṇa (see HOUBEN 1991).

Rigveda Brāhmaṇas: The Aitareya and Kauṣītaki Brāhmaṇas of the Rigveda (trans. Arthur Berriedale KEITH) (1925), (Harvard Oriental Series, Vol. 25). Cambridge, Massachusetts: Harvard University Press.

Śatapatha-Brāhmaṇa, according to the text of the Mādhyandina school (parts I–V) (trans. and ed. Julius EGGELING) (1995) [1882–1900]. (*Sacred Books of the East*, Vols 12, 26, 41, 43, 44, ed. F. Max MÜLLER). Delhi: Motilal Banarsidass/[Oxford: Clarendon Press].

Taittirīya-Brāhmaṇa (see DUMONT 1951).

BRAHMAVARCAS (2000). *Jaṛī būṭiyoṇ dvārā svāsthya saṃrakṣaṇ.* Mathurā: Yug Nirmāṇ Yojnā.

——— (2001). *Vanauṣadhi: ek saṃkṣipt mārgdarśikā.* Haridvār: Śāntikuñj.

BRAID, James (1850). *Observations on Trance: or Human Hibernation.* Edinburgh: Adam and Charles Black.

BRANDIS, Dietrich (1907). *Indian Trees: An Account of Trees, Shrubs, Woody Climbers, Bamboos and Palms Indigenous or Commonly Cultivated in the British Empire.* London: Archibald Constable & Co. Ltd.

BRERETON, Joel P. (2004) '*Bráhman, Brahmán*, and Sacrificer'. In GRIFFITHS and HOUBEN (eds), pp.325–344).

——— (2005). 'Soma'. In Lindsay JONES (ed.), *Encyclopedia of Religion*, 2nd edn., Vol. 12, pp.8521–8522. USA/London/Munich: Thomson/Gale.

BROCKINGTON, J. L. (1996) [1981]. *The Sacred Thread: Hinduism in its Continuity and Diversity.* Edinburgh: Edinbugh University Press.

BRONKHORST, Johannes (2001). 'The Perennial Philosophy and the Law of Karma'. In BARFOOT (ed.), pp.175–189.

BROUGH, John (1971). 'Soma and *Amanita Muscaria*'. *Bulletin of the School of Oriental and African Studies.* Vol. XXXIV, part II, pp.331–362.

——— (1973). 'Problems of the "Soma-Mushroom" Theory'. *Indologica Taurinensia,* Vol. 1, part 1, pp.21–32.

BROWN, George W. (2010) [1890]. *Researches in Oriental History*, 2nd edn. Kessinger Publishing's Rare Mystical Reprints/[Rockford, Illinois: the author].

BROWN, Jerry B., and Julie M. BROWN (2016). *The Psychedelic Gospels: The Secret History of Hallucinogens in Christianity.* Rochester, Vermont/Toronto: Park Street Press.

BUDHANANDA, Swami (ed.) (1974). *The Life of Swami Vivekananda by His Eastern and Western Disciples*, 8th edn. Calcutta: Advaita Ashrama.

BURKERT, Walter (trans. Peter BING) (1983) [1972]. *Homo Necans: The Anthropology of Ancient Greek Sacrificial Ritual and Myth.* Berkeley/Los Angeles/London. University of California Press.

——— (trans. John RAFFAN) (1985) [1977]. *Greek Religion: Archaic and Classical.* Malden, Massachusetts/Oxford/Carlton, Victoria (Australia): Blackwell Publishing Ltd./Harvard University Press.

——— (1987). *Ancient Mystery Cults.* London/Cambridge, Massachusetts: Harvard University Press.

BURMAN, J. J. Roy (2003). *Tribal Medicine: Traditional Practices and Changes in Sikkim.* New Delhi: Mittal Publications.

BURROUGHS, William S., and Allen GINSBERG (1971) [1963]. *The Yage Letters.* San Francisco: City Lights Books.

CALAND, W., and V. HENRY (1906). *L'Agniṣṭoma: Description complète de la forme normale du sacrifice de soma dans la culte védique.* Paris: Ernest Leroux.

CALLAWAY, J. C. (1993). 'Tryptamines, Beta-carbolines and You'. *Newsletter of the Multidisciplinary Association for Psychedelic Studies [MAPS]*, Vol. 2, no. 2 (Summer). http://www.maps.org/news-letters/v04n2/04230cal.html (accessed 22/04/2014).

——— (1999). 'Phytochemistry and Neuropharmacology of Ayahusaca'. In METZNER (ed.), pp.250–275.

CARAKA (trans. and eds Ram Karan SHARMA and Vaidya Bhagwan DASH) (1983). *Agniveśa's Caraka Saṃhitā (Text with English Translation and Critical Exposition Based on Cakrapāṇidatta's Āyurveda Dipikā)* (Chowkhamba Sanskrit Studies, Vol. XCIV), Vols 1–2. Varanasi: Chowkhamba Sanskrit Series Office.

CASSADIO, Giovanni, and Patricia A. JOHNSTON (eds) (2009). *Mystic Cults in Magna Graecia.* Austin, Texas: Texas University Press.

CASTLEDEN, Rodney (1990). *Minoans: Life in Bronze Age Crete.* London/New York: Routledge.

CEMIN, Arneide (2010). 'The Rituals of Santo Daime: Systems of Symbolic Construction'. In LABATE and MACRAE (eds), pp.39–63.

CHEEK, Charles D., Jacqueline DE DURAND-FOREST, Doris HEYDEN, and Balaji MUNDKUR (1979). 'On the Alleged Diffusion of Hindu Symbols to Mesoamerica'. *Current Anthropology*, Vol. 20, no. 1, March, pp.167–171.

CHRISTIE, Ben (2014). 'The Egyptians Had Their Own Version Of Ayahuasca They Called "The Tree of Life"'. http://www.collective-evolution.com/2014/05/31/the-tree-of-life-acacia-nilotica/ (accessed 8/01/2015).

CLARK, Matthew (2006). *The Daśanāmī-Saṃnyāsīs: The Integration of Ascetic Lineages into an Order.* Leiden/Boston: E. J. Brill.

——— (2015). 'Soma & Ayahuasca'. In Dave KING *et al.* (eds), pp.149–160.

——— (2016). 'Religious Sects, Syncretism, and Claims of Antiquity: The Dashanami-Sannyasis and South-Asian Sufis'. In Raziuddin AQUIL and David L. CURLEY (eds), *Literary, Religious and Political Cultures in Medieval and Early Modern India*, pp.61–92. New Delhi: Manohar.

CLARK, Raymond J. (2009). 'The Eleusian Mysteries and Vergil's "Appearance-of-a-Terrifying-Female-Apparition-in-the-Underworld" Motif in *Aeniad* 6'. In CASSADIO and JOHNSTON (eds), pp.190–203.

CLARK, Walter Houston (1969). *Chemical Ecstasy: Pychedelic Drugs and Religion.* New York: Sheed and Ward.

CLARKE, Robert C., and Mark D. MERLIN (2013). *Cannabis: Evolution and Ethnobotany.* Berkeley/Los Angeles/London: University of California Press.

CLINTON, Kevin (2003). 'Stages of Initiation in the Eleusian and Samothracian Mysteries'. In COSMOPOULOS (ed.), pp.50–78).

COLE, Krystle A. (2007) [2004]. *Lysergic*, 2nd edn. Amazon (print-on-demand).

COOPER, Samuel (1797). *Dissertation on the Properties and Effects of the Datura Stramonium or Common Thorn-Apple and on its Uses in Medicine.* Philadelphia: Samuel H. Smith.

COSTA, Carlo, Antonella BERTAZZO, Graziella ALLEGRI, Ornella CURCURATO, and Pietro TRALDI (1992). 'Indole alkaloids from the roots of an African plant *securidaca longipedunculata.* I. Isolation by column chromatography and preliminary structural characterization by mass spectronomy'. *Journal of Heterocyclic Chemistry*, Vol. 29, Issue 6 (October/November), pp.1641–1647.

COSMOPOULOS, Michael B. (ed.) (2003). *Greek Mysteries: The Archaeology and Ritual of Ancient Greek Secret Cults.* London/New York: Routledge.

——— (2015). *Bronze Age Eleusis and the Origin of the Eleusian Mysteries.* New York: Cambridge University Press.

CROWLEY, Mike (1996). 'When Gods Drank Urine: A Tibetan myth may help solve the riddle of *soma*, sacred drug of ancient India'. *Fortean Studies*, Vol. 3, pp.1–19. https://www.erowid.org/plants/amanitas/amanitas_writings1.shtml (accessed 19/02/2015).

CULPEPPER, Larry (2013). 'Reducing the Burden of Difficult-to-Treat Major Depressive Disorders: Revisiting Monoamine Oxidase Inhibitor Therapy'. *The Primary Care Companion For CNS Disorders*, Vol. 15 (5), pp.1–12. http://www.ncbi.nlm.nih.gov/pmc/articles/PMC3907330 (accessed 27/03/2014).

DANDEKAR, R. N. (1958–1962). *Śrautakośa (Based on the Śrautasūtras* [Part 1] *and Kalpasūtras* [Part 2] *belonging to the various Vedic Schools)* (English Section, Vol. 1, Parts 1 & 2). Poona: Vaidika Saṃśodhana Maṇḍala.

——— (1994). 'Soma is not Fly-Agaric'. In S. S. BAHUKAR and Sucheta PARANJPE (eds), *Śruti-cintāmaṇiḥ (Prof. C. G. Kashikar Felicitation Volume)*, pp.21–28. Pune: Tilak Maharashtra Vidyapeeth.

DANGE, Sadashiv Ambadas. (1988/9). 'Soma and the Ritual-Waters'. In A. KUMAR *et al.* (eds), *Studies in Indology (Professor Rasik Vihari Joshi Felicitation Volume)*, pp.73–83. New Delhi: Shree Publishing House.

——— (2000). *Images from Vedic Hymns and Rituals.* New Delhi: Aryan Books International.

DANNAWAY, Frederick R., Alan PIPER, and Peter WEBSTER (2006). 'Bread of Heaven or Wines of Light: Entheogenic Legacies and Esoteric Cosmologies'. *Journal of Psychoactive Drugs* (December). https://www.academia.edu/1376609/Bread_of_heaven_or_wines_of_light_Entheogenic_legacies_and_esoteric_cosmologies (accessed 21/08/2015).

DAS, Rahul Peter (2001) [1987]. 'On the identification of a Vedic plant'. In G. Jan MEULENBELD and Dominik WUJASTYK (eds), *Studies on Indian Medical History* (Indian Medical Tradition, Vol. 5; International Workshop on the Study of Indian Medicine, 1985, Wellcome Institute, London), 2nd edn., pp.17–38). Delhi: Motilal Banarsidass.

DASH, Vaidya Bhagwan (1989) [1978]. 'Cannabis in Ancient Medical Texts'. In DASH (ed.), *Fundamentals of Ayurvedic Medicine*, 7th (revised) edn., pp.142–156. Delhi: Konark Publishers/Bansal & Co.

DASH, Vaidya Bhagwan, and Vaidya Lalitesh KASHYAP (1980). *Materia Medica of Ayurveda, based on* Ayurveda Saukhyaṃ *of Toḍarānanda.* New Delhi: Concept Publishing Company.

DAVENPORT–HINES, Richard (2001). *The Pursuit of Oblivion: A Global History of Narcotics 1500–2000.* London: Wiedenfield & Nicholson.

DAVIS, Wade (1985). *The Serpent and The Rainbow.* New York: Simon & Schuster Paperbacks.

DEEG, Max (1993). 'Shamanism in the Veda: The *Keśin*-Hymn (10.136), the Journey to Heaven of *Vasiṣṭa* (ṚV. 7.88) and the *Mahāvrata*-Ritual'. *Nagoya Studies in Indian Culture and Buddhism (Saṃbhāṣā)*, Vol. 14, pp.95–144. Nagoya: Department of Indian Philosophy, University of Nagoya.

DEKORNE, Jim (2011) [1994]. *Psychedelic Shamanism: The Cultivation, Preparation and Shamanic Use of Psychotropic Plants*, 2nd edn. Berkeley: North Atlantic Books.

DEKORNE, Jim, David AARDVARK, and K. TROUT (2002) [2000] (eds). *Ayahuasca Analogues and Plant-Based Tryptamines: The Best of The Entheogen Review 1992–1999*, 2nd edn. Sacramento, California: The Entheogen Review.

Dēnkard: see WEST (2010) [1897].

DELATTE, Armand (1954). 'Le Cycéon, beuvrage ritual des mystères d'Éleusis'. *Bulletin de la Classe des Lettres et des Sciences Morales* (Académie royale de Belgique), 5th series, Vol. 40, pp.690–748.

DEMIR AKCA, Ayşe Semra, and Fatih Ozan KAHVECI (2012). 'An indispensible toxin known for 2500 years: victims of mad honey'. *Turkish Journal of Medical Science*, Vol. 42 (Sup. 2), pp.1499–1504.

DE MORI, Bernd Brabec (2011). 'Tracing Hallucinations: Contributing to a Critical Ethnohistory of Ayahuasa Usage in the Peruvian Amazon'. In LABATE and JUNGABERIE (eds), pp.23–47.

DEVEREUX, Paul. (2008) [1997]. *The Long Trip: A Prehistory of Psychedelia.* Brisbane: Daily Grail Publishing.

DÍAZ, José Luis. (1975). 'Etnofarmacologia de Algunas Psicotropicos Vegetales de Mexico'. In José Luis DÍAZ (ed.), *Etnofarmacologia de Plantas Alucinógenas Latinoamericanas* (Cuaderno Cientifico Cemef, no. 4). Mexico City: Centro Mexicano de Estudios en Farmacodependencia (CEMEF), pp.135–201.

——— (1977). 'Ethnopharmacology of sacred psychoactive plants used by the Indians of Mexico'. *Annual Review of Pharmacological Toxicology*, Vol. 17, pp.647–675.

DICKINSON, Jonathan (2014). 'Feeding the Hungry Ghosts: Ibogaine and the Psychospiritual Treatment of Addiction'. In Rick DOBLIN and Brad BURGE (eds), *Manifesting Minds: A Review of Psychedelics in Science, Medecine, Sex, and Spirituality*, pp.104–107. Berkeley, California: Evolver Editions/ North Atlantic Books.

DIGBY, Simon (1984). 'Qalandars and Related Groups: Elements of Social Deviance in the Religious Life of the Delhi Sultanate of the Thirteenth and Fourteenth Centuries'. In Yohanan FRIEDMANN (ed.), *Islam in Asia* (Vol. 1, South Asia), pp.60–108. Jerusalem/ Boulder, Colorado: The Magnes Press, The Hebrew University/Westview Press.

DI MAIO, Paula (2013a). 'Ethnobotanical Identification of Echinopsis Pachanoi in Himachal Pradesh. A New Candidate for the Soma Plant?'. https://www.academia.edu/5399240/Ethnobotanical_study_identifies_native_cactus_in_Asia_new_candidate_for_vedic_Soma_Plant (accessed 15/02/2014).

——— (2013b). 'Preliminary Observations and hypotheses from the Ethnobotanical identification of *Euphorbia Royleana VS Echinopsis Pachanoi* in Himachal Pradesh'. https://www.academia.edu/5352927/Ethnobotanic_Observation_of_White_Flowering_Cactus_Like_Plant_in_Himachal_Pradesh (assessed 17/08/2014).

DIOSCORIDES, Padanius (trans. Tess Anne OSBALDESTON and R. P. A. WOOD) (2000). *De Materia Medica.* Johnnesburg: Ibidis.

DITMAN, K. S., M. HAYMAN, and J. R. B. WHITTLESAY (1962). 'Nature and Frequency of Claims Following LSD'. *Journal of Nervous and Mental Diseases*, Vol. 134, pp.336–352.

DITTRICH, A. (1998). 'The standardized psychometric assessment of altered states of consciousness (ASCs) in humans'. *Pharmopsychiatry*, Vol. 31, suppl. 2 (July), pp.80–84.

DOBKIN DE RIOS, Marlene (1972). *Visionary Vine: Psychedelic Healing in the Peruvian Amazon.* San Francisco/Seranton/London/Toronto: Chandler Publishing Company.

DOBLIN, Rick (1991). 'Pahnke's "Good Friday Experiment": A long-term follow-up and methodological critique'. *Journal of Transpersonal Psychology*, Vol. 23, no. 1, pp.1–28.

DOIDGE, Norman (2016). *The Brain's Way of Healing: Stories of Remarkable Recoveries and Discoveries.* UK/USA/Canada/Ireland/Australia/India/New Zealand/South Africa: Penguin Books.

Doniger, Wendy (1997). ''Somatic' Memories of R. Gordon Wasson'. In Riedlinger (ed.), pp.55–59.

Drower, E. S. (1956). *Water into Wine: A Study of Ritual Idiom in the Middle East.* London: John Murray.

Duchesne-Guillemin, Jacques (1962). *La religion de l'Iran ancien.* Paris: Presses Universitaires de France.

——— (1988). 'Haoma proscrit et réadmis'. In Marie-Madeleine Mactoux and Evelyne Geny (eds), *Mélanges Pierre Levêques*, Vol. 1 (Religion) (Centre de Recherches d'Histoire Ancienne, Vol. 79), pp.127–131. Paris/Besançon: Les Belles Lettres/ Annales Littéraires de l'Université de Besançon.

Dumont, Paul-Emile (1951). 'The Special Kinds of Agnicayana (or Special Methods of Building the Fire-Altar) According to the Kaṭhas in the Taittirīya-Brāhmaṇa'. *Proceedings of the American Philosophical Society*, Vol. 95, no. 6, December 21, pp.628–675.

Dupré, Louis (2005) [1987]. 'Mysticism'. In Lindsay Jones (ed.), *Encyclopedia of Religion*, 2nd edn., Vol. 9, pp.6341–6355. New York/London/Munich: Thomson Gale.

Earleywine, Mitch (ed.) (2005). *Mind-Altering Drugs: The Science of Subjective Experience.* Oxford/New York: Oxford University Press.

——— (2005). 'Cannabis: Attending to Subjective Effects to Improve Drug Safety'. In Earleywine (ed.), pp.240–257.

Eduljee, K. E. (2014). 'Cave Dwellings of Shanidar'. *Zoroastrian Heritage*, 2005–2014, pp.1–4. http://www.heritageinstitute.com/zoroastrianism/cavedwellings/shanidar.htm (accessed 21/10/2016).

Eliade, Mircea (trans. Willard R. Trask) (1974) [1964]. *Shamanism: Archaic Techniques of Ecstacy* (Bollingen Series LXXVI). Princeton: Princeton University Press.

Elizarenkova, Tatiana (1996). 'The problem of Soma in the light of language and style of the Ṛgveda'. In Nalini Balbir and Georges-Jean Pinault (eds), avec Jean Fezas, *Langue, style et structure dans le monde indien (Centenaire de Louis Renou)* (Actes du Colloque international, Paris, 25–27 janvier 1996), pp.13–31. Paris: Editions Champion.

Ellis Davidson, H. R. (1973) [1964]. *Gods and Myths of Northern Europe.* Harmondsworth, Middlesex: Penguin Books.

Emboden, William A. (1979). 'Sacred Narcotic Water Lily of the Nile: *Nymphaea caerulea* Sav.'. *Economic Botany*, 33 (1), pp.395–407.

——— (1981). 'Transcultural Use of Narcotic Water Lillies in Ancient Egyptian and Maya Drug Ritual'. *Journal of Ethnopharmacology*, Vol. 3, pp.39–83.

——— (1982). 'The Mushroom and the Water Lily: Literary and Pictoral Evidence for *Nymphaea* as a Ritual Psychotogen in Mesoamerica'. *Journal of Ethnopharmacology*, Vol. 5, pp.139–148.

——— (2008) [1995]. 'Art and Artifact as Ethnobotanical Tools in the Ancient Near East with Emphasis on Psychoactive Plants'. In Schultes and von Reis (eds), *Ethnobotany: Evolution of a Discipline*, pp.93–107. Portland, Oregon: Timber Press.

Erdosy, George (ed.) (1997). *The Indo-Aryans of Ancient South Asia: Language, Material Culture and Ethnicity.* New Delhi: Munshiram Manoharlal.

Escohotado, Antonio (trans. and ed. G. B. Robinette) (2010). *The General History of Drugs*, Vol. 1. Valparaiso, Chile: Graffiti Militante Press.

Euripides (1997) [1908] (trans. Henry Hart). *Bacchae.* New York: Dover Publications, Inc.

EWING, Katherine Pratt (1997). *Arguing Sainthood: Modernity, Psychoanalysis, and Islam.* Durham/London: Duke University Press.

FADIMAN, James (2011). *The Psychedelic Explorer's Guide: Safe, Therapeutic, and Sacred Journeys*. Rochester, Vermont: Park Street Press.

FAHEY, Bede (2004). 'Mayan: A Sino-Tibetan Language? A Comparative Study'. *Sino-Platonic Papers*, no. 130, February, pp.1–61.

FALK, Harry (1989). 'Soma I and II'. *Bulletin of the School of Oriental and African Studies*, Vol. LII, Part 1, pp.77–90.

——— (1997). 'The Purpose of Ṛgvedic Ritual'. In WITZEL (ed.), pp.69–88.

——— (2002/3). 'Decent Drugs for Decent People: Further Thoughts on the Nature of Soma'. *Orientalia Suecana*, Vol. LI–LII, 2002–2003, pp.141–155.

FEENEY, Kevin (2013). 'The Significance of Pharmacological and Biological Indicators in Identifying Historical Uses of Amanita Muscaria'. In RUSH (ed.), pp.279–316.

FERGUSON, John (1989). *Among the Gods: An archeological exploration of ancient Greek religion.* London/New York: Routledge.

FERNANDEZ, James W. (1982). *Bwiti: An Ethnography of the Religious Imagination in Africa,* Princeton: Princeton University Press.

FESTER, Uncle (2006). *Practical LSD Manufacture*, 3rd edn. Green Bay, Wisconsin: Festering Publications.

FESTI, Francesca, and Giorgio SAMORINI (1993). 'Alcaloidi indolici psicoattivi nei generi *Phalaris* e *Arundo* (*Graminaceae*): una rassegna'. *Annali dei Musei Civici di Roverto*, Vol. 9, pp.239–287.

——— (1999). '*Claviceps paspali* and the Eleusian *Kykeon*: A Correction'. *The Entheogen Review*, Vol. VIII, no. 2 (Autumnal Equinox), pp.96–97, 122–124.

——— (2004). '"Ayahuasca-like" effects obtained with Italian plants'. In *Actas II Congreso Internacinal para el Estudio de los Estados Modificados de la Consciencia,* Llèida, octobre 3–7, 1994, pp.62–71. Barcelona: Instituto de Prospectiva Antropológica.

FIACCONI, Marta, and Chris O. HUNT (2015). 'Pollen taxonomy at Shanidar Cave (Kurdish Iraq): an initial evaluation'. *Review of Palaeobotany and Palynology*, Vol. 223, December, pp.87–93.

FIELDING, Amanda (ed.) (trans. Jonathan OTT) (2008). *Hofmann's Elixir: LSD and the New Eleusis (Talks and Essays by Albert Hofmann and Others).* Oxford: Beckley Foundation Press.

FOTIOU, Evgenia (2014). 'On the Uneasiness of Tourism: Considerations on Shamanic Tourism in Western Amazonia'. In LABATE and CAVNAR (eds), pp.159–181.

FLATTERY, David Stophlet, and Martin SCHWARTZ (1989). *Haoma and Harmaline: The Botanical Identity of the Indo-Iranian Hallucinogen "Soma" and its Legacy in Religion, Language and Middle Eastern Folklore* (Near Eastern Studies, Vol. 21). Berkeley/Los Angeles/London: University of California Press.

FONTENROSE, Joseph (1959). *Python: A Study of Delphic Myth and its Origins.* Berkeley/Los Angeles: University of California Press.

FORMAN, Robert K. C. (ed.) (1990). *The Problem of Pure Consciousness: Mysticism and Philosophy.* Oxford/New York: Oxford University Press.

——— (1990). 'Introduction: Mysticism, Constructivism, and Forgetting'. In FORMAN (ed.), pp.3–49.

FRAWLEY, David (2013). *Soma in Yoga and Ayurveda: The Power of Rejuvenation and Immortality.* Delhi: Motilal Banarsidass.

FRECSKA, Ede, Petra BOKOR, and Michael WINKELMAN (2016). 'The Therapeutic Potentials of Ayahuasca: Possible Effects against Various Diseases of Civilization'. *Frontiers in Pharmacology*, Vol. 7 (March), article 35, pp.1–17.

FREUD, Sigmund (trans. James STRACHEY) (1960) [1950]. *Totem and Taboo: Some Points of Agreement between the Mental Lives of Savages and Neurotics*. London: Routledge & Keegan Paul.

FRIEDRICH, Walter L. (trans. Alexander R. MCBIRNEY) (2009). *Santorini: Volcano, Natural History, Mythology*. Aarhus: Aarhus University Press.

FURST, Peter T. (ed.) (1972). *Flesh of the Gods: The Ritual Use of Hallucinogens*. New York/Washington: Praeger Publishers.

——— (1972). 'To Find Our Life: Peyote Among the Huichol Indians of Mexico'. In FURST (ed.), pp.136–184.

——— (1976). *Hallucinogens and Culture*. San Francisco: Chandler & Sharp Publishers, Inc.

——— (1988) [1986]. *Mushrooms: Psychedelic Fungi* (*Encyclopedia of Psychoactive Drugs: Hallucinogens*). London: Burke Publishing Company Limited.

GALANI, V. J., B. G. PATEL, and N. B. PATEL (2010). '*Argyreia speciosa* (Linn. f.) sweet: A comprehensive review. *Pharmacognosy Review*, Vol. 4 (8), pp.172–178.

GALLIMORE, Andrew R. (2015). 'Restructuring Consciousness – the psychedelic state in light of integrated information theory'. *Frontiers in Human Neuroscience*, Vol. 9 (June), Article 346, pp.1–16.

GAUTIER, Théophile (trans. Ralph J. GLADSTONE) (1969) [1846]. 'The Hashish Club'. In SOLOMON (ed.), pp.200–218.

GERSHEVITCH, Ilya (1974). 'An Iranianist's View of the Soma Controversy'. In Ph. GIGNOUX and A. TAFAZZOLI (eds), *Mémorial de Jean Menasce*, pp.45–75. Louvain: Imprimerie Orientaliste.

GHOSAL, S., S. K. DUTTA, A. K. SANYAL, and S. K. BHATTACHARYA (1969). 'Arundo donax L. (Graminae), Phytochemical and Pharmacological Evaluation'. *Journal of Medical Chemistry*, Vol. 12, p.480.

GHOSAL, S., S. SINGH, and S. K. BHATTACHARYA (1971). 'Alkaloids of *Mucuna pruriens*: Chemistry and Pharmacology'. *Planta Medica*, Vol. 19 (3), pp.279–294.

GHOSAL, S. N. (1980/81). 'Haoma as a Plant in the Avestan Text'. *Sambodhi*, Vol. 9, nos. 1–4, April 1980–January 1981, pp.52–55.

GNOLI, Gherado (1988) 'Bang'. In *Encyclopedia Iranica*, Vol. 3, Fasc. 7. pp.689–691 http://www.iranicaonline.org/articles/bang-middle-and-new-persian-in-book-pahlavi-also-mang-arabicized-banj-a-kind-of-narcotic-plant (accessed 6/10/2014).

——— (1989). Review of FLATTERY and SCHWARZ (1989). *East and West*, Vol. 39, no. 1/4 (December), pp.320–324.

——— (1993). 'On the Iranian Soma and Pers. *sepand* 'Wild Rue''. *East and West*, Vol. 43, no. 1/4 (December), pp.235–236.

——— (trans. Roger DEGARIS) (2005) [1987]. 'Haoma'. In Lindsay JONES (ed.), *Encyclopedia of Religion*, Vol. 6, 2nd edn., pp.3775–3776. New York/London/Munich: Thomson Gale.

GOLEMAN, Daniel (1977). *The Varieties of the Meditative Experience*. New York: E. P. Dutton.

GOLLA, Upendarrao, and Solomon Sunder Raj BHIMATHATI (2014). 'Evaluation of Antioxidant and DNA Damage Protection Activity of the Hydroalcaholic Extract of *Desmostachya bipinnata* L. Stapf'. *The Scientific World Journal*, Vol. 2014, Article ID 2315084, pp.1–8.

GONDA, J. (1975). *Vedic Literature* (*Saṃhitās and Brāhmaṇas*) (*A History of Vedic Literature*, Vol. 1, ed. Jan GONDA). Wiesbaden: Otto Harrassowitz.

——— (1980). *Vedic Ritual: The Non-Solemn Rites*. Leiden/Köln: E. J. Brill.

——— (1982). *The Haviryajñāḥ Somāḥ: The Interrelations of the Vedic Solemn Sacrifices; Śāṅkhāyana Śrautasūtra 14, 1–3, Translation and Notes* (Verhandelingen der Mededelingen der Koninklijke Nederlandse Akademie van Wetenschapen, AFD. Letterkunde, Nieuwe Reeks, Deel 113). Amsterdam/Oxford/New York: North-Holland Publishing Company.

——— (1983). *Soma's Metamorphoses (The Identifications in the Oblatory Rites of Śatapatha Brāhmaṇa 12, 6, 1)* (Mededelingen der Koninklijke Nederlandse Akademie van Wetenschapen, AFD. Letterkunde, Nieuwe Reeks, Deel 46, no. 2). Amsterdam/Oxford/New York: North-Holland Publishing Company.

——— (1985). *The Ritual Functions and Significance of Grasses in the Religion of the Veda*. Amsterdam/Oxford/New York: North-Holland Publishing Company.

——— (1989). *The Indra Hymns of the Ṛgveda*. Leiden/New York/København/ Köln: E. J. Brill.

——— (1994). 'Soma Unnamed'. In S. S. BAHULKAR and Sucheta PARANJPE (eds), *Śruti-cintāmaṇiḥ (Prof. C. G. Kashikar Felicitation Volume)*, pp.61–63. Pune: Tilak Maharashtra Vidyapeeth.

——— (1997) [1965]. *Change and Continuity in Indian Religion*. New Delhi: Munshiram Manoharlal.

GOULART, Sandra Lucia (2010). 'Religious Matrices of the União de Vegetal'. In LABATE and MACRAE (eds), pp.107–133.

GRACIE and ZARKOV (1985). 'Three Beta-Carboline Containing Plants as Potentiators of Synthetic DMT and Other Indole Psychedelics', pp.1–7. (Reprint based on the text of 'Notes from the Underground' no. 7, as archived at www.erowid.org and deoxy.org) (accessed 7/5/2015).

GRAF, Fritz (2003). 'Lesser Mysteries – Not Less Mysterious'. In COSMOPOULOS (ed.), pp.241–262.

GRAY, David B. (2007). *The* Cakrasamvara Tantra *(The Discourse of Śrī Heruka): A Study and Annotated Translation*. New York: The American Institute of Buddhist Studies, Columbia University/Columbia University's Centre for Buddhist Studies and Tibet House US.

GREENE, Mott T. (1992). *Natural Knowledge in Preclassical Antiquity*. Baltimore/London: The Johns Hopkins University Press.

GRIERSON, George Abraham (1894). 'The Hemp Plant in Sanskrit and Hindi Literature'. *The Indian Antiquary*, September, pp.260–262.

GRIEVE, M. (1995/2014). 'Mandrake'. In *Botanical.com: A Modern Herbal*. http://www.botanical.com/botanical/mgmh/m/mandra10.html (accessed 24/04/2014).

——— (1995/2014) 'Asclepias'. In *Botanical.com: A Modern Herbal*. https://www.botanical.com/botanical/mgmh/a/ascle072.html (accessed 29/12/2015).

GRIFFITHS, Arlo, and Jan E. M. HOUBEN (eds) (2004). *The Vedas: Texts, Language and Ritual (Proceedings of the Third International Vedic Workshop, Leiden 2002)*. Groningen: Egbert Forsten.

GRIFFITHS, R. R., W. A. RICHARDS, U. MCCANN, and R. JESSE (2006). 'Psilocybin can occasion mystical-type experiences having substantial and sustained personal meaning and spiritual significance'. *Psychopharmacology*, Vol. 187, pp.268–283.

GRIFFITHS, R. R., M. W. JOHNSON, W. A. RICHARDS, B. D. RICHARDS, U. MCCANN, and R. JESSE (2011). 'Psilocybin occasioned mystical-type experiences: Immediate and persisting dose-related effects'. *Psychopharmacology*, Vol. 218 (4), December, pp.649–655.

GRINSPOON, Lester, and James B. BAKALAR (1997). *Marihuana, the Forbidden Medicine* (revised edn.). New Haven/London: Yale University Press.

——— (1998) [1979]. *Psychedelic Drugs Reconsidered.* New York: The Lindesmith Centre.

GROF, Stanislav (1979) [1975]. *Realms of the Human Unconscious: Observations from LSD Research.* London: Souvenir Press (Educational & Academic) Ltd.

GUERBER, H. A. (1953) [1938]. *The Myths of Greece and Rome*, 2nd edn. London/Toronto/Wellington/Sydney: George G. Harrap & Co. Ltd.

GUPTA, Shakti M. (2010). 'Woman and Tree Motifs'. In S. K. JAIN (ed.), *Manual of Ethnobotany*, 2nd revised edn., pp.112–118. Jodhpur: Scientific Publications (India).

GUZMÁN, Gastón (1995). 'Supplement to the monograph of the genus *Psilocybe*'. *Bibliotheca Mycologica*, Vol. 190, pp.91–141. Berlin/Stuttgart: J. Cramer in der Gebrüder Borntraeger Verlagsbuchhandlung.

——— (2002). 'A Successful Coincidence: The Hallucinogenic Mushrooms, The Genus *Psilocybe*, The Traditions and the Development of Mycology in Mexico'. In José E. SÁNCHEZ and Elizur MONTIEL (eds), *Mushroom Biology and Mushroom Products (Proceedings of the Fourth International Conference, February 20–23, 2002, Cuernavaca, Morelos, Mexico)*, pp.9–14. Cuernavaca: Universidad Autónoma del Estado de Morelos.

GYANSHRUTI, Sannyasi, and Sannyasi SRIVIDYANANDA (2006). *Yajna: A Comprehensive Survey.* Munger, Bihar: Yoga Publications Trust.

HAJICEK-DOBBERSTEIN, Scott (1995). 'Soma siddhas and alchemical enlightenment: psychedelic mushrooms in Buddhist tradition'. *Journal of Ethnopharmacology*, Vol. 48, pp.99–108.

HALBFASS, Wilhelm (2001). 'Mescaline and Indian Philosophy: Aldous Huxley and the Mythology of Experience'. In BARFOOT (ed.), pp.221–235.

HARNER, Michael J. (ed.) (1973). *Hallucinogens and Shamanism.* London/Oxford/New York: Oxford University Press.

——— (1973). 'The Sound of Rushing Water'. In HARNER (ed.), pp.15–27.

HARSHANANDA, Swami (2001) [1997]. *Vedic Sacrifices: An Outline.* Bangalore: Ramakrishna Math.

[Haṭhapradīpikā] Hatha Yoga Pradipika (trans. Brian Dana AKERS) (2002). Woodstock, New York: YogaVidya.com.

HATSIS, Thomas (2014). 'Psychoactive Potions in Medieval Magic and Witchcraft'. In Robert DICKINS (ed.), *Psypress*, Vol. II, pp.67–80. Falmouth: Psychedelic Press.

——— (2016). 'Born of a Version: Parthenogenesis and The Holy Mushroom'. In Robert DICKINS (ed.), *Psychedelic Press*, Vol. XVII, pp.21–39. London: Psychedelic Press.

HAVELL, E. E. (1920). 'What is Soma?'. *Journal of the Royal Asiatic Society of Great Britain and Ireland*, no. 3 (July), pp.349–351.

HAY, David (1990). *Religious Experience Today: Studying the Facts.* London: Mowbray.

HEESTERMAN, Jan C. (2005). 'Brāhmaṇas and Āraṇyakas'. In Lindsay JONES (ed.), *Encyclopedia of Religion*, 2nd edn., Vol. 2, pp.1026–1028. New York/London/Munich: Thomson Gale.

HEGDE, Medha M., K. LAKSHMAN, K. GIRIJA, B. S. Ashok KUMAR, and V. LAKSHMIPRASANNA (2010). 'Assessment of antidiarrhoeal activity of *Desmostachya bipinnata* L. (Poaceae) root extracts'. *Boletin Latinameicano y del Caribe de Plantas Medicinales y Aromáticas*, Vol. 9 (4), pp.312–318.

HERODOTUS (trans. and intro. Aubrey DE SÉLINCOURT) (1968) [1954]. *The Histories.* Harmondsworth, Middlesex: Penguin Books.

HEINRICH, Clark (1995). *Strange Fruit: Alchemy, Religion and Magical Foods. A Speculative History.* London: Bloomsbury Publishing.

HILLEBRANDT, Alfred (trans. Sreeramula Rajeswara SARMA) (1980–1981) [1927–1929]. *Vedic Mythology*, Vols 1–2. Delhi: Motilal Banarsidass.

HILLMAN, D. C. A. (2008). *The Chemical Muse: Drug Use and the Roots of Western Civilization.* New York: Thomas Dunne Books/St. Martin's Press.

HINZ, Walter (1975). 'Zu den Mörsern und Stösseln aus Persepolis'. In *Acta Iranica* 4, deuxième série (Hommages et Opera Minora; Monumentum H. S. Nyberg), pp.371–385. Leiden: E. J. Brill.

HINZE, Almut (2004). 'On the Ritual Significance of the Yasna Haptaŋhāiti'. In STAUSBERG (ed.), pp.291–316.

HINTZEN, Annelie, and Torsten PASSIE (2010). *The Pharmacology of LSD: A Critical Review.* Oxford: Oxford University Press/Beckley Foundation Press.

HOERNLE, A. F. Rudolph (1893). *The Bower Manuscript (Facsimile Leaves, Nagari Transcript, Romanised Transliteration and English Translation with Notes).* Calcutta: Office of the Superintendent of Government Printing, India (Archeological Survey of India).

——— (1909). 'Studies in Ancient Indian medicine (V): The Composition of the *Caraka Samhita* in the Light of the Bower Manuscript'. *Journal of the Royal Asiatic Society,* Vol. 19, pp.857–893.

——— (2011) [1912]. *The Bower Manuscript (Facsimile Leaves, Nagari Transcript, Romanised Transliteration and English Translation with Notes).* New Delhi: Aditya Prakashan [Calcutta: Superintendent Government Printing].

HOFMANN, Albert (2005) [1979] (trans. Jonathan OTT). *LSD, My Problem Child: Reflections on Sacred Drugs, Mysticism and Science.* Sarasota, Florida: MAPS.

——— (2011) (trans. Annabel MOYNIHAN). *LSD and the Divine Scientist: The Final Thoughts and Reflections of Albert Hofmann.* Rochester, Vermont/Toronto: Park Street Press.

HÖLLER, Carsten (eds Udo KITTELMANN and Dorothée BRILL) (2011). *Soma: Dokumente/ Documents.* Ostfildern: Hatje Cantz Verlag.

HOPKINS, E. Washburn (1929). 'Soma'. In James HASTINGS (ed.), *Encyclopedia of Religion and Ethics*, Vol. XI, pp.685–687. Edinburgh/New York: T. & T. Clark/Charles Scribner's Sons.

HOUBEN, Jan E. M. (1991). *The Pravargya Brāhmaṇa of the Taittirīya Āraṇyaka: An Ancient Commentary on the Pravargya Ritual.* Delhi: Motilal Banarsidass.

——— (2003). 'The Soma-Haoma problem: Introductory overview and observations on the discussions'. *Electronic Journal of Vedic Studies [EJVS]*, Vol. 9, Issue 1a (May 4).

HOUGHTON, Peter J., and Melanie-Jayne HOWES (2005). 'Natural Products and Derivatives Affecting Neurotransmission Relevant to Alzheimer's and Parkinson's Disease'. *Neurosignals*, Vol. 14, pp.6–22.

HOUSTON, Robert, and Jean MASTERS (2000) [1966]. *The Varieties of Psychedelic Experience (The Classic Guide to the Effects of LSD on the Psyche).* Rochester, Vermont: Park Street Press.

HOUTZAGER, Guus (2006). *The Complete Encyclopedia of Greek Mythology.* Lisse, Holland: Rebo International b.v.

HSÜ, Kenneth J. (1998). 'Did the Xinjiag Indo-Europeans Leave Their Home Because of Global Cooling?'. In MAIR (ed.), pp.683–696.

HUA, Lei, Ya LI, Fei WANG, Dan-feng LU, and Kun GAO (2012). 'Biologically active steroids from the aerial parts of *Vernonia anthelmintica* Willd'. *Fitoterapia*, Vol. 83, pp.1036–1041.

HUGHES, Dewi Arwel (2003). 'Mysticism: The Perennial Philosophy?'. In PARTRIDGE (ed.), pp.306–324.

Hulin, Michel (2014) [1993]. *La mystique sauvage: Aux antipodes de l'esprit.* Paris: Quadrige/Presses Universitaires de France.

Hume, David (2007) [1748]. *An Enquiry concerning Human Understanding.* Oxford/New York: Oxford University Press.

Hummel, Karl (1997). Besprechungsaufsatz [review] of Wasson (1969). *Studien zur Indologie und Iranistik*, Band 21, pp.79–90.

Hunter, Jack, and David Luke (eds) (2014). *Talking With the Spirits: Ethnographies From Between the Worlds.* Brisbane: Daily Grail Publishing.

Hutter, M. (1996). 'Weltliche und geistliche Berauschung: die Bedeutung von Haoma im Zoroastrismus'. *Mitteilungen für Anthropologie und Religionsgeschichte*, Vol. 11, pp.186–208.

Huxley, Aldous (1973) [1954]. *The Doors of Perception* and *Heaven and Hell.* Harmondsworth, Middlesex (UK)/Ringwood, Victoria (Australia): Penguin Books.

——— (eds Michael Horowitz and Cynthia Palmer) (1999) [1977]. *Moksha: Aldous Huxley's Classic Writings on Psychedelics and the Visionary Experience.* Rochester, Vermont: Park Street Press.

——— (2009) [1945]. *The Perennial Philosophy.* New York/London: HarperCollins Publishers.

Indian Tobacco: A Monograph (1960). Madras: Indian Central Tobacco Committee (Ministry of Food and Agriculture, Government of India).

International Plant Names Index (IPNI) (2005) http://www.ipni.org/ipni/plantnamesearchpage.do (accessed 2/01/2015).

Jacobs, Alan (2010). *Sri Ramana Maharshi: The Supreme Guru.* Mumbai: Yogi Impressions.

Jain, Usha (1983). 'The Custom of Biting Grass in Retrospect'. In G. C. Tripathi and Maya Malaviya (eds), *Baladeva Upādhyāya Felicitation Volume* (*Journal of the Ganganatha Jha Kendriya Sanskrit Vidyapeetha*, Vol. XXXVII, January–December 1981, Parts 1–4), pp.243–248. Allahabad: Ganganatha Jha Kendriya Sanskrit Vidyapeetha.

James, William (1985) [1902]. *The Varieties of Religious Experience: A Study in Human Nature.* London/New York: Penguin Books.

Jay, Mike (1999). *Blue Tide: The Search for Soma.* Brooklyn, New York: Automedia.

——— (2010). *High Society: Mind-Altering Drugs in History and Culture.* London: Thames & Hudson Ltd.

Jayasekara, T. K., P. C. Stevenson, S. R. Belmain, D. I. Farman, and D. R. Hall (2002). 'Identification of methyl salicylate as the principal volatile component in the methanol extract of *Securidaca longifolia* Fres'. *Journal of Mass Spectronomy*, Vol. 37, pp.577–580.

Jaynes, Julian (1976). *The Origins of Consciousness in the Breakdown of the Bicameral Mind.* Boston: Houghton Mifflin Company.

Jiang, Hong-En, Xiao Li, You-Xing Zhao, David K. Ferguson, Francis Hueber, Subir Bera, Yu-Fei Wang, Liang-Chen Zhao, Chang-Jiang Liu, and Cheng-Sen Li (2006). 'A new insight into *Cannabis sativa* (Cannabaceae) utilization from 2500-year-old Yanghai Tombs, Xinjiang, China'. *Journal of Ethnopharmacology*, Vol. 108, pp.414–422.

Jones, Rex L. (1995). *The Soma Plant and the Possible Connections to the Genus Datura (Thornapple Tree).* Pennsylvania: Dept. of South Asian Studies, University of Pennsylvania.

Jones, Terry L., Alice A. Storey, Elizabeth A. Matisoo-Smith, and José Miguel Ramírez-Aliaga (eds) (2011). *Polynesians in America.* Lanham/New York/Toronto/Plymouth (UK): Altamira Press.

Jordan, Peter (1994). 'Woodrose vs Ipomoea'. https://www.erowid.org/plants/hbw/hbw_info1.shtml (accessed 24/08/2015).

Josephson, Judith (1997). *The Pahlavi Translation Technique as Illustrated by* Hōm Yašt (Studia Iranica Upsaliensis 2). Uppsala, Sweden: Uppsala Universitetsbibliotek.

Jouveau Dubreuil, G. (1926). 'Soma'. *The Indian Antiquary*, Vol. 55, September, p.176.

Jung, C. G. (2008) [1955]. *Synchronicity: An Acausal Connecting Principle*. London/New York: Routledge.

Kalyanaraman, S. (2004). *Indian Alchemy: Soma in the Veda*. New Delhi: Munshiram Manoharlal.

Kamal, Rajiv (1988). *Economy of Plants in the Vedas*. New Delhi: Janaki Prakashan/Commonwealth Publishers.

Kane, Pandurang Vaman. (1977–1997) [1930–1962]. *History of Dharmaśāstra*, Vols 1–5 (Government Oriental Series, Class B, no. 6), 3rd edn. Poona: Bhandarkar Oriental Research Institute.

Kapadia, B. H. (1959). *A Critical Interpretation and Investigation of Epithets of Soma*. Vallabh Vidyanagar: Dr. B. H. Kapardia.

Karamustafa, Ahmet T. (2006) [1994]. *God's Unruly Friends: Dervish Groups in the Islamic Middle Period 1200–1550*. Oxford: Oneworld Publications.

Karayil, Sudha (2011). 'Somalata – A Pioneer Herb in the entire Plant Kingdom: Ethnopharmacological Perspective Through Vedic Literature'. *International Journal of Research in Pharmaceutical and Biomedical Science*, Vol. 2 (3), July–September, pp.977–981.

Karnick, C. R. (1969). 'True Identity of Soma Plant – The Famous Ayurvedic Rejuvenating and Longevity-Promoting Drug. *Quarterly Journal of Crude Drug Research*, Vol. 9, part 4, pp.1473–1479.

Kashikar, C. G. (1990). *Identification of Soma*. Pune: Tilak Maharashtra Vidyapeeth.

Kashivishvanathan, T. S. (ed.) (trans. A. R. Parthasarathi) (2012) [2003]. *Yajurveda Trikāla Sandhyāvandanam*. Mumbai: Giri Trading Agency Private Limited.

Katz, Steven T. (1978). 'Language, Epistemology, and Mysticism'. In Katz (ed.), pp.22–74.

——— (ed.) (1978). *Mysticism and Philosophical Analysis*. London: Sheldon Press.

Kaul, M. K. (1997). *Medicinal Plants of Kashmir and Ladakh*. New Delhi: Indus Publishing Company.

Kensinger, Kenneth M. (1973). '*Banisteriopsis* Usage Among the Peruvian Cashinahua'. In Harner (ed.), pp.9–14.

Kerényi, C. (trans. Ralph Manheim) (1977) [1967]. *Eleusis: Archetypal Image of Mother and Daughter.* New York: Schocken Books.

Keith, Arthur Berriedale (1925). *The Religion and Philosophy of the Veda and Upanishads*, Vols 1–2 (Harvard Oriental Series, Vols 31–32). Cambridge, Massachusetts/London: Harvard University Press/Oxford University Press.

Khanizadeh, Mehrbod (2016). 'The exegesis of a Zoroastrian sacred text: Aspects of the Pahlavi version of the hymns to Haoma'. Unpublished research presentation at SOAS, January 2016.

Khlopin, Igor N. (1980). 'Mandragora Turcomanica in der Geschichte der Orientalvölker'. *Orientalia Lovaniensia Periodica*, Vol. 11, pp.223–231.

King, Dave (2014). 'Epilogenesis'. In Robert Dickins (ed.), *Psypress*, Vol. V, pp.47–60. Falmouth: Psychedelic Press.

King, Dave, David Luke, Ben Sessa, Cameron Adams, and Aimee Tollan (eds) (2015). *Neurotransmissions: Essays on Psychedelics from Breaking Convention*. London: Strange Attractor Press.

KIRTIKAR, K. R., and B. D. BASU (1984) [1935]. *Indian Medicinal Plants*, Vols 1–4. Dehra Dun: Bishen Singh Mahendra Pal Singh.

KISHORE, Prem (Director) (1999). *An Appraisal of Tribal-Folk Medicines*. New Delhi: Central Council for Research in Ayurveda and Siddha.

KNIPE, David M. (1967). 'The Heroic Theft: Myths from Ṛgveda IV and the Ancient Near East'. *History of Religions*, Vol. 6, no. 4, pp.328–360.

——— (2015). *Vedic Voices: Intimate Narratives of a Living Andhra Tradition*. Oxford/New York: Oxford University Press.

KORYAKOVA, Ludmila, and Andrej EPIMAKHOV (2014) [2007]. *The Urals and Western Siberia in the Bronze and Iron Ages*. Cambridge/New York: Cambridge University Press.

KOTWAL, Dastur Firoze M, and James W. BOYD (1991). *A Persian Offering, the Yasna: A Zoroastrian High Liturgy* (Studia Iranica – Cahier 8). Paris: Association pour l'avancement des études iranienne.

KRAMSISCH, Stella (1975). 'The Mahāvīra Vessel and the Plant Pūtika'. *Journal of the American Oriental Society*, Vol. 95, pp.222–235.

KUIPER, Franciscus Bernados Jacobus (1969). Review of WASSON (1969). *Indo-Iranian Journal*, Vol. 12, pp.279–285.

——— (1984). 'Was the *putíka* a Mushroom?'. In S. D. JOSHI (ed.), *Amṛtadhārā: Professor R. N. Dandekar Felicitation Volume*, pp.219–227. Delhi: Ajanta Publications (India).

KUMAR, K. Ashok, SHARVANEE, Jitendra PATEL, and Ram Kumar CHOUDHARY (2010). 'Chemical composition and antimicrobial activity of the essential oil of *Desmostachya bipinnata* Linn'. *International Journal of Phytomedicine*, Vol. 2, pp.436–439.

KUMAR, P. Suresh, K. SONI, S. R. JADHAV, and M. N. SARAF (2007). 'Mechanism of spasmolytic activity of a fraction of *Sarcostemma brevistigma* Wight'. *Indian Journal of Experimental Biology*, Vol. 45, May, pp.419–424.

'Kumbh'- parv (viśeṣāṅk) (2001). Ramādatt ŚUKL and Ṛtśīl ŚARMĀ (eds). Prayāg: Parāvāṇī Ādhyātmik Śodh-Saṃsthān.

KURUP, P. N. V. (Director) (1999) [1978]. *Hand Book of Domestic Medicine and Common Ayurvedic Remedies*. New Delhi: Central Council for Research in Ayurveda & Siddha (Ministry of Health and Family Welfare, Govt. of India).

LABATE, Beatriz Caiuby, and Clancy CAVNAR (eds) (2014). *Ayahuasca Shamanism in the Amazon and Beyond*. Oxford/New York: Oxford University Press.

——— (2016). *Peyote: History, Tradition, Politics, and Conservation*. Santa Barbara/Denver: Praeger.

LABATE, Beatriz Caiuby, and Henrik JUNGABERIE (eds) (2011). *The Internationalization of Ayahuasca* (Intercultural Studies on Ritual, Play and Theatre, Vol. 16). Zürich/Berlin: LIT Verlag.

LABATE, Beatriz Caiuby, and Edward MACRAE (eds) (2010). *Ayahuasca Ritual and Religion in Brazil*. London/Oakville: Equinox.

LABATE, Beatriz Caiuby, and Gustavo PACHECO (2010). *Opening the Portals of Heaven: Brazilian Ayahuasca Music* (Brazilian Studies, Vol. 4). Berlin/New Brunswick/London: LIT Verlag/Transaction Publishers.

——— (2011). 'The Historical Origins of Santo Daime: Academics, Adepts, and Ideology'. In LABATE and JUNGABERIE (eds), pp.71–84.

LABATE, Beatriz Caiuby, Rafael Guimarães SANTOS, Brian ANDERSON, Marcelo MERCANTE, and Paulo César Ribeiro BARBOSA (2010). 'The treatment and handling of substance dependence with ayahuasca: reflections on current and future research'. In LABATE and MACRAE (eds), pp.205–227.

LAHIRI, Ajoy Kumar (1984). *Vedic Vṛtra*. Delhi: Motilal Banarsidass.

Lamberg-Karlovsky, C. C. (2013). 'The Oxus Civilization/La Civilización del Oxus'. *Cuadernos de Prehisoria y Arqueología de la Universidad Autónoma de Madrid [CuPAUM]*, Vol. 39, pp.21–63.

Laski, Marghanita (1980). *Everyday Ecstasy (some observations on the possible social effects of major and minor ecstatic experiences in our daily secular lives).* London: Thames and Hudson.

Leary, Timothy (1964). 'The Religious Experience: Its Production and Interpretation'. *Psychedelic Review*, Vol. 1, no. 3. Reprinted in Penner (ed.) (2014), pp.205–232 ('The Good Friday Experiment').

Leary, Timothy, George H. Litwin, and Ralph Metzner (1963). 'Reactions to Psilocybin Administered in a Supportive Environment'. *Journal of Nervous and Mental Diseases*, Vol. 137, no. 6, pp.561–573. Reprinted in Penner (ed.) (2014), pp.74–98 ('On Set and Setting Theory').

Leary, Timothy, Ralph Metzner, and Richard Alpert (1992) [1964]. *The Psychedelic Experience: A manual based on the Tibetan Book of the Dead.* New York: Citadel Press/Kensington Publishing Corp.

Leggett, Trevor (1990). *The Complete Commentary by Śaṅkara on the Yoga Sūtra-s: A Full Translation of the Newly Discovered Text.* London/New York: Kegan Paul International.

Lees, A. J. (2016). *Mentored by a Madman: The William Burroughs Experiment.* London: Notting Hill Editions.

Leonti, Marco, and Laura Casu (2014). 'Soma, food of the immortals according to the Bower Manuscript (Kashmir, 6th century AD)'. *Journal of Ethnopharmacology*, Vol. 155, June, pp.373–386.

Leprechaun (2008). 'Cheap Sweet Sufiuasca New World Style: Arundo donax & Passion Flower (Passiflora Incarnata)' https://www.erowid.org/experiences/exp.php?ID=75834 (accessed 7/04/2015).

Letcher, Andy (2007). *Shroom: A Cultural History of the Magic Mushroom.* London: Faber and Faber.

——— (2016). 'Mad Thoughts on Mushrooms: Discourse and Power in the Study of Psychedelic Consciousness'. In Robert Dickins (ed.), *Psychedelic Press*, Vol. XVIII, pp.1–26. London: Psychedelic Press.

Lewin, Louis (trans. P. H. A. Wirth) (1998) [1927]. *Phantastica: A Classic Survey on the Use and Abuse of Mind-Altering Plants.* Rochester, Vermont: Park Street Press.

Lewis, I. M. (1995) [1971]. *Ecstatic Religion: A study of shamanism and spirit possession*, 2nd edn. London/New York: Routledge.

Lilly, John C. (1974) [1967]. *The Human Biocomputer: Theory and Experiments.* London: Abacus.

——— (1997) [1988]. *The Scientist: A Metaphysical Autobiography.* Berkeley, California: Ronin Publishing Inc.

Lipski, Alexander (1993) [1977]. *The Life and Teaching of Ānandamayī Mā.* Delhi: Motilal Banarsidass Publishers Private Ltd.

Littleton, C. Scott (1998). 'Were Some of the Xinjiang Mummies "Epi-Scythians"? An Excursus in Trans-Eurasian Folklore and Mythology'. In Victor H. Mair (ed.), pp.746–766.

Long, J. Bruce (1976). 'Life out of Death: A Structural Analysis of the Myth of the 'Churning of the Ocean of Milk'. In Bardwell L. Smith (ed.), *Hinduism: New Essays in the History of Religions* (Studies in the History of Religions, Supplements to *Numen*, Vol. XXXIII), pp.171–207. Leiden: E. J. Brill.

LUBIN, Timothy (2016). 'The Vedic *Homa* and the Standardization of Hindu *Pūjā*'. In PAYNE and WITZEL (eds), pp.143–166.

LUKE, David (2011). 'Discarnate Entities and Dimethyltryptamine (DMT): Psychopharmacology, Phenomonology and Ontology'. *Journal of the Society of Psychical Research*, Vol. 75.1, no. 902 (January), pp.26–42.

LUNA, Luis Eduardo (2011). 'Some Reflection on the Global Expansion of Ayahuasca'. In LABATE and JUNGABERIE (eds), pp.123–129.

LUNA, Luis Eduardo, and Pablo AMARINGO (1999) [1991]. *Ayahuasca Visions: Iconography of a Peruvian Shaman.* Berkeley, California: North Atlantic Books.

MACDONELL, A. A. (1995) [1898]. *Vedic Mythology*. Delhi: Motilal Banarsidass.

MACLEAN, Katherine A., Jeannie-Marie S. LEOUTSAKOS, Matthew W. JOHNSON, and Roland R. GRIFFITHS (2012). 'Factor Analysis of the Mystical Experience Questionnaire: A Study of Experiences Occasioned by the Hallucinogen Psilocybin'. *Journal of the Scientific Study of Religion*, Vol. 51 (4) (December), pp.721–737.

MADHIHASSAN, S. (1986). 'Ephedra as Soma Meaning Hemp Fibres with Soma Later Misidentified as the Hemp Plant Itself'. *Indian Journal of Science*, 21 (1), pp.1–6.

——— (1987a). *The History and Natural History of Ephedra as Soma.* Islamabad: Pakistan Science Foundation.

——— (1987b). 'Three Important Vedic Grasses'. *Indian Journal of History of Science*, Vol. 22 (4), pp.286–291.

MAHADEVAN, T. P., and Frits STAAL (2003). 'The Turning-Point in a Living Tradition: *Somayāgam* 2003'. *Electronic Journal of Vedic Studies [EJVS]*, Vol. 10, Issue 1a (Sept. 21).

MAIR, Victor H. (ed.) (1998). *The Bronze Age and Early Iron Age Peoples of Eastern Central Asia,* Vols 1–2 (Journal of Indo-European Studies Monograph, no. 26). Washington/Philadelphia: Institute for the Study of Man/University of Pennsylvania Museum Publications.

MAJUPURIA, Trilok Chandra, and Indra MAJUPURIA (1978). *Sacred and Useful Plants and Trees of Nepal.* Kathmandu: Sahayogi Prakashan Tripureswar.

MALAMOUD, Charles (trans. Gerald HONIGSBLUM) (1991a). 'Soma as Sacrificial Substance and Divine Figure in the Vedic Mythology of Exchange'. In *Mythologies* (A Restructured Translation of *Dictionnaire des mythologies et des religions des sociétés traditionelles et du monde antique*, compiled by Yves BONNEFOY), Vol. 2, pp.803–806. Chicago/London: Chicago University Press.

——— (1991b) 'Le soma et sa contrepartie: Remarques sur les stupéfiants et les spiritueux dans les rites de l'Inde ancienne'. In Dominique FOURNIER and Salvatore D'ONOFRIO (eds), *Le Ferment Divin*, pp.19–33. Paris: Éditions de la maison des sciences de l'homme.

MALANDRA, William W. (1979). 'Atharvaveda 2.27: Evidence for a Soma Amulet'. *Journal of the American Oriental Society*, Vol. 99, pp.220–224.

——— (trans. and ed.) (1983). *An Introduction to Ancient Iranian Religion: Readings from the Avesta and Achaemenid Inscriptions.* Minneapolis: University of Minnesota Press.

MALLINSON, James (2007). *The Khecarīvidyā of Ādinātha: A critical edition and annotated translation of an early text of* haṭhayoga. London/New York: Routledge.

MALLORY, J. P. (1998). 'A European Perspective on Indo-Europeans in Asia'. In MAIR (ed.), pp.175–201.

MANANDHAR, N. P. (1989). *Useful Wild Plants of Nepal* (Nepal Research Centre Publications, no. 14). Stuttgart: Franz Steiner Verlag Wiesbaden GMBH.

MANI, Vettam (1989) [1975]. *Purāṇic Encyclopedia.* Delhi: Motilal Banarsidass.

MANNICHE, Lise (1999) [1989]. *An Ancient Egyptian Herbal.* London: British Museum Press.

[Manusmṛti] The Law Code of Manu (trans. and ed. Patrick OLIVELLE) (2004). Oxford/New York: Oxford University Press.

MASLOW, Abraham H. (1970) [1964]. *Religions, Values, and Peak-Experiences.* New York: The Viking Press.

MAYOR, Adrienne (1995). 'Bees and the Baneful Rhododendron: Mad Honey!'. *Archaeology*, November/December, pp.32–40. https://www.academia.edu/966648/Mad_Honey_ (accessed 7/01/2015).

——— (2010). *The Poison King: The Life and Legend of Mithradates, Rome's Deadliest Enemy.* Princeton/Oxford: Princeton University Press.

MAZZIO, E., S. DELAB, K. PARK, and K. F. A. SOLLMAN (2013). 'High throughput Screening to Identify Natural Monoamine Oxidase B Inhibitors'. *Phytotherapy Research*, June, Vol. 27 (6), pp.818–828 http://www.ncbi.nlm.nih.gov/pubmed/22887993 (accessed 10/11/2014).

MCDONALD, Andrew (2004). 'A Botanical Perspective on the Identity of Soma (*Nelumbo Nucifera* Gaertn.) Based on Scriptural and Iconographic Records'. *Economic Botany*, Vol. 58, Supplement (Winter), pp.S147–S173.

MCGILCHRIST (2010). *The Master and His Emissary: The Divided Brain and the Making of the Western World.* New Haven/London: Yale University Press.

MCGREGOR, R. S. (ed.) (1995). *The Oxford Hindi-English Dictionary.* Oxford/Delhi: Oxford University Press.

MCKAY, Alex (2016). *Kailas Histories: Renunciate Traditions and the Construction of Himalayan Sacred Geography.* Leiden/Boston: E. J. Brill.

MCKENNA, Dennis J. (1999). 'Ayahuasca: An Ethnopharmacologic History'. In METZNER (ed.), pp.187–213.

MCKENNA, Terence (1992) [1984]. *Food of the Gods.* London: Rider.

MEGGERS, Betty J. (1975). 'The Transpacific Origin of Mesoamerican Civilization: A Preliminary Review of the Evidence and its Theoretical Implications'. *American Anthropologist*, Vol. 77, Issue 1 (March), pp.1–27.

MENZIES, Gavin (2012) [2011]. *The Lost Empire of Atlantis.* London: Phoenix.

MERCUR, Dan (2013). 'The Soma Function in Jung's Analytical Psychology'. In RUSH (ed.), pp.519–564.

METZNER, Ralph (ed.) (1968). *The Ecstatic Adventure.* New York/Toronto: The Macmillan Company/Collier-Macmillan Canada Ltd.

——— (ed.) (1999). *Ayahuasca: Hallucinogens, Consciousness, and the Spirits of Nature.* New York: Thunder's Mouth Press.

——— (2005a) 'Psychedelic, Psychoactive, and Addictive Drugs and States of Consciousness'. In EARLEYWINE (ed.), pp.25–48.

——— (ed.) (2005b). *Sacred Mushrooms of Visions: Teonanácatl.* Rochester, Vermont: Park Street Press.

——— (2005c). 'Introduction: Visionary Mushrooms of the Americas'. In METZNER (ed.) (2005b), pp.1–48.

——— (2009). *Mind Space and Time Stream: Understanding and Navigating Your States of Consciousness.* Berkeley, California: Regent Press/Green Earth Foundation.

MEULENBELD, G. Jan (1974). *The Mādhavanidāna and its Chief Commentary, Chapters 1–10* (Introduction, Translation and Notes). Leiden: E. J. Brill.

——— (1989). 'The search for clues to the chronology of Sanskrit medical texts, as illustrated by the history of *bhaṅgā* (Cannabis sativa Linn.)'. *Studien zur Indologie und Iranistik*, Vol. 15, pp.59–70.

MILLS, James H. (2012) [2003]. *Cannabis Britannica: Empire, Trade, and Prohibition, 1800–1928.* Oxford: Oxford University Press.

MINKOWSKI, Christopher Z. (1991). *Priesthood in Ancient India: A Study of the Maitrāvaruṇa Priest* (Publications of the De Nobili Research Library Vol. XVIII). Vienna: De Nobili.

MITCHENER, John E. (1982). *Traditions of the Seven Ṛṣis.* Delhi: Motilal Banarsidass.

MODI, Jivanji Jamshedi (1913). 'Haoma'. In James HASTINGS (ed.), *Encyclopedia of Religion and Ethics*, Vol. VI, pp.506–510. Edinburgh/New York: T. & T. Clark/ Charles Scribner's Sons.

——— (1922). *The Religious Ceremonies and Customs of the Parsis.* Mazagaon, Bombay: British India Press.

MONIER-WILLIAMS, Monier (1994) [1899]. *Sanskrit-English Dictionary.* New Delhi: Munshiram Manoharlal.

MONROE, Robert A. (1974). *Journeys out of the Body.* London: Corgi Books.

MOORE, Michael (1989). *Medicinal Plants of the Desert and Canyon West.* Santa Fe, New Mexico: Museum of New Mexico Press.

MOORE, Peter (2005). 'Mysticism [Further Considerations]'. In Lindsay JONES (ed.), *Encyclopedia of Religion*, 2nd edn., Vol. 9, pp.6355–6359. New York/London/ Munich: Thomson Gale.

MUKHERJEE, Braja Lal (1921). 'The Soma Plant'. *Journal of the Royal Asiatic Society of Great Britain and Ireland*, no. 2 (April), pp.241–244.

MUKHOPADHYAY, Biswanath (1978). 'On the Significance of Soma'. *Vishveshvaranand Indological Journal* (Panjab University, Hoshiapur), Vol. XVI, part 1, March, pp.6–9.

MUKTANANDA Paramahansa, Swami (1974). *The Play of Consciousness (Chitshakti Vilas).* California: Shree Gurudev Siddha Yoga Ashram.

MULHOLLAND, Jean (1976). 'Soma. An Attempt to Classify the Plant and the Drug'. *Journal of the Asiatic Society*, Vol. XVIII, nos. 1–4, pp.47–55.

MÜLLER-EBELING, Claudia, Christian RÄTSCH, and Wolf-Dieter STORL (trans. Annabel LEE) (2003) [1998]. *Witchcraft Medicine: Healing Arts, Shamanic Practices, and Forbidden Plants.* Rochester, Vermont: Inner Traditions.

MYERS, Luke A. (2011). *Gnostic Visions: Uncovering the Greatest Secret of the Ancient World.* Bloomington: iUniverse.

MYLONAS, George E. (1974) [1961]. *Eleusis and the Eleusian Mysteries.* Princeton: Princeton University Press.

NADKARNI, K. M. (1954) [1908]. *Indian Materia Medica*, Vols 1–2, 3rd edn. Bombay/ Panvel: Popular Book Depot/Dhootapapeshwar Prakashan Ltd.

——— (1998) [1910]. *Indian Plants and Drugs with their Medical Properties and Uses.* Delhi: Asiatic Publishing House.

NARANJO, Claudio (1973). *The Healing Journey: New Approaches to Consciousness.* New York: Ballantine Books.

——— (1997). 'A Posthumous 'Encounter' with R. Gordon Wasson'. In RIEDLINGER (ed.), pp.177–181.

NEMU, Reverend (2016). 'Exodrugs'. In Robert DICKINS (ed.), *Psychedelic Press*, Vol. XVI, pp.9–23. London: Psychedelic Press.

NICHOLSON, Philip T. (2002). 'The Soma Code, Parts I–III'. *Electronic Journal of Vedic Studies [EJVS]*, Vol. 8, Issue 3 (March 27), pp.31–92.

NIKHILANANDA, Swami (1977) [1942]. *The Gospel of Ramakrishna (translated into English with an Introduction).* New York: Ramakrishna-Vivekananda Centre.

Noro, Tadataka, Toshio Miyase, Masanori Kuroyanagi, Akira Ueno, and Sego Fukushima (1983). 'Monoamine Oxidase Inhibitor from the Rhizome of *Kaempferia galanga* L.'. *Chemical and Pharmaceutical Bulletin*, Vol. 31, no. 8, pp.2708–2711.

Nyberg, Henrik Samuel (trans. H. H. Schraeder) (1938). *Die Religionen des alten Iran* (Mittleitung der Vorderasiatisch-Aegyptischen Gesellschaft, E. V., Band 43). Leipzig: J. C. Hinrichs Verlag.

Nyberg, Harri (1997). 'The problem of the Aryans and the Soma: The botanical evidence'. In Erdosy (ed.), pp.382–406.

Oberlies, Thomas (1989). 'König Somas Kriegzeug – Eine Untersuchen zur Kompositionstechnik der Pavamāna-Hymnen'. *Studien zur Indologie und Iranistik*, Vol. 15, pp.71–96.

——— (1995). Review of Kashikar (1990). *Wiener Zeitschrift für die Kunde Südasiens*, Vol. 39, pp.235–238.

——— (1998–1999). *Die Religion des Ṛgveda*, Vols 1–2 (Vol. 1, *Das Religiöse System des Ṛgveda*; Vol. 2, *Kompositsionanalyse der Soma-Hymnen des Ṛgveda*), (Publications of the De Nobili Research Library, Vol. XXVI). Wien: De Nobili.

Oesterreich, Traugott K. (trans. D. Ibberson) (1974) [1921]. *Possession and Exorcism: Among Primitive Races, in Antiquity, the Middle Ages, and Modern Times.* New York: Causeway Books.

O'Flaherty, Wendy Doniger (1969) [1968]. 'The Post-Vedic History of the Soma Plant'. In Wasson, pp.95–147.

——— (1981). *The Rig Veda: An Anthology.* London/New York: Penguin Books.

Oizumi, Masafumi, Larissa Albantakis, and Guilio Tononi (2014). 'From the Phenomenology to the Mechanisms of Consciousness: Integrated Information Theory 3.0'. *PLOS Computational Biology*, Vol. 10, Issue 5 (May), e1003588, pp.1–25.

Oort, Marianne S. (1995). 'Surā and Other Spirits in Ritual and Non-Ritual Context'. In N. V. Gurov and Ya. V. Vasil'kov (eds), *Sthāpakaśrāddham (Professor G. A. Zograph Commemorative Volume)*, pp.221–231. St. Petersburg: Russian Academy of Sciences, Institute of Oriental Sciences.

Ornstein, Robert E. (1975) [1972]. *The Psychology of Consciousness.* New York/ Harmonsdsworth, Middlesex, UK: Penguin Books.

Oroc, James (2009). *Tryptamine Palace: 5-MeO-DMT and the Sonoran Desert Toad.* Rochester, Vermont: Park Street Press.

Ott, Jonathan (1975). 'Amanita Muscaria: Usos y Quimica'. In José Luis Díaz (ed.), *Etnofarmacologia de Plantas Alucinógenas Latinoamericanas* (Cuaderno Cientifico Cemef, no. 4), pp.203–221. Mexico City: Centro Mexicano de Estudios en Farmacodependencia (CEMEF).

——— (1996a) [1993]. *Pharmacotheon: Entheogenic Drugs, their Plant Sources and History*, 2nd edn. Kennewick, WA: Natural Products Co.

——— (1996b). 'Pharmahuasca: On Phenethylamines and Potentiation'. *Newsletter of the Multidisciplinary Association for Psychedelic Studies [MAPS]*, Vol. 6, no. 3, Summer, pp.32–34.

——— (1997). 'Pharmahuasca, Anahuasca and Vinho da Jurema: Human Pharmacology of Oral DMT Plus Harmine'. (Originally published in *Yearbook of Ethnomedicine 1997/98*.) http://ibogaine.mindvox.com/Articles/JO-Pharmahuasca.htm (accessed 3/06/2014).

——— (1998a). 'The Delphic Bee: Bees and Toxic Honeys as pointers to Psychoactive and other Medicinal Plants'. *Economic Botany*, Vol. 52 (3), pp.260–266.

——— (1998b). 'The Post-Wasson History of the *Soma* Plant'. *Eleusis*, n.s., no. 1, pp.9–37.

——— (2001). 'Applied Psychonautics: Ayahuasca to Pharmahuasca to Anahuasca'. http://ibogaine.mindvox.com/Articles/JO-AppliedPsychonautics.htm (accessed 3/06/2014).

——— (2006). *Análogos de la Ayahuasca: Enteógenos Pangeicos.* Madrid: Ediciones Amargord.

——— (2011). 'Psychonautic uses of "Ayahuasca" and its Analogues: Panacæa or *Outré* Entertainment'. In Labate and Jungaberie (eds), pp.105–122.

Ott, Jonathan, and Patricia Neely (1980). 'Entheogenic (Hallucinogenic) Effects of Methylergonovine'. *Journal of Psychedelic Drugs*, Vol. 12 (2), April–June, pp.165–166.

Otto, Rudolf (trans. John W. Harvey) (1978) [1923]. *The Idea of the Holy: An Inquiry into the non-rational factor in the idea of the divine and its relation to the rational,* 2nd edn. London/Oxford/New York: Oxford University Press.

Packialakshmi, N, and Alwin (2014). 'Analysis of Phytochemical and High Performance Liquid Chromatography in *Desmostachya bipinnata*'. *BMR Biotechnology*, Vol. 1, Issue 1, pp.1–6.

Padhy, Sachidananda, and Santosh Kumar Dash (1997). 'Mushrooms as Prohibited Food in *Manusmṛti vis-à-vis Amanita Muscaria* as Vedic Soma Plant'. *Ethnobotany*, Vol. 9, p.129.

——— (2004). 'The *Soma* Drinker of Ancient India: An Ethno-Botanical Retrospection'. *Journal of Human Ecology*, 15 (1), pp.19–26.

Padma Purāṇa (trans. and annotation N. A. Deshpande) (1992). Delhi: Motilal Banarsidass.

Page, D. L. (1970). *The Santorini Volcano and the Destruction of Minoan Crete* (Supplementary Paper no. 12). London: The Society for the Promotion of Hellenic Studies.

Pal, D. C. and S. K. Jain (1989). 'Notes on Lodha Medicine in Midnapur District, West Bengal, India'. *Economic Botany*, Vol. 43, Issue 4, pp.464–470.

Pandanus Database of Indian Plants (1998–2009). http://iu.ff.cuni.cz/pandanus/ (accessed 21/03/2016). Prague: Seminar of Indian Studies, Institute of South and Central Asia, Faculty of Arts, Charles University.

Pandey, Ashish, Satish Kumar Sharma, Lalit Singh, and Tanuja Singh (2013). 'An overview on Desmostachya Bipinnata'. *Journal of Drug Discovery and Therapeutics*, Vol. 1 (7), pp.67–68.

Pandey, Brahma Prakash (1989). *Sacred Plants of India.* New Delhi: Shree Publishing House.

Pandey, Rajbali (1994) [1969]. *Hindu Saṃskāras: Socio-Religious Study of the Hindu Sacraments.* Delhi: Motilal Banarsidass Publishers Private Limited.

Pāṇini (trans. and ed. Srisa Chandra Vasu) (1977). *The Ashṭādhyāyī of Pāṇini.* Delhi/Varanasi/Patna: Motilal Banarsidass.

——— (trans. and ed. Sumitra M. Khatre) (1989). *Aṣṭādhyāyī of Pāṇini.* Delhi: Motilal Banarsidass.

Parker, R. C., and Lux (2008). 'Psychoactive Plants in Tantric Buddhism: Cannabis and Datura Use in Indo-Tibetan Esoteric Buddhism'. *Erowid Extracts,* no. 14 (June), pp.6–11.

Parpola, Asko (1997a). 'The problem of the Aryans and the Soma: Textual-linguistic and archeological evidence'. In Erdosy (ed.), pp.353–381.

——— (1997b). 'The Dāsas and the Coming of the Aryans'. In Witzel (ed.), pp.193–202.

——— (1998). 'Aryan Languages, Archaeological Cultures and Sinkiang: Where Did Proto-Iranian Culture Come into Being, and How Did It Spread?'. In Mair (ed.) pp.114–147.

——— (2002). 'Pre-Proto-Iranians of Afghanistan as Initiators of Śākta Tantrism: on the Scythian/Saka Affiliations of the Dāsas, Nuristanis and Magadhians'. *Iranica Antiqua*, Vol. XXXVII, pp.233–324.

——— (2004). 'From Archaeology to a Stratigraphy of Vedic Syncretism: The banyan tree and the water buffalo as Harappan-Dravidian symbols of royalty, inherited in succession by Yama, Varuṇa and Indra, divine kings of the first three layers of Aryan speakers in South Asia'. In GRIFFITHS and HOUBEN (eds), pp.470–515.

——— (2015). *The Roots of Hinduism: The Early Aryans and the Indus Civilization.* Oxford/New York: Oxford University Press.

PARRINDER, Geoffrey (1976). *Mysticism in the World's Religions.* London: Sheldon Press.

PARTRIDGE, Christopher (2003). 'Sacred Chemicals'. In PARTRIDGE and GABRIEL (eds), pp.96–131.

PARTRIDGE, Christopher, and Theodore GABRIEL (eds) (2003). *Mysticisms East and West: Studies in Mystical Experience.* Carlisle (UK)/Waynesboro, GA (USA): Paternoster Press/Authentic Media.

Pāśupata Sūtram with Pañchārtha-bhāṣya of Kauṇḍinya, translated with an Introduction on the history of Śaivism in India (trans. and ed. Haripada CHAKRABORTI) (1970). Calcutta: Academic Publishers.

PATAÑJALI (trans. Rāma PRASĀDA) (1978) [1912]. *Patañjali's Yoga Sūtras with the commentary of Vyāsa and the gloss of Vāchaspati Miśra.* New Delhi: Oriental Books Reprint Corporation.

——— (trans. and comm. Sāṃkyha-yogāchārya Swāmi Hariharānanda ĀRAṆYA; trans. into English P. N. MUKHERJI) (1985) [1965]. *Yoga Philosophy of Patañjali.* Albany: State University of New York Press.

PATIL, Gajanam M. (1960). 'Soma, The Vedic Deity'. *Oriental Thought*, Vol. 4, January, April, nos 1 & 2, pp.69–79.

PAUL, N. C. (1884). *A Treatise on the Yoga Philosophy.* Benares: E. J. Lazarus and Co., Medical Hall Press.

PAYNE, Richard K., and Michael WITZEL (eds) (2016). Homa *Variations: The Study of Ritual Change Across the* Longue Durée. Oxford/New York: Oxford University Press.

PENDELL, Dale (2010a) [1995]. *Pharmako/Poeia: Plant Powers, Poisons, and Herbcraft.* Berkeley, California: North Atlantic Books.

——— (2010b) [2002]. *Pharmako Dynamis: Stimulating Plants, Potions and Herbcraft.* Berkeley, California: North Atlantic Books.

——— (2010c) [2005]. *Pharmako Gnosis: Plant Teachers and the Poison Path.* Berkeley, California: North Atlantic Books.

PENNACCHIO, Marcello, Lara Venessa JEFFERSON, and Kayri HAVENS (2010). *Uses and Abuses of Plant-Derived Smoke: Its Ethnobotany as Hallucinogen, Perfume, Incense, and Medicine.* Oxford/New York: Oxford University Press.

PENNER, James (ed.) (2014). *Timothy Leary, The Harvard Years: Early Writings on LSD and Psilocybin with Richard Alpert, Huston Smith, Ralph Metzner and others.* Rochester, Vermont/Toronto, Canada: Park Street Press.

PERRINE, Daniel M. (1996). *The Chemistry of Mind-Altering Drugs: History, Pharmacology, and Cultural Context.* Washington, DC: American Chemical Society.

PETERSON, Barbara Bennett (2011). *Peopling the Americas, Currents, Canoes, and DNA.* New York: Nova Science Publishers.

PINCHBECK, Daniel (2003). *Breaking Open the Head: A visionary journey from cynicism to shamanism.* London: Flamingo/HarperCollins.

PIPER, Alan (2005). 'The mysterious origin of the word "marihuana"'. *Sino-Platonic Papers*, no. 153, July, pp.1–17.

PLATO (trans. Walter HAMILTON) (1973). *Phaedrus and Letters VII and VIII*. Harmondsworth, Middlesex, UK: Penguin Books.

PLINY (trans. W. H. S. JONES) (1961). *Natural History*, Books 20–23, 24–27 (Vols VI and VII, Loeb Classical Library). Cambridge, Massachusetts/London: Harvard University Press/William Heinemann Ltd.

PLOWMAN, Timothy G., Adrian LEUTCHMANN, Carol BLANEY, and Keith CLAY (1990). 'Significance of the Fungus *Balansia cyperi* Infecting Medicinal Species of *Cyperus* (Cyperaceae) from Amazonia'. *Economic Botany*, Vol. 44, Issue 4, pp.452–462.

POSSEHL, Gregory L. (2002). 'Indus-Mesopotamian Trade: The Record in the Indus'. *Iranica Antiqua*, Vol. XXXXVII, pp.325–342.

PRANAVANANDA, Swami (1983) [1949]. *Kailās-Mānasarovar*, 2nd edn. New Delhi: Swami Pranavananda.

The Psychonaut.org (2013). 'LSA (d-lysergic Acid Amide)', pp.1–7. http://www.thepsychonaut.org/entheopedia/lsa/ (accessed 7/09/2015).

PRANUTHI, E. Kamala, K. NARENDRA, J. SWATHI, K. M. SOWJANYA, K. V. N. Rathnakar REDDI, Rev Fr. S. EMMANUEL S. J., and A. Krishna SATYA (2014). 'Qualititive assessment of bioactive compounds from a very rare medicinal plant *Ficus dalhousiae* Miq'. *Journal of Pharmacognosy and Phytochemistry*, Vol. 3, no. 1, pp.57–61.

PRESTI, David E., and David E. NICHOLS (2005). 'Biochemistry and Neuropharmacology of Psilocybin Mushrooms'. In METZNER (ed.) (2005b), pp.93–112.

RAMANATHAN, A. S. (1995). *Vedic Concept of Soma* (The Logic of Vedic Thought – 2). Jaipur: Rajasthan Patrika Limited.

RĀMĀNUJA (trans. Svāmī ĀDIDEVĀNANDA) (2007). *Śrī Rāmānuja Gītā Bhāṣya*. Chennai: Sri Ramakrishna Math.

RANADE, R. D. (1988) [1933]. *Mysticism in Maharashtra: Indian Mysticism*. Delhi: Motilal Banarsidass.

RÄTSCH, Christian (2005). *Encyclopedia of Psychoactive Plants: Ethnopharmacology and its Applications*. Rochester, Vermont: Park Street Press.

RAU, Wilhelm (1997). 'The Earliest Literary Evidence for Permanent Vedic Settlements'. In WITZEL (ed.), pp.203–206.

RAUSING, Gad (1988). 'Soma'. *Orientalia Suecana*, Vols XXXVI–XXXVII (1987–1988), pp.125–126.

RAVALEC, Vincent, MALLENDI, and Agnès PAICHELER (trans. Jack CAIN) (2007). *Iboga: The Visionary Root of African Shamanism*. Rochester, Vermont: Park Street Press.

RAWALA, G. S., K. RAWALA, and M. P. SHARMA (2002). 'Medicinally Important Agarics in Himalaya'. In S. S. SAMANT, U. DHAR, and L. M. S. PALNI (eds), *Himalayan Medicinal Plants: Potential and Prospects*, pp.33–43. Nainital: Gyanodaya Prakashan.

RENFREW, Colin (1998). 'The Tarim Basin, Tocharian, and Indo-European Origins: A View from the West'. In MAIR (ed.), pp.202–212.

RENOU, Louis (1961). *Études Védiques et Pāṇinéennes*, Tome IX. Paris: Éditions E. de Boccard.

——— (2004). *History of Vedic India*. New Delhi: Sanjay Prakashan.

RIEDLINGER, Thomas J. (ed.) (1997) [1990]. *The Sacred Mushroom Seeker: Tributes to R. Gordon Wasson*. Rochester, Vermont: Park Street Press.

——— (2005) [1993]. 'Wasson's Alternative Candidates for Soma'. *The Journal of Psychoactive Drugs*, Vol. 25, issue 2, pp.149–156. https://www.erowid.org/entheogens/entheogens_article2.shtml (accessed 2/03/15).

ROBINSON, Trevor (1968). *The Biochemistry of Alkaloids (Molecular Biology, Biochemistry and Biophysics 3).* New York: Springer-Verlag New York Inc.

ROHAS-ARÉCHIGA, Mariana, and Joel FLORES (2016). 'An Overview of Cacti and the Controversial Peyote'. In LABATE and CAVNAR (eds), pp.21–42.

ROSENTHAL, Franz (1971). *The Herb: Hashish versus Muslim Society.* Leiden: E. J. Brill.

ROTH, R. (1881). 'Über den Soma'. *Zeitschrift der Deutschen Morgenländischen Gesellschaft*, Band 35, pp.680–692.

RUCK, Carl A. P. (2006). *Sacred Mushrooms of the Goddess and the Secrets of Eleusis.* Berkeley, California: Ronin Publishing Inc.

——— (2008) [1997]. 'Gods and Plants in the Classical World'. In Richard Evans SCHULTES and Siri VON REIS (eds), *Ethnobotany: Evolution of a Discipline*, pp.131–143. Portland, Oregon: Timber Press.

——— (2013). 'Democracy and the Dionysian Agenda'. In RUSH (ed.), pp.343–385).

RUCK, Carl A. P., Mark A. HOFFMAN, José Alfredo González CEDRÁN (2011). *Mushrooms, Myth & Mithras: The Drug Cult that Civilized Europe.* San Francisco: City Lights Books.

RUCK, Carl A., and Robert LARNER (2013). 'Virgil's Edible Tables'. In RUSH (ed.), pp.387–449.

RUDGLEY, Richard (1998). *The Alchemy of Culture: Intoxicants in Society.* London: The British Museum Press.

——— (1999). *The Encyclopaedia of Psychoactive Substances.* London: Abacus.

RUKMANI, T. S. (1998). 'The *Yogasūtrabhāṣyavivaraṇa* is not a work of Śaṅkarācārya the author of the *Brahmasūtrabhāṣya*'. *Journal of Indian Philosophy*, Vol. 26, no. 3, pp.263–274.

RUSH, Benjamin (1771). 'An Account of the Effects of the Strammonium, or Thorn-Apple'. *Transactions of the American Philosophical Society*, Vol. 1 (Jan. 1, 1769–Jan. 1, 1771), pp.318-322.

RUSH, John A. (ed.) (2013). *Entheogens and the Development of Culture: The Anthropology and Neurobiology of Ecstatic Experience.* Berkeley, California: North Atlantic Books.

RUSSELL, James R. (1987). *Zoroastrianism in Armenia* (Harvard Iranian Series, Vol. 5). Cambridge, Massachusetts/London: Harvard University Press.

RUSSO, Ethan (2005). 'Cannabis in India: ancient lore and modern medicine'. In Ralph MECHOULAM (ed.), *Cannabinoids as Therapeutics (Milestones in Drug Therapy)*, pp.1–22. Basel/Boston/Berlin: Birkhäuser Verlag.

RYMLAND, Lizbeth (1999). 'Huantuj 3: Into the Datura Realms We Go'. In Thomas LYTTLE (ed.), *Psychedelics ReImagined*, pp.75–78. Brooklyn, New York: Automedia.

SACKS, Oliver (2012). *Hallucinations.* London: Picador.

SAÉS, Oscar Calavier (2011). 'A Vine Network'. In LABATE and JUNGABERIE (eds), pp.131–144.

SAMORINI, Giorgio (1995). 'Umbrella-stones or mushroom-stones? (Kerala, southern India)'. *Integration, Journal of Mind-Moving Plants and Culture*, no. 6, pp.33–40.

——— (1996). 'An African kykeon?' *Eleusis*, Vol. 4 (April), pp.40–41.

——— (1997). '*Aspergillus Fumigatus* Fres. G'. *Eleusis*, no. 8 (August), pp.38–43.

——— (1998). 'The Pharsalus Bass-Relief and the Eleusian Mysteries'. *The Entheogen Review*, Vol. 7, no. 2, pp.60–63.

——— (2000). 'A Contribution to the Discussion of the of the Ethnobotany of the Eleusian Mysteries'. *Eleusis* (New Series), no. 4, pp.1–53.

——— (trans. Tami CALLIOPE) (2002). *Animals and Psychedelics: The Natural World and the Instinct to Alter Consciousness.* Rochester, Vermont: Park Street Press.

Sanderson, Alexis (2003). 'The Śaiva Religion among the Khmers, Part 1'. *Bulletin de l'École française d'Extrême-Orient*, Vols 90–91 (2003–2004), pp.349–463.

Santosh, M. K., D. Shaila, T. Chandrakumar, I. Rajyalakshmi, and I. Sanjeeva Rao (2005). 'Physicochemical and Phytochemical Examination of Medicinal Plants Used in Indigenous System of Medicine'. *E-Journal of Chemistry*, Vol. 2, no. 2, pp.142–151.

Sarasvatī, Ācārya Rāmānand (n.d.). *Śrīyantra Rahasya*. Delhi: Manoj Poket Buks.

Sarianidi, Victor (1994). 'Temples of Bronze Age Margiana: traditions of ritual architecture'. *Antiquity*, Vol. 68, no. 259, June, pp.388–397.

——— (1999). 'Near Eastern Aryans in Central Asia'. *The Journal of Indo-European Studies*, Vol. 27, nos 3 & 4, Fall/Winter, pp.295–326.

——— (2003). 'Margiana and Soma-Haoma'. *Electronic Journal of Vedic Studies [EJVS]*, Vol. 9, Issue 1d (May 5).

——— (trans. Inna Sarianidi) (2007). *Necropolis of Gonur.* Athens: Kapon Editions.

Saunders, Nicholas, Anja Saunders, and Michelle Pauli (2000). *In Search of the Ultimate High: Spiritual Experience through Psychoactives.* London/Sydney/Auckland/Johannesburg: Rider.

Savage, Charles, William W. Harman, and James Fadiman (1972) [1969]. '*Ipomoea Purpurea*: A Naturally Occurring Psychedelic'. In Charles T. Tart (ed.), *Altered States of Consciousness*, pp.452–454. New York: Anchor Books.

Scandola, Marina, David E. Games, Carlo Costa, Graziella Allegri, Antonella Bertazzo, Ornella Curcuruto, and Pietro Traldi (1994). 'Structural Study of Alkaloids from *Securidaca Longipedunculata* Roots (II). Isolation and Characterization by Supercritical Fluid Chromatography/Mass Spectrometry'. *Journal of Heterocyclic Chemistry*, Vol. 32, January–February, pp.219–224.

Schleiffer, Hedwig (trans. and ed.) (1979). *Narcotic Plants of the Old World Used in Rituals and Everyday Life: An Anthology of Texts from Ancient Times to the Present.* Monticello, New York: Lubrecht & Cramer.

Schmidt, Hanns-Peter (2009). 'Ṛgveda 1.28 and the Alleged Soma-Pressing'. *Electronic Journal of Vedic Studies [EJVS]*, Vol. 16, Issue 1, pp.3–13.

Schmitt, Rüdiger (2015) [2003]. 'Haomavarga'. In *Encyclopædia Iranica*, Vol. 12, Fasc. 1, pp.63–64. Winona Lake, Indiana: Encyclopædia Iranica Foundation/Eisenbrauns Inc. http://www.iranicaonline.org/articles/haumavarga (accessed 27/02/15).

Schultes, Richard Evans (1972). 'An Overview of Hallucinogens in the Western Hemisphere'. In Furst (ed.), pp.3–54.

Schultes, Richard Evans, and Albert Hofmann (1980). *The Botany and Chemistry of Hallucinogens.* Springfield, Illinois: Charles C. Thomas.

Schultes, Richard Evans, Albert Hofmann, and Christian Rätsch (2001) [1992]. *Plants of the Gods: Their Sacred, Healing, and Hallucinogenic Powers,* 2nd edn. Rochester, Vermont: Healing Arts Press.

Schultes, Richard Evans, and Robert A. Raffauf (2004) [1992]. *Vine of the Soul: Medicine Men, their Plants and Rituals in the Colombian Amazonia.* Santa Fe, New Mexico: Synergetic Press.

Seaford, Richard (2004). *Money and the Early Greek Mind: Homer, Philosophy, Tragedy.* Cambridge: Cambridge University Press.

——— (2006). *Dionysos.* London/New York: Routledge.

Sen, Chitrabhanu (1978). *A Dictionary of the Vedic Rituals (Based on the Śrauta and Gṛhya Sūtras).* Delhi: Concept Publishing Company.

Shah, Niti T., Tarulata N. Pandya, Parameshwar P. Sharma, Bhupesh R. Patel, and Rabinarayan Acharya (2012). '*Mootrala Karma* of *Kusha* (*Imperata cylindrica*

Beauv.) and *Darbha* (*Desmostachya bipinnata* Stapf.) – A comparative study'. *Ayu*, Vol. 33, Issue 3 (July–Sept), pp.387–390.

SHANON, Benny (2010) [2002]. *The Antipodes of the Mind: Charting the Phenomenology of the Ayahuasca Experience.* Oxford/New York: Oxford University Press.

SHARMA, P. V. (1996). 'Original Concept of Soma'. *Indian Journal of History of Science*, 31(2), pp.109–130.

SHARON, Douglas (1972). 'The San Pedro Cactus in Peruvian Folk Healing'. In FURST (ed.), pp.114–135.

SHELDRAKE, Rupert (2013). *The Science Delusion: Freeing the Spirit of Enquiry.* London: Coronet.

SHELLEY, William Scott (1995). *The Elixir: An Alchemical Study of the Ergot Mushrooms.* Notre Dame, Indiana: Cross Cultural Publications.

SHEPARD, Glenn (2005). 'Psychoactive botanicals in ritual, religion and shamanism'. In E. ELIZABETSKY and N. ETKIN (eds), *Ethnopharmacology: Encyclopedia of Life Support Systems (EOLSS)*, Vol. 2, Theme 6.79, pp.128–182. Oxford: UNESCO/Eolss Publishers.

——— (2014). 'Will the Real Shaman Please Stand Up?: The Recent Adoption of Ayahuasca Among Indigenous Groups of the Peruvian Amazon'. In LABATE and CAVNAR (eds), pp.16–39.

SHERRATT, Andrew (1991). 'Sacred and Profane Substances: the Ritual Use of Narcotics in Later Neolithic Europe'. In P. GARWOOD, D. JENNINGS, R. SKEATES, and J. TOMS (eds), *Sacred and Profane: Proceedings of a Conference on Archaeology, Ritual and Religion, Oxford, 1989* (Monograph no. 32), pp.50–64. Oxford: Oxford University Committee for Archaeology.

——— (1995). 'Alcohol and its Alternatives: Symbol and Substance in Pre-Industrial Cultures'. In Jordan GOODMAN, Paul E. LOVEJOY, and Andrew SHERRATT (eds), *Consuming Habits: Drugs in History and Anthropology*, pp.11–46. London/New York: Routledge.

SHULGIN, Alexander, and Ann SHULGIN (1997). *TiHKAL: The Continuation.* Berkeley: Transform Press.

——— (2000) [1991]. *PiHKAL: A Chemical Love Story.* Berkeley: Transform Press.

SIEGAL, Ronald K. (2005) [1989]. *Intoxication: The Universal Drive for Mind-Altering Substances.* Rochester, Vermont: Park Street Press.

SIKLÓS, Bulcsu (1993). '*Datura* Rituals in the Vajramahabhairava Tantra'. *Curare*, Vol. 18, pp.71–76.

SILVER, Gary (ed.), Michael A. ALDRICH (Intro.) (1979). *The Dope Chronicles 1850–1950.* New York/Hagerstown/San Francisco/London: Harper & Row.

SINGH, Bhagwan (1981). 'Identification of Soma'. *Purātattva (Bulletin of the Indian Archeological Society)*, Number 12 (1980–81), pp.154–156.

SINGH, Rita (2006). *Psychoactive Medicinal Plants: Hallucinogenic and Narcotic Drugs.* New Delhi: Global Vision Publishing House.

SINHA, Kirti, N. P. MISHRA, J. SINGH, and S. P. S. KHANUJA (2004). '*Tinospora cordifolia* (Guduchi), a reservoir plant for therapeutic applications: A Review'. *Indian Journal of Traditional Knowledge*, Vol. 3 (3), July, pp.257–270.

SKJÆRVØ, Prods Oktor (2004). 'Smashing Urine: On *Yasna* 45.10'. In STAUSBERG (ed.), pp.253–281.

——— (2011) (Intro., trans. and ed.) *The Spirit of Zoroastrianism.* New Haven/London: Yale University Press.

SMART, Ninian (1978). 'Understanding Mystical Experience'. In KATZ (ed.), pp.10–21.

SMITH, Frederick M. (2006). *The Self Possessed: Deity and Spirit Possession in South Asian Literature and Civilization.* New York: Columbia University Press.

Smith, Huston (2000). *Cleansing the Doors of Perception: The Religious Significance of Entheogenic Plants and Chemicals.* New York: Jeremy P. Tarcher/Putnam.

Smith, Terrence A. (1977). 'Review: Tryptamine and Related Compounds in Plants'. *Phytochemistry*, Vol. 16, pp.171–175.

Solomon, David (ed.) (1969). *The Marijuana Papers.* London: Panther Books Ltd.

Sood, S. K., Sarita Rana, and T. N. Lakhanpal (2005). *Ethnic Aphrodisiac Plants.* Jodhpur: Scientific Publishers (India).

Sorensen, John L., and Carl L. Johannessen (2004). 'Scientific Evidence for Pre-Columbian Transoceanic Voyages'. *Sino-Platonic Papers*, no. 133, April, pp.1–258.

Sourvinou-Inwood (2003). 'Festival and Mysteries: aspects of the Eleusian Cult'. In Cosmopoulos (ed.), pp.25–49.

Spess, David L. (2000). *Soma: The Divine Hallucinogen.* Rochester, Vermont: Park Street Press.

Spinella, Marcello (2001). *The Psychopharmacology of Herbal Medicine: Plant Drugs That Alter Mind, Brain and Behavior.* Cambridge, Mass./London: The MIT press.

Śrautasūtras: see Dandekar (1958–1962).

Srivastava, J. G. (1966). 'The Soma plant'. *Quarterly Journal of Crude Drug Research*, Vol. 6, no. 1, pp.811–818.

——— (1970) 'Some further observations on the 'Soma' plant'. *Quarterly Journal of Crude Drug Research*, Vol. 10, no. 3, pp.1590–1600.

Staal, Frits (1975). *Exploring Mysticism.* UK/Canada/Australia/New Zealand: Penguin Books.

——— (1996) [1990]. *Ritual and Mantras: Rules without Meaning.* Delhi: Motilal Banarsidass.

——— (2001a). 'How a Psychoactive Substance Became a Ritual: The Case of Soma'. *Social Research*, Vol. 68.3, pp.745–778.

——— (2002). 'Vedic Mantras'. In Alper (ed.), pp.48–95.

——— (2008). *Discovering the Vedas: Origins, Mantras, Rituals, Insights.* New Delhi: Penguin Books.

Staal, Frits, with C. V. Somayajipad, and M. Itti Ravi Nambudiri (2001b) [1983]. *Agni: The Vedic Ritual of the Fire Altar*, Vols I–II. Berkeley: Asian Humanities Press.

Stace, W. T. (1960). *Mysticism and Philosophy.* Los Angeles: Jeremy & Tarcher, Inc.

Stafford, Peter (1977). *Psychedelics Encyclopedia.* Berkeley: And/Or Press.

Stamets, Paul (2005). 'Global Ecologies, World Distribution, and Relative Potency of Psilocybian Mushrooms'. In Metzner (ed.) (2005b), pp.69–75.

Stausberg, Michael (ed.) (2004). *Zoroastrian Rituals in Context.* Leiden/Boston: E. J. Brill.

——— (2004). 'Contextualizing the Contexts: On the Study of Zoroastrian Rituals'. In Stausberg (ed.), pp.1–56.

Stein, Aurel (1932). 'On the Ephedra, the Hūm Plant, and the Soma'. *Bulletin of the School of Oriental and African Studies*, Vol. VI (1930–1932), pp.501–514.

Stepan, Vladimir (2016). 'Heart of Darkness: Sensory Deprivation and Darkness Retreat as a Psychedelic Experience'. In Robert Dickins (ed.), *Psychedelic Press*, Vol. XVIII, pp.61–80. London: Psychedelic Press.

Stolaroff, Myron J. (2004) [1997]. *The Secret Chief Revealed.* Sarasota, Florida: Multidisciplinary Association for Psychedelic Studies (MAPS).

——— (2015). 'Do We Still Need Psychedelics?'. In Badiner (ed.), pp.198–205.

Storey, Alice A., Daniel Quiróz, and Elizabeth A. Matisoo-Smith (2011). 'A Reappraisal of the Evidence for Pre-Columbian Introduction of Chickens to America'. In Jones *et al.* (eds), pp.139–170.

Strassman, Rick (2001). *DMT: The Spirit Molecule*. Rochester, Vermont: Park Street Press.

——— (2005). 'Hallucinogens'. In Earleywine, pp.49–85.

Studerus, Erich, Alex Gamma, and Franz X. Vollenweider (2010). 'Psychometric Evaluation of the Altered States of Consciousness Rating Scale (OAV)'. *Plos One*, Vol. 5, issue 8 (August), pp.1–19.

Stuhrman, Rainer (1985). 'Worum handelt es sich beim Soma'. *Indo-Iranian Journal*, Vol. 28, pp.85–93.

——— (2006). 'Capturing Light in the Ṛgveda: Soma seen botanically, pharmacologically, and in the eyes of the Kavis'. *Electronic Journal of Vedic Studies [EJVS]*, Vol. 13, Issue 1 (April), pp.1–93.

Suryawanshi and Patel (2011). 'Traditional Uses, Medicinal and Phytopharmacological Properties of Caesalpinia crista Linn. – An Overview'. *International Journal of Research in Pharmacy and Chemistry*, Vol. 1 (4), pp.1179–1183.

Suśruta (trans. and ed. Kaviraj Kunjalal Bhishagratna) (1963). *Sushruta Samhitā: An English Translation Based on Original Sanskrit Text,* Vol. 2 (The Chowkhamba Sanskrit Studies, Vol. XXX). Varanasi: The Chowkhamba Sanskrit Series Office.

Swamy, B. G. L. (1976). 'Sources for a History of Plant Sciences in India, II: The *Ṛg Vedic Soma* Plant'. *Indian Journal of History of Science*, Vol. 11, no. 1, May, pp.11–32.

Taillieu, Dieter (1995) [1994]. 'Old-Iranian *Haoma-*: A Note on its Pharmacology'. *Acta Orientalia Belgica*, Vol. IX (Guerre et Paix/War and Peace), pp.187–191.

——— (2012) [1998]. 'Haoma i. Botany'. In *Encyclopædia Iranica*, Vol. XI, Fasc. 6, pp.659–662. http://www.iranicaonline.org/articles/haoma-i (accessed 27/02/2015).

Tattersall, Ian (1995). *The Last Neanderthal: The Rise, Success, and Mysterious Extinction of our Closest Human Relatives.* New York: Macmillan.

Temple, Robert (1989). *Open to Suggestion: The Uses and Abuses of Hypnosis.* Wellingborough, Northamptonshire: The Aquarian Press.

Thakur, Arun Kishore, and Jainendra Kumar (n.d.). '*Kusha* – the Holy grass'. www.harmonybihar.org/Kusha.pdf (accessed 2/01/2015).

Theophrastus (trans. Arthur Hort) (1916). *Enquiry into Plants and Minor Works on Odours and Weather Signs*, Vols 1–2 (The Loeb Classical Library). London/New York: William Heinemann/G. P. Putnam's Sons.

Thomas, Benjamin (2000). 'Psychoactive Plant Use in Papua New Guinea: A Review'. *Science in New Guinea*, Vol. 25 (1.2.3), pp.33–59.

Thomas, Keith (1978) [1971]. *Religion and the Decline of Magic: Studies in Popular Beliefs in Sixteenth- and Seventeenth-Century England.* London/New York/ Ringwood, Victoria, Australia: Penguin Books.

Thompson, George (2003). 'Soma and Ecstasy in the Rgveda'. *Electronic Journal of Vedic Studies [EJVS]*, Vol. 9, Issue 1e (May 6).

——— (2007). 'On the Nāmarūpa of Soma'. *Nāmarūpa*, Vol. 5, Fall 2006–Spring 2007, pp.65–69.

Tigunāit, Paṇḍit Rājmaṇi (2012). *Himālay ke siddh yogi Śrī Svāmī Rām*, Vol. 1. Ilāhābād: Himalayan Institute.

Tirumular (trans. and notes B. Natarajan) (1991). *Tirumantiram.* Mylapore, Chennai: Sri Ramakrishna Math.

Tononi, Guilio, and Christof Koch (2015). 'Consciousness: here, there and everywhere?' *Philosophical Transactions of the Royal Society B*, Vol. 370: 20140167, pp.1–18.

Toro, Gianluca, and Benjamin Thomas (2007). *Drugs of the Dreaming, Oneirogens:* Salvia Divinorum *and other Dream-Enhancing Plants.* Rochester, Vermont: Park Street Press.

Tortel, Christiane (2009). *L'Ascète et le Bouffon:* qalandars, *vrais ou faux renonçants en islam, ou l'Orient indianisé.* Actes Sud.

Törzsök, Judit (2007). 'Search for Meaning in Tantric Ritual in the Śaiva Scriptures'. In Dominic Goodall and André Padoux (eds), *Mélanges Tantriques à la mémoire de'Hélène Brunner/Tantric Studies in Memory of Hélène Brunner*, pp.449–479. Pondicherry/Paris: Institut français de Pondichéry/École français d'Extrême-Orient.

Tregar (2010). 'The Sacred Brew of Eleusis? adduct-ed ergonovine'. https://mycotopia.net/topic/62420-the-sacred-brew-of-eleusis-adduct-ed-ergonovine/ (accessed 21/08/2015).

Trout, K., and friends (2002) [1993–2001]. *Trout's Notes on Some Simple Tryptamines: A brief overview & resource compendium* (Trout's Notes #FS-X7, Version 4-2002). Mydriatic Productions/Better Days Publishing.

——— (2004a) [2002]. *Trout's Notes on the Genus* Desmodium *(Chemistry, Ehnomedicine, Pharmacology, Synonyms and Miscellany)* (Trout's Notes #D-2). Austin, Texas: Better Days Publications. http://troutsnotes.com/sc/TNinfo.htm (accessed 22/10/2014).

——— (2004b). *A-5: Ayahuasca: alkaloids, plants & analogs*, 2nd edn. https://www.erowid.org/library/books_online/ayahuasca_apa/ (accessed 29/10/2014).

——— (2004c) *Trout's Notes: Tryptamine Content of Arundo donax.* http://www.erowid.org/plants/arundo_donax/arundo_donax_info1.shtml (accessed 30/10/2014).

Turner, D. M. (1994). *The Essential Psychedelic Guide.* San Francisco: Panther Press.

——— (1996). *Salvinorin: The Psychedelic Essence of Salvia Divinorum.* San Francisco: Panther Press.

Upādhyāy, Rāmkṛṣn (n.d.). *Kumbh Mahātmya, aur pāvan tīrth Haridvār-Kankhāl-Ṛṣikeś.* Haridvār: Raṇdhīr Book Sales.

Upaniṣads: (trans. and ed. Robert Ernest Hume) (1998) [1877]. Oxford: Oxford University Press.

——— (trans. and ed. Patrick Olivelle) (1996). Oxford/New York: Oxford University Press.

——— (trans. and ed. Valerie J. Roebuck) (2003). London: Penguin Books.

——— (eds V. P. Limaye and R. D. Vadekar) (1958). Aṣṭādaśa-Upaniṣadaḥ*/Eighteen Principal Upaniṣads*, Vol. 1. Poona: Vaidika Saṃśodhana Maṇḍala.

Usdin, Earl, and Daniel H. Efron (1967). *Psychotropic Drugs and Related Compounds* (Public Health Service Publication no. 1589). Washington, D. C.: U. S. Department of Health, Education, and Welfare.

Vahman, Fereydun (1986). *Ardā Wirāz Nāmag: The Iranian 'Divina Commedia'* (Scandanavian Institute of Asian Studies Monograph Series, no. 53). London/ Malmo: Curzon Press.

Valencic, Ivan (1994). 'Has the Mystery of the Eleusian Mysteries been solved?'. *Yearbook for Ethnomedicine and the Study of Consciousness/Jahrbuch für Ethnomedizin und Bewußteinsforschung*, Issue 3, pp.325–336. Berlin: Verlag für Wissenschaft und Bildung.

Valiathan, M. S. (2003). *The Legacy of Caraka.* Chennai: Orient Longman Private Limited.

Vayne, Julian (2006). *Pharmakon: Drugs and the Imagination.* Oxford: Mandrake of Oxford.

Vedas: *Atharva Veda*, Vols 1–6 (trans. and ed. R. L. Kashyap) (2011–2012). Bangalore. Sri Aurobindo Kapāli Sāstri Institute of Vedic Culture (SAKSHI).

The Atharva Veda, Vols 1–2 (trans. and ed. Acharya Vaidya Nath Shastri) (1984). New Delhi: Sarvadeshik Arya Pratinidhi Sabha.

Atharva-Veda-Saṃhitā, (books VIII–XIX) (trans. William Dwight Whitney, revised and ed. Charles Rockwell Lanman) (1993) [1905]. Delhi: Motilal Banarsidass.

Rig Veda Samhitā, Vols 1–12 (trans. and ed. R. L. KASHYAP) (2007–2009). Bangalore: Sri Aurobindo Kapāli Sāstri Institute of Vedic Culture (SAKSHI).

Sāma Veda, Vols 1–2 (trans. and ed. R. L. KASHYAP) (2008–2011). Bangalore: Sri Aurobindo Kapāli Sāstri Institute of Vedic Culture (SAKSHI).

Texts of the White Yajurveda, translated with a popular commentary (trans. and ed. Ralph T. H. GRIFFITH (2012) [1899]. [Benares]: [E. J. Lazarus and Co.]/Forgotten Books.

The Yajur Veda (Taittirya Sanhita) (trans. and ed. Arthur Berriedale KEITH) (2008) [1914]. Forgotten Books.

Yajur Veda (Taittirīya-Samhitā), Vols 1–4 (trans. and ed. R. L. KASHYAP) (2011). Bangalore: Sri Aurobindo Kapāli Sāstri Institute of Vedic Culture (SAKSHI).

[Viṣṇusmṛti] The Institutes of Vishnu (trans. Julius JOLLY) (1986) [1880] (*Sacred Books of the East*, Vol. 7, ed. F. Max MÜLLER). Delhi: Motilal Banarsidass.

WAGENAAR, Henk W. (compiler) (1996). *Hindi—Transliterated Hindi—English Dictionary.* New Delhi: Allied Publishers Limited.

WALSH, Roger (2015). 'Mysticism: Contemplative and Chemical'. In BADINER (ed.), pp.19–25.

WARADPANDE, N. R. (1995). *The Rgvedic Soma* (Research Monograph II). Nagpur: Sanskrit Bhasha Pracharini Sabha.

WASSON, R. Gordon (1969) [1968]. *Soma: Divine Mushroom of Immortality.* New York: Harcourt Brace Jovanovich, Inc.

——— (1971). 'The Soma of the Rig Veda. What Was It?'. *Journal of the American Oriental Society*, Vol. 91, no. 2 (April–June), pp. 169–187.

——— (1972a). 'The Divine Mushroom of Immortality'. In FURST (ed.), pp.185–200.

——— (1972b). 'What Was the Soma of the Aryans?' In FURST (ed.), pp.201–213.

——— (1972c). *Soma and the Fly-Agaric: Mr. Wasson's Rejoinder to Professor Brough.* Cambridge, Mass.: Botanical Museum of Harvard University.

WASSON, R. Gordon, Albert HOFMANN, and Carl A. P. RUCK. (1978). *The Road to Eleusis: Unveiling the Secret of the Mysteries* (Ethno-mycological Studies, no. 4). London/ New York: First Harvest/HBJ edition/Harcourt Brace Jovanovich Inc.

WASSON, R. Gordon, Stella KRAMRISCH, Jonathan OTT, and Carl A. P. RUCK (1986). *Persephone's Quest: Entheogens and the Origins of Religion.* New Haven/London: Yale University Press.

WATKINS, Calvert (1978). 'Let Us Now Praise Famous Grains'. *Proceedings of the American Philosophical Society*, Vol. 122, no. 1, pp.9–17.

WATSON, Peter (2013) [2012]. *The Great Divide; Nature and Human Nature in the Old World and the New.* New York: HarperCollins.

WATTS, Alan W. (1970) [1962]. *The Joyous Cosmology: Adventures in the Chemistry of Consciouness.* New York: Vintage Books.

——— (2011) [1968]. 'Qualities of Transcendent Experience: Four Dominant Characteristics'. In FADIMAN, pp.39–44 (reprint of an article entitled 'Psychedelics and the Religious Experience', *California Law Review*, Vol. 56, no. 1, January 1968, pp.74–85).

WEBSTER, Peter, Daniel M. PERRINE, and Carl A. P. RUCK (2000). 'Mixing the *Kykeon*'. *Eleusis* (New Series), Vol. 1, no. 4, pp.55–86.

WEIL, Andrew (1975) [1972]. *The Natural Mind.* Harmondsworth, Middlesex, UK/ Ringwood, Victoria, Australia/Auckland, New Zealand: Penguin Books Ltd.

WERNER, Karel (1989). 'The Longhaired Sage of *Ṛg Veda*, 10.136'. In Karel WERNER (ed.), *The Yogi and the Mystic: Studies in Indian and Comparative Mysticism* (Durham Indological Series, no. 1), pp.33–53. Richmond, UK: Curzon Press.

WEST, E. W. (trans. and ed.) (2010) [1897]. *Pahlavi Texts*, Part V (*Marvels of Zoroastrianism*) (*Sacred Books of the East*, Vol. XLVII, ed. F. Max MÜLLER). Delhi: Low Price Publications/[Oxford: Clarendon Press].

WEZLER, Albrecht (2001). '"Psychedelic" Drugs as a Means to Mystical Experience'. In BARFOOT (ed.), pp.191–220.

WHITAKER, Jarod L. (2004). 'Ritual Power, Social Prestige, and Amulets (*maṇi*) in the Atharvaveda'. In GRIFFITHS and HOUBEN (eds), pp.565–580.

——— (2007). 'Does Pressing *Sóma* Make you an Āryan?: A Brief Review of *súṣvi-* and *ásuṣvi-* in the *Ṛgveda*'. *Zeitschrift der Deutschen Morgenländischen Gesellschaft*, Vol. 157, part 2, pp.417–426.

WILLIAMS, A. V. (trans. and ed.) (1990). *The Pahlavi Rivāyat Accompanying the Dādestān ī Dēnīg*, Parts I–II (Historisk-filosofiske Meddelelser 60:1–2). Copenhagen: Munksgaard/Det Kongelige Danske Videnskabernes Selskab (The Royal Danish Academy of Sciences and Letters).

WILSON, Peter Lamborn (1999). *Ploughing The Clouds: The Search for Irish Soma.* San Francisco: City Lights.

WINDFUHR, Gernot L. (1985). 'Haoma/Soma: The Plant'. In *Papers in Honour of Professor Mary Boyce* (Acta Iranica 25), pp.699–726). Leiden: E. J. Brill.

WINTERNITZ, Maurice (trans. V. Srinivasa SARMA) (1981). *A History of Indian Literature*, Vol. 1*: Introduction, Veda, Epics, Purāṇas and Tantras.* Delhi: Motilal Banarsidass.

WITZEL, Michael (ed.) (1997). *Inside the Texts, Beyond the Texts: New Approaches to the Study of the Vedas (Proceedings of the International Vedic Workshop, Harvard University, June 1989)* (Harvard Oriental Series, Opera Minora, Vol. 2). Cambridge, Massachusetts: Department of Sanskrit and Indian Studies, Harvard University.

——— (1997). 'The Development of the Vedic Canon and its Schools: The Social and Political Milieu'. In WITZEL (ed.), pp.297–345.

——— (1999). 'Early Sources for South Asian Substrate Languages'. *Mother Tongue*, Special Issue, October, pp.1–76.

——— (2000). 'The Home of the Aryans'. In Almut HINZE and Eva TICHY (eds), *Anusantatyai: Festschrifft für Johanna Narten* (Münchener Studien zur Sprachtwissenschaft, Beiheft 19), pp.283–338. Dettelbach: J. H. Röll Verlag.

——— (2003). 'Linguistic Evidence for Cultural Exchange in Prehistoric Western Central Asia'. *Sino-Platonic Papers*, no. 129, December, pp.1–70.

——— (2004). 'The Ṛgvedic Religious System and its Central Asian and Hindukush Antecedents'. In GRIFFITHS and HOUBEN (eds), pp.581–636.

——— [E. J.] Michael (2012). *The Origins of the World's Mythologies.* Oxford/New York: Oxford University Press.

——— (2016). '*Agnihotra* Rituals in Nepal'. In PAYNE and WITZEL (eds), pp.371–406.

WOHLBERG, Joseph (1990). 'Haoma-Soma in the World of Ancient Greece'. *The Journal of Psychoactive Drugs*, Vol. 2, issue 3 (July–Sept), pp.333–342.

WRIGHT, Dudley (2011) [1919]. *The Eleusian Mysteries and Rites.* [London/Denver: The Theosophical Publishing House].

WRÓBEL, J. T., M. MATUSZEWSKA, J. SZYCHOWSKI, A. BERTAZZO, P. TRALDI, C. V. L. COSTA, and G. ALLEGRI (1996). 'Indole alkaloids and other constituents from the plant *Securidaca longipedunculata fres* [sic]'. In Graziella Allegri FILIPPINI, Carlo V. L. COSTA, and Antonella BERTAZZO (eds), *Recent Advances in Tryptophan Research: Tryptophan and Serotonin Pathways* (Proceedings of the Eighth International Meeting on Tryptophan Research, held June 25–29, in Padova, Italy), pp.685–689. New York: Plenum Press.

WUJASTYK, Dominic (1998). *The Roots of Ayurveda.* London: Penguin Books.

——— (2002). 'Cannabis in Traditional Indian Herbal Medicine'. In A. SALEMA (ed.), *Ayurveda at the Crossroads of Care and Cure: Proceedings of the Indo-European Seminar on Ayurveda held at Arrabida, Portugal, in November 2001*, pp.45–73. Lisbon: Universidade Nova.

——— (2004). 'Agni and Soma: A Universal Classification'. *Studia Asiatica*, IV–V (2003–2004), pp.347–369.

YI, Tao, Zhong-Zhen ZHAO, Zhi-Ling YU, and Hu-Biao CHEN (2010). 'Comparison of the anti-inflammatory and anti-nociceptive effects of three medicinal plants known as "Snow Lotus" herb in traditional Uighur and Tibetan medicines'. *Journal of Ethnopharmacology*, March 24, Vol. 128 (2), pp.405–411.

ZAEHNER, R. C. (1969 [1957]). *Mysticism Sacred and Profane: An Inquiry into some Varieties of Praeternatural Experiences.* London/Oxford/New York: Oxford University Press.

——— (1972) [1960]. *Hindu and Muslim Mysticism.* New York: Schocken Books

ZVELEBIL, Kamil V. (1996). *The Siddha Quest for Immortality.* Oxford: Mandrake of Oxford.

ZYSK, Kenneth G. (1985). *Religious Healing in the Veda* (Transactions of the American Philosophical Society, Vol. 7, part 7). Philadelphia: The American Philosophical Society.

——— (2002). '*Mantra* in Āyurveda: A Study of the Use of Magico-Religious Speech in Ancient Indian Medicine'. In ALPER (ed.), pp.123–143.

List of abbreviations

AB	*Aitareya Brāhmaṇa*
AV	*Atharvaveda*
EJVS	*Electronic Journal of Vedic Studies*
MS	*Manusmṛti*
IPNI	International Plant Names Index
MW	MONIER-WILLIAMS
ṚV	*Ṛgveda*
ŚB	*Śatapatha Brāhmaṇa*
S.B.E.	*Sacred Books of the East* (ed. Friedrich Max Müller)
SV	*Sāmaveda*
TB	*Taittirīya Brāhmaṇa*
TS	*Taittirīya Saṃhitā*
Vd.	*Vīdēvdād*
Y	*Yasna*
YV	*Yajurveda*

APPENDIX 1

The Vedic sacrificial arena for *agniṣṭoma* rites

(modified diagram and key from HOUBEN 1991:136–137)
Less complex arenas are constructed for *iṣṭi* and *paśuyajña* rites.
For diagrams of all three arenas, see MINKOWSKI 1991:13–15.

Gārh	*gārhapatya* (domestic fire)
Āhav.	*āhavanīya* (offering fire)
Dakṣiṇ.	*dakṣiṇāgni* (southern fire)
R.	*rājāsandī*, the king's throne for the *soma* stalks
S.	*saṃrāḍ-āsandī*, the emperor's throne for the *pravargya* vessels
m.	*methī* and *mayūkhas*, the peg and pins for the cow, the calf, the she-goat, and the lamb
kh.	*kharas*, the mounds
Utt.v.	*uttaravedi* (*vedi* = altar)
n.	*nābhi* (navel)
sadas	The temporary shelter where brahmans assemble for Vedic recitation
havirdhāna	The *soma* hall
pravargya	Clay pots that are filled with milk and ghee, and heated
yūpa	A post to which sacrificial animals are tied

APPENDIX 2

Arundo donax (giant reed)

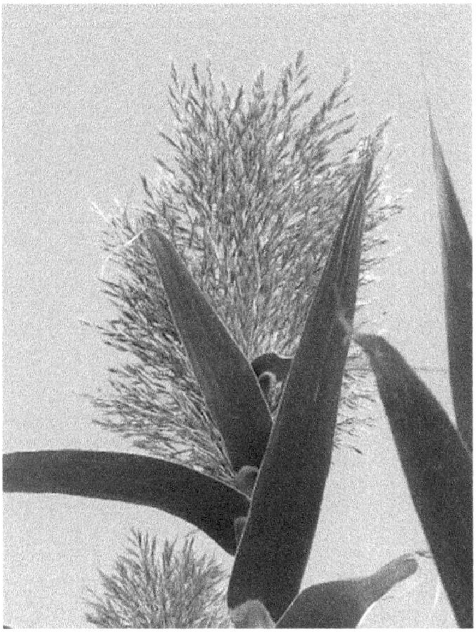

APPENDIX 3

Darbha/Kuśa grass

(photograph by Janette BUSHELL)

APPENDIX 4

Brief outline of the three largest Brazilian ayahuasca churches

Santo Daime was founded by Raimundo Irineu SERRA (*Mestre* Irineu, 1892–1971) around 1930 in Rio Branco (Acre Province, Brazil). It currently has two principal branches (and several sub-branches), the much smaller Alto Santo, and CEFLURIS (Centro Eclético de Fluente Luz Universal Raimundo Irineu Serra), created in 1972 by one of Irineu's followers, Sebastião Mota DE MELO (Padrinho Sebastião, 1920–1990). After the demise of Sebastião, the leadership was assumed by Alfredo Gregório DE MELO (Padrinho Alfredo). CEFLURIS—which split with Alto Santo partly due to CEFLURIS' use of cannabis—was recently renamed 'Igreha do Culto Eclético da Fluente Luz Universal Patrono Sebastião Mota de Melo'. CEFLURIS is more influenced by the Africa-derived *umbanda* 'possession' cult, and by KARDEC (see below) than is Alto Santo.

The UDV was officially founded (as Centro Espírita Beneficiente União do Vegetal) in 1961 by José Gabriel DA COSTA (*Mestre* Gabriel, 1922–1971), who established his first temple in 1965 in Port Velho (Rondônia Province, Upper Amazon, Brazil). The Santo Daime and UDV combine elements of Catholicism, Afro-Brazilian religions, the mid-19th century Spiritism (of the Frenchman and educator, Allan KARDEC), European esotericism, Masonry (particularly in the UDV), and a belief in reincarnation and 'karma'.

Barquinha ('little boat') was instituted by Daniel Pereira DE MATOS (*Mestre*—or 'Frei'—Daniel, 1888–1958) in 1945 near Rio Branco. This group focuses primarily on 'cleansings' (*limpezas*), alleviating sickness, countering witchcraft, and exorcising bad spirits. Current estimates for the membership of these churches are, approximately: UDV, 15,000; Santo Daime, 8,000; Alto Santo, 600; Barquinha, 500.

APPENDIX 5

States of consciousness (diagram from Metzner 2009:64)

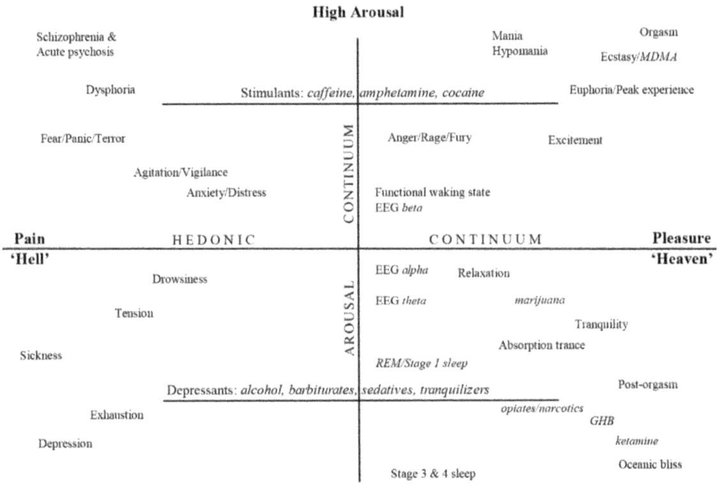

High Arousal
Schizophrenia &
Acute psychosis
Mania
Hypomania
Orgasm
Ecstasy/*MDMA*
Dysphoria
Stimulants: *caffeine, amphetamine, cocaine*
Euphoria/Peak experience
Fear/Panic/Terror
Anger/Rage/Fury
Excitement
Agitation/Vigilance
Anxiety/Distress
Functional waking state
EEG *beta*
CONTINUUM
Pain
'Hell'
HEDONIC
CONTINUUM
Pleasure
'Heaven'
Drowsiness
EEG *alpha*
Relaxation
Tension
EEG *theta*
marijuana
Tranquility
AROUSAL
Sickness
Absorption trance
REM/Stage 1 sleep
Depressants: *alcohol, barbiturates, sedatives, tranquilizers*
Post-orgasm
Exhaustion
opiates/narcotics
GHB
Depression
ketamine
Oceanic bliss
Stage 3 & 4 sleep

APPENDIX 6

Pre-Columbian trans-Pacific contact?

There appears to be have been at least some intercontinental trade between Egypt, some regions of Asia, and South America in the pre-Columbian ancient world. However, this claim needs to be understood as highly speculative and improbable; nevertheless, I believe it is worthy of at least some consideration.

Nicotine, cannabis and coca were identified in samples of hair, skin, bone and muscle taken from Egyptian mummies that date between 1070 BCE and 395 CE (BALABANOVA, PARSCHE and PIRSIG 1992:358), demonstrating that already by 1000 BCE, coca, which, historically, only grew in South America, was being imported into Egypt. This surprising discovery has been subsequently validated by other scientists (SORENSEN and JOHANNESSEN 2004:13), and indicates the possibility that other plants could conceivably have arrived in Asia at least 3,000 years ago from South America or Mesoamerica, where there was a highly developed use of intoxicating plants.

DÍAZ (1977) catalogues and provides chemical analysis and identifications of about forty psychoactive plants belonging to some fifteen botanical families—including psychedelic mushrooms and cacti, and also psychoactive varieties of fig—used ritually or regarded as sacred by Mesoamericans, from 8000 BCE up to the time of the Spanish conquest of Mexico (1521–1525). There is evidence of the use of *Dermatophyllum secundiflorum/Sophora secundiflora* (Texas mountain laurel), which is a hallucinogen, since 8000 BCE. BALABANOVA *et al.* have also found traces of coca, nicotine and cannabis in Peruvian mummies dating from 115 CE–1500 CE (PIPER 2005:9), indicating, what appears to be—if the analysis is correct—the pre-Columbian importation of cannabis to the New World.

FAHEY (2004) analyses the structure, vocabulary and grammar of the Mayan language, which has no known relatives in the Americas—except for a proposed relation to Mixe-Zoqueen and to Tototnacan—and concludes that the striking similarities to and parallels with Old Chinese, more specifically the Chinese of the 2nd millennium BCE Shang period (the Shang Dynasty was founded in 1766 BCE), can only be interpreted as the result of settlement by Sino-Tibetan-speaking people in Mesoamerica before 900 BCE, the time of the initial development of the Mayan civilization, whose iconography suddenly appears, puzzling archaeologists. FAHEY suggests that the Mayans may have been displaced agriculturist Shang people. MEGGERS (1975), similarly endorses the theory of ancient Chinese settlement in Mesoamerica, noting some interesting parallels between Shang culture and the Olmec civilization, which also erupted, somewhat inexplicably, "in full flower" in Mexico in 1200 BCE. The use of what appear to be oblong, jade 'tablets' of authority, the similarity of feline and dragon imagery, and some similarities between Shang and Olmec scripts lead MEGGERS to conclude that Shang settlers established Olmec culture in Mesoamerica.

A large body of evidence for pre-Columbian transatlantic trade between Asia and the New World is provided by SORENSEN and JOHANNESSEN (2004). Some of their findings, in particular the case made for the introduction of species of domestic chicken to South America from Asia, have alternative, pre-Columbian explanations. In the case of the chicken—specifically the Araucana breed (*Gallus inauris*), evidence for which has been found in Al Arenal in Chile—STOREY *et al.* (2011) make a strong case for the introduction of this species of chicken from Polynesia, rather than from Asia. However, although some of the evidence that SORENSEN and JOHANNESSEN provide of transported plants, animals or parasites is disputable, there are nevertheless several significant anomalies in the conventional, historical view of pre-Columbian 'non-contact' between continents, so that at least a few of their findings cannot, in my view, be explained otherwise than by ancient transatlantic voyages and exchange of goods and aspects of culture.

Another, recent publication by PETERSON (2011) also makes extensive, though unproven and often unsubstantiated, diffusionist claims, based on very speculative evidence. Rather than Shang Chinese influences on Olmec (and subsequently Mayan) culture,

PETERSON sees evidence of influences from Hinduism ('Hinduism in the Americas', pp.74ff.).

Disagreements continue between those either for or against pre-Columbian cultural diffusionism, both generally and also in regard to specific plants, animals, parasites and features of language, particularly between Asia and Mesoamerica (for a brief example, see CHEEK *et al.* 1979). However, given the presence of coca in Egypt in 1000 BCE, perhaps it behoves us to be open-minded about the possible use of non-native psychoactive plants in ancient Asia.

Index

A

Abraham, Karl, 110, 110n.357
acacia (tree), 153n.488, 158, 158n.511
Acacia catechu (*khadira*, catechu tree), 42n.166, 139n.450, 158n.511
Acacia nilotica (gum Arabic tree), 158n.511
Acacia polyacantha (*Senegalia polyacantha*/*Mimosa suma*, *śamī*, white thorn tree), 14n.42
Acacia polyantha, see *Albizia inundata*
Acosta, Cristoval, 68n.253
ādāra (plant), 37, 37n.147, 38n.147, 41, 41n.159, 42
adhvaryu (priest), 7n.7, 11, 14n.43, 150n.482
Aditi, 8n.13
adrenaline, 116. 118, 143n.461, 144n.465
Ādur, 56
Afanas'evo culture, 30n.116
Afghanistan, 29, 34n.138, 72, 114, 116, 117, 123n.396
Agari, 120n.383
Agni, 8, 8n.11, 8n.13, 8n.15, 14, 19n.61, 117n.376
agnicāyana (rite), 8n.13, 16n.51
agnihotra (rite), 13n.40, 13n.41, 49n.193, 165n534, 207n.643
agniṣṭoma (rite), 8n.11, 11n.25, 13n.41, 15n.50, 42n.159, 46, 46n.185
Agrostis linearis (Bermuda/couch grass), see *Panicum*/*Cynodon dactylon*
ahīna (rite), 16n.53, 118
Ahura Mazda, 26n.97, 27, 28n.108, 28n.110, 56n.224, 57
Akkadian seals, 197n.628, 200
Alaric I (king), 173
Albizia inundata (*timbó blanco* tree), 136n.442
Albizia lebbeck (*Mimosa speciosa*, lebbeck tree), 44n.177
Alburz (mountain), 26n.93
alchemy/alchemical, 72n.266, 106n.341, 112, 112n.361, 157
alcohol, 1, 16n.62, 19, 19n.63, 50, 50n.196, 63n.239, 77n.278, 113n.362, 113n.366, 129, 130n.419, 135, 161n.522, 171, 183, 186
ALD-52, 195n.624
Alexander the Great, 174n.563
Alfredo, *Mestre*, 167n.539, 168, 169n.548, 257
Al-Ghazali, 101n.330
Alkybiades, 177n.572
Alpert, Richard, 88
Altai (mountains), 67n.247, 67n.250
Alto Santo (church), 257

āmalaka/āmalakī (*Phyllanthus embilica*, emblic myrobalan), 22, 22n.84
Amanita muscaria (fly-agaric mushroom), 61, 120, 120n.384, 120n.385, 121, 121n.387, 121n.389, 122, 123n.392, 123n.396, 124, 124n.399, 125, 125n.401, 125n.402, 125n.405, 126, 126n.406, 126n.407, 127n.411, 128n.411, 128, 129n.414, 130, 182, 182n.585, 186, 186n.601, 196, 198, 206, 212, 213; alkaloids in, 121n.388; effects of, 121n.390; in Christianity, 126n.409; in Greek religion, 127, 127n.411, 181, 181n.583, 182n.584; in Siberia, 123
Amaranthus spinosus (spiny amaranth), 108n.349
Amazon/Amazonia, 3, 94n.313, 105, 105n.337, 105n.338, 107n.348, 116, 138, 155, 155n.494, 155n.495, 156n.499, 156n.501, 157n.505, 159, 159n.516, 160, 160n.517, 161, 161n.522, 161n.525, 162n.526, 162n.530, 163n.531, 167n.538, 168, 190, 191, 196, 208, 212, 213, 257
ambrosia, 18n.60, 110n.357, 150, 175n.565, 187, 187n.604
amphetamine, 116, 145
amṛta (nectar of immortality), 18n.60, 20, 21, 21n.76, 21n.79, 22, 22n.79, 44, 46, 110, 127n.410, 140, 141, 144, 145, 145n.467, 146, 146n.468, 151n.487, 187, 187n.604, 208; endogenous, 23, 23n.85
amulet, 44, 44n.180, 45, 45n.181, 70, 149, 152
Ānandamayī Mā, 90n.306
Anatolia, 8n.12, 115n.370, 201
Angra Mainyu, 27n.97, 27n.100
Antinoos, 172n.559
aphrodisiac, 19n.63, 44n.176, 103, 103n.332, 117, 130. 136n.442, 145n.467, 185, 188n.605, 207, 207n.643, 207n.644, 207n.645
apomorphine, 109, 144n.464
aporphine, 109, 109n.353, 144n.464
apsarasa, 43n.175
aptoryāma (rite), 15n.50
Āraṇyaka (text), 7n.7
Ardā Wirāz Nāmag (text), 56, 57, 58
Arethusa, 172n.558
Argyreia nervosa, see Hawaiian baby woodrose
Argyreia speciosa (elephant creeper), 188n.605
Aristotle, 104n.336, 178n.576, 190
arjun (tree), see *Terminalia arjuna*
arjuna (grass), 40n.158, 41
arjunāni (grass), 40
Armenia, 9n.18, 26n.97
Artaxerxes I, 31n.119
Artemis, 172n.559
Artemisia nilagirica, see Indian wormwood
Arundo donax (giant reed), 35, 35n.141, 148, 148n.476, 153n.488, 154n.492, 209; DMT in, 36n.142, 36n.143
Ašavahišt, 28

Asclepiad sp., 62n.235, 136
Asgard, 22n.79
associative thinking, 97, 97n.321, 100
Assyria, 130n.418
aśvattha, see peepal tree
Atharvaveda, 7n.7, 43, 43n.172, 44, 44n.180, 45, 138, 151n.485, 207; cannabis in, 69, 69n.257, 70
Athens, 6, 128n.411, 171, 173n.561, 174n.563, 174n.564, 176, 176n.567, 177, 177n.572, 178
atirāta (rite), 15n.50
Atlantis, 202n.639
atropine, 57n.226, 104n.335, 131n.422
Attis, 172n.559
atyagniṣṭoma (rite), 15n.50
avabhṛta (purificatory bath), 17
Avalon, Arthur (= John Woodroffe), 71n.263
Avesta, 5, 9n.18, 11n.26, 18n.60, 25, 26, 26n.96, 26n.97, 27, 27n.97, 28, 29, 30n.117, 32, 34n.138, 49, 50, 52n.200, 63, 120n.385, 133, 140, 147, 148, 187, 199, 203, 205, 206; cannabis in, 67; composition of, 25n.92; many *haomas* in, 140n.451; translation of, 31, 61
ayahuasca, 2, 2n.3, 2n.5, 3n.6, 5, 6, 36, 75, 78, 102, 104, 116, 118, 133, 134, 141, 142, 142n.457, 143, 147, 148, 153n.489, 154, 155n.495, 155n.496, 156, 160n.517, 160n.520, 162n.527, 162n.530, 163, 163n.531, 167n.538, 170, 171, 171n.554, 183n.592, 191, 196, 197, 205, 206, 208, 208n.646, 209, 211, 212, 213, 257; additives to, 44n.176, 138; ancient rejuvenation treatment, 46n.187, 47; cold preparation of, 160; discovery of chemistry, 155n.493; effects of, 157n.508, 161, 162, 166n.527; in Egypt, 158n.511; legal status of, 155n.497; Sūfī ayahuasca, 35; use by churches, 155; use by indigenous people, 155n.494; use by Santo Daime church, 166, 167, 168, 169; various uses of, 161, 161n.523, 161n.524, 162, 162n.525, 162n.526
azalea, 19n.63
Azerbaijan, 26n.93
Aztec, 188n.605

B

bacchant, 174n.562
Bactria, 10n.20, 30n.115, 30n.118, 114, 114n.368, 201
Bahrain, 201
Balansia cyperi (sedge), 107n.348, 190, 191, 191n.613
Balanta (people), 190
Balochistan, 117, 200n.633, 200n.634
Balzac, Honoré de, 73n.270
Banisteriopsis caapi (vine), 2, 156, 157n.506, 158n.509, 159, 159n.514, 159n.516, 160, 169n.550, 171n.554, 208
banyan tree (*Ficus bengalensis*/

benghalenis/indica, nyagrodha), 3, 42, 42n.170, 43, 43n.174, 43n.175, 139n.450, 146, 146n.470, 207, 207n.643, 207n.644; mythology of, 42n.170
Barquinha (church), 155, 155n.496, 257
barsom, 33
Basella alba/cordifolia (Malabar/ vine spinach), 41n.159, 42
Baudelaire, Charles, 73n.270, 74
Beleric myrobalan, see *Terminalia bellirica*
belladonna, 57n.226
Bergson, Henri, 96n.320
Bermuda grass, see *Panicum/ Cynodon dactylon*
β-carboline, 131, 142n.457, 142n.459, 156, 157n.505, 158n.509, 159n.514, 171n.554
bhāṃg/bhaṅga/bhaṅgā, see cannabis
Bible, 126n.409
Black Sea, 9n.20, 19n.63, 67
BMAC (Bactria Margiana Archeological Complex), 10n.20, 30, 69, 114, 199, 200, 200n.633, 200n.634, 201, 201n.635
boar, 9n.18, 45n.181, 152n.487
bodhi tree, see peepal tree
Bolivia, 107n.348, 155n.494
Boswellia glabra (Indian frankincense), 139n.450
Bower Manuscript, 23n.84, 45, 140, 140n.454, 141, 146, 207, 208
brahman (cosmic principle), 43, 79, 84n.293, 85n.295, 101n.330
brahman/Brāhmaṇa (priest/caste), 7, 7n.7, 10n.23, 13n.39, 13n.40, 13n.41, 14n.43, 15, 16, 24, 49n.193, 55, 117, 127, 137, 145n.467, 150, 166n.535; size of population, 24n.86
Brāhmaṇa (text), 6, 7n.7, 9, 10, 10n.24, 14, 19, 19n.62, 20, 39, 40n.158, 41, 42, 47, 50, 107n.347, 139n.450, 140, 146, 152, 165, 166n.536, 203, 205, 206, 207, 209, 212
Brazil, 19n.63, 94n.315, 107n.348, 138, 155, 155n.494, 155n.496, 160n.521, 170n.553, 257
Bṛhaspati, 8n.13, 54
Briza bipinnata, see *Desmostachya bipinnata*
Broad, Charles, 96n.320
Brough, John, 123, 124
Brugmansia sp., see also datura, 104, 104n.334; varieties of, 105n.338, 156n.503
Bucharest, 67
Buddha, 152n.487
bufotenidine, 148n.475
bufotenin, 36n.142, 142n.459, 148m.475
Bulgaria, 173n.559
Burroughs, William, 157n.506
Bu-ston, 105n.340
Butea frondosa/monosperma (flame of the forest tree), 14n.42, 42, 44n.180, 207, 207n.643
Bwiti (religion), 77n.278

C

Caesalpinia sp., 37n.147
Caesalpinia bonduc/crista, see gray nicker

Caesalpinia sepiaria (*Yun-shih*), 37n.147
caffeine, 116, 118
Cakrapaṇidatta, 71
Calonyction muricatum, see *Ipomoea muricata*
Cameroon, 77n.278
canary grass, 152n.488
cannabis, 35, 44n.179, 51n.196, 58, 58n.229, 63n.239, 65, 65n.241, 65n.242, 66, 66n.244, 67, 67n.247, 67n.249, 67n.250, 68, 68n.251, 69, 69n.253, 69n.255, 69n.257, 70, 70n.259, 70n.260, 71, 71n.263, 71n.264, 71n.265, 72, 72n.266, 72n.267, 72n.269, 74n.272, 76, 76n.276, 77, 109n.352, 114, 114n.369, 127n.410, 129, 129n.414, 135, 136, 138, 160n.516, 197, 198, 198n.629, 257, 261; medical discovery of, 68n.253; effects of, 73, 74, 74n.271, 75, 75n.273; kinds of, 66n.246
Cappodocia, 130n.420
Caraka, 45n.184
Caravaca crucifix, 170n.553
Cashinahua (people), 163n.531
Caspian Sea, 26n.93
Çatal Huyuk, 173n.559
Caucasus, 26n.93, 67, 130, 199
CEFLURIS (Santo Daime branch), 168n.546, 257
Centella asiatica (Indian pennywort), 136n.442
Ceropegia decaisneana (lantern flower/snake creeper), 63n.238
chacrona (plant), see *Psychotria viridis*
Chenavard, Paul, 73n.270
Chieh (king), 202
Chile, 262
China, 10n.20, 11n.26, 67, 67n.247, 68, 103n.332, 109, 113, 115, 116, 118, 141, 201, 202
Christian/Christianity, 21n.76, 34n.136, 82n.289, 85n.295, 113n.362, 127n.409, 155
Circe, 186
Claviceps (fungus), 106, 189n.608
Claviceps paspali, 107, 187, 189
Claviceps purpurea, 107, 189, 190, 193, 194
Club des Hashischins, 73, 73n.270, 74
cluster fig tree, see *Ficus glomerata*
Clypea hernandifolia (kind of jasmine), 45
coca, 138, 261, 263
cocaine, 134n.438
Cocculus cordifolius, see *Tinospora cordifolia*
Cocculus hirsutus (broom creeper), 136n.442
Coelachyrum longiglume (grass), 38n.149
Cohen, Sydney, 75n.275
Colombia, 65n.241, 105n.338, 107n.348, 155n.494
Conessi tree, see *Holarrhena antidysenterica*
consciousness, scales of, 100n.329, 101n.329
cordgrass, 38n.149
Costus speciosus (wild ginger), 43n.172, 139n.449

couch grass, see *Panicum dactylon*
cowhage (*Mucuna pruriens*), 141, 142
Crete, 173n.560, 197, 198, 201, 202n.639
Crinum latifolium (kind of amaryllis), 63n.239, 136n.442
Cyclopes, 128n.411
Cynodon dactylon, see *Panicum dactylon*
Cynosurus durus (dogstail grass), see *Desmostachya bipinnata*
Cyperus articulatus (sedge), 191
Cyperus plolixus (sedge), 191
Cyprus, 199

D

Daniel, *Mestre*, 257
Danube (river), 67
darbha (grass), see also *kuśa* and *Desmostachya bipinnata*, 17, 40, 40n.159, 43, 44n.180, 69n.257, 149n.477, 150n.483, 151n.485, 152, 206n.641; as a drug, 151; identification of, 38n.149, 39n.149, 40n.156, 40n.157; mythology of, 151n.487, 152n.487; numinous power of, 149, 149n.480, 150, 150n.482
Darius, 30n.118
Dāsa (people), 9, 10n.20, 26n.96
Dasyu (people), 9, 10n.20
datura, 58n.230, 105n.339, 105n.340, 155n.495, 156n.503; alkaloids in, 104n.335; effects of, 104, 104n.336; indigenous use of, 105, 105n.337; kinds of, 104n.334, 105n.338
Daumier, Honoré, 73n.270
Demeter, 171, 172, 172n.557, 172n.558, 172n.559, 173, 173n.559, 173n.560, 173n.561, 174n.564, 175, 175n.565, 176, 176n.567, 177n.573, 184, 186, 186n.602, 196
Demophon, 175n.565
Dermatophyllum secundifloram (Texas mountain laurel), 261
Desmanthus illinoensis (prairie bundleflower), 152n.488
Desmodium sp., 133n.434, 153n.488
Desmodium gangeticum, see *śālaparṇī*
Desmostachya bipinnata (grass), see also *kuśa* and *darbha*, 38n.149, 39n.149, 40n.156, 146
Dhanvantari, 151n.487
dhava, see *Grislea tomentosa*
dīkṣā (initiation), 17
Dionysos, 127n.411, 172n.599, 173n.599, 174, 174n.562, 176n.569, 177n.571
Diplopterys cabrerana (vine), 156n.501
DMT, 2, 4, 119n.381, 133, 133n.434, 134, 134n.438, 136n.442, 137, 140, 141, 142, 145n.467, 146, 148, 152, 152n.488, 154, 154n.492, 156, 157, 157n.507, 158, 158n.511, 159, 159n.512, 159n.513, 160n.521, 198, 206, 207n.642, 208, 209, 212n.647, 213; DMT entities, 98n.323; DMT experiences, 101n.329, 133n.430, 156n.504; endogenous,

23n.85, 157n.505; extracting from plants, 153n.488; first isolation from plants, 158n.510; in *Arundo donax*, 36, 36n.142, 36n.143; in *Desmodium gangeticum*, 142n.457, 145; in *Phalaris* grass 153n.489, 153n.491; 5-MeO-DMT, 36n.142, 142, 142n.457, 148n.475, 153n.488, 153n.489, 153n.491, 154, 154n.492, 157n.505
Doblin, Rick, 89n.303
dopamine, 143n.461, 144n.464, 144n.465
d'Orta, Garcia, 68n.253
drug addiction, 77n.278, 161n.524
drugs, effects of, 76n.276, 100n.329, 158
Dumas, Alexandre, 73n.270
Dzogchen, 105n.340

E

eagle, 18n.60, 22n.79, 39n.152, 166n.535, 197n.628
Ecuador, 107n.348, 155n.494, 163n.531
Egypt, 67, 103, 109, 109n.352, 130n.418, 158n.511, 173n.559, 173n.560, 202n.639, 261, 263
Elam, 199, 200
elephant creeper, see *Argyreia speciosa*
Eleusis, 6, 108, 171, 172n.557, 173, 173n.559, 174, 174n.563, 174n.564, 175n.565, 176n.568, 182n.584, 183, 186n.603, 189n.607, 192, 195, 196, 196n.627, 197, 203; conditions for initiation, 175; experiences of initiates, 179, 180, 180n.581; origins of cult, 173n.560; payment to, 174n.564; procedures for initiation/rites, 176n.567, 177, 178
elymoclavine, 188n.605, 191
emblic myrobalan, see *āmalaka*
ephedra, 58, 61, 66n.245, 76, 76n.276, 113, 113n.362, 113n.363, 113n.365, 114, 114n.366, 114n.369, 115, 115n.371, 116n.373, 117, 117n.375, 118, 118n.380, 125n.405, 129, 134, 134n.436, 134n.438, 136, 138, 140, 167n.538, 198, 212; effects of, 118; in Zoroastrianism, 34, 34n.138; use by Mormons, 116
ephedrine, 117, 118, 134, 134n.438, 138, 143, 145, 197; effects of, 116, 116n.374; first isolation of, 113n.365
Eragrostis bipinnata, see *Desmostachya bipinnata*
Eragrostis cynosuroides, see *Desmostachya bipinnata*
Erasixenus, 183n.587
ergine (D-lysergic acid amide = LSA), 107, 107n.346, 136n.442, 146n.468, 181, 187n.605, 188n.605, 192n.618, 194, 194n.622, 194n.624, 195, 195n.624; effects of, 192, 193, 193n.619, 193n.620
ergonovine (ergometrine), 188n.605, 192n.618
ergot, 6, 42, 106, 106n.341, 106n.342, 106n.344,

106n.345, 107, 108, 123n.392, 181, 185n.595, 187, 189, 189n.607, 190n.611, 192n.614, 192n.618, 193, 194, 195, 195n.624, 195n.625, 196, 196n.627; alkaloids in, 187n.605, 188n.605; as medicine, 107n.348, 190n.612, 191, 192n.614; effects of, 191, 192, 196n.626; for intoxication, 107n.349, 190, 190n.612
ergotamine, 192n.618, 195n.624
ergotism/Saint Anthony's fire (ergot poisoning), 106, 106n.345, 186n.600, 192, 194n.621
ergotoxine, 190n.611, 194
Etana, 197n.628
Eubuleus, 172n.557
Eumolpos, 177n.573, 178
Euphorbia royleana (sullu spurge), 111
Evans-Prichard, E. E., 97n.321

F

falcon, 16n.51, 18, 18n.58, 18n.60, 37n.146, 42n.166
Ficus sp., 43n.176, 44n.177
Ficus bengalensis/benghalensis/indica, see banyan tree
Ficus carica (common fig tree), 41n.163
Ficus dalhousiae, 136n.442
Ficus glomerata/racemosa (*udumbara*, cluster fig tree), 14n.42, 42, 43, 43n.171, 44, 44n.180, 66n.244, 146, 146n.470, 207
Ficus infectoria (*plakṣa*, wavy-leaf fig tree), 43, 43n.173, 44, 44n.176, 66n.244, 139n.450, 146, 151, 207
Ficus insipida (*figueira branca*), 44n.176
Ficus religiosa, see peepal tree
Ficus ruiziana, 44n.176
flame of the forest tree, see *palāśa*
fly-agaric mushroom, see *Amanita muscaria*
Foucault, Michel, 79n.285
frankincense, 33, 139n.450
Fraxinus floribunda (kind of ash tree), 136n.442
Frazer, James, 97n.321
Freud, Sigmund, 97, 110, 110n.337

G

Gabon, 77n.278
Gabriel, *Mestre*, 257
Gandhāra, 11n.26
gandharva, 43n.175
Gaṇeśa, 149n.478
Garuḍa, 18n.60, 21n.79
Gautier, Théophile, 73, 73n.270, 74
Gibbons, Simon, 3, 154
Gilund, 201n.635
ginger, 43n.172, 138n.446, 139n.449
ginseng, 103, 103n.332, 129n.414
glechon, 184, 184n.595, 185, 185n.595
Gonur, 114, 114n.367, 200
grail, 126n.409
gray nicker (*Caesalpinia bonduc/crista*), 37n.147, 38n.147, 41, 41n.160, 42
grayanotoxin, 19n.63
Grislea tomentosa (*Woodfordia floribunda*, *dhava*, fire flame bush), 139n.450
guaraná, 138
Guinea Bissau, 190

Gynergen, 195n.624

H

hadhānaēpata (plant in *Avesta*), 148, 148n.473, 148n.474
halfa grass, 38n.149
Haraiti, 25
Harappa (city), 200, 200n.634, 202n.639
Hardy, Alister, 81n.289, 99, 99n.325
Haridvār, 21n.79
harmaline/harmine, 4, 131, 133, 142n.457, 146, 156, 158, 159, 160n.520, 207n.642, 208; effects of, 132, 132n.428; history of discovery, 131n.425
havirdhāna (Vedic sacrificial shed), 11, 12n.30, 12n.37, 14n.43
Hawaiian baby woodrose, 188n.605, 192n.618
Haydarī (Sūfī), 72
Hekate, 172n.559
hemispheres of the brain, 97n.323, 98n.323
hemlock, 22n.80, 58n.228, 131n.422
henbane, 57, 57n.226, 58, 117n.375
Hera, 172n.559
Heracles, 128n.411
Hermes, 172n.558
hierophant (priest), 174n.564, 177, 177n.573, 178, 189n.607, 194
Himachal Pradesh, 50n.196, 65n.241, 111
Hindu Kush (mountains), 26n.93
Hittite, 173n.559
Hofmann, Albert, 106, 106n.342, 108, 181, 185n.595, 187, 188n.605, 189, 192n.616, 193
Holarrhena antidysenterica (Conessi tree), 145n.467
Hōm Yasht, 27, 28, 52; origin of, 28n.106
honey, 12n.36, 19, 52n.203, 176n.567, 184, 186; mad honey, 19n.63
hotar (priest), 7n.7, 13, 14n.43, 32n.124, 52n.202
Howes, Melanie-Jayne, 3, 146n.471
Hugo, Victor, 73n.270
Hume, David, 98
Huxley, Aldous, 83, 83n.292, 85n.295, 87n.299, 88, 88n.299, 88n.300, 88n.301, 96, 96n.320, 113n.362
hypnosis, 80, 90n.304, 95, 95n.318, 95n.319

I

Iakchos, 176n.567, 177, 177n.571
iboga, 77, 77n.278, 144
ibogaine, 77n.278, 144, 145
ibotenic acid, 120, 120n.387, 121n.388
Imperata cylindrica (blady grass), 38n.149, 40n.156
India, 1, 7, 18n.59, 29, 34, 35, 36n.143, 38n.149, 42n.169, 49, 58n.228, 62, 63, 63n.238, 68n.253, 72, 84n.293, 85n.295, 98n.323, 103, 104n.336, 112n.359, 117, 117n.375, 119, 120n.384, 122, 127n.410, 133n.430, 134, 139n.449, 145n.467, 146, 152n.487, 153n.488, 153n.489, 154, 188n.605, 190n.610, 199, 202, 206; smoking in, 66n.244

Indian wormwood (*Artemisia nilagirica*), 108n.349
Indra, 8, 8n.12, 8n.13, 8n.15, 9, 9n.16, 9n.18, 10n.20, 10n.21, 11n.27, 12n.33, 14, 18n.60, 26, 26n.97, 29, 30, 44, 52n.203, 54n.217, 55, 55n.220, 111, 124n.400, 145n.467, 197n.628; derivation of name, 198n.630
Indus river, 47n.191
Indus valley (civilization/culture), 13n.40, 42n.170, 199, 199n.631, 199n.632, 200, 200n.634, 201, 201n.635, 202n.639
Integrated Information Theory, 99, 99n.327
Ipomoea sp., see also morning glory, 146n.468, 188n.605
Ipomoea digitata (milky yam), 146n.468
Ipomoea muricata/muricatum/turbinate (*Calonyction muricatum*, lavender moonvine), 63n.239
Ipomoea pupurea, 193n.619
Ipomoea tricolor, 188n.605
Ipomoea violacea, 188n.605, 193n.620
Iran, 1, 9n.18, 17n.57, 21, 26n.93, 26n.97, 28, 29, 29n.113, 31, 34, 49, 56, 67, 69, 72, 117, 118, 134, 140n.452, 148, 153n.488, 199, 200, 200n.633, 201, 209, 213
Irineu, *Mestre*, 167n.539, 168, 168n.548, 169n.548, 169n.550, 257
Isis, 172n.559, 173n.559
isocarboxazid, 139n.449
isoergine, 188n.605, 193, 194, 194n.622, 195, 195n.624
iṣṭi (rite), 15, 15n.47, 251

J

jaguar, 159n.516
James, William, 82n.291, 92, 102n.331
Jesus, 167n.539, 168n.545, 169n.550
jhāna/dhyāna (states of Buddhist meditation), 93n.312
Jivaro, 163n.531
Jones, Rufus M., 85n.294
Jones, William, 61, 62, 122, 130
Joseph, Saint, 168n.545, 169
Jung, Carl G., 99, 110, 110n.357
Juramidam (entity), 168, 168n.545, 168n.547, 169n.548

K

Kabeiroi, 172n.559
Kadrū, 151n.487
Kaempferia galanga (aromatic ginger), 139n.449
Kāfir (people), 10n.20
Kālacakra (rite), 152n.487
Kālī, 43n.170
kāliṅga (plant), 145n.467
karañja (plant/tree), 41n.159
Kardec, Allan, 257
Kātyāyana, 70
Katz, Steven T., 83, 84, 85, 86, 92
Keleos (king), 173n.560, 175n.565
Kərəsāspa, 26n.96, 27n.97
Kerman, 200, 200n.633
Kerykes (family), 178n.574
Keryx, 178n.574
khadira, see *Acacia catechu*
Khām (valley), 123n.392

khecarī mudrā (yoga technique), 23, 23n.85, 90n.304
Khyber Pass, 116
Kleomenes (king), 182n.587
Kodaikanal, 120n.384, 123n.392
Krakatao/Krakatoa, 202
Kṛśānu, 39n.152
Kubaba, 173n.559
kuśa (grass), see also *darbha* and *Desmostachya bipinnata*, 4, 38, 38n.149, 39, 39n.149, 40, 40n.156, 40n.157, 41, 140, 146, 149, 149n.477, 149n.478, 151, 151n.485, 152, 154, 206, 207n.642; identification of, 38n.149; mythology of, 151n.487
kuṣṭha (plant), 138, 139, 207; identification of, 43n.172, 139n.449
Kybele, 172n.559, 173n.559
kykeōn (Greek mixed potion), 6, 33n.128, 106n.342, 108, 171, 175, 177, 177n.572, 181, 183, 184, 184n.592, 184n.593, 184n.595, 185, 185n.596, 185n.597, 185n.598, 186, 186n.600, 186n.601, 186n.603, 187, 189, 191, 194, 195, 195n.625, 196, 203; kinds of, 183n.590

L

Labasūkta (song of the lapwing), 53, 118
Lagochillus inebriens (Turkish mint), 123n.392
Lahore, 35n.140, 90n.304
Lamarck, Jean-Baptiste, 66n.246
Laserpitium latifolium (broad-leaved sermountain), 63n.239
Lava, 152n.487
L-DOPA, 143, 143n.461
Leary, Timothy, 75n.275, 76n.275, 88, 88n.301, 89n.303
Lees, Andrew, 143n.461
Leibniz, 83n.292, 102n.331
leprosy, 43n.172, 138n.447, 158n.511
Leptochoa bipinnata (grass), 38n.149
Lévy-Bruhl, Lucien, 97n.321
Lilly, John C., 92n.309
Lima, Gonçales de, 158n.510
Lodha (people), 107n.349, 108n.349
Lolium temulentum (darnel/ryegrass), 189
Lonitzer, Adam, 106n.345
lotus (plant), 108, 108n.350, 109, 109n.352, 110, 125n.405, 143
Loulan (people), 116n.372
Lovatelli urn, 182n.584
LSD, 57n.225, 76n.276, 78n.282, 86, 92n.309, 99, 181, 192, 192n.618, 193, 193n.620, 195n.624, 212n.647; and mystical experience, 88, 88n.301, 89n.303, 91; discovery of, 106, 106n.343
lysergic acid amide (LSA), see ergine
lysergol, 188n.605

M

Machaon, 185, 185n.597
mada/madha (elation/intoxication), 31, 50, 51, 72, 118, 147
Madagascar, 112n.359

Madārī, Badī ad-dīn Shāh, 72
magnoflorine, 144n.464
Malabar spinach, see *Basella alba*
mandrake, 57n.226, 103, 121n.390
Maṅgala, 152n.487
mango tree, 43
mania, 96, 104n.336
Manthara/Mandara (mountain), 151n.487
MAO inhibitor/MAOI/MAO-I, 2, 4, 44n.176, 131, 134, 134n.438, 139n.449, 140, 141, 142, 142n.457, 144, 145n.466, 145n.467, 146, 148n.476, 154, 156, 157, 157n.507, 158, 159n.514, 161n.522, 167, 183n.592, 185n.595, 198, 206, 207, 207n.642, 208, 208n.646, 212, 213; kinds of, 144n.465
Margiana (see also BMAC), 10n.20, 30n.115, 114, 114n.368, 115
Marhashi, 200, 200n.633
Maruts, 124n.400
Maslow, Abraham, 86, 87, 87n.296, 87n.298, 89n.303
Maya (civilization)/Mayans, 108n.351, 109n.352, 188n.605
Mehrgarh, 200
Menispermum glabrum (moonseed vine), 63n.239
Mentha pulegium (pennyroyal mint), 184n.595
Meru (mountain), 25n.93
mescaline, 77n.277, 78n.282, 85n.295, 87n.299, 111
Mesoamerica, 121n.390, 208n.646, 261, 262
Mesopotamia, 199, 199n.631, 200, 200n.633, 201
Metaneira, 175n.565
methylergonovine, 192, 192n.617, 193
Metzner, Ralph, 80n.286, 88
Mexico, 94n.315, 109, 119, 119n.381, 131, 188n.605, 207n.643, 262
Miguel, São 169n.548
milk, 12, 16n.52, 19, 26, 32n.124, 33, 33n.128, 46n.187, 50n.196, 65n.241, 107, 140, 140n.451, 148n.473, 148n.474, 150n.483, 176n.567, 184, 186, 186n.599, 207n.643, 251; ocean of, 21, 21n.77, 151n.487
millet, 16n.52, 38n.147, 39, 42, 63n.239, 107, 107n.347, 107n.349
Mimosa catechu, see *Acacia catechu*
Mimosa hostilis (*Mimosa tenuiflora, vinho da jurema*), 158
Mimosa suma, see *Acacia polyacantha*
Mimosaceae sp., 136n.442
Minoa, 197, 199, 202
Mithra, 9n.18, 17n.57, 27n.97, 31, 31n.120, 56n.224
Mithras, 172n.559, 181n.583
Mitra, 8n.13
moclobemide, 134
Mohenjo Daro (city), 200, 202n.639
moly (plant), 130n.420
Mongolia, 30n.116, 201
moon (and *soma*), 18n.61, 19n.61
Mormon tea, 116, 118

morning glory (vine), see also *Ipomoea*, 63n.239, 123n.392, 136n.442, 188n.605, 192, 192n.618, 193n.619, 193, 194, 195n.624
Mucuna pruriens, see cowhage
Mūjavat (mountain), 10; location of, 11n.26, 18n.59
Müller, Friedrich Max, 62
mullet (fish), 183, 183n.591, 183n.592, 184n.592
Mumbai, 34, 62
muñja (grass), 39, 39n.154, 46n.185, 47n.189
muscarine, 120, 120n.386, 131n.422
muscazone, 121n.388
muscimol, 120n.387, 121, 121n.388
mushroom, see also *Amanita muscaria* and psilocybin, 5, 40n.159, 45n.181, 70n.259, 78, 110, 111, 111n.358, 119, 119n.381, 119n.382, 120, 120n.383, 120n.384, 120n.385, 121, 121n.387, 121n.388, 121n.389, 121n.390, 122n.391, 123, 123n.392, 123n.393, 124, 124n.399, 125, 125n.405, 126, 126n.407, 127, 127n.409, 127n.410, 127n.411, 128, 181, 181n.583, 182, 182n.584, 182n.586, 186, 196, 261; brahmanical prohibition of, 122, 125n.404
Muz/Muzh Tagh Ata, see Mūjavat
Mycenae, 128n.411, 173, 173n.560, 199
myrrh, 34n.136
mystagogue, 175
mystai, 177, 177n.570, 179
mysteria/mystery rites, 6, 82n.290, 106n.342, 108, 128, 128n.411, 156, 171, 172, 172n.557, 172n.558, 172n.559, 173n.559, 173n.561, 174, 174n.562, 174n.563, 175, 175n.566, 176, 177, 177n.572, 178, 178n.576, 179, 179n.577, 180, 181, 181n.582, 182, 182n.584, 183, 184, 187, 189, 191, 196n.627; prohibition of, 173

N

Nambudiri (brahmans), 117
Nāsatya, 52n.203
nāy (flute), 35n.141
Nelumbo nucifera, see also lotus, 108, 141, 143, 145
Nepal, 7, 13n.39, 19n.63, 63, 65n.241, 103n.332
Nerval, Gérard de, 73n.270
Nestor, 185, 185n.597
nicotine, 142n.459, 261
Nietzsche, 110n.357
noradrenaline, 143n.461, 144n.465
nuciferine, 109, 145
norepinephrine, 144n.465
nornuciferine, 109
numinous power, 79n.284, 82n.289, 149
nyagrodha, see banyan tree
Nymphaea sp., see lotus
Nymphaea ampla, 109n.352

O

Odin, 22n.79
O'Flaherty, Wendy (Doniger), 61, 63, 63n.240, 103, 120n.385

oleander, 19n.63
Olmec, 262
ololiuqui, 188n.605, 193, 193n.620, 194, 195n.624
Olympus (mountain), 172, 172n.558
Oman, 201
opiate, 76n.276, 143
opium/papaver, 67, 71, 109, 114, 114n.369, 129n.414, 130n.419, 160n.516, 186, 186n.600, 197, 198, 198n.629
Oraon (people), 107n.349, 108n.349
Ordos (plateau), 201
Orphism, 180n.570
oṣadhi (herb/drug), 22, 22n.81, 40n.156, 41n.159, 112n.361, 138
Osmond, Humphry, 1n.2, 193
Ott, Jonathan, 1n.2
Oxus (civilization/river), 11n.26, 30n.118, 114, 115n.370, 203

P

Paederia foetida (stinkvine), 63n.239, 136n.442
Pahnke, Walter, 89n.303
palāśa (*parṇa*, flame of the forest tree), 14n.42, 39n.152, 44n.180, 207, 207n.643
Panicum/Cynodon dactylon (Bermuda/couch grass), 38n.148, 38n.149, 40n.156, 41n.164
Pāṇini, 70
papaver (poppy), see opium
parahaoma/parahōm, 33
Parkinson's disease, 143, 144n.464, 192n.614
parṇa, see *palāśa*
Parsi, 34, 34n.136
Paspalum distichum (knotgrass), 181, 187, 189n.606, 189, 189n.607
Paspalum scrobiculatum (kodo millet), 107, 107n.349
Passiflora incarnata (passion flower), 159n.514
paśubandha (rite), 15, 15n.47
pāṭā (plant), 44, 45, 45n.182
PCE (pure consciousness event), 85, 86
peepal/bodhi tree (*Ficus religiosa, aśvattha*), 3, 14n.42, 43, 43n.172, 43n.174, 43n.175, 44, 66n.244, 138, 139, 146, 146n.470, 149, 152n.487, 207, 207n.642
Peganum harmala (Syrian/ mountain rue), 35, 35n.141, 61, 62, 66n.245, 114n.369, 117n.375, 130, 130n.414, 130n.416, 130n.417, 130n.418, 130n.420, 131, 131n.421, 131n.422, 131n.423, 131n.424, 132n.428, 132n.429, 133, 133n.430, 134, 134n.436, 135, 136, 142n.457, 153n.489, 158, 158n.511, 159, 159n.514, 160n.521, 186, 212
Peganum nigellastrum (rue), 133n.430
Periploca aphylla (vine), 62n.235, 62n.236, 63n.239, 113n.362, 129, 129n.414
Persephone, 128n.411, 171, 172, 172n.557, 172n.558, 173, 173n.560, 175n.565, 176n.567, 177n.573, 178

Persepolis, 31, 31n.119
Perseus, 128n.411
Persia, 19n.63, 26n.93, 27n.100, 31n.120, 34, 35n.141, 58, 133n.431, 182n.584
Peru, 105n.337, 107n.348, 155n.494, 162n.526, 163n.531, 190, 191, 261
peyote, 77, 77n.277, 88, 88n.301, 111, 212n.647
Phalaris grass, DMT in, 4, 152, 152n.488, 153, 153n.488, 153n.489, 153n.491, 154n.491, 154n.492, 160n.521
Pharsalus bas relief, 182n.584
phenelzine, 139n.449
philosophia perennis, 83, 83n.292
Phragmitis australis/communis (*Arundo phragmites*, common reed), 153n.488
Phrygia, 172n.559
Phyllostachis sp. (bamboo), 153n.488
Piper chaba (creeper), 136n.442
plakṣa (wavy-leaf fig tree), see *Ficus infectoria*
Plato, 102n.331, 174n.562, 177n.572, 179, 183, 202n.639
Pluton, 172, 172n.558
Poa cynosuroides (grass), see also *Desmostachya bipinnata*, 38n.149, 39n.149, 40n.156
Pogonarthria bipinnata, see *Desmostachya bipinnata*
Polyalthia cerasoides (cherry Ashok), 136n.442
pomegranate, 33, 130n.417, 148, 172n.558, 176n.567, 184
Pongamia glabra/pinnata (Pongam oil tree/Indian beech), 41n.159
Pont-Saint-Esprit, 106n.345
Pourushapa, 28n.110
Pradier, Jean-Jacques, 73n.270
Prajāpati, 20n.66
prāṇāyāma, 90n.304
Prayāg (Allahabad), 21n.79
psilocybin, 78, 78n.282, 86, 88, 89n.303, 101n.329, 111n.358, 119, 123n.392, 132n.428, 182n.584, 186n.601, 196, 212n.647; global distribution of mushroom, 119n.381
Psoralea corylifolia, see *Serratula anthelmintica*
psychosis, 76n.275, 96, 143n.461, 157n.508, 193n.620
Psychotria viridis (*chacrona* plant), 2, 156, 156n.501, 157n.506, 160, 171n.554
puroḍāśa (ritual bread/cake), 13, 56
Pūṣan, 8n.15
pūtīka, 37n.147, 38n.147, 39, 39n.155, 40, 41, 41n.159, 42, 42n.167; identification of, 40

Q

Qalandar (Sūfī), 35, 35n.139, 35n.140, 72, 74n.271, 74n.272, 134
Qāwrighal (people), 116n.372
Quechua, 155n.494
Quetta, 200
Quincey, Thomas de, 197

R

ṛājasūya (rite), 16n.52, 52n.204, 150n.482

Rāma, 145n.467, 152n.487
Rāmakṛṣna Paramahaṃsa, 80n.287, 90n.304, 91
Rāmana Mahārshi, 90n.306, 91
Rāmānuja, 101n.330
Rašnu, 56n.224
Rastafarian, 74n.272
Ṛgveda, 8, 8n.15, 9n.16, 10n.20, 14, 14n.46, 15, 15n.50, 18n.61, 20n.73, 25n.92, 37n.144, 39, 39n.152, 50n.194, 51, 52, 53, 58, 69, 106n.341, 112, 112n.361, 114n.366, 117n.376, 122n.391, 123n.395, 124, 124n.400, 125n.402, 125n.404, 126, 126n.407, 138, 151, 165n.532, 199, 206n.641; composition of, 7n.7
Rhipsalis (cactus), 112n.359
rhododendron, 19n.63
rhubarb, 113n.366, 129n.414
Rio Branco, 257
Rita, Madrinha, 167n.539
rohiṣa (plant), 37n.147, 38n.147
ṛṣi (seer), 8, 8n.10, 168
Ruck, Carl, 1n.2, 106n.342, 108, 181, 182, 192n.616
Rudra, 8n.15, 198n.630
rue, see *Peganum harmala* and *Ruta graveolens*
Russell, Bertrand, 102n.331
Ruta graveolens (garden rue), 62, 63, 133n.430
ryegrass (darnel), see *Lolium temulentum*

S

Sabazios, 127, 127n.411, 173n.559
Sabina, Maria, 111n.358, 119n.382
Saccharum arundinaceum (a reed-like grass), 39, 39n.153
Saccharum cylindricum (blady grass), 39, 40n.156
Saccharum officinarum (sugarcane), 146n.469
Saccharum sara (tall cane), 146n.469
Saccharum spontaneum (wild sugarcane), 40n.156, 146n.469
sādhu (Indian ascetic), 74n.272
Sakā (people), 9n.20, 11n.26, 30n.118
śālaparṇī (*Desmodium gangeticum*, sal leaved gangeticum), 141, 142, 142n.457, 145, 153n.488, 206
Salvia divinorum (Mexican sage), 77
salvinorin, 78n.279
samādhi (yogic trance), 22, 90, 90n.304, 90n.305, 90n.306, 91, 93, 93n.312
Sāmaveda, 7, 7n.7, 15, 15n.50, 16n.55; and sorcery, 18
śamī, see *Acacia polyacantha*
Samothrace, 172n.559, 173n.559
saṃskāra (life-ritual), 149
San Pedro (cactus), 77, 77n.277, 111, 212n.647
Sansert (drug), 195n.624
Santal (language/people), 40n.159, 107n.349
Santo Daime (church), 5, 6, 138, 155, 155n.496, 155n.498, 161n.523, 166, 166n.537, 167, 168, 168n.546, 169, 169n.548, 169n.550, 170, 170n.553, 198, 212, 213, 257
Santorini, 201, 201n.636, 202, 202n.639

Sarcopetalum tomentosum, 136n.442
Sarcostemma bevistigma (vine), 62, 62n.236, 63n.238, 113n.362, 129, 129n.414, 136, 137n.443
Sarianidi, Victor, 69, 114, 115, 115n.370, 116, 199
Saussurea sp., 43n.172, 139n.449
sautrāmaṇī (rite), 52, 52n.203, 52n.204
Sāyaṇa, 40, 69n.257
Schetul (valley), 123n.396
schizophrenia, 96, 98n.323
Schopenhauer, 102n.331
Schultes, Richard Evans, 157n.506, 188n.605
scopolamine, 57n.226, 104n.335, 193n.620
Scythian (people), 9n.20, 10n.20, 30, 30n.118, 67, 72, 72n.269, 116n.372, 120n.383, 182n.587, 183n.587
Sebastião, Padrinho, 167n.539, 168, 257
Securidaca longipedunculata (violet tree), 190
sedge, 107n.348, 191
sensory deprivation, 80, 92, 92n.309
Serapis, 172n.559
serotonin, 119n.381, 142n.459, 144n.464, 144n.465
Serratula anthelmintica (*Vernonia anthelmintica/Psoralea corylifolia, kuṣṭhanāśinī/ somarāja*), 63n.239, 136n.442
Setaria glauca (yellow foxtail), 63n.239
Shahdad, 200
shaman/shamanic/shamanism, 53n.207, 88n.301, 93, 94n.313, 94n.314, 95n.317, 105n.339, 111n.358, 117, 120n.383, 123, 129n.413, 155, 155n.494, 155n.495, 159, 166, 188n.605, 200, 201
Shang (dynasty), 262
Shanidar (caves), 115n.371
Shanon, Benny, 162n.527
Shuar (people), 155n.494
Shulgin Scale, 100n.329
Siberia, 30n.116, 67n.250, 121n.387, 121n.390, 123, 124, 124n.400
Sida sp. (*acuta/cordifolia/ rhombifolia/spinosa*), 141, 143, 143n.462, 145
siddha (people/tradition), 23, 127, 152n.487
siddhi (occult power), 22, 24
silācī (plant), 139n.450, 207
Simashki, 200, 200n.633
Simlipal (hills), 123n.392
Sintashta, 199
śiva (plant), 22n.84
Śiva (god), 43n.170, 149n.478
Skardu, 11n.26
Skinner, Gordon Todd, 196n.626
smilax (plant), 171n.554
snake, 9, 26, 26n.97, 47n.189, 56, 143n.460, 151n.487, 162, 162n.527, 185n.595, 190
snow lotus, 43n.172, 138n.446, 139n.449
ṣodaśin (rite), 15n.50
Sogdia, 30n.118
Solanaceae sp., 57n.226
Solecki, Ralph, 115n.371
soma function, 22, 110, 110n.357, 111, 111n.358, 135

somarāja (plant), 63, 136
somalatā (plant), 63, 134n.437, 136n.442
somarayen (plant), 134n.437
somavallī (plant), 63, 136n.442, 144
Somnāth, 201n.635
spirit possession, 80, 82, 93, 93n.312, 94, 94n.313, 94n.315, 95, 95n.316, 95n.317, 95, 95n.317, 257
Sraoša, 27n.97, 56, 56n.224
śrauta (rites), 13n.41, 14, 14n.43, 14n.44, 15
Śrautasūtra, 7n.7, 10, 14, 41
Sri Lanka, 112n.359
Stace, W. T., 84n.293, 86, 89n.303, 92
staggers, 154n.492
Stapfiola bipinnata, see *Desmostachya bipinnata*
Stearns, John, 106n.345
Steuchus, Augustinus, 83n.292
Strawson, G. J., 102n.331
Stropharia cubensis (psilocybin mushroom), 122, 123
Sūfī, 35, 35n.141, 72, 74n.271, 74n.272, 93n.312, 134, 135n.440
Sumatra, 202
sun (and *soma*), 18n.61
suparṇa (eagle), 18n.60, 39n.152
surā, 16n.52, 50, 50n.195, 50n.196, 52, 52n.203, 52n.204, 129
Susiana, 200n.634
Suśruta, 45n.184, 46, 47, 71, 71n.264
śyāmāka (millet), 38n.147, 39, 41, 42, 107n.347
śyena (falcon), 16n.51, 18, 18n.58, 18n.60
śyenahṛta, 37, 37n.146, 41
Syrian rue, see *Peganum harmala*

T

Tabernaemontana divaricata (pinwheelflower/crape jasmine), 141, 143, 145
Tajik/Tajikistan, 11n.26, 129n.414
Tantra/Tantric rites, 23, 24, 43n.170, 71, 71n.263, 72, 72n.266, 105, 105n.340, 145n.467, 149n.478
tapas (austerities), 22
Tartar, 129n.414
Tashkent, 30n.118
Terminalia arjuna (*arjun* tree), 40n.158
Terminalia bellirica (Beleric myrobalan), 108n.349
Terminalia chebula (chebulic myrobalan), 68, 68n.252
tetrahydroharmine, 131, 156
Tetrapterys methystica (vine), 156n.502
Texas mountain laurel, see *Dermatophyllum secundifloram*
Thebes, 174n.563
Themis, 172n.559
Theodosius (emperor), 173
Theophrastus, 104n.336, 190
Thespesia lampas (*vanakārpasi* [Sanskrit], *jaṅglī bhiṇḍī/ ban kapās* [Hindi], common mallow/wild cotton tree), 136n.442
Thespesia populnea (Indian tulip tree), 44n.177
Thessaly, 173n.560, 182n.584
thorn-apple, see datura
Thrace, 172n.559, 173n.560
Thraētaona, 26n.96, 27n.97

Three Kings, 167n.539, 169
Tibet, 88n.301, 103n.332, 117n.375, 123n.392, 127; medicine, 43n.172; rites, 23, 105, 127n.410, 152n.487
Tinospora cordifolia (*Cocculus cordifolius*, heart-leaved moonseed), 63n.239, 136n.442, 141, 144, 144n.464, 145
tobacco, 66n.244, 155n.495, 156n.503
tortoise, 151n.487
trance, 22, 84n.293, 90, 90n.304, 90n.306, 91, 93, 94, 95, 95n.318, 95n.319, 96, 180n.581, 187
tranylcypromine, 139n.449
Triptolemus, 172n.557, 175n.565
Trophonius, 180, 184
truffle, 45n.181
Tryambakeśvar, 21n.79
tryptamine, 2, 36n.142, 78n.282, 119n.381, 133, 143, 148n.476, 152, 153n.488, 156, 157n.505, 159n.512, 159n.513, 171n.554
Tūra (tribe), 30n.118
Turkey, 19n.63, 172n.559, 173n.559
Turkmen, 129n.414
Turkmenistan, 10n.20, 28, 30n.115, 69, 114, 114n.368, 116, 197, 199, 201, 203
Tvaṣṭrī, 55n.220
Tylor, Edward Burnett, 97n.321
tyramine, 144n.465, 161n.522

U

udgātar (priest), 7n.7, 14n.43, 16n.55
udumbara (cluster fig tree), see *Ficus glomerata*
Ujjain, 21n.79
ukthya (rite), 15n.50
Ulysses, 186
União de Vegetal (UDV), 155, 257
Uniola bipinnata (grass), 38n.149, 39n.149
Upaniṣad, 7n.7, 85n.295, 90n.305
uparava (sound hole), 12n.32
Ural (mountains), 67, 199
Ural (river), 199
urine, intoxicants in, 124n.401, 125n.402, 127, 127n.410, 157n.505
uśānā (plant), 44, 44n.179, 65n.242, 140
Utah, 116
Uzbek, 129n.414

V

Vāghbaṭa, 45n.184
Vāgīśvārī, 149n.478
vājapeya (rite), 13n.38, 15n.50, 16n.52, 52n.204
Vajrayāna, 127n.410
Yaminawa (people), 162n.525, 162n.530
Vaṅgasena, 71, 141n.455
Varāhamihira, 71
Varuṇa, 8n.13
Vatica robusta (*śāl/sāl,* plane tree) 50n.196
Vāyu (wind god), 12n.33
Veda, see also *Atharvaveda, Ṛgveda, Sāmaveda, Yajurveda*, 6, 7, 7n.7, 8, 8n.14, 9, 9n.18, 10, 10n.20, 14, 15, 18, 19, 19n.62, 20, 21, 21n.77, 24, 26, 26n.96, 26n.97, 27, 42n.170 46, 49,

50, 52n.203, 55n.217, 62, 63, 69, 111, 116n.373, 119, 124, 129, 129n.413, 133, 138, 141, 147, 169, 185, 186, 206, 208; writing of, 7n.8
vedi (Vedic altar), 16, 16n.51, 149, 251
Venezuela, 107n.348, 155n.494
Vĕrĕthragna/*verethrajan*, 9n.18, 26, 26n.97
Vernonia anthelmintica, see *Serratula anthelmintica*
vijayā, see also cannabis, 68, 71, 72, 72n.267
vinho da jurema, see also *Mimosa hostilis*, 158, 160n.521
Virgin Mary, 168, 169n.550
Visigoth, 174
Viṣṇu, 151n.487, 152n.487
Vitex negundo (Chinese chastetree), 63n.239
Vitis vinifera (common grape vine), 136n.442
Vivekānanda, 80n.287
Vohuman, 28
Vṛtra, 9, 9n.18, 9n.19, 26, 26n.97, 56

W

Wales, 75n.274
Waoroni (people), 155n.494
Wasson, R. Gordon, 45n.181, 61, 103, 106n.342, 108, 110, 119, 119n.382, 120, 120n.384, 120n.385, 121n.390, 122, 123, 123n.392, 123n.393, 123n.395, 124, 125, 125n.403, 126, 126n.406, 127, 128, 147, 181, 182n.584, 186n.601, 187, 188, 192n.616
water-lily, see also lotus and *Nymphaea*, 108, 109, 109n.352, 110, 125n.405
Watts, Alan, 88, 88n.302
wavy-leaf fig tree, see *Ficus infectoria*
Whitehead, A. N., 102n.331
wine, 57, 57n.226, 57n.227, 131n.421, 171, 174n.562, 176n.567, 181, 182, 183, 183n.587, 183n.588, 183n.589, 184, 185, 186, 187, 194, 195; ergot wine, 196n.626
witchcraft, 95n.317, 162, 175, 191, 257
Woodroffe, John, see Avalon, Arthur

X

Xerxes, 30n.118, 31
Xinjiang, 10n.20, 69, 115

Y

yāga/yajña (rite), 8, 14n.43, 16n.53, 49, 54, 165, 165n.534, 166; *soma yāga*, 15n.50, 166
Yahya, 200
yajamāna, 11, 14n.43, 15n.50, 17, 18, 118, 166n.535
Yajurveda, 7n.7, 10n.25, 11n.27, 12n.32, 14, 15, 15n.48, 52, 70n.260, 124, 129n.413
yakṣa/yakṣini (spirit), 42n.170
Yama (commentator), 122
Yama (god), 26n.96
Yamnaya (people), 67
yasht (hymn), 25n.92
yasna (rite), 25n.92, 26n.94,

28n.106, 29n.113, 32, 32n.123, 33, 33n.126, 33n.129, 33n.131, 33n.134, 34, 49, 140, 147
yūpa (Vedic sacrificial post), 13, 13n.40, 251

Z

Zādsparam, 29n.113
Zaehner, R. C., 85n.295, 86n.295, 87n.299, 114n.366
zaotar (priest), 32, 32n.124, 147
Zarathustra, 25n.92, 28, 28n.108, 28n.110, 30, 30n.117, 32, 56, 57, 58, 58n.227, 58n.228; and *haoma*, 29n.113; date of, 28n.107
Zeus, 171, 172, 172n.557, 172n.558, 179n.577, 182n.584
Zoroastrian (religion/rites), 1, 4, 5, 24, 25, 25n.89, 25n.91, 25n.92, 26n.97, 27n.98, 28, 29, 29n.113, 30, 30n.117, 33n.130, 34, 36, 49, 49n.192, 56, 56n.224, 115, 117, 118, 130n.417, 148, 163, 167n.538, 170, 198, 212, 213

www.ingramcontent.com/pod-product-compliance
Ingram Content Group UK Ltd.
Pitfield, Milton Keynes, MK11 3LW, UK
UKHW020146191125
465181UK00006B/139

9 781913 274399